MORNING
THOUGHTS

GREAT CHRISTIAN BOOKS
LINDENHURST, NEW YORK

MORNING
THOUGHTS

OCTAVIUS
WINSLOW

Great Christian Books
is an imprint of Rotolo Media
160 37th Street Lindenhurst, New York 11757
(631) 956-0998

Winslow, Octavius, 1808 —1878
Morning Thoughts / by Octavius Winslow
p. cm.
A "A Great Christian Book" book
GREAT CHRISTIAN BOOKS an imprint of Rotolo Media
ISBN 978-1-61010-008-3
Recommended Dewey Decimal Classifications: 200, 202, 230, 234
Suggested Subject Headings:
1. Religion—Christianity & Christian theology—Devotional
2. Christianity—Bible—Christian Living
I. Title

Book and cover design are by Michael Rotolo, www.michaelrotolo.com. This book is typeset in the Minion typeface by Adobe Inc. and is quality-manufactured on acid-free paper stock. To discuss the publication of your Christian manuscript or out-of-print book, please contact us.

Manufactured in the United States of America

CONTENTS

PREFACE

*"My voice shall You hear in the morning, O
Lord; in the morning will I direct my prayer
unto You, and will look up." Psalm 5:3*

In compliance with a request frequently, and from various quarters,
preferred, that the author would allow selections from some of his published
works to appear in the form of Daily Readings, he ventures to offer to
the Christian Church the following pages. They have been gleaned—with
much care, and with a strict regard to variety, yet consecutiveness, of
topic; presenting a spiritual, and occasionally a critical, exposition of each
Scripture motto. In the large family of similar productions which have
issued from the press, he trusts that his little volume—not quite a stranger
to some who will peruse it—may find a humble place. Should it, with the
Holy Spirit's blessing, drop occasionally a Christ-endearing, heart-soothing,
soul—guiding, word in seasons of daily toil, conflict, or trial, his utmost
wish in its publication will be realized.

Robert Hall was wont to define domestic prayer as "that border which
keeps the web of my life from unraveling." With equal appropriateness
this beautiful remark will apply to morning religion. To begin the day
with God is the great secret of walking through the day with God. What a
privilege this the moment that "slumber's chain" is broken, and we wake to
duty and toil—perchance to temptation and trial—to raise the soul to God,
and seek to fill it at this Infinite Fountain of life, love, and bliss, with such
thoughts, and feelings, and purposes as will exert a hallowing, soothing,
and controlling influence upon the day! Before the secular commences,
to begin with the spiritual. Before care insinuates, to preoccupy the mind
with peace. Before temptation assails, to fortify the heart with prayer.
Before sorrow beclouds, to irradiate the soul with Divine sunshine. What
a precious privilege this! A morning without God is the precursor of a

uneasy, cloudy, and dark day. It is like a morning around whose eastern horizon thick vapors gather, veiling the ascending sun, and foreshadowing a day of storm. "The first thing I do when I awake in the morning," remarks an aged saint of God, "is to ask the Holy Spirit to take possession of my mind, my imagination, my heart, directing, sanctifying, and controlling my every thought, feeling, and word." (See "Life in Jesus, Memoir of Mrs. Mary Winslow.") What profound spiritual wisdom is there in this conception! What a God-descending, heaven—returning spirit does it betray! How the well of water in the soul springs up! "In the morning will I direct my prayer unto You, and will look up." "Look up!" Ah! here is the true and befitting attitude of the spiritual soul. Looking up for the day's supply of grace to restrain, of power to keep, of wisdom to guide, of patience to suffer, of meekness to endure, of strength to bear, of faith to overcome, of love to obey, and of hope to cheer. Jesus stands at the Treasury of Infinite grace, ready to meet every application, and to supply every need. His fullness is for a poor, needy, asking people. He loves for us to bring the empty vessel. Oh, to have our "morning thoughts" occupied with God, and Christ, and the Holy Spirit, and heaven! Truly this is the border which keeps the web of daily life from unraveling! Dear reader, let your first thought be of God, and your first incense be to Jesus, and your first prayer be to the Holy Spirit, and thus anointed with fresh oil, you will glide serenely and safely through the day, beginning, continuing, and ending it with God.

"Direct, control, suggest, this day,
All I design, or do, or say,

That all my powers, with all their might, In Your sole glory may unite."

JANUARY

JANUARY 1

"You have not passed this way heretofore." Joshua 3:4

How solemn is the reflection that with a new cycle of time commences, with each traveler to Zion, a new and untrodden path! New events in his history will transpire—new scenes in the panorama of life will unfold—new phases of character will develop—new temptations will assail—new duties will devolve—new trials will be experienced—new sorrows will be felt—new friendships will be formed—and new mercies will be bestowed. How truly may it be said of the pilgrim journeying through the wilderness to his eternal home, as he stands upon the threshold of this untried period of his existence, pondering the unknown and uncertain future, "You have not passed this way heretofore!"

Reader! if you are a believer in the Lord Jesus, you will enter upon a new stage of your journey by a renewed surrender of yourself to the Lord. You will make the cross the starting-point of a fresh setting-out in the heavenly race. Oh, commence this year with a renewed application to the "blood of sprinkling." There is vitality in that blood; and its fresh sprinkling on your conscience will be as a new impartation of spiritual life to your soul. Oh, to begin the year with a broken heart for sin, beneath the cross of Immanuel! looking through that cross to the heart of a loving, forgiving Father. Do not be anxious about the future; all that future God has provided for. "All my times are in Your hands." "Casting all your care upon Him, for He cares for you." "Cast your burden upon the Lord, and He shall sustain you." Let it be a year of more spiritual advance. "Speak to the children of Israel that they go forward." Forward in the path of duty—forward in the path of suffering—forward in the path of conflict—forward in the path of labor—and forward in the path to eternal rest and glory. Soon will that rest be reached, and that glory appear. This new year may be the jubilant year of your soul—the year of your release. Oh spirit—stirring, ecstatic thought—this year I may be in heaven!

JANUARY 2

"He knows the way that I take." Job 23:10

Untried, untrodden, and unknown as your future path may be, it is, each step, mapped, arranged, and provided for in the everlasting and unchangeable covenant of God. To Him who leads us, who accepts us in the Son of His love, who knows the end from the beginning, it is no new, or uncertain, or hidden way. We thank Him that while He wisely and kindly veils all the future from our reach, all that future—its minutest event—is as transparent and visible to Him as the past. Our Shepherd knows the windings along which He skillfully, gently, and safely leads His flock. He has traveled that way Himself, and has left the traces of His presence on the road. And as each follower advances—the new path unfolding at each step—he can exultingly exclaim, "I see the footprint of my Lord; here went my Master, my Leader, my Captain, leaving me an example that I should follow His steps." Oh, it is a thought replete with strong consolation, and well calculated to gird us for the coming year—the Lord knows and has ordained each step of the untrodden path upon which I am about to enter.

Another reflection. The infinite forethought, wisdom, and goodness which have marked each line of our new path, have also provided for its every necessity. Each exigency in the history of the new year has been anticipated. Each need will bring its appropriate and adequate supply—each perplexity will have its guidance—each sorrow its comfort—each temptation its shield—each cloud its light. Each affliction will suggest its lesson—each correction will impart its teaching—each mercy will convey its message of love. The promise will be fulfilled to the letter, "As your day, so shall your strength be."

JANUARY 3

"For it pleased the Father that in him should all fullness dwell." Colossians 1:19

All wisdom to guide, all power to uphold, all love to soothe, all grace to support, all tenderness to sympathize, dwells in Christ. Let us, then, gird ourselves to a fresh taking hold of Christ. We must walk through this year not by sight, but by faith—and that faith must deal simply and directly, with Jesus. "Without me you can do nothing." But with His strength made perfect in our weakness, we can do all things. Oh, be this our course and our posture—"coming up from the wilderness leaning on her Beloved." Living in a world of imperfection and change, we must expect nothing perfect, nothing stable, in what we are, in what we do, or in what we enjoy. But amid the dissolving views of the world that "passes away," let us take firm hold of the unchangeableness of God. The wheels may revolve, but the axle on which they turn is immoveable. Such is our covenant God. Events may vary—providences may change—friends may die—feelings may fluctuate—but God in Christ will know "no variableness, neither the shadow of a turning." "Having loved His own that were in the world, He loved them unto the end."

JANUARY 4

"The grace of our Lord Jesus Christ, and the love of God, and the communion of the Holy Spirit, be with you all. Amen." 2 Corinthians 13:14

The doctrine of the Trinity is to the Christian the key of the Bible. The Spirit imparting skill to use it, and the power, when used, it unlocks this divine arcade of mysteries, and throws open every door in the blest sanctuary of truth. But it is in the light of salvation that its fitness and beauty most distinctly appear—salvation in which Jehovah appears so inimitably glorious—so like Himself. The Father's love appears in 'sending' His Son; the Son's love in 'undertaking' the work; the Holy Spirit's love in 'applying' the work. Oh, it is delightful to see how, in working out the mighty problem of man's redemption, the Divine Three were thus deeply engaged. With which of these could we have dispensed? All were needed; and had one been lacking, our salvation would have been incomplete, and we would have been eternally lost. In bringing to glory the church they thus have saved, the sacred Three are solemnly pledged. And in the matter of prayer, how sustaining to faith, and how soothing to the mind, when we can embrace, in our ascending petitions, the blessed Three in One. "For through Him (the Son) we both have access by one Spirit unto the Father."

JANUARY 5

"He that believes (on the Son of God) has the witness in himself." 1 John 5:10

The Spirit of God breaking, humbling, healing the heart; taking his own truth and transcribing it upon the soul; witnessing, sealing, sanctifying; opening the eye of the soul to the holiness of God's law—to its own moral guilt, poverty, helplessness, and deep need of Christ's blood and righteousness, thus leading it to rest on Him as on an all-sufficient Savior; thus producing "righteousness, peace, and joy in the Holy Spirit"—this is the truth experienced—this is the religion of the heart; and all other religion, beautiful as may be its theory, and orthodox as may be its creed, is worth nothing! Without this experience there is no true belief in God's Word. The revelation of God asks not for a faith that will merely endorse its divine credentials; it asks not merely that skepticism will lay aside its doubts, and receive it as a divine verity; it asks, yes, it demands, more than this—it demands a faith that will fully, implicitly, practically receive the momentous and tremendous facts it announces—a faith that brings them home with a realizing power to the soul, and identifies it with them—a faith that believes there is a hell, and seeks to escape it—a faith that believes there is a heaven, and strives to enter it—a faith that credits the doctrine of man's ruin by nature, and that welcomes the doctrine of man's recovery by grace—in a word, a faith that rejects all human dependence, and accepts as its only ground of refuge "the righteousness of Christ, which is unto all, and upon all those who believe." Oh, this is the true faith of the gospel! Do you have it, reader?

JANUARY 6

"In the world you shall have tribulation." John 16:33

Could we draw aside, for a moment, the thin veil that separates us from the glorified saints, and inquire the path along which they were conducted by a covenant God to their present enjoyments, how few exceptions, if any, would we find to that declaration of Jehovah—"I have chosen you in the furnace of affliction." All world tell of some peculiar cross; some domestic, relative, or personal trial which attended them every step of their journey; which made the valley they trod, truly, "a valley of tears," and which they only threw off when the spirit, divested of its robe of flesh, fled where sorrow and sighing are forever done away. God's people are a sorrowful people. The first step they take in the divine life is connected with tear's of godly sorrow; and, as they, travel on, sorrow and tears do but trace their steps. They sorrow over the body of sin which they are compelled to carry with them; they sorrow over their perpetual proneness to depart, to backslide, to live below their high and holy calling. They mourn that they mourn so little; they, weep that they weep so little; that over so much indwelling sin, over so many and so great departures, they yet are found so seldom mourning in the posture of one low in the dust before God. In connection with this, there is the sorrow which results from the needed discipline which the correcting hand of the Father who loves them almost daily employs. For, in what light are all their afflictions to be viewed, but as so many correctives, so much discipline employed by their God in covenant, in order to make them "partakers of His holiness." Viewed in any other light, God is dishonored, the Spirit is grieved, and the believer is robbed of the great spiritual blessing for which the trial was sent.

JANUARY 7

"Thanks be unto God for his unspeakable gift." 2 Cor. 9:15

The Atonement itself precludes all idea of human merit, and, from its very nature, proclaims that it is free. Consider the grandeur of the Atonement—contemplate its costliness: incarnate Deity—perfect obedience—spotless purity—unparalleled grace and love—acute and mysterious sufferings—wondrous death, resurrection, ascension, and intercession of the Savior, all conspire to constitute it the most august sacrifice that could possibly be offered. And shall there be anything in the sinner to merit this sacrifice? Shall God so lower its dignity, underrate its value, and dishonor Himself, as to 'barter' it to the sinner? And if God were so disposed, what is there in the sinner that could purchase it? Where is the equivalent, where the price? "Alas!" is the exclamation of a convinced soul, "I am a spiritual bankrupt; I lost everything in my first parent who fell; I came into the world poor and helpless; and to the sin of my nature I have added actual transgression of the most aggravated character. I have nothing to recommend me to the favor of God; I have no claim upon His mercy; I have no price with which to purchase it; and if redemption is not free, without money and without price, I am undone." The very costliness, then, of the Atonement puts it beyond all price, and stamps it with infinite freeness.

JANUARY 8

"Who gave himself for us, that he might redeem us from all iniquity, and purify unto himself a peculiar people, zealous of good works." Titus 2:14

There is no victory, over the indwelling power of sin, and there is no pardon for the guilt of sin, but as the soul deals with the blood of Christ. The great end of our dear Lord's death was to destroy the works of the devil. Sin is the great work of Satan. To overcome this, to break its power, subdue its dominion, repair its ruins, and release from its condemnation, the blessed Son of God suffered the ignominious death of the cross. All that bitter agony which He endured—all that mental suffering—the sorrow of His soul in the garden—the sufferings of His body on the cross—all was for sin. See, then, the close and beautiful connection between the death of Christ, and the death of sin. All true sanctification comes through the cross. Reader, seek it there. The cross brought into your soul by the eternal Spirit will be the death of your sins. Go to the cross—oh, go to the cross of Jesus. In simplicity of faith, go. With the strong corruption, go. With the burden of guilt, go, go to the cross. You will find nothing but love there—nothing but welcome there—nothing but purity there. The precious blood of Jesus "cleanses us from all sin." And while you are kept low beneath the cross, your enemy dares not approach you, sin shall not have dominion over you, nor shall Satan, your accuser, condemn you.

JANUARY 9

"And the Lord turned, and looked upon Peter. And Peter remembered the word of the Lord." Luke 22:61

His Lord's solemn prediction of his sin he seemed quite to have forgotten. But when that look met his eye, it summoned back to memory the faded recollections of the faithful and tender admonitions that had forewarned him of his fall. There is a tendency, in our fallen minds to forget our sinful departures from God. David's threefold backsliding seemed to have been lost in deep oblivion, until the Lord sent His prophet to recall it to his memory. Christ will bring our forgotten departures to view, not to upbraid or to condemn, but to humble us, and to bring us afresh to the blood of sprinkling. The heart searching look from Christ turns over each leaf in the book of memory; and sins and follies, inconsistencies and departures, there inscribed, but long forgotten, are read and re-read, to the deep sin-loathing and self-abasement of our souls. Ah! let a look of forgiving love penetrate your soul, illuminating memory's dark cell, and how many things, and circumstances, and steps in your past life will you recollect to your deepest humiliation before God. And oh! how much do we need thus to be reminded of our admonitions, our warnings, and our falls, that we may in all our future spirit and conduct "walk humbly with God."

JANUARY 10

"They took knowledge of them, that they had been with Jesus." Acts 4:13

We have a right to look for one or more of the moral features of our dear Lord's character in His people. Some resemblance to His image; something that marks the man of God; some lowliness of mind—gentleness of temper—humility of deportment—charity—patience in the endurance of affliction—meekness in the suffering of persecution—forgiveness of injuries—returning good for evil—blessing for cursing—in a word, some portion of "the fruit of the Spirit," which is "love, joy, peace, long-suffering, gentleness, goodness, faith, meekness, temperance." If one or more of these are not "in us and abound, so that they make us that we shall neither be barren nor unfruitful in the knowledge of our Lord Jesus Christ," and in a resemblance to His likeness, we have great reason to doubt whether we have ever "known the grace of God in truth." That is indeed a melancholy profession in which can be traced nothing that identifies the man with Jesus; nothing in his principles, his motives, his tone of mind, his spirit, his very looks, that reminds one of Christ—that draws the heart to Him, that makes the name of Immanuel fragrant, and that lifts the soul in ardent desires to be like Him too. This is the influence which a believer exerts, who bears about with him a resemblance to his Lord and Master. A holy man is a blessing, go where he may. He is a savor of Christ in every place.

JANUARY 11

"We have not a high priest which cannot be touched with the feeling of our infirmities; but was in all points tempted like as we are, yet without sin." Hebrews 4:15

See Him bearing our sicknesses and our sorrows; more than this, carrying our iniquities and our sins. Think not that your path is a isolated one. The incarnate God has trodden it before you, and He can give you the clear eye of faith to see His footprint in every step. Jesus can say, and He does say to you, "I know your sorrow; I know what that cross is, for I have carried it. You have not a burden that I did not bear, nor a sorrow that I did not feel, nor a pain that I did not endure, nor a path that I did not tread, nor a tear that did not bedew my eye, nor a cloud that did not shade my spirit, before you, and for you. Is it bodily weakness? I once walked forty miles, to carry the living water to a poor sinner at Samaria. Is it the sorrow of bereavement? I wept at the grave of my friend, although I knew that I was about to recall the loved one back again to life. Is it the frailty and the fickleness of human friendship? I stood by and heard my person denied by lips that once spoke kindly to me; lips now renouncing me with an oath that once vowed affection unto death. Is it straitness of circumstance, the galling sense of dependence? I was no stranger to poverty, and was often nourished and sustained by the charity of others. Is it that you are houseless and friendless? So was I. The foxes have their shelter, and the birds their nests; but I, though Lord of all, had nowhere to lay my head; and often day after day passed away, and no soothing accents of friendship fell upon my ear. Is it the burden of sin? Even that I bore in its accumulated and tremendous weight when I hung accursed upon the tree."

JANUARY 12

"With You is the fountain of life." Psalm 36:9

Behold, what a fountain of life is God! All intelligences, from the highest angel in heaven to the lowliest creature on earth, drawing every breath of their existence from Him. "In Him we live, and move, and have our being." But He is more than this to the Church. He is the fountain of love, as well as of life. The spirits of "just men made perfect," and the redeemed on earth, satiate their thirsty souls at the overflowing fullness of the Father's love. How much do we need this truth! What stinted views, unjust conceptions, and wrong interpretations have we cherished of Him, simply because we overlook His character as the Fountain of living waters! We "limit the Holy One of Israel." We judge of Him by our poor, narrow conception of things. We think that He is such a one as we ourselves are. We forget, in our approaches, that we are coming to an Infinite Fountain. That the heavier the demand we make upon God, the more we shall receive, and that the oftener we come, the more are we welcome. That we cannot ask too much. That our sin and His dishonor are, that we ask so little. We forget that He is glorified in giving; and that the more grace He metes out to His people, the richer the revenue of praise which He receives in return. How worthy of such an infinite Fountain of love and grace is His "unspeakable gift." It came from a large heart; and the heart that gave Jesus will withhold no good thing from those who walk uprightly.

JANUARY 13

And when He (the Comforter) has come, He will reprove (marg. convince) the world of sin." John 16:8

This is the great office of the Spirit—this is His first work, prior to His bringing the soul to rest on the great sacrifice for sin. Not a step will the soul take to Christ, until that soul has been brought in guilty and condemned by the law of God. And this is the work of the Spirit. "No man," says the excellent Newton, "ever did or ever will feel himself to be a lost, miserable, and hateful sinner, unless he is powerfully and supernaturally convinced by the Spirit of God." And what is the instrument by which the Spirit thus powerfully and supernaturally convinces of sin? We reply, the Law. "By the law is the knowledge of sin." "The law was our schoolmaster to bring us unto Christ." The law, brought into the conscience by the Holy Spirit; condemns the man, and leads him to condemn himself; it holds up to view the holiness of God—the purity and inflexibility of every precept— contrasts it with the unrighteousness, guilt, and misery, of the sinner, and thus prostrates the soul in the dust, exclaiming in all the lowliness of self—accusation, "the law is holy, just, and good—I am guilty, guilty, guilty." Through this instrument—the law of God—and thus effectually, does the Holy Spirit convince the soul of sin, and lay it low before God.

JANUARY 14

"Sufficient unto the day is the evil thereof." Matthew 6:34

It is a matter of much practical importance, that you take heed not to anticipate or to forestall the promised grace. For every possible circumstance in which you may be placed, the fullness of Christ and the supplies of the covenant are provided. That provision is only meted out as the occasions for whose history it was provided occur. Beware of creating trouble by ante-dating it. Seen through the mist, the advancing object may appear gigantic in size, and terrific in appearance; and yet the trouble you so much dread may never come; or coming, it will assuredly bring with it the "word spoken in due season." In the case of every child of God, calamity never comes alone; it invariably brings Jesus with it.

JANUARY 15

"Christ is all, and in all." Colossians 3:11

Anything, even if it be the blessed production of the Eternal Spirit of God, which takes the place of Christ, which shuts out Christ from the soul, is dangerous. In the great work of salvation, Christ must be everything or nothing; from Him solely, from Him entirely, from Him exclusively, must pardon and justification be drawn. Whatever, then, rises between the soul and Christ—whatever would tend to satisfy the soul in His absence—whatever would take His place in the affections, must be surrendered. Is it as the plucking out of a right eye? It must be yielded. Is it as the cutting off of a right hand? Let it go. Christ in his Godhead, Christ in his humanity, Christ in his great and finished work, Christ in his mediatorial fullness, must be all in all to the believer.

JANUARY 16

"If his children forsake my law, and walk not in my judgments; If they break my statutes, and keep not my commandments; Then will I visit their transgression with the rod, and their iniquity with stripes. Nevertheless my loving-kindness will I not utterly take from him, nor suffer my faithfulness to fail." Psalm 89:30-33

Divine love chastens, because it sees the necessity for the correction. The Lord's love is not a blind affection. It is all-seeing and heart-searching. When has He ever shown Himself blind to the follies of His people?

When has His love been ignorant of their sinful departures? Was He blind to the unbelief of Abraham? He chastened him for it. Was He blind to the deception of Jacob? He chastened Him for it. Was He blind to the impatience of Moses? He chastened him for it. Was He blind to the self-applause of Hezekiah? He chastened him for it. Was He blind to the adultery and murder of David? He chastened him for it. Was He blind to the idolatry of Solomon? He chastened him for it. Was He blind to the disobedience of Jonah? He chastened him for it. Was He blind to the self-righteousness of Job? He corrected him for it. Was He blind to the denial of Peter? He rebuked him for it. It is our mercy to know that love marks our iniquity, and that love and not justice, grace and not vengeance, holds the rod and administers the correction. Do you think, O chastened child of the Lord, that your Father would have touched you where your feelings are the acutest, where your anguish is the deepest, had He not seen a real necessity? Had He marked no iniquity, no flaw, no departure, no spot, you would have known what the "kisses of His mouth" were, rather than the strokes of His rod. And yet believe it, for he has declared it, those stripes of His rod are as much the fruit and the expression of His love as are the "kisses of His mouth;" "For whom the Lord loves he chastens."

JANUARY 17

"And it shall come to pass, that before they call, I will answer: and while they are yet speaking, I will hear. Isaiah 65:24

Remember, the throne of grace is near at hand. You have not to travel far to reach it: no lengthy and painful journey; no wearisome and mortifying pilgrimage. It is near at hand. Lying down or rising up—going out or coming in—in the streets or in the house—in public or in private—in the chamber or in the sanctuary, God is everywhere; and where He is, there is a prayer-hearing and a prayer-answering God. In a moment, in the greatest emergency, you may lift up your heart to the Lord, and in a moment your cry shall be heard, and your request shall be granted. Remember, the throne of grace is everywhere. On the land and on the sea—at home or abroad—in the publicity of business or in the privacy of retirement, "the eyes of the Lord are upon the righteous, and His ears are open unto their cry." Wherever a believer goes, he bears about with him the intercession of the Spirit below, and he has the consolation of knowing that he has the intercession of Jesus above.

JANUARY 18

"Mighty to save." Isaiah 63:1

Let us glance at the authoritative manner with which He executes His mighty acts of grace. Mark His deportment. Was there anything that betrayed the consciousness of an inferior, the submission of a dependant, the weakness of a mortal, or the imperfection of a sinner? Did not the God shine through the man with majestic awe, when to the leper He said, "I will, be clean;"—to the man with the withered hand, "Stretch forth your hand;"—to the blind man, "Receive your sight;"—to the dead man, "I say unto you, Arise;"—and to the tumultuous waves, "Peace, he still"? Dear reader, are you an experimental believer in Jesus? Then this omnipotent Christ is wedded to your best interests. He is omnipotent to save—omnipotent to protect—omnipotent to deliver—omnipotent to subdue all your iniquities, to make you humble, holy, and obedient. All power resides in Him. "It pleased the Father that in Him"—in Him as the Mediator of His Church—"all fullness should dwell." Not a corruption, but He is omnipotent to subdue it: not a temptation, but He is omnipotent to overcome it: not a foe, but He is omnipotent to conquer it: not a fear, but He is omnipotent to quell it. "All power," is His own consoling language, "all power is given unto Me in heaven and in earth."

JANUARY 19

"We know that we have passed from death unto life." 1 John 3:14

For it is a thing of whose possession the believer may be assured. He can speak of its possession with holy boldness and with humble confidence. The life of God in the soul authenticates itself. It brings with it its own evidence. Is it possible that a believer can be a subject of the quickening grace of the Holy Spirit, and not know it? Possess union with Christ, and not know it? The pardon of sin, and not know it? Communion with God, and not know it? Breathing after holiness, and not know it? Impossible! The life of God in the soul evidences itself by its actings. Are you sensible of your sinfulness? Do you love the atoning blood? Is Jesus precious to your soul? Do you delight in God, and in retirement for communion with Him? Then, for your encouragement we remind you, that these are not the actings of a soul lying in a state of moral death, nor are these the productions of a soil still unregenerate. They proceed from the indwelling life of God, and are the ascendings of that life to God, the Fountain from where it flows. Thus the weakest believer in Jesus may humbly exclaim, "This one thing I know, that whereas I was blind, now I see."

JANUARY 20

"Partakers of the inheritance of the saints in light." Col. 1:12

The glorified saints are "the saints in light." No more veilings of the Father's countenance—no more "walking in darkness, having no light,"—no more mourning over Divine desertions, the suspensions of the Father's experienced love—no more tears to dim the eye—no more clouds of unbelief to darken the mind—no more mental despondency to enshroud the spirit; they leave the gloom, and the mist, and the fog, and the darkness of ignorance, error, and pollution behind them, and they flee to the regions of light, to "the inheritance of the saints" of which "the Lamb is the light thereof."

But it will be observed, that these glorified saints are said to be "partakers of the inheritance." There is something very emphatic in the word. We are "partakers" of it now, in Christ our Head. In consequence of our union to Christ, the exalted Head of the Church, we are at present "partakers" of this inheritance. We have the first dawnings of it in our soul: the foretaste and the antepast, and, what is best of all, the indwelling of the Spirit, who is the earnest of its possession; and if we have the "earnest" of the inheritance in the possession of the Spirit, we must, and shall assuredly, have the inheritance itself.

"Partakers of the inheritance of the saints in light." "Partakers" with all the saints of God; "partakers" with the whole family of the elect; "partakers" with all the children of adoption; "partakers" with Abraham, Isaac, and Jacob; with David, and Solomon, and with all who have gone before us, with all who have entered heaven a little in advance; and "partakers" with all the "ransomed of the Lord," who shall yet "come to Zion with songs, and everlasting joy upon their heads, obtaining joy and gladness, their sorrow and their sighing fleeing away!" Oh, who would not be a "partaker of the inheritance of the saints in light"? Reader, if you are a humble possessor of the inner life, you shall be a happy partaker of this glorious inheritance—the life which is to come.

JANUARY 21

"This also we wish, even your perfection." 2 Cor. 13:9

Seek larger degrees of grace. Let your standard be the loftiest, and your aim the highest. Place no limit to that which God has not limited. Never cease expecting until He ceases giving. If you are satisfied with your present measure of grace, a worse sign you could not have. To be content with being stationary in the divine life places you in a doubtful position. It is an essential property of grace that it grows. It is the immortal seed of God, and must, from its very nature, germinate. If your faith does not increase, your doubts will increase; and if your grace does not strengthen, your fears will strengthen. Fill the measure with pure wheat, as one has said, and there will be no room for chaff. Aim after elevated principles, if you desire elevated practice. Low principles invariably lead to low practice. Watch against that which tends to impair the vigor of your grace. Watch against your besetting sins—your greatest infirmities—your strongest temptations. Beware of your own heart—beware of self-confidence—beware of creature idolatry—beware of the world. Beware, too, of any neglect of the means of grace. God has appointed His channels of conveyance. Beware that you do not despise any one of them. A neglected sanctuary—a forsaken throne of grace—an unread Bible—will soon bring leanness into your soul. God has as much ordained the means of grace, as He has appointed the grace of the means.

JANUARY 22

"This is a faithful saying, and worthy of all acceptation, that Christ Jesus came into the world to save sinners." 1 Timothy 1:15

He came into the world to save sinners—and He will save you. His compassion inclines Him to save sinners—His power enables Him to save sinners—His promise binds Him to save sinners. And, oh, how easy is it to be saved when the Holy Spirit draws the heart to Christ! It is not great faith, nor deep experience, nor extensive knowledge that are required. The dimmest eye that ever looked to Christ—the feeblest hand that ever took hold of Christ—the most trembling step that ever traveled to Christ, has in it present salvation—has in it life eternal. The smallest measure of real faith will take the soul to heaven. Yes! there is hope for the trembling penitent. Jesus suffered to the uttermost, therefore He is able to "save to the uttermost all that come unto God by Him."

JANUARY 23

"Christ shall be magnified in my body, whether it be by life or by death." Phil. 1:20

You shall not lack a Christ when most you need Him. He, who has been with you all your earthly pilgrimage, will be with you in its last step. The Shepherd, who has guided you through the wilderness, will not leave you when just emerging from it into the promised land. The Pilot, who has conducted you across the stormy main, will not resign the government just as the vessel enters the haven of rest. The Captain, who has conquered for and conquered in you, will not leave you when on the eve of the final conflict and the

certain victory. Oh no! Jesus will be with you to the last. Do not be painfully anxious about a dying hour. Let all your solicitude be how you may best glorify Him in your life—He will glorify Himself in your death. All grace, all strength, all glory is laid up for you against that moment. And when it comes, and not until then, will Jesus unlock the treasury and bring it forth. But oh, to live to Him! To be able to say, "To me to live is Christ." Strive for this. Whatever opposes it, take it to His grace, lay it beneath, yes, fasten it to His cross. Oh! let Christ be everything to you in life, then will He be everything to you in death.

JANUARY 24

"Take heed, brethren, lest there be in any of you an evil heart of unbelief, in departing from the living God." Hebrews 3:12

Observe to what cause He traces all departure from God—unbelief. This is the sin which, in another place, he exhorts the Christian to "lay aside," as "the sin which does so easily beset us." What is the easy besetting sin of every child of God? Let any believer testify. Ask him to point to his most subtle, constant, powerful, and dangerous foe. Ask him what has the most easy access to his mind; what most entangles his feet, and so impedes him in the race that is set before him; what has most easily and frequently vanquished him; what has brought most distress to his soul, and dishonor to God—and he will unhesitatingly reply, "My evil heart of unbelief." He may have constitutional infirmities, and be assailed by peculiar temptations, and may yield to "presumptuous sins," and these, in secret and close transaction with God, may cause him deep bitterness and humiliation of soul. But the sin which does so easily and so perpetually beset him is the sin of unbelief, the fruitful cause of all other sin. For as faith is the parent of all holiness, so is unbelief the parent of all unholiness.

JANUARY 25

"In all things it behooved him to be made like unto his brethren." Hebrews 2:17

Partaking of our nature, nothing that was human was foreign to Him but the sin that tainted and defaced it. Separate from it all that is fallen, exorcize every evil spirit from the soul, expel every low sentiment from the mind, extirpate every selfish feeling from the heart, and let all that remains of our humanity, be its pure affections, its exquisite sensibilities, its refined feelings, its noble purposes, its lofty, generous, and delicate sentiments of sympathy and love, and you have a perfect portrait of our Lord and Savior. Our Lord, as man, was truly and purely human. Entering Himself into every affinity of our nature, He became intimate with each thought and feeling, with each sentiment and emotion, with each sorrow and pang, with each tear, groan, and sigh of our humanity—all, all were His, but its sin. Nor was it essential to the exquisite and perfect tenderness and sympathy of His nature that He should, like us, be sinful. No, this would have but beclouded, blunted, and impaired all the gentle sensibilities and intellectual perceptions of His human soul, as in us it has woefully done. The human susceptibilities which Jesus possessed were all the deeper, richer, and intenser from the very fact of their perfect purity, their entire sinlessness. How perfect, then, must be His love, how tender His compassion, how exquisite His sympathy, since it flows from a humanity all immaculate as His Godhead!

JANUARY 26

"My times are in your hand." Psalm 31:15

Let this precious truth divest your mind of all needless, anxious care for the present or the future. Exercising simple faith in God, "Do not be anxious about anything." Learn to be content with your present lot, with God's dealings with, and His disposal of, you. You are just where His providence has, in its inscrutable but all-wise and righteous decision, placed you. It may be a position painful, irksome, trying, but it is right. Oh, yes! it is right. Only aim to glorify Him in it. Wherever you are placed, God has a work for you to do, a purpose through you to be accomplished, in which He blends your happiness with His glory. And, when you have learned the lessons of His love, He will transfer you to another and a wider sphere, for whose nobler duties and higher responsibilities the present is, perhaps, but disciplining and preparing you. Covet, then, to live a life of daily dependence upon God. Oh, it is a sweet and holy life! It saves from many a desponding feeling, from many a corroding care, from many an anxious thought, from many a sleepless night, from many a tearful eye, and from many an imprudent and sinful scheme. Repairing to the "covenant ordered in all things and sure," you may confide children, friends, calling, yourself, to the Lord's care, in the fullest assurance that all their 'times' and yours are in His hand.

JANUARY 27

"If Christ has not been raised, your faith is vain; you are yet in your sins." 1 Corinthians 15:17

Here was the grand evidence of the perfection and acceptance of His sacrifice. The atoning work of Jesus was in itself perfect and complete. It was all that God demanded, all that the Church required, and all that law and justice asked. Yet there lacked one proof that this work was accepted by God, and was satisfactory to divine justice. On the cross He had uttered that wondrous cry, which sent gladness through all heaven, and dismay through all hell—"It is finished." But, lo, He dies! The Captain of our salvation is conquered! The promised Victor is vanquished! He is laid in the grave! The stone covers Him! The earth imprisons Him! What proof have we now that He was more than mortal? What evidence that He was

God? What divine seal is affixed to the great charter of redemption? What pledge have we that it is complete? What security against the law's loud thunder, and the consuming flames of justice—against the wrath of an offended God, and the condemnation that is to come? In a word, how may we know that all the divine perfections are harmonized in our salvation, and that "whoever believes in Jesus shall not perish, but have everlasting life"? Behold, the Father raises Him from the dead! This is the evidence—this is the seal—this is the pledge—and this is the security. We need even ask no more. It satisfied God; it satisfies us. At that moment all created intelligences were summoned to witness the great and final seal affixed to redemption's perfect work; and while every eye was thus intently bent upon the yielding grave, the Father, in that stupendous act of His power and love, utters His solemn voice, "This is my beloved Son, in whose person I delight, and with whose work I am well satisfied." Oh, what majesty now encircled the rising form of the incarnate God! Never had He appeared so truly a Savior, never so illustrious a Redeemer, and never so perfectly the Mediator and Advocate as now—sealed by God the Father, quickened by God the Spirit, and radiant with the beams of His own divine glory.

JANUARY 28

"Who was delivered for our offences, and was raised
again for our justification." Romans 4:25

Obeying, suffering, and rising as the Representative, the Surety, the Head of His Church, may we not say, that what He did was not so much His own act, as that of the Church in Him? He obeyed not for Himself, nor for Himself did He die and rise again, but for His "body, the Church." His resurrection, therefore, was as much His Church's entire release, discharge, and justification, as it was His own. Then was the glorious sentence of acquittal passed, then transpired the great act of justification. The emerging of the Redeemer from the grave was the emerging of the redeemed from all condemnation. His release from the cold grasp of the destroyer was their release from the iron hand of the law. "He was taken from prison and from judgment," and as He passed out of the court of God's justice, and from the prison-house of death, the Church, purchased with His blood, passed out with Him, legally and fully discharged, exclaiming, as the last barrier yielded and the last fetter broke, "Who is he that condemns? It is Christ who died; yes, rather, who has risen again!" Precious Redeemer! what surpassing glory beams forth from your emptied sepulcher!

JANUARY 29

"We shall be like Him, for we shall see Him as He is." 1 John 3:2

Who can fully tell of all the Redeemer's glory in heaven? Or, were it fully revealed, what power to grasp, what faculties to comprehend, what eye to behold, and what tongue to describe so lofty a theme and so sublime a spectacle as this? But we shall behold it! We, too, shall be glorified. The mind shall be adjusted to the mightiness of the theme, and the eye shall be strengthened for the dazzling magnificence of the spectacle. With every physical and mental and moral faculty perfectly developed and sanctified, we shall be a glorified Church, placed in the presence, and contemplating through eternity the glory, of a glorified Head. We shall behold the Redeemer's glory. "Shall I see the King in His beauty? What! my eye behold His glory?" Yes! if you see beauty in Jesus now, if your eye beholds glory in Immanuel, feeble and dim though the view may be, so surely shall you be with Him where He is, and shall contemplate the ceaseless unfoldings of His unclouded glory, and that through all eternity.

JANUARY 30

"I have loved you with an everlasting love; therefore with loving-kindness have I drawn you. Jeremiah 31:3

The law of love is the law of God's moral government of His people. By this, and by this alone, He rules them. All that is disciplinary in His conduct is resolvable into love. It is by kindness, "loving-kindness," yes, "marvelous loving-kindness," that He wins back their truant hearts, and binds them closer to Himself. "I am the Lord, who exercise loving-kindness." Oh, to imitate Him in this particular!—to be like God in His kindness to the children of men. Then would there be less sitting in the judgment-seat; less readiness to cast the first stone; less harshness and censoriousness in our conduct and spirit towards others; and more of that self-judging, self—condemning, and self-abasement, before the holy, heart-searching, all-seeing Lord God, without which we may be awfully deceived.

JANUARY 31

*"Therefore glorify the Lord in the fires, even the
name of the Lord God of Israel." Isaiah 24:15*

Great is the glory brought to our incarnate God by the sanctified
afflictions of His saints. How deep these often are, let many testify; and
yet the deeper the affliction, the deeper the glory. Behold the glory brought
to God by Daniel in the den of lions; by Shadrach, Meshach, and Abednego
in the fiery furnace; and by Paul and Silas in the prison. And what is
their history but a type of all the afflicted members of God's family? The
Lord will be glorified in His people: therefore does He afflict, and try,
and chasten them. "The Lord tries the righteous." He has His den, His
prison, His furnace. He has His own mode, His appointed way, of proving
His work in their hearts; and, whether by the lions' den, or the prison,
or the furnace, He is glorified in them. To see how Christ can shut the
mouth of the lion, and can temper the devouring flame, and can unbar the
doors of the prison-house; how glorious thus appears His power! To mark
the resigned will, the subdued spirit, the mute submission, the cheerful
acquiescence in the deepest affliction—how glorious thus appears His grace!
To behold the daily strength imparted, the precious promises applied, the
soothing consolation experienced, how glorious thus appears his love! To
see the chaff scattered, and the dross consumed, and the mind brought
into perfect harmony with God's will; to say with David, " My soul is even
as a weaned child,"—how glorious thus appears His wisdom! Oh, if these
are the blessings which blossom upon the rod, then welcome the rod! If
this is the glory brought to the name of Jesus by a process of sanctified
affliction, then welcome the affliction! Only see that He is truly glorified
in you by it. See that He is glorified, while you are in the furnace, by your
passive graces; see that He is glorified, when you have come forth from
the furnace, by your active graces. "When he has tried me, I shall come
forth as gold."

FEBRUARY

FEBRUARY 1

"It is God who justifies." Romans 8:33

Behold the eternal security of the weakest believer in Jesus. The act of justification, once passed under the great seal of the resurrection of Christ, God can never revoke without denying Himself. Here is our safety. Here is the ground of our dauntless challenge, "Who shall lay anything to the charge of God's elect? It is God who justifies." What can I need more? What more can I ask? If God, the God of spotless purity, the God of inflexible righteousness, justifies me, "who is he that condemns? " Sin may condemn, but it is God that justifies! The law may alarm, but it is God that justifies! Satan may accuse, but it is God that justifies! Death may terrify, but it is God that justifies! "If GOD is for us, who can be against us?" Who will dare condemn the soul whom He justifies? How gloriously will this truth shine forth in the great day of judgment! Every accuser will then be dumb. Every tongue will then be silent. Nothing shall be laid to the charge of God's elect. GOD Himself shall pronounce them fully, and forever justified: "And those He justifies, He also glorifies."

FEBRUARY 2

"Who went about doing good." Acts 10:38

Earnestly would I endeavor to impress upon the reader what Henry Martyn beautifully terms "the pleasure of doing good." Next to direct communion with God, the loftiest and purest source of enjoyment opened to us on earth is found in the expression of human sympathy, in the exercise of Christian benevolence. No selfish pleasure ever brought to the heart the peace, the joy, the happiness which one solitary act of kindness to another did. God is happy in the exercise of His boundless love. Angels are happy in the discharge of their beneficent mission, and man is happy as his affections and sympathies travel forth in quest of objects upon which they may repose. Oh! the luxury of effacing one sorrow from the heart, one shadow from the brow, one tear from the eye. It is in this living for the good of others, especially in seeking their spiritual and eternal happiness, we have found a most powerful means of advancing vital godliness in our own souls. The religion of many of the Lord's people is sickly and feeble, cold and gloomy, just because it is so selfish. Would they be more vigorous in their souls? Would they make greater progress in the divine life? Would they combat more successfully the many doubts and fears that assail them? Would they have a happier, sunnier religion, walking more fully in the light of the Lord's countenance? Then let them be up and doing in their Lord's vineyard. Let them seek the conversion of lost sinners, the comforting of poor saints, the betterment of human misery in some of its many forms, thus, like their Master, going about doing good, and then would be fulfilled in their souls' happy experience the precious promise: "You come to the help of those who gladly do right, who remember your ways."

FEBRUARY 3

"There remains, then, a rest for the people of God." Hebrews 4:9

Not yet come to the heavenly rest, we still are approaching it, and, oh ecstatic thought! we shall reach it at last. Everything in our present course reminds us that we are nearing home, as the seaweed washed from the rocks, and as the land-birds venturing from their bowers and floating by the vessel, are indices to the voyager that he is nearing his port. Are you bereaved? Weep not! earth has one tie the less, and heaven has one tie more. Are you impoverished of earthly substance? Grieve not! your imperishable treasure is in heaven. Are you sailing over dark and stormy waters? Fear not! the rising flood but lifts your ark the higher and nearer the mount of perfect safety and endless rest. Are you battling with disease, conscious that life is ebbing and eternity is nearing? Tremble not! there is light and music in your lone and shaded chamber—the dawn and the chimings of your heavenly home. "I am going home! Transporting thought!—True, I leave an earthly one, all so sweet and attractive, but I exchange it for a heavenly one infinitely brighter, more sacred and precious. I am going to Jesus—to the Church Triumphant—to Apostles, Prophets, and Martyrs—to the dear ones who line the shore on the other side, prepared to welcome me there. Death, from which I have so often recoiled, is but the triumphal arch—oh, how bright a risen Christ has made it!—through which I pass into 'my Father's house.'"

FEBRUARY 4

*"Who his own self bore our sins in his own body
on the tree," or, to the tree. 1 Peter 2:24*

Blessed announcement! Not the less hateful, nor hated, is the sin because it is forgiven and entirely blotted out. Oh no! Let the Lord touch your heart, Christian reader, with a sense of His pardoning love, with the assurance of His forgiveness, and you will go and hate, and mortify, and forsake it, more resolutely and effectually than ever. And must the Son of God become the Son of man, that those who are by nature children of wrath, might become the sons of God! Must God, the eternal God, the high and lofty One, stoop so low as to become incarnate, and that for sinners; for me, a poor worthless sinner! To save me from eternal woe, must the Son of Man suffer, agonize, and die; die in my stead, die for my sins, die an accursed death! Ah! Lord, what must sin be, what must my sin be! How little have I thought of it, how little have I mourned for it, still less have I hated it as I ought to have hated it! Lord, how vile, how unutterably vile I am! Oh hated sin! Do You forgive it, Father of my mercies? This only makes it more hateful still. Never, never, can I forgive myself.

FEBRUARY 5

"Without Me you can do nothing." John 15:5

Oh, that the Church of Christ, and each individual member, would but realize this truth; that simpler, closer, more experimental views of Jesus would essentially strengthen the tone of inward spirituality and comfort! The great secret of all comfort in seasons of affliction is to take the affliction, as it comes, simply to Christ; and the great secret of all holiness is to take the corruption, as it rises, simply to Christ. It is this living upon Christ for all he needs, this going to Christ under all circumstances, and at all seasons, which forms the happy and holy life of a child of God. There is no other path for him to walk in. The moment he turns from Christ he becomes like a vessel loosed from its moorings, and driven at the mercy of the winds from billow to billow. Christ must be all in all to him; friends, domestic comforts, Church privileges, ordinances, means of grace, nothing must suffice for Jesus. And why does the Lord so frequently discipline the soul? Why remove friends, why blight domestic comforts, why rob us of

Church privileges, why close up the ordinances, and write death upon the means of grace? Oh, why? but to open a way through which He Himself might enter the believer, and convince that lonely, bereaved, and desolate heart that He is a substitute for everything, while nothing shall ever be a substitute for Him. He will have the supreme affection of His saints; they shall find their all in Him; and to this end He sends afflictions, crosses, and disappointments, but to wean them from their idols and draw them to Himself.

FEBRUARY 6

"Except a man be born again, he cannot
see the kingdom of God." John 3:3

Regeneration is a work standing alone and distinct from all the other operations of the Divine Spirit. It is to be carefully distinguished from conversion, adoption, justification, and sanctification; and yet must be regarded as forming the basis and the spring-head of them all. For instance, there can be no conversion without a principle of life in the soul; for conversion is the exercise of a spiritual power implanted in man. There can be no sense of adoption, apart from a renewed nature; for adoption confers the privilege only, not the nature of sons. There can be no comforting sense of acceptance in the Beloved, until the mind has passed from death unto life; nor can there be the smallest advance in a conformity of the will and of the affections to the image of God, while there is lacking in the soul the very root of holiness. Faith is a purifying grace, but faith is only found in the heart "created anew in Christ Jesus." There must necessarily be the spiritual renewal of the whole man, before the soul can pass into an adopted, justified, and sanctified state. Reader, ponder seriously this solemn truth.

FEBRUARY 7

"When He, the Spirit of truth, has come, He
will guide you into all truth." John 16:13

New and enlarged views of the Holy Spirit mark a regenerate mind. Having received the Holy Spirit as a quickener, he feels the need of Him now as a teacher, a sanctifier, a comforter, and a sealer. As a teacher, discovering to him more of the hidden evil of the heart, more knowledge of God, of His word, and of His Son. As a sanctifier, carrying forward the work of grace in the soul, impressing more deeply on the heart the Divine image, and bringing every thought and feeling and word into sweet, holy, and filial obedience to the law of Jesus. As a comforter, leading him, in the hour of his deep trial, to Christ; comforting, by unfolding the sympathy and tenderness of Jesus, and the exceeding preciousness and peculiar fitness of the many promises with which the word of truth abounds for the consolation of the Lord's afflicted. As a sealer, impressing upon his heart the sense of pardon, acceptance, and adoption; and entering himself as the "earnest of the inheritance, until the redemption of the purchased possession." Oh! what exalted views does he now have of the blessed and eternal Spirit—of His personal glory, His work, His offices, His influences, His love, tenderness, and faithfulness! The ear is open to the softest whisper of His voice; the heart expands to the gentlest impression of His sealing, sanctifying influence. Remembering that He is "a temple of the Holy Spirit," he desires so to walk—lowly, softly, watchfully, and prayerfully. Avoiding everything that would "grieve the Spirit," resigning every known sin that would dishonor and cause Him to withdraw, the one single aim of his life is to walk so as to please God, that "God in all things may be glorified."

FEBRUARY 8

"He will rest in his love." Zephaniah 3:17

The marginal reading of the passage is exceedingly beautiful and expressive: "He will be silent because of His love." Divine wrath is silent, because love has hushed it. Divine justice is silent, because love has satisfied it. Sin is silent, because love has condemned it. Satan is silent, because love has vanquished him. God's love has silenced every voice but its own. When an accusation was brought against a poor sinner in the presence of Jesus, and He was called upon to judge in the case, it is recorded that He "stooped down, and with His finger wrote on the ground, as though He heard them not." He was silent, because of His love! And have we no accusers? Ah, yes! many and just. Conscience accuses, and Satan accuses, and sin accuses, and the world accuses, but Jesus does not accuse; He is silent, because of His love. They condemn loudly, fiercely, justly, but He never condemns. "And again he stooped down and wrote on the ground." Still not a word of condemnation breathed from His lips. He had been wronged, He had been sinned against, His own holy law had been broken, and the witnesses, many and malignant, are there to testify in truth against the sinner—but Jesus is silent, and silent in His love.

FEBRUARY 9

"This sickness is not unto death, but for the glory of God, that the Son of God might be glorified thereby." John 11:4

The season of sickness is the schooling of the soul. More of God is unfolded then, and more of his truth is learned, than perhaps in any other circumstances. Oh, how the character, and the perfections, and the government of God become unfolded to his mind by the teachings of the Spirit of truth! His dim views are cleared, his crude ideas are ripened, his erroneous ideas are rectified; he contemplates God in another light, and truth through another medium. But the sweetest effect of all is the personal appropriation of God to his own soul. He can now say, "This God is my God, and is my Father, and is my portion forever,"—words of assurance hitherto strange to his lips. The promises of God were never realized as so precious, the doctrines of grace were never felt to be so establishing, and the precepts were never seen to be so obligatory and so sanctifying as now; blessed results of a hallowed possession of the season of sickness! And what a pruning of this living branch has taken place! What weanedness from the engrossing claims of the earthly calling, from an undue attachment to created good, from the creature, from the world, and what is the greatest weanedness of all, from the wedded idol, self! What humility of mind, what meekness of spirit, and self-renunciation follow! He entered that chamber as a proud man; he leaves it as a little child. He went into it with much of the spirit of a grasping, covetous, worldly-minded professor; he emerges from it with the world under his feet: "Consecration to Christ and Holiness to God", written upon his substance, and engraved upon his brow. He has been near to eternity! He has been looking within the veil! He has been reading his own heart! He has been dealing with Christ! He has seen and felt how solemn a thing it was to approach the gate of death, to enter the presence of God—and from that dreadful point of vision, he has contemplated the world, and life, and human responsibility, as they are; and he has come back like a spirit from another sphere, clothed with all the solemnities of eternity—to live now as one soon in reality to be there. Truly, his sickness was "for the glory of God, that the Son of God might be gloried thereby."

FEBRUARY 10
"He ever lives to make intercession for them." Hebrews 7:25

How sweet and consolatory to the believer is this view of our exalted Immanuel in the hour of bereavement—when confined to his chamber of solitude, or languishing upon his bed of "pining sickness"! Too deeply absorbed in sorrow, it may be, to give utterance to his anguished spirit in prayer—his bodily frame so weakened by disease, and racked by pain, as to render the mind unfit for close and connected spiritual thought—oh, how sweet is then the intercession of Jesus, to know that, in the hour of the soul's extremity, when human sympathy and power are exhausted, "Jesus has entered into heaven, now to appear in the presence of God" for His suffering child! And, when all utterance has failed on earth—and the heart is broken—and the lips are sealed, then to look up and see our elder Brother—the Brother born for our adversity—the exalted High Priest, waving the golden censer before the throne, while the cloud of His atoning merit goes up before the mercy-seat, bearing as it ascends the person, the name, the circumstances, and the needs of the sufferer below. Precious gospel, that opens to the eye of faith so sweet a prospect as this! When you cannot think of Him, afflicted soul, He is thinking of you—when you cannot pray to Him, He is praying for you, for "He ever lives to make intercession."

FEBRUARY 11
"Every one that does righteousness is born of him." 1 John 2:29

Negative holiness—the abstaining from outward sins—does not always describe a regenerate soul; associated with this there must be the positive evidence—"Every one that does righteousness is born of him." Where there is life, there is action, motion, energy. The life of a regenerate man is a life of the highest activity. The principles that influence him are divine and heavenly; their tendency is to holy action. The more we resemble Christ "in righteousness and true holiness," the stronger the evidence to ourselves and to others that we are born again. We possess, professedly, and, if not self-deceived, actually, the life of Christ. That life is holy in its tendency and vigorous in its acting. The renewed soul longs for holiness. He pants for divine conformity. He rests not in the mere longing; he arises and labors for the blessing; he "works out his salvation with fear and trembling." He prayerfully and diligently uses the means the Lord of sanctification has given him for the attainment of holiness; he is active in his pursuit of the blessing.

FEBRUARY 12

"Whom He did foreknow, He also did predestinate to be conformed to the image of His Son." Romans 8:29

Here is the glorious pattern of a child of God. Sanctification is a conformity to the image and the example of Christ. The more the believer is growing like Jesus, the more he is growing in holiness. On the contrary, the less resemblance there is to Christ in his principles, in the habit of his mind, spirit, temper, daily walk, yes, in every action and in every look, the less is he advancing in the great work of holiness. Oh, how many who profess His dear name, and who are expecting to be with Him forever, never pause to consider what resemblance they bear to Him now! And were they to deal faithfully, with conscience in the much—neglected duty of self-examination; were they to bring themselves to this great standard, how far below it would they be found to have come! How much in their principles, in their governing motives, in their temper, spirit, and daily conduct—how much in their walk in the world, in their deportment in the Church, and in their more concealed conduct in their families, would be discovered that was unlike Christ! How much that was "from beneath," how little that was "from above,"—how much of the "image of the earthly," how little of the "image of the heavenly!" But look at the image of our dear Lord—how lowly, how holy it is! Look at His poverty of spirit—lowliness of heart—humility of deportment—tenderness—forgiveness of injuries—self-denial—prayerfulness—zeal for His Father's glory—yearnings for the salvation of men. Oh to be like Jesus! to grow up into Him in all things! this is to "walk worthy of the Lord unto all pleasing." This is to realize "the will of God, even our sanctification." Let it not then be forgotten, that an advancing believer is one growing in a resemblance and conformity to the image and example of Christ.

FEBRUARY 13

"The wind blows where it wills, and you hear the sound thereof, but cannot tell where it comes, and where it goes: so is every one that is born of the Spirit." Jn. 3:8

Mark how striking is the figure. The wind bids defiance to man's governing power. It is as sovereign in its influence as it is irresistible in its strength. We cannot command it, nor can we control it. It is alike out of our power to summon it, as it is to soothe it. It comes, we know not where; it goes, we know not where. "So is every one that is born of the Spirit." We do not say that the Spirit is not resisted—He is resisted, strongly and perseveringly. But He is not overpowered. All the enmity and carnality of the heart rises in direct opposition to Him; but, when bent upon a mission of love, when, in accordance with the eternal purpose, He comes to save, not all the powers on earth or in hell can effectually resist Him. Like the mighty force, He bears down all opposition, sweeps away every barrier, overcomes every difficulty, and the sinner, "made willing in the day of His power," is brought to the feet of Jesus, there meekly and gratefully to sit, "clothed, and in his right mind." Who can withstand the power of the Spirit? Whether He speaks in the "still small voice" of tender, persuasive love, or whether He comes in the "mighty rushing wind" of deep and overwhelming conviction, His influence is quenchless, His power is irresistible. He effectually works in those who believe.

But His operation is as sovereign as it is mighty. He comes to whom He will; He comes when He will; He comes in the mode He will. He blows where He wills; we hear the sound, we see the effects; but how He works, why He works, and why in a particular way He works, He reveals not to mortals. Even so, O blessed and eternal Spirit, for so it seems good in Your sight.

FEBRUARY 14

"Herein is love, not that we loved God, but that He loved us, and sent his Son to be the propitiation for our sins." 1 John 4:10

"Herein is love!" as though John would say, "and nowhere else but here!" That God should punish the innocent for the guilty—that He should exact the blood of His Son to cancel the guilt of His rebels—that He should lay an infinite weight of wrath on His soul, in order to lay an infinite weight of love on ours—that He should sacrifice His life of priceless value for ours—worthless, forfeited, and doomed—that He should not only give His

Son, but should bruise Him, put Him to grief, afflict Him, should make His soul an offerinq for sin—that the 'Lord of Glory' should become a 'man of sorrows', the Lord of Life should die, and the Heir of all things should be "as him that serves." Oh depth of love unfathomable! Oh height of love unsearchable! Oh length and breadth of love unmeasurable! Oh love of God, which passes knowledge!

FEBRUARY 15

"He that spared not His own Son, but delivered Him up for us all, how shall He not with him also freely give us all things?" Romans 8:32

Look at the cross; behold His precious Gift transfixed to it, and that by His own hand, and for your sins. Then look at your present circumstances, survey your needs, your trials, your chastisements, your bereavements, your heart-sickening, heartbreaking tribulations, and know that God still is love. If He had love strong enough, deep enough, to give you Jesus—to tear Him, as it were, from His bosom, and to transfix Him on yonder accursed tree for your iniquities—has He not love enough to bow His ear to your cry, and His heart to your sorrow? Will He not rescue you from this difficulty, deliver you out of this trouble, shield you in this temptation, supply this need, and support, succour, and comfort you in this grief? Oh yes, He will! doubt it not! The cross of Calvary is a standing pledge—standing until sin and guilt, need and woe, shall be known no more—that God, who "spared not His own Son, but delivered Him up for us all, will with Him also freely give us all things" necessary to our good, and promotive of His glory.

FEBRUARY 16

"I am not alone, because the Father is with Me." John 16:32

Oh, what words are these! Who can harm you now? What can befall you? When and where can you be alone, if your heavenly Father is with you? He is with you on the ocean; He is with you on the land. He is with you in your exile; He is with you at home. Friends may forsake, and kindred may die, and circumstances may change—but "my Father is with me!" may, still be your solace and your boast. And, oh, to realize the presence of that Father—to walk with God in the absorbing consciousness of His loving eye never removed, of His solemn presence never withdrawn, of His encircling arm never untwined—welcome the solitude, welcome the loneliness, welcome the sorrow, cheered, and sweetened, and sanctified by such a realization as this! "I am not alone, because the Father is with Me."

FEBRUARY 17
"Precious in the sight of the Lord is the death of his saints." Psalm 116:15

It is solemnly true that there is a "time to die." Ah! affecting thought—a "time to die!" A time when this mortal conflict will be over—when this heart will cease to feel, alike insensible to joy or sorrow—when this head will ache and these eyes will weep no more—best and holiest of all—a time "when this corruptible shall put on incorruption, and this mortal shall put on immortality," and we shall "see Christ as He is, and be like Him." If this be so, then, O Christian, why this anxious, trembling fear? Your time of death, with all its attendant circumstances, is in the Lord's hand. All is appointed and arranged by Him who loves you, and who redeemed you—infinite goodness, wisdom, and faithfulness consulting your highest happiness in each circumstance of your departure. The final sickness cannot come, the "last enemy" cannot strike, until He bids it. All is in His hand. Then calmly, confidingly, leave life's closing scene with Him. You cannot die away from Jesus. Whether your spirit wings its flight at home or abroad, amid strangers or friends, by a lingering process or by a sudden stroke, in brightness or in gloom, Jesus will be with you; and, upheld by His grace, and cheered with His presence, you shall triumphantly exclaim, "Though I walk through the valley of the shadow of death, I will fear no evil; for you are with me: your rod and your staff, they comfort me," bearing your dying testimony to the faithfulness of God, and the preciousness of His promises. My time to die is in Your hand, O Lord, and there I calmly leave it.

FEBRUARY 18
"Looking unto Jesus." Hebrews 12:2

If Jesus is especially glorified in the faith of His people, let yours be a life of faith in all its minute detail. Live upon Him for spiritual supplies; live upon Him for temporal supplies. Go to Him in dark providences, that you may be kept from sinking: go to Him in bright providences, that you may be kept from falling. Go to Him when the path is rough, that you may walk in it contentedly: go to Him when the path is smooth, that you may walk in it surely. Let your daily history be a traveling to Jesus empty, and a coming from Jesus filled. Keep the truth constantly and prominently before your eye, "The just shall live by faith." If this be so, do not expect that God will ever permit you to live by sight. Bend your whole soul submissively to Him in this matter. Let His will and yours be one. If, in the course of your wilderness journeyings, He has brought you into a great difficulty, yes, to the very margin of the sea, still, at His bidding, "go forward," though it be into that sea. Trust Him to cleave asunder its waters, making a dry passage for your feet, and causing those very waves that threatened to engulf you, now to prove as a cloud canopying you above, and as walls of strength fencing you in on every side.

FEBRUARY 19

"You know the grace of our Lord Jesus Christ, that, though He was rich, yet for your sakes He became poor, that you through His poverty might be rich." 2 Corinthians 8:9

How little do we associate our most costly mercies, and even those which we are accustomed to esteem of a more ordinary character (although every mercy is infinitely great), with the abasement of our Lord! How seldom do we trace our happy moments, and hallowed joys, and high delights, and sacred scenes, and precious privileges, to this dark part of His eventful history! And yet all flow to us through this very channel, and, but for this, would never have been ours. When the ocean of His goodness rolls in upon me, wave on wave—when I feel the cheering warmth of creature smiles beaming sweetly and fondly—when I review, one by one, my personal, domestic, and relative mercies—when even the cup of cold water, presented by the hand of Christian kindness, moistens my lips, what is the thought that forces itself upon my mind? "All this springs from the deepest humiliation of my adorable Christ!"

And when I ascend into the higher region of grace, and survey the blessings so richly and so freely bestowed—a rebel subdued—a criminal pardoned—a child adopted—a royal priest anointed—union with Christ—covenant relationship with God—access within the Holy of Holies—conformity to the Divine image—still more deeply am I overwhelmed with the thought, "all this proceeds from the infinite abasement of the incarnate God!"

And when yet higher still I ascend, and, passing from grace to glory, contemplate the heaven of bliss that awaits me—in one moment absent from a body of sin, and present with the Lord—away from a world, beautiful though it is, because God has made it, yet the throne of Satan, the empire of sin, the scene of sorrow, pollution, suffering, and death; and eternally shut in with God, where all is joy, and all is holiness—made perfectly holy, and, consequently, perfectly happy, to sin no more, to sorrow no more, to weep no more, to wander no more, to fall no more—oh, how full of glory then becomes the humiliation of my incarnate Lord! Beloved, when God exalts you, remember it is because your Savior was abased. When your cup is sweet, remember it is because His cup was bitter. When you press your mercy fondly and closely to your heart, remember it is because He pressed His heart to the spear. And when your eye of faith and hope looks forward to the coming glory, oh, do not forget that, because He endured your hell, you shall enjoy His heaven!

FEBRUARY 20

"You have not as yet come to the rest and to the inheritance which the Lord your God gives you." Deuteronomy 12:9

It is a richly instructive and deeply sanctifying thought—the futurity of the heavenly rest. When told that we are not as yet come to the rest and to the inheritance which the Lord our God gives us, we are gently reminded that we have each one a niche in life to occupy, a sphere to fill, a mission to perform. The idea of personal responsibility, of individual influence, and of untiring action, instantly starts up before the mind. "Not yet in heaven—then for what am I here? Surely it is for an object in harmony with my intellectual and spiritual being, and worthy of Him who still detains me on earth. It must be that I have something to do, or something to endure, for Christ—an active or a passive part to fill. Lord, what will You have me to do or suffer for You?" Oh, there is a fathomless depth of divine wisdom in the arrangement that keeps us so long out of heaven. The world needs us, and we need the world. It needs us to illumine and sanctify it; we need it as the field of our conflict, and as the school of our graces. We need the world, not as a hermit's cell, but as a vast theater, where before angels and men our Christianity is developed in the achievements of prayer, in the triumphs of faith, in the labors of love, and in the endurance of suffering.

FEBRUARY 21

"If so be that we suffer with Him." Romans 8:17

Not as He suffered. Oh, no! there is no curse, no wrath, no hell in the cup of sorrow which we drink. All these ingredients composed His bitter draught. Yet He suffers with us, and permits our afflictions to be called the "afflictions of Christ." He is with you on that bed of sickness; He is with you on that couch of languishing; He is with you in that darkened room; He kneels with you at that coffin; and He weeps with you by the side of that sepulcher. Oh, may it not reconcile us to all the suffering we have ever endured, or may yet be called to endure, to feel the perfect oneness, the presence, the sympathy, the succourings of such a Savior? Who would wish to shun the shame of His cross, the scorn of His name, the lowliness of His kingdom, the self—denial of His religion, allied in the tenderest sympathy at every step with this illustrious Martyr—this Prince of sufferers—this Brother born for adversity?

FEBRUARY 23

"And this is the confidence that we have in Him, that, if we ask anything according to His will, He hears us: and if we know that He hear us, whatever we ask, we know that we have the petitions that we desired of Him." 1 John 5:14, 15

When we draw near to God, and ask for more love, more zeal, an increase of faith, a reviving of God's work within us, more resemblance to Christ, the subjection of some enemy, the mortification of some evil, the subduing of some iniquity, the pardon of some guilt, more of the spirit of adoption, the sprinkling of the atoning blood, the sweet sense of acceptance, we know and are assured that we ask for those things which are according to the will of God, and which it is in the heart of God fully and freely to bestow. There need be no backwardness here—there need be no restraint here—there may be no misgiving here. The believer may, when pleading for such blessings, spreading out such needs before the Lord, with "boldness enter into the holiest, by the blood of Jesus." He may draw near to God, not standing afar off, but, in the spirit of a child, drawing near to God, he may come with large requests, large desires, hopeful expectations; he may open his mouth wide, because he asks those things which it is glorifying to God to give, which glorify Him when given, and which we know, from His own word, are according to His blessed will to bestow. Oh, the unspeakable encouragement of going to God with a request which we feel assured it is in His heart and according to His will freely to grant!

FEBRUARY 23

"For this thing I besought the Lord thrice, that it might depart from me." 2 Corinthians 12:8

When Paul prayed for the removal of the thorn in the flesh, he asked that of God which betrayed a lack of judgment in his estimate of the thing which he petitioned for. Who would have suspected this in the apostle of the Gentiles? But the Lord knew best what was for the good of His dear servant. He saw that, on account of the peculiar revelations that were given him in his visit to glory, the discipline of the covenant was needed to keep him low in the dust. And, when His child petitioned thrice for the removal of the thorn in the flesh, he for a moment overlooked, in the painful nature of the discipline, its needed influence to keep him "walking humbly with God." So that we see even an inspired apostle may ask those things of God, which He may see fit to refuse. We may frequently expect some trial, something to keep us low before God, after a season of peculiar nearness to Him, a manifestation of His loving-kindness to our souls. There is a proneness to rest in self-complacency after close communion with God, that the gentle hand of our Father is needed to screen us from ourselves. It was so with Paul—why may it not be with us? In withholding, however, the thing we ask of Him, we may be assured of this, that He will grant us a perfect equivalent. The Lord saw fit to deny the request of the apostle; but He granted him an equivalent—yes, more than an equivalent, to that which He denied him—He gave him His all-supporting grace. "My grace is suffcient for you." Beloved reader, have you long asked for the removal of some secret, heavy, painful cross? Perhaps you are yet urging your request, and yet the Lord seems not to answer you. And why? Because the request may not be in itself wise. Were He now to remove that cross,

He may, in taking away the cross, close up a channel of mercy which you would never cease to regret. Oh, what secret and immense blessing may that painful cross be the means of conveying into your soul!

FEBRUARY 24

"For I am the Lord, I change not; therefore you sons of Jacob are not consumed." Malachi 3:6

It is no small attainment to be built up in the faithfulness of God. This forms a stable foundation of comfort for the believing soul. Mutability marks everything outside of God. Look into the Church, into the world, into our families, ourselves, what innumerable changes do we see on every hand! A week, one short day, what alterations does it produce! Yet, in the midst of it all, to repose calmly on the unchangeableness, the faithfulness of God. To know that no alterations of time, no earthly changes, affect His faithfulness to His people. And more than this—no changes in them—no unfaithfulness of theirs, causes the slightest change in God. Once a Father, ever a Father; once a Friend, ever a Friend. His providences may change, His heart cannot. He is a God of unchangeable love. The promise He has given, He will fulfil; the covenant He has made, He will observe; the word that has gone out of His mouth, He will not alter. "He cannot deny Himself." Peace then, tried believer! Are you passing now through the deep waters? Who kept you from sinking when wading through the last?

Who brought you through the last fire? Who supported you under the last cross? Who delivered you out of the last temptation? Was it not God, your covenant God—your faithful, unchangeable God? This God, then, is your God now, and your God forever and ever, and He will be your guide even unto death.

FEBRUARY 25

"Rest in the Lord, and wait patiently for Him." Psalm 37:7

It is just this simple, patient waiting upon God in all our straits that certainly and effectually issues in our deliverance. In all circumstances of faith's trial, of prayer's delay, of hope deferred, the most proper and graceful posture of the soul—that which insures the largest revenue of blessing to us and of glory to God—is a patient waiting on the Lord.

Although our impatience will not cause God to break His covenant, nor violate His oath, yet a patient waiting will bring down larger and richer blessings. The moral discipline of patience is most costly. It keeps the soul humble, believing, prayerful. The mercy in which it results is all the more prized and precious from the long season of hopeful expectation. It is possible to receive a return too speedily. In our eagerness to grasp the mercy with one hand, we may lose our hold on faith and prayer and God with the other. A patient waiting the Lord's time and mode of appearing in our behalf will tend to check all unworthy and unwise expedients and attempts at self-rescue. An immediate deliverance may be purchased at a price too costly. Its present taste may be sweet, but afterwards it may be bitter—God embittering the blessing that was not sought with a single eye to His glory. God's time, though it tarry, and God's deliverance, though delayed, when it comes proves always to have been the best: " My soul, wait only upon God, for my expectation is from him."

FEBRUARY 26
"Go, and sin no more." John 8:11

See how Christ manifests His abhorrence of the sin, while He throws His shield of mercy around the sinner. The Lord does not justify the sinner's transgression, though He justifies the sinner's person. In the great matter of salvation, justification and sanctification, pardon and holiness, are essentially and inseparably united. When the Lord Jesus dismisses a sinner with a sense of acquittal in his conscience, it is ever accompanied with that most affecting of all exhortations, "Sin no more." And as he passes out from the presence of Jesus, pardoned, justified, saved, the Savior's tender, soul-subduing words from that moment seem to vibrate upon his ear every step of his onward way. "Go, admire, and publish abroad the glory of that grace that has done such great things for you. Go, and spread His fame, and with your latest breath dwell upon His name, who, when sin and Satan and conscience accused you, and would have consigned you to eternal woe—then appeared your Friend, your Advocate, and your Savior. Go, and when tempted to wound afresh the bosom that sheltered you, remember Me; from Gethsemane, from Calvary, and from the hallowed spot where I spoke to you, I condemn you not. Go, and sin no more."

FEBRUARY 27

"With You is the fountain of life." Psalm 36:9

What a fountain of life is Jesus! The dead, on whose ear falls the sound of His voice, live. There is grace in Christ—quickening, regenerating, life-giving grace; and to whomsoever that grace is imparted, he that was lying cold and inanimate in the valley begins to move, to live, to breathe, and to arise. One touch of Christ, a whisper of His voice, a breath of His Spirit, begets a life in the soul that never dies. What a fountain of life is Jesus! Think of its superabundance . There is a fulness of life in Christ. The grace that is welled in Jesus is as infinite in its source, as it is divine in its nature. An uncreated fulness, it must possess an inexhaustible overabundance. Had the Father deposited this life-giving grace in all the angels in heaven, it had long since been exhausted. Think of the myriads, thirsting for holiness and for happiness, who have knelt and slaked their thirst at this fountain—think of the myriads who have here filled their empty vessels, and have gone away with joy and hope springing high in their minds. Think of the myriads whose sins His blood has washed, whose souls His righteousness has clad, whose corruptions His grace has subdued, and whose sorrows His love has comforted. Think of the iniquities which He has pardoned; of the backslidings which He has healed; of the grief which He has removed; of the tears which He has dried; of the souls which He has saved. Think of the myriads once drinking from the stream below, but who are now drinking from the fountain head in glory. And yet is this fountain as full as ever! Not one hair's breadth has it sunk. Jesus is as full of pardoning grace for the guilty, and of justifying grace for the vile, and of sanctifying grace for the unworthy, as ever. He is full enough to meet the needs of every poor, thirsty, panting soul who ventures near. Oh, what a precious truth is this! Precious, indeed, to him who feels his own insufficiency, poverty, and need. What, reader, is your need? what your sorrow? what your trial? what your infirmity? what your burden? Whatever it may be, repair with it to this fountain of living water, and despair not of a gracious welcome and of an adequate supply. It is a fountain, and a living fountain. It needs no persuasion to flow, for it flows spontaneously; and wherever it flows there is life.

FEBRUARY 28

*"I will give unto him that is athirst of the fountain
of the water of life freely." Revelation 21:6*

The grace that is in Christ Jesus must, from its very nature, be unpurchasable. It implies absolute poverty in the creature, and infinite affluence in God. Could it, by any possibility, be purchased, it would cease to be what it now is, the "grace of God." Because it is so great, so rich, and infinite, God has made it as free as the sun, the light, and the air. Nothing can procure it. Tears cannot—convictions cannot—faith cannot—obedience cannot—prayer cannot—yes, not even can the most costly work of God's Spirit in the soul procure a drop of this "living water." God gives it, and He gives it, as the word implies, freely. This is its glory—it is an unpurchasable and a freely bestowed gift. Upon no other terms is it granted. Consequently, no condition of human character, and no case of human guilt, is excluded. The vilest of the vile, the poor insolvent sinner, the needy, the wretched, the penniless; the voice of free grace welcomes to the "living waters." What has kept you so long from this fountain? You have thirsted, and panted, and desired; but still your soul has not been replenished. You have, perhaps, long been seeking the Lord, asking the way, and desiring salvation. Why have you not found Him? You have borne the heavy burden of sin, month after month and year after year, knowing nothing of a sense of pardon, of acceptance, of adoption, of rest. And why? Because you have stumbled at the freeness of the gift. You have expected to receive it as a saint, not seeing that God will only give it to you as a sinner. But hear the word of the Lord: "By grace are you saved;" "Redeemed without money;" "Nothing to pay;" "Whoever will, let him take of the water of life freely." Oh! receive into your heart this truth, and you will be happy. All creation will seem to smile upon you—the heavens will smile—the earth will smile—yes, God himself will smile. Dropping its chain, your emancipated soul will spring into the glorious liberty of the sons of God. What sovereignty, sweetness, and glory will now appear in the very act that forgives all, forgets all, and which introduces you into a new world, redolent of joy and delight!

FEBRUARY 29

"God is our refuge and strength, a very present help in trouble."
Psalm 46:1

It is one of the most blessed truths of the covenant of grace, that the God of the covenant is a very present help in every time of trouble. Loving His people as He does, dwelling in them by His Spirit, their people and circumstances continually before Him in the person and the intercession of His dear Son, how can He possibly lose sight of them for a single moment? They may, and they often do, lose sight of Him. They, do not, alas! set the Lord always before their face. They do not train and discipline themselves to see Him in every event, circumstance, and incident of life. They are not clear-sighted to recognize, nor prompt to acknowledge, Him in every providence that darkens or lightens upon their way. Were they but right-minded, they, would exclaim of every good and of every evil as it came, "The Lord is in this!" But they are never for an instant out of His heart, out of His thoughts, out of His hands, or out of His eye. How near to them, too, is the Holy Spirit! Dwelling in and overshadowing them, He is at their side to guide, to uphold, and to cheer; bringing to their memory a precious promise, or writing upon their heart an animating truth, or opening before their eye some endearing glimpse of Jesus, just at the moment it was needed. What a happy, what a favored people are the Lord's! "Happy is he that has the God of Jacob for his help, whose hope is in the Lord his God. Happy is that people that is in such a case: yes, happy is that people whose God is the Lord."

MARCH

MARCH 1

"Search the scriptures; for in them you think you have eternal life: and they are they which testify of me." John 5:39

The word of God is full of Christ. He is the Sun of this divine system, the Fountain of its light and beauty. Every doctrine derives its substance from His person, every precept its force from His work, every promise its sweetness from His love. Is it not to be feared, that in the study of the Scriptures it is a much-forgotten truth, that they testify of Jesus? Are they not read, searched, and examined, with a mind too little intent upon adding to its wealth by an increased knowledge of His person, and character, and work? And thus it is we lower the character of the Bible. We may read it as a mere uninspired record; we may study it as a book of human literature. Its antiquity may interest us, its history may inform us, its philosophy may instruct us, its poetry may charm us; and thus, while skimming the surface of this Book of books, the glorious Christ, who is its substance, its subject, its sweetness, its worth—and but for whom there had been no Bible—has been deeply and darkly veiled from the eye.

But it is the office of the blessed and eternal Spirit to unfold, and so to glorify, Jesus in the Word. All that we spiritually and savingly learn of Him, through this revealed medium, is by the sole teaching of the Holy Spirit, opening up this word to the mind. He shows how all the luminous lines of Scripture truth emanate from, return to, and center in, Christ—how all the doctrines set forth the glory of His person, how all the promises are written in His heart's blood, and how all the precepts are embodied in His life.

MARCH 2

"Open you mine eyes, that I may behold wondrous things out of your law." Psalm 119:18

To the question often earnestly propounded—"What is the best method of reading, so as to understand the Scriptures?" I would reply—Read them with the one desire and end of learning more of Christ, and with earnest prayer for the teaching of the Spirit, that Christ may be unfolded in the Word. With this simple method persevered in, you shall not fail to comprehend the mind of the Holy Spirit, in portions which previously may have been unintelligible and obscure. Restrict not yourself to fixed rules, or to human helps. Rely less upon dictionaries, and maps, and annotations. With singleness of aim, with a specific object of research, and with fervent prayer for the Holy Spirit's teaching, "you need not that any man teach you;" but collating Scripture with Scripture, "comparing spiritual things with spiritual," you may fearlessly enter upon the investigation of the greatest mysteries contained in the sacred volume, assured that the Savior, for whose glories and riches you search, will reveal Himself to your eye, "full of grace and truth." Precious Bible! so full of a precious Jesus! How do all its clouds and darkness melt into light and beauty, as He, the Sun of righteousness, rises in noontide glory upon its page! Search it, my reader, with a view of seeing and knowing more of your Redeemer, compared with whom nothing else is worth knowing or making known. Love your Bible, because it testifies of Jesus; because it unfolds a great Savior, an almighty Redeemer; because it reveals the glory of a sin-pardoning God, in the person of Jesus Christ. Aim to unravel Jesus in the types, to grasp Him amid the shadows, to trace Him through the predictions of the prophet, the records of the evangelist, and the letters of the apostles. All speak of, and all lead to, Jesus. "They are they which testify of me."

MARCH 3

"If you then be risen with Christ, seek those things which are above, where Christ sits on the right hand of God. Set your affection on things above, not on things on the earth." Col. 3:1-2

To win heaven, the mind must become heavenly; and to be heavenly, it must habituate itself to heavenly things and heavenly pursuits. It is a law of our mental constitution, that the mind assimilates in its tone and habits of thought with the subject which most engrosses its study. Hence it is that we sometimes become men of one idea. Now the contemplation of divine and spiritual themes has a powerful tendency to spiritualize and sanctify the mind. It seems impossible to breathe a heavenly atmosphere, and not be heavenly; to study holy things, and not be holy; to admire the image of Christ, and not resemble Christ; to have frequent communion with Jesus upon the throne, and not catch some stray beam of His glory. And apart from Christ nothing is really pleasant and satisfying to the heavenly mind. Without Him, what a dreary, lonesome wilderness would this be! But with Christ in the heart, and the heart resting in Christ—He in the center of our souls, and our affections and desires centering on Him—the desert loses its solitude and its desolateness. To have the eye resting on Jesus—all our heart-springs in Him—the spirit in frequent excursions where He dwells in light and glory—to lean upon Him and converse with Him as though He were actually walking by our side, sitting at our table, associating with us in our callings—this, this is heavenly-mindedness. Such is the counter—attraction to the "things on the earth,"—the secularizing pursuits, the low-thoughted cares, the carnal enjoyments—which we so deeply need. And this powerful counteracting influence which we possess is a realization of our resurrection with Christ, and His enthronement in glory.

MARCH 4

*"Looking unto Jesus the author and finisher
of our faith." Hebrews 12:2*

Be careful of making a savior of faith. There is a danger, and it cannot be too vigilantly guarded against, of substituting the work of the Spirit for the work of Christ; this mistake it is that leads so many of God's saints to look within, instead of outside of themselves, for the evidences of their calling and acceptance; and thus, too, so many are kept, all their spiritual course, walking in a state of bondage and fear, the great question never fully and fairly settled; or, in other words, never quite sure of their sonship. The work of Christ is a great and finished work; it is so glorious that it can admit of no comparison, so complete that it can allow of no addition, and so essential that it can give place to no substitution. Precious as is the work of the Holy Spirit in the heart, and essential as it is to the salvation of the soul, yet he who places it where the work of Jesus ought only to be, deranges the order of the covenant, closes up the legitimate source of evidence, and will assuredly bring distress and uncertainty into his soul. "Righteousness, peace, and joy" are the fruit of a full belief in the Lord Jesus Christ, and he who looks for them away from the cross will meet with disappointment; but they are found in Jesus. He who looks away from himself, from his vileness, guiltiness, emptiness, and poverty, fully, and believingly unto Jesus, shall know what the forgiveness of sin is, and shall experience the love of God shed abroad in his heart.

If, then, your faith is feeble and tried, do not be cast down. Faith does not save you; though it be an instrument of salvation, and, as such, is of vast importance, it is but the instrument. The finished work of Immanuel is the ground of your salvation, yes, it is your salvation itself. Then, make not a savior of your faith; despise it not if it is feeble, exult not in it if it is strong, trample not on it if it is small, deify it not if it is great: such are the extremes to which every believer is exposed. If your faith is feeble and sharply tried, it is no evidence that you are not a believer; but the evidence of your acceptance in the Beloved is to arise from Jesus alone; then let your constant motto be, "looking unto Jesus;" looking to Him just as you are; looking unto Him when faith is feeble; looking unto Him when faith is tried; looking unto Him when faith is declining; yes, looking unto Him when you fear you have no faith. Look up, tried and tempted soul! Jesus is the Author, the Sustainer, and He will become the Finisher of your faith. All you need is in Him; one glimpse, dim though it be, of His cross, one touch, trembling though it be, of His garment, will lift you from your lowest depths, lighten your heaviest burden, gild your darkest prospect, and when you arrive at Jordan's brink, will bear you safely through its swellings, and land you on the sunny and verdant shores of Canaan.

MARCH 5

"The spirit is life because of righteousness." Romans 8:10

What are we to understand by the term spirit? Our reply will at once exclude the idea of the Holy Spirit. Of the Third Person of the blessed Trinity it cannot be of whom the apostle speaks. The only remaining interpretation, then, is that which restricts its meaning to the spiritual and immortal part of the believer—the regenerated spirit of man, and not the regenerating Spirit of God. The cheering declaration, then, of the apostle is, that the spiritual and immortal part of our nature is recovered from the curse, renewed and quickened with a divine and heavenly life. If the body is dead because of sin, the spirit is life because of righteousness. The spirit is life—instinct with a new and deathless principle—because Christ is the righteousness of His people. On the broad basis of God's method of justification our spirit lives. In every point of view Christ is identified with our spiritual life. We live a life of justification by Christ—a life of holiness from Christ—a life of faith in Christ—and a life of immortality with Christ. Thus, in all its phases, "Christ is our life." Oh glorious truth! Welcome death—the spirit lives! Welcome the grave—the spirit is beyond it! Death! you can but touch the material fabric—the inner life towers above your reach, hid with Christ in God. Grave! you can but imprison the body—the soul is at home with Jesus. I live, not because of any righteousness which I have wrought, but because Christ is my righteousness. I live on account of the Righteous One—I live in the Righteous One—and I shall live forever with the Righteous One. Thus is the spirit life because of righteousness. Oh, what a glorious immortality unveils to the eye of faith! If through the gloomy portals of death the spirit of the believer must pass, in its transit to eternity, life attends it, and life awaits it, and life crowns it. Animated with a deathless existence, clothed with the robe of a new-born immortality, it bursts from its enthralment, and, smiling back upon death, speeds its way to glory, honor, and endless life. To this life let us look forward. From a life now experienced, let us live for a life so soon to be enjoyed. The body must die. But what of that? the spirit is life. And the life-inspired spirit will come back again, re-enter and re-animate the slumbering dust; and now, remodeled and spiritualized, it will be with Christ and all the saints in the new heaven and the new earth, wherein will dwell righteousness.

MARCH 6

"Let us therefore come boldly unto the throne of grace, that we may obtain mercy, and find grace to help in time of need." Hebrews 4:16

The throne of grace is for the needy. It is always a time of need with a child of God. "Without me," says Jesus, "you can do nothing." There is not a moment, but, if he knows his real state, he is in need of something. What a blessing, then, is the throne of grace! It is for the needy. It is for those who are in need—upon whom all other doors are closed, with whom all other resources have failed, who have nowhere else to look, nowhere else to fly. To such is the throne of grace always open. Is it a time of trial with you? then it is a time of need. Take your trial, whatever it be, simply to God.

Do not brood over it. Do not cherish it. This will not make it sweeter, or more easy to be borne. But taking it to Jesus will. The very act of taking it will lighten it, and casting it upon His tenderness and sympathy will make it sweet. Is it a time of spiritual darkness with you? then it is a time of need. Take your darkness to the throne of grace, and "in His light" who sits upon it you "shall see light." Is it a time of adverse providences? then it is a time of need. And where can you go for guidance, for direction, for counsel, for light upon the intricacies of the way, but to the God of grace? Is it a time of temporal distress with you? then it is a time of need. Take your temporal cares and necessities to the Lord, for He who is the God of grace is also the God of providence.

Thank the Lord for every errand that takes you to the throne of grace. Whatever it is that sends you to prayer, count it one of your choice blessings. It may be a heavy cross, a painful trial, a pressing need; it may be a broken cistern, a cold look, an unkind expression; yet, if it leads you to prayer, regard it as a mercy sent from God to your soul. Thank God for an errand to Him.

MARCH 7

"Your will be done on earth, as it is heaven." Matthew 6:10

The holy Leighton has remarked, that to say from the heart, "your will be done," constitutes the very essence of sanctification. There is much truth in this; more, perhaps, than strikes the mind at the first view. Before conversion, the will, the governing principle of the soul, is the seat of all opposition to God. It rises against God—His government, His law, His providence, His grace, His Son; yes, all that appertains to God, the unrenewed will of man is hostile to. Here lies the depth of man's unholiness. The will is against God; and so long as it refuses to obey Him, the creature must remain unholy. Now, it needs no lengthened argument to show that the will, being renewed by the Holy Spirit, and made to submit to God, in proportion to the degree of its submission must be the holiness of the believer. There could not be perfect holiness in heaven, were there the slightest preponderance of the will of the creature towards itself. The angels and "the spirits of just men made perfect," are supremely holy, because their wills are supremely swallowed up in the will of God. "Your will be done on earth, even as it is in heaven." The will of God is supremely obeyed in heaven, and in this consists the holiness and the felicity of its glorious inhabitants.

Now, in exact proportion as God's will "is done on earth" by the believer, he drinks from the pure fountain of holiness; and as he is enabled, by the grace of Christ, in all things to look up to God with filial love, and to say, "not my will," O my Father, "but your, be done," he attains the very essence of sanctification.

MARCH 8

"Let this mind be in you, which was also
in Christ Jesus." Philippians 2:5

What is it to have "the mind that was in Christ"? We answer, it is to be ever aiming after the highest perfection of holiness. It is to have the eye of faith perpetually on Jesus as our model, studying Him closely as our great example, seeking conformity to Him in all things. It is to be regulated in all our conduct by His humble spirit. First, with regard to others, to choose the low place, to acknowledge God in, and to glorify Him for, the grace, gifts, and usefulness bestowed on other saints, and to exemplify in our social communion the self-denying, expansive benevolence of the Gospel, which enjoins the duty of not seeking paramountly our own interests, but to sacrifice all self-gratification, and even honor and advantage, if, by so doing, we may promote the happiness and welfare of others; thus it is to live, not for ourselves, but for God and our fellow men; for "no man lives to himself, and no man dies to himself;" in the spirit of Him, who, on the eve of returning to His glory, took a towel and girded Himself, and washed His disciples' feet, it is to serve the saints in the most lowly acts and offices. Second, it is to exemplify, with regard to ourselves, the same humble spirit which He breathed. It is to be little in our own eyes, to cherish a humble estimate of our gifts, attainments, usefulness, and station—to be meek, gentle, and submissive under rebuke and correction—to "seek not great things for ourselves,"—to court not human praise, watching our hearts with perpetual vigilance and jealousy, lest we thirst for the honor which comes from man, and not "the honor that comes from God only." It is to contribute to the necessities of saints without begrudging, to give to Christ's cause without ostentation, to do good in secret—to seek, in all our works of zeal, and benevolence, and charity, to hide ourselves, that self may be perpetually mortified—in a word, it is to hunger and thirst after righteousness, to be poor in spirit, lowly in mind, to walk humbly with God, and to live to, and labor for, and aim after, the glory of God in all things. This is to have the "mind which was also in Christ Jesus."

MARCH 9

"God was in Christ, reconciling the world unto himself." 2 Cor. 5:19

The great glory of our Immanuel is his essential glory. When our faith can firmly grasp the Deity of our adorable Lord—and on this precious doctrine may it never waver!—there is a corresponding confidence and repose of the mind in each particular of His sacrificial work. Then it is that we talk of Him as a Mediator, and love to view Him as the great Sin-bearer of His people. In vain do we admire His righteousness, or extol His death, if we look not upon Him in the glory which belongs to Him as essentially God. From this truth, as from a fountain of light, beams forth the glory, which sheds its soft halo around His atoning work. Oh, when, in the near view of death, memory summons back the past, and sin in battle array passes before the eye, and we think of the Lord God, the Holy One, into whose dreadful presence we are about to enter, how will every other support sink beneath us but this! And, as the Holy Spirit then glorifies Christ in His essential glory, testifying that the blood and righteousness—the soul's great trust—are of the incarnate God, we shall rise superior to fear, smile at death, and pass in peace and triumph to glory. Yes, reader, we shall be satisfied with nothing short of absolute Deity, when we come to die. And, in proportion as you find this great truth the substance of your life, you will experience it the support of your death.

MARCH 10

"You are come...to the spirits of just men made perfect." Hebrews 12:22, 23

That the saints will recognize and have communion with each other immediately on their entrance into glory is, we think, clear from these words of the apostle, when enumerating the privileges of the released believers. We indulge, therefore, the fond hope that, should death remove us before the coming of the Lord, we shall meet, know, and have delightful communion with our friends who departed this life in Jesus. But the recognition and the communion must necessarily do not be so perfect and full as when Christ shall appear, and the risen saints shall cluster together around the person and in the kingdom of their Lord; since neither we nor they have attained our state of full knowledge and capacity until that great event take place, and the "blessed hope" is realized. We argue the recognition of the saints from the fact of the perfection of knowledge to which the coming glory will advance us. Our dear Lord reminds His saints that they shall be equal to the angels. They know each other. It would seem impossible, living together for so many years, that they would not. If, then, the saints are equal to them at all, they must be in this sweet privilege. And is it reasonable to suppose that in all other respects our knowledge will be perfected, but in this one particular only? Shall we possess an element of mental power here, which we shall lose in a gradation towards perfection, and, consequently, shall not possess in a higher degree hereafter? Assuredly not. When, therefore, the dead in Christ shall rise at His coming, every intellectual faculty will be enlarged, and not only retaining all our former, but increasing the amount by a larger degree of additional knowledge, we shall "know even as we are known." The perfection of happiness, which glorification implies, involves this blessing. What a rich source of high and holy delight does the communion of saints supply, even in our present state! How it elevates, chastens, expands, and soothes the mind and heart, so much beclouded by care and chafed by sorrow! But heaven will perfect this bliss. Does it not heighten the beauty of the prospect, and strengthen the expectation of the scene?

MARCH 11

"Them also which sleep in Jesus will God bring with him." 1 Thes. 4:14

Will it add nothing to the glory of that event, and to the happiness of that moment, when the Son of God descends, and, dissolving the soft slumbers of the holy dead, will reanimate each with its former occupant, that then we shall perfectly recognize those we once knew and loved, and renew the sweet communion, before imperfect and limited, but now complete and eternal? Dry, then, your tears, and cease to mourn, you saints of God. They are "not lost, but gone before." Their spirits live with Jesus. And when He comes, He will bring them with Him, and you shall see and know them with a cloudless sight and a perfect knowledge. The very eyes which once smiled upon you so kindly—the very tongue which spoke to you so comfortingly—the very hands which administered to you so skillfully—the very feet which traveled by your side so faithfully—the very bosom which pillowed you so tenderly—you shall meet again. "The coming of the Lord draws near," and those who "sleep in Jesus will God bring with Him." Let us "comfort one another with these words."

Will it not be added joy to meet and to know those eminent servants of God whose histories and whose writings stimulated, instructed, and cheered us, shedding light and gladness on our way? Abraham, whose faith had animated us—David, whose experimental psalms had comforted us—Isaiah, whose visions of Jesus had gladdened us—Paul, whose doctrinal epistles had instructed us—John, whose letters of love had subdued us; to gaze upon the "Magdalene" that sat at Jesus' feet—upon the beggar that reposed in Abraham's bosom—upon the repentant thief that Christ promised Paradise—Oh! will not this add to the happiness of heaven? Will this be no joy, no bliss, no glory? Assuredly it will! At Christ's coming, will not His ministers, too, and those to whom their labors had been useful rejoice in each other? The pastor and the flock, will there be no certain and permanent reunion? no sweet, and fond, and holy recognition? Shall their union in the Church below exceed, in its beauty and sweetness, their reunion in the Church above? Here it is necessarily marred by sin. Much concealment is connected with their united labors in the vineyard of Christ. They go forth weeping, bearing precious seed, and often are called to their rest before the fruit of their prayers, and tears, and toil appears. Here, too, seasons of sickness and of separation frequently transpire, enshrouding the spirit with gloom, and wringing the heart with anguish. And then, at last, death itself rudely breaks the tender bond, leaving the affectionate flock to gaze with streaming eyes upon the lessening spirit of their pastor as it ascends and flys away to glory. But the coming of Jesus, with all His saints, will restore this happy union, invest it with new and richer glory, and place it upon an everlasting basis. "For what is our hope, or joy, or crown of rejoicing? Are not even you in the presence of our Lord Jesus Christ at His coming? For you are our glory and joy." Yes, beloved, we shall know each other again, altered and glorified though we will be.

MARCH 12

"Let me fall now into the hand of the Lord; for very great are his mercies: but let me not fall into the hand of man." 1 Chron. 21:13

Well did the trembling king of Israel so exclaim, when with an air of tender faithfulness the prophet placed before him the choice of those evils which should mark his sin. Every point of light in which his decision can be viewed justifies both its wisdom and its holiness. It was wise: he knew that the Lord was his God; as such, He had long been wont to deal with him in transactions the most solemn and confiding, and thus, from knowledge and experience, he felt he could now safely trust in Him. It was holy: he saw that God was most righteous in punishing his sin, and that in meekly submitting to that punishment which came more immediately from the Lord, he was sympathizing with the equity of the divine government, and was upholding the character of the "Judge of all the earth" as "most upright.

Guided by these considerations, he would rather fall into the hands of the Lord, uplifted though they were to scourge. Who has not made this prayer his own, and breathed it at the footstool of mercy? The "tender mercies of the wicked are cruel," but the severest corrections of our Father are love. To be smitten by God is infinitely better to the believer than to be blest by man. The creature's affection often brings with it a snare; and the honor which comes from man tends to nourish the corrupt principle of depraved self. But whatever, in the experience of a child of God, that may be which comes more directly from the Lord, it brings with it its concealed but its certain and often unutterable blessing. Oh, how safe are we in the Lord's hands! Though He frown, we yet may love. Though He scourge, we yet may cling. Though He slay, we yet may trust. "I will cause you to pass under the rod, and I will bring you into the bond of the covenant." With such an issue, welcome the discipline that leads to it. "Let me fall into the hand of the Lord; for very great are His mercies."

MARCH 13

"O you of little faith, wherefore did you doubt?" Matthew 14:31

Doubting faith is not doubtful faith. If the believer has not the faith of assurance, he may have the faith of reliance, and that will take him to heaven. All the doubts and fears that ever harassed a child of God cannot erase his name from the Lamb's book of life, nor take him out of the heart of God, nor shut him out of glory. "Unbelief," says Rutherford, "may perhaps tear the copies of the covenant which Christ has given you; but He still keeps the original in heaven with Himself. Your doubts and fears are no parts of the covenant; neither can they change Christ."

"The doubts and fears of the elect," remarks another, "are overruled by almighty grace to their present and eternal good; as conducing to keep us humble at God's footstool, to endear the merits of Jesus, and to make us feel our weakness and dependence, and to render us watchful unto prayer." Did ever an unregenerate, lifeless soul entertain a doubt or fear of its spiritual condition? Never. Was it ever known anxiously and prayerfully to question or to reason about its eternal state? Never. Do I seek to strengthen your doubts? No; but I wish to strengthen your tried and doubting faith. I would tell you, for your encouragement, that the minutest particle of grace has eternal glory in it, even as the smallest seed virtually contains all that proceeds from it—the blade, the ear, and the full corn in the ear. Faint not, nor be discouraged in your trial of faith. There is not a sweeter way to heaven than along the path of free grace, paved with hard trials. It was the way which He trod who was "full of grace." Rich though He was in grace, yet see how deeply He was tried. Think not, then, that your sore trials are signs of a graceless state. Oh no! The most gracious saints have been the most tried saints. But do not rest here. There is still richer, surer comfort for you—even the fulness of grace that is in Jesus—grace, ever flowing, and yet ever full. Disclose to Him your doubts and fears. Tell Him you desire Him above all good. Plunge into the sea of His fulness; and He, who has created in your soul a thirst for grace, will assuredly and bountifully give you the grace for which you thirst.

MARCH 14

"I will make an everlasting covenant with you,
even the sure mercies of David." Is. 55:3

God had promised David that he would sit upon the throne of his fathers—that the kingdom of Israel, rent from Saul, should be transferred to his government. But the crown and the scepter thus promised loomed in the distance, almost enshrouded from view by dark intervening clouds. The promise seemed as a dead letter. The providence of God appeared to clash with and to contradict the promise of God. But, in the history of His

Church, the providences of the divine government are not the exponents of the promises of the Divine Governor. It is not so much by what God does, as by what God has said, that He is to be judged. Christian mourner, in the divine promises you have an equal proprietorship. They are as much yours as they were David's, of whose "sure mercies" you are the possessor. These promises are exceedingly great and precious in their nature—they are personal and particular in their application—they are absolute and infallible in their fulfilment. Death may appear to be written upon the promise, and upon all the means leading to its accomplishment, but there is a life in the promise that cannot die. See how God wrote the sentence of death upon the promise, as in the case of the age of Abraham—the sterility of Sarah—the abduction of Joseph—the demand for Benjamin—the banishment of David; and yet, in all the instances, the word upon which God caused those waiting souls to hope was made good to the letter; and the promise that appeared dead rose again with a life, all the more vigorous and glorious from its long and gloomy entombment. It is the believer's mercy to know that he has to do with a Divine Promiser, whose faithfulness has been proved, and with a promise whose power has been tested. There is not a promise with which the Holy Spirit the Comforter seeks to support and console you, but has passed through the crucible, and has been "tried as silver is tried." "The word of the Lord is tried." And if it be a fearful sin to doubt what God has declared, it is a tenfold aggravation of that sin not to believe, when a thousand times over He has made good what He has promised, and when a great cloud of witnesses testify that He has never once falsified His word.

MARCH 15

"Trust in the Lord with all your heart; and lean not unto your own understanding. In all your ways acknowledge him, and he shall direct your paths." Proverbs 3:5-6

The constant exercise of prayer makes every burden light, and smooths every rugged step of a child of God: it is this only that keeps down his trials; not that he is ever exempt from them—no, it is "through much tribulation that he is to enter the kingdom;"—he is a disciple of the cross, his religion is that of the cross, he is a follower of Him who died upon the cross, and entire exemption from the cross he never expects until he passes to the possession of the crown. But he may pray down his crosses: prayer will lessen their number, and will mitigate their severity. The man whose walk is far from God, whose frame is cold, and worldly, and careless, if he be a true child of the covenant, one of the Lord's family, may expect crosses and trials to increase upon every step he advances towards the kingdom. Ah! little do many of the tried, afflicted, and constantly disappointed believers think how closely related are these very trials, and afflictions, and disappointments, to their restraining of prayer before God; every step seems attended with some new cross—every scheme is blasted by some adverse wind—every effort is foiled—disappointment follows disappointment, wave attends upon wave—nothing they attempt prospers, all they enter upon fails, and everything seems against them. Oh, could we pass behind the scene, what should we discover? a deserted throne of grace! Were we to divulge the secret, and place it in the form of a charge against the believer, what would it be? "You have restrained prayer before God!" The scheme was framed without prayer; the enterprise was entered upon without prayer; the effort was made without prayer—God has blown upon it, and all has come to nothing. No marvel—God was not consulted—the Lord was not acknowledged, His permission was not asked, His wisdom was not sought, His blessing was not craved; and so He blew upon it all! The precious injunction is—"In all your ways acknowledge Him, and He shall direct your paths." Where this is honored, there is the divine blessing; where it is slighted, there is the divine curse.

MARCH 16

"He shall glorify me." John 16:14

One essential and important office of the Spirit is to glorify Christ. And how does He most glorify Christ, but by exalting His atoning work, giving to it the preeminence, the importance, and the glory it demands; leading the sinner, whom He has first convinced of sin, to accept of Jesus as a willing, an all-sufficient Savior; to cast away all trust in self, all reliance upon a covenant of works, which is but a covenant of death, and thus going entirely outside of himself, to take up his rest in the blood and righteousness of Immanuel, the God-man Mediator. Oh, what sweet, holy delight must it be to the Spirit of God when a poor sinner, in all his conscious nothingness, is led to build upon Jesus, the "tried stone, the precious corner-stone, the sure foundation!"

Let the reader, then, imagine how grieving it must be to the Spirit, when there is any resting in His work in the soul, either for acceptance, or for comfort, or for peace, or for strength, or even for evidence of a state of grace, and not solely and entirely in the atoning work which Jesus has wrought out for the redemption of sinners. The work of the Spirit and the work of Christ, though they form parts of one glorious whole, are yet distinct, and to be distinguished in the economy, of grace and in the salvation of a sinner. It is the work of Jesus alone, His perfect obedience to the broken law of God, and His sacrificial death as a satisfaction to divine justice, that forms the ground of a sinner's acceptance with God—the source of his pardon, justification, and peace. The work of the Spirit is not to atone, but to reveal the atonement; not to obey, but to make known the obedience; not to pardon and justify, but to bring the convinced, awakened, penitent soul to receive the pardon, and embrace the justification already provided in the work of Jesus. Now, if there is any substitution of the Spirit's work for Christ's work—any undue, unauthorized leaning upon the work within, instead of the work outside of the believer, there is a dishonor done to Christ, and a consequent grieving of the Holy Spirit of God. It cannot be pleasing to the Spirit to find Himself a substitute for Christ; and yet this is the sin which so many are constantly falling into. If I look to convictions of sin within me, to any motion of the indwelling Spirit, to any part of His work, as the legitimate source of healing, of comfort, or of evidence, I turn my back upon Christ, I remove my eye from the cross, and slight His great atoning work; I make a Christ of the Spirit! I make a Savior of the Holy Spirit! I convert His work into an atoning work, and draw the evidence and the consolation of my pardon and acceptance from what He has done, and not from what Jesus has done! Oh, is not this, again we ask, dishonoring to Christ, and grieving to the Holy Spirit of God? Do not think that we undervalue the Spirit's work—great and precious is it. Viewed as a Quickener—as an Indweller—as a Sanctifier—as a Sealer—as a Witness—as a Comforter—as the Author of prayer—His person cannot be too ardently loved, nor can His work be too highly prized; but the love we bear Him, and the honor we give Him, must not be at the expense of the honor and glory and love due to the Lord Jesus Christ, whom it is His office and His delight to glorify. The crown of redemption must be placed upon the head of Jesus; He alone is worthy to wear it—He alone has a right to wear it. "You have redeemed us by Your blood," is the song they sing in glory; and "You shall wear the crown," should be the song echoed back from the redeemed on earth.

MARCH 17

"And the same day Pilate and Herod were made friends together;
for before they were at enmity between themselves." Luke 13:12

How striking and solemn the instruction conveyed in this incident! Pilate and Herod, standing in the attitude of the deadliest hate to each other, are now made friends! And what strange but mighty power has thus suddenly subdued their animosity, and turned their hatred into love? What mystic chain has drawn and bound together these hostile rulers? Their mutual and deep enmity against Jesus! Believers in Christ! are the enemies of our glorious Redeemer, inspired by a natural and kindred feeling of hatred, induced to forget their private quarrels, and merge their differences in one common confederation to crush the Son of God, the object of their mutual hostility; and shall not the friends of the Redeemer, constrained by that divine principle of love which dwells in the hearts of all who are born of God, quench their heart-burnings, bury their antipathies, and draw more closely together in one holy, vigorous, and determined alliance to exalt the Son of God, the glorious and precious Object of their mutual affection? Oh, if Jesus is the bond of union to those who hate Him, how much more should He be the bond of union to those who love Him! Beneath His cross how should all unholy jealousy and bitterness, and wrath and anger, and clamor and all uncharitableness, be mourned over, confessed, abhorred, and renounced by the children of the one family; and how should all who love the Lord Jesus Christ in sincerity be unhesitatingly and cordially recognized as such, thus "endeavoring to keep the unity of the Spirit in the bond of peace."

MARCH 18

"I John, who also am your brother, and companion in tribulation, and in the kingdom and patience of Jesus Christ, was in the isle that is called Patmos, for the word of God, and for the testimony of Jesus Christ. I was in the Spirit on the Lord's day." Rev. 1:9-10

Our adorable Immanuel frequently reveals the most brilliant beams of His glory in seasons of the most painful trial and deepest gloom. The dark providential dispensations of God often bring out in richer radiance the glories of His beloved Son, as the darkness of night reveals more distinctly and brightly the existence and beauty of the heavenly bodies. For the manifestation of this remarkable revelation of His risen glory to His servant, our Lord selects precisely such an occasion—an occasion which, to the eye of reason, would appear the most unfavorable and improbable; but to faith's eye, ranging beyond second causes, the most appropriate for such a revelation of Jesus. The emperor Domitian, though not released from his fearful responsibility for the act, was but the instrument of executing the eternal purpose of grace and love. God's hand was moving, and moving too, as it often does, in the "thick darkness." Exiled as John was by this Roman emperor to a desolate island of the Aegean Sea, "for the word of God, and for the testimony of Jesus Christ," the Redeemer was but preparing the way for the revelation of those visions of glory, than which, none more sublime or more precious ever broke upon the eye of mortal man. God was not only placing His beloved servant in a right posture to behold them, but was also most wisely and graciously training and disciplining His mind spiritually and humbly to receive them.

But mark how this dark and trying incident was making for the good of this holy exile. Banished though he was from the saints, from society, and from all means of grace, man could not banish him from the presence of God; nor persecution separate him from the love of Christ. Patmos, to his view, became resplendent with the glory of a risen Savior—a reconciled God and Father was his Sanctuary—the Holy Spirit, the Comforter, overshadowed him—and the Lord's day, already so hallowed and precious to him in its association with the resurrection of the Lord, broke upon him with unwonted effulgence, sanctity, and joy. Oh, how richly favored was this beloved disciple! Great as had been his previous privileges—journeying with Christ, beholding His miracles, hanging on His lips, reposing on His bosom—yet never had he been so privileged—never had he learned so much of Jesus, nor had seen so much of His glory, nor had drunk so deeply of His love, nor had experienced so richly His unutterable tenderness, gentleness, and sympathy; and never had he spent such a Lord's day as now, the solitary in habitant of an isolated isle though he was. Oh, where is there a spot which Jesus cannot irradiate with His glory; where is there solitude which He cannot sweeten with His presence; where is there suffering, privation, and loss, which He cannot more than recompense by His sustaining grace and soothing love; and where is there a trembling and prostrate soul, which His "right hand" cannot lift up and soothe? This, then, was the occasion on which the Lord appeared in so glorious a form, with such soothing words and sublime revelations, to His beloved servant.

MARCH 19

"And he led them out as far as to Bethany, and he lifted up his hands, and blessed them." Luke 24:50

Let us approach the spot where the Redeemer ascended. It was from Mount Olivet, near to Bethany; so that the two accounts of Christ's ascension recorded by Luke, the one in his Gospel, and the other in his Acts of the Apostles, 1:12, perfectly, agree. How full of great, and holy, and solemn, yes, awful, associations would be that spot to Jesus! It was no strange, unfamiliar, untrodden ground to Him. At the foot of that mount, from whose summit He entered into glory, He had been wont to resort with His disciples for holy meditation and prayer. There, too, His sufferings commenced. There He endured the fearful conflict, when His soul was "exceeding sorrowful, even unto death." It was there, prostrate in the dust, the cup of trembling in His hand, the sweat of blood falling to the ground, He thrice poured out His soul in that touching prayer—"O my Father, if it be possible, let this cup pass from me: nevertheless, not as I will, but as You will." Yes, it was from Mount Olivet, the scene of His deep mental agony, and near to Bethany (which signifies the house of affliction), our blessed Lord took His flight to His Father and His God, to enjoy His presence forever, and to drink deeply and eternally of the pleasures which are at His right hand. And so will it be with all His members. As if to heighten, by contrast with the sufferings of earth, the glories of heaven—as if to give a deeper melody to their song, and a richer sweetness to their joy, and a higher character to their ecstasy, and a profounder sense of the grace that brought them there, it often pleases the Lord that affliction, in various forms, should throw its deepest gloom around the path of the children of God, when just on the eve of translation to glory. And when, in anticipation of a smooth descent and a cloudless sunset, they have said, with Job, "I shall die in my nest," God their Father has seemed to have reserved the bitter dregs of affliction's cup for the dying lips; and, like Jacob, they have been constrained to anticipate that with sorrow their grey hairs will be brought down to the grave. Thus, through much tribulation they enter the kingdom; out of the house of affliction, and, as it were, from Mount Olivet, they ascend to Mount Zion, borne up as in a chariot of fire. Be it so; "He does all things well." Compared with the sufferings of Jesus, it is, in its heaviest form, but a "light affliction;" and measured with an eternity of bliss, in its longest duration, is but "for a moment."

MARCH 20

"And it came to pass, while he blessed them, he was parted from them, and carried up into heaven." Luke 24:51

How touching and instructive was the parting interview! Oh, how worthy of Himself was this His final blessing! How harmonious with every previous act of His life was this its closing one! Blessing to the last, and while with outstretched hands that blessing was yet breathing from His lips, "received up into glory." Oh, how full of grace and love is our adorable Immanuel! What a heart of overflowing tenderness and blessing is His! Knowing this, knowing it from observation and from experience, supported by the innumerable proofs which crowd every page of the New Testament, is it not a marvel that we should seek our blessing from any other source than Jesus, or that we should breathe our sighs, or pour our sorrows, or repose our aching head, on any other bosom than His? Ah! our acquaintance with Him—our best, our dearest, our most loving Friend—is so limited, we walk with Him so coldly, we follow Him so distantly, we believe in Him so feebly; the greatest wonder is; that in the midst of all, His patience forbearance, tender and unchangeable love, towards us should still be so unwearied and so great.

But who can describe the parting interview and the last blessing? Clustering around Him a lonely timid band, saddened as they must have been by the thought that they were about to separate forever on earth from Him whom they loved—as many of them afterwards proved—better than life itself—to whom they had been wont to look for guidance, on whom they had leaned for strength, and to the shelter of whose bosom they had fled in danger and in sorrow, they needed His blessing—they needed that which none but Jesus could give to them. They were oppressed, and He only could undertake for them. They were in sorrow, and He only could comfort them. They were tried and perplexed, and He only could sustain and counsel them. And what, may we suppose, would that blessing contain, which He now breathed over them? The richer anointing of the Spirit to fit them for their work—a larger measure of grace to shield them in temptation, and to uphold them in trial—increased light in the understanding respecting the spiritual nature of His kingdom, and the meaning of the Holy Scriptures of truth; and—what to them, at that moment, would be of unspeakable preciousness—a deeper discovery of His own pardoning love, a fuller assurance of their personal acceptance in Himself, and a richer bestowment of the "peace of God, which passes all understanding." Thus blessing, He was "parted from them, and carried up into heaven," to intercede for them there; and thus blessed, "they worshiped Him, and returned to Jerusalem with great joy," to spread the fragrance and to manifest the power of His name through all the world.

MARCH 21

"It is I; do not be afraid." John 6:20

Imagine yourself threading your way along a most difficult and perilous path, every step of which is attended with pain and jeopardy, and is taken with hesitancy and doubt. Unknown to you and unseen, there is one hovering each moment around you, checking each false step, and guiding each doubtful one; soothing each sorrow, and supplying each need. All is calm and silent. Not a sound is heard, not a movement is seen; and yet, to your amazement, just at the critical moment the needed support comes—you know not from where, you know not from whom. This is no picture of fancy. Are you a child of God, retracing your steps back to Paradise by an intricate and a perilous way? Jesus is near to you at each moment, unseen and often unknown. You have at times stood speechless with awe at the strange interposition, on your behalf, of providence and of grace. No visible sign betokened the source of your help. There was no echo of footfall at your side, nor flitting of shadow across your path. No law of nature was altered or suspended, the sun did not stand still, nor did the heavens open; and yet deliverance, strange and effectual deliverance, came at a moment most unexpected, yet most needed. It was Jesus, your Redeemer, your Brother, your Shepherd, and your Guide. He it was who, hovering round you, unknown and unobserved, kept you as the apple of His eye, and sheltered you in the hollow of His hand. It was He who armed you with courage for the fight, who poured strength into your spirit, and grace into your heart, when the full weight of calamity pressed upon them. Thus has He always been to His saints. The incident of the disciples in the storm presents a striking instance of this. Behold Him standing upon the shore, eyeing, with riveted gaze, the little boat as it struggled amid the sea. They were often invisible to human eye, but not a moment were they lost to His. Not even when in the mount alone in prayer, were they forgotten or unobserved. He beheld from thence their peril, He knew their fears, and He hastened to their support. Stepping from the shore, He approached them. Oh how majestic did His form now appear—walking like a man; and upon the water, like a God! They did not realize that it was Jesus, and were afraid. But their knowledge of Him was not necessary to their safety. It was enough that He knew them. And just as the storm was at its height, and their fears rose with their peril, He drew near and said, in His own gentle, soothing tone, unto them, "It is I; do not be afraid."

MARCH 22

"One God and Father of all, who is above all, and
through all, and in you all." Ephesians 4:6

All who?—the one Church of God. One covenant God and Father unites the one family in heaven and in earth. They are one in His choice, one in His purpose, one in His covenant, one in His heart. The same will chose them—the same affection loved them—the same decree predestinated them: they are one in Him. Blessed truth! "One God and Father." Behold them clustering together around the mercy-seat: they come from various parts of the world, they speak different languages, they express opposite feelings, they unfold needs and sorrows; yet listen! they all address Him as "Our Father." Every heart bows in love to Him, every heart is fixed in faith upon Him, and every tongue breathes the lofty, and endearing, and holy name of "Abba, Father." There, in the glowing light amid which the throne of mercy, stands, all sectarian feeling dies, all denominational distinction is lost, and Christians of every name meet, and embrace, and love as brethren. Holy thought! One God loves all, and protects all; one Father pities all, supplies all, bears with all, and, with an impartial affection, binds all together and alike in His heart.

MARCH 23
"One Lord." Ephesians 4:5

The Church is also one in the Son—"There is one Lord." The Lord Jesus is the one Head, as He is the one Foundation, of the Church. All believers are chosen in Christ, blessed in Christ, saved in Christ, preserved in Christ, and in Christ will be glorified. The work of Christ is the one resting-place of their souls. They rely for pardon upon the same blood, for acceptance upon the same righteousness, and for sanctification upon the same grace. One in Christ, all other differences and distinctions are merged and forgotten: "There is neither Jew nor Greek; there is neither bond nor free; there is neither male nor female for you are

all one in Christ Jesus." Blessed truth! the "righteousness of God, which is unto all and upon all those who believe," imparts the same completeness to all believers in Christ. Upon the breastplate of the great High Priest, now within the veil, every, name is alike written—not a sectarian appellation dims the luster of the "Urim and the Thummin," in whose glowing light the names of all the saints are alike enshrined. What a uniting truth is this! Jesus is the one Head of life, light, and love, to all His saints. He carried the transgression of all—He bore the curse of all—He endured the hell of all—He pardons the sin of all—He supplies the need of all—He soothes the sorrows of all, and He lives and intercedes for all. To Him all alike repair, it is true, with different degrees of knowledge and of faith, and from different points; yet, to Jesus, as to one Savior, one Brother, one Lord, they all alike come. Oh! what a cementing principle is this! The body of Christ—the purchase of the same blood, loved with the same affection, and in heaven represented by the same Advocate, and soon, oh, how soon, to be "gloried together" with Him. What love, then, ought I to bear towards Him whom Jesus has so loved! How can I feel coldly, to, or look unkindly at, or speak uncharitably of, one whom Jesus has redeemed with the same precious blood, and whom He carries each moment in the same loving heart?

MARCH 24

"By one Spirit are we all baptized into one body, whether we be Jews or Gentiles, whether we be bond or free; and have been all made to drink into one Spirit." 1 Cor. 12:13

The Church of God is equally one in the Holy Spirit. One Spirit regenerating all, fashioning all, teaching all, sealing all, comforting all, and dwelling in all. Degrees of grace and "diversities of gifts" there are, "but the same Spirit." That same Spirit making all believers partakers of the same divine nature, and then taking up his abode in each, must necessarily assimilate them in every essential quality, and feature, and attribute of the Christian character. Thus, the unity of the Church is an essential and a hidden unity. With all the differences of opinion, and the varieties of ceremonial, and the multiplicity of sects into which she is broken and divided, and which tend greatly to impair her strength, and shade her beauty, she is yet essentially and indivisibly one—her unity consisting, not in a uniformity of judgment, but better far than this, in the "unity of the Spirit." Thus, no individual believer can with truth say that he possesses the Spirit exclusively, boasting himself of what other saints have not; nor can any one section of the Christian Church lay claim to its being the only true Church, and that salvation is found only within its pale. These lofty pretensions, these exclusive claims, this vain-glory and uncharitableness, are all demolished by one lightning touch of truth, even by that blessed declaration, "For by one Spirit are we all baptized into one body."

MARCH 25

"The love of Christ constrains us." 2 Cor. 5:14

Love is the great influential principle of the gospel. The religion of Jesus is preeminently a religion of motive: it excludes every compulsory principle; it arrays before the mind certain great and powerful motives with which it leads captive the understanding, the will, the affections, and enlists them all in the active service of Christ. Now the law of Christianity is not the law of coercion, but of love. This is the grand lever, the great influential motive, "the love of Christ constrains us." This was the apostle's declaration, and this his governing motive; and the constraining love of Christ is to be the governing motive, the influential principle, of every believer. Apart from the constraining influence of Christ's love in the heart, there cannot possibly be a willing, prompt, and holy obedience to His commandments. A conviction of duty and the influence of fear may sometimes urge forward the soul, but love can only prompt to a loving and holy obedience; and all obedience that springs from an inferior motive is not the obedience that the gospel of Jesus inculcates. The relation in which the believer stands to God, under the new covenant dispensation, is not that of a slave to his master, but of a child to its father. "And because you are sons, God has sent forth the Spirit of his Son into your hearts, crying, Abba, Father." "Wherefore you are no more a servant (a slave), but a son." With this new and spiritual relation, we look for a new and spiritual motive, and we find it in that single but comprehensive word—Love. And thus has our Lord declared it: "If you love me, keep my commandments;" "If a man love me, he will keep my words;" and "he that loves me not, keeps not my sayings." It is, then, only where this love is shed abroad in the heart by the Holy Spirit that we may expect to find the fruit of obedience. Swayed by this divine principle, the believer labors not for life, but from life; not for acceptance, but from acceptance. A holy, self—denying, cross-bearing life, is not the drudgery of a slave, but the filial, loving obedience of a child; it springs from love to the person, and gratitude for the work of Jesus, and is the blessed effect of the spirit of adoption in the heart.

Under the constraining influence of this principle, how easy becomes every cross for Jesus! how light every burden, and how pleasant every yoke! Duties become privileges, difficulties vanish, fears are quelled, shame is humbled, and delay is rebuked.

MARCH 26

"It is good for me to draw near to God." Psalm 73:28

The more any object is to us a source of sweet delight and contempla-tion, the more strongly do we desire its presence, and the more restless are we in its absence. The friend we love we want constantly at our side; the spirit goes out in longings for communion with him; his presence sweetens, his absence embitters every other joy. Precisely true is this of God. He who knows God, who with faith's eye has discovered some of His glory, and, by the power of the Spirit, has felt something of His love, will not be at a loss to distinguish between God's sensible presence and absence in the soul. Some professing people walk so much without communion, without fellowship, without daily, filial, and close communion with God; they are so immersed in the cares, and so lost in the fogs and mists of the world; the fine edge of their spiritual affection is so blunted, and their love so frozen by contact with worldly influences and occupations—and no less so with cold, formal professors—that the Sun of Righteousness may cease to shine upon their soul, and they not know it! God may cease to visit them, and His absence not be felt! He may cease to speak, and the stillness of His voice not awaken an emotion of alarm! Yes, a more strange thing would happen to them if the Lord were suddenly to break in upon their soul with a visit of love, than were He to leave them for weeks and months without any token of His presence. Reader, are you a professing child of God? Content not yourself to live thus; it is a poor, lifeless existence, unworthy of your profession, unworthy of Him whose name you do bear, and unworthy of the glorious destiny towards which you are looking. Thus may a believer test the character of his love. He in whose heart divine affection deepens, increases, and expands, finds God an object of increasing delight and desire, and communion with Him the most costly privilege on earth; he cannot live in the neglect of constant, secret, and close fellowship with his God, his best and most faithful friend.

MARCH 27

"We walk by faith, not by sight." 2 Cor. 5:7

This walk of faith takes in all the minute circumstances of every day's history; a walking every step by faith; a looking above trials, above necessities, above perplexities, above improbabilities and impossibilities, above all second causes; and, in the face of difficulties and discouragements, going forward, leaning upon God. If the Lord were to roll the Red Sea before us, and marshal the Egyptians behind us, and thus hemming us in on every side, should yet bid us advance, it would be the duty and the privilege of faith instantly to obey, believing that, before our feet touched the water, God, in our extremity, would divide the sea and take us dry—shod over it. This is the only holy and happy life of a believer; if he for a moment leaves this path and attempts to walk by sight, difficulties will throng around him, troubles will multiply, the smallest trials will become heavy crosses, temptations to depart from the simple and uptight walk will increase in number and power, the heart will sicken at disappointment, the Holy Spirit will be grieved, and God will be dishonored. Let this precious truth ever be before the mind, "We walk by faith, not by sight."

MARCH 28

"The children of Manasseh could not drive out
the inhabitants of those cities; but the Canaanites
would dwell in the land." Joshua 17:12

You will recollect that when the children of Israel took possession of Canaan, although they conquered its inhabitants and took supreme possession and government of the country, yet they could not entirely dispossess the former occupants of the soil. Now, what these Canaanites, these heathenish idolaters, were to the children of Israel, the natural corruptions of the heart are to the called children of God. After all that divine and sovereign mercy has done for the soul, though the inhabitants of the land have been conquered, and the heart has yielded to the power of omnipotent grace, and the "strong man armed" has been deposed, and Jesus has taken the throne, yet the Canaanites still dwell in the land, and we cannot expel them thence. These are the natural corruptions of our fallen nature, the evils of a heart that is but partially renewed, the heathenish lusts and passions and infirmities that formerly were the sole occupants of the soil, and still dwell there, and which we shall never, in the present state, entirely dispossess. But what did the children of Israel do to these Canaanites, whom they could not give out of the cities, but who would dwell in the land? We read in the 13th verse: "Yet it came to pass when the children of Israel were waxen strong, that they put the Canaanites to tribute; but did not utterly drive them out." Now this is what the children of God must do with the spiritual Canaanites that yet dwell in the renewed heart: they cannot be driven out, but they may be put to tribute; they cannot be entirely extirpated, yet they may be brought into complete subjection, and even made to contribute to the spiritual advance of the soul, and to the glory of God. Yes, even these very indwelling and powerful Canaanites, these strong corruptions that war and fight in the renewed soul, may be made subservient to the spiritual benefit of a child of God. Will it not be so, if they lead him to put no confidence in himself, to draw largely from the fulness of grace in Jesus, to repair often to the throne of mercy, to deal much and closely with the atoning blood, to cultivate a watchful, prayerful, tender spirit, and daily and hourly to rejoice in Christ Jesus, having no confidence in the flesh? Thus may the renewed soul—often led to exclaim, "O wretched man that I am! who shall deliver me from the body of this death?"—through a supply of the Spirit of Christ Jesus, and becoming more thoroughly versed in the are of the holy war, be able to turn the risings of his indwelling sins into occasions of more holy and humble walk with God.

MARCH 29

"I know, O Lord, that your judgments are right, and that you in faithfulness have afflicted me." Psalm 119:75

The mark of a vigorous love to God is when the soul justifies God in all His wise and gracious dealings with it; rebels not, murmurs not, repines not, but meekly and silently acquiesces in the dispensation, be it ever so trying. Divine love in the heart, deepening and expanding towards that God from where it springs, will, in the hour of trial, exclaim, "My God has smitten me, but He is my God still, faithful and loving. My Father has chastened me sorely, but He is my Father still, tender and kind. This trying dispensation originated in love, it speaks with the voice of love, it bears with it the message of love, and is sent to draw my heart closer and yet closer to the God of love, from whom it came." Dear reader, are you one of the Lord's afflicted ones? Happy are you if this is the holy and blessed result of His dealings with you. Happy if you hear the voice of love in the rod, winning your lonely and sorrowful heart to the God from whom it came. But when love to God has declined, the reverse of this is the state of a tried and afflicted believer; and hard thoughts of God in His dispensations may be regarded as an undeniable symptom of such declension.

MARCH 30

"Having therefore, brethren, boldness to enter into the holiest by the blood of Jesus." Hebrews 10:19

In all true prayer great stress should be laid on the blood of Jesus; perhaps no evidence distinguishes a declension in the power and spirituality of prayer more strongly than an overlooking of this. Where the atoning blood is kept out of view, not recognized, not pleaded, not made the grand plea, there is a deficiency of power in prayer. Words are nothing, fluency of expression nothing, niceties of language and brilliancy of thought nothing, and even apparent fervor nothing, where the blood of Christ—the new and the living way of access to God, the grand plea that moves Omnipotence, that gives admission within the holy of holies—is slighted, undervalued, and not made the groundwork of every petition. Oh, how much is this overlooked in our prayers, how is the atoning blood of Immanuel slighted! How little mention we hear of it in the sanctuary, in the pulpit, in the social circle! whereas it is this that makes prayer what it is with God. All prayer is acceptable with God, and only so, as it comes up perfumed with the blood of Christ; all prayer is answered as it urges the blood of Christ as its plea; it is the blood of Christ that satisfies justice, and meets all the demands of the law against us; it is the blood of Christ that purchases and brings down every blessing into the soul; it is the blood of Christ that sues for the fulfilment of His last will and testament, every precious legacy of which comes to us solely on account of His death; this it is, too, that gives us boldness at the throne of grace. How can a poor sinner dare approach without this? How can he look up, how can he ask, how can he present himself before a holy God, but as he brings in the hand of faith the precious blood of Jesus? Outside of Christ, God can hold no communication with us; all communion is suspended, every avenue of approach is closed, all blessing is withheld. God has crowned His dearly beloved Son, and He will have us crown Him too; and never do we place a brighter crown upon His blessed head, than when we plead His finished righteousness as the ground of our acceptance, and His atoning blood as our great argument for the bestowment of all blessing with God. If, then, dear reader, you feel yourself to be a poor, vile, unholy sinner; if a backslider, whose feet have wandered from the Lord, in whose soul the spirit of prayer has declined, and yet still feel some secret longing to return, and dare not, because so vile, so unholy, so backsliding; yet you may return, "having boldness to enter into the holiest by the blood of Jesus." Come, for the blood of Jesus pleads; return, for the blood of Christ gives you a welcome. "If any man sin, we have an Advocate with the Father, Jesus Christ the righteous."

MARCH 31

"And for sin, condemned sin in the flesh." Romans 8:3

As sin is the great condemning cause, let us aim to condemn sin, if we would rank with those for whom there is no condemnation. Most true is it, that either sin must be condemned by us, or we must be condemned for sin. The honor of the Divine government demands that a condemnatory sentence be passed, either upon the transgression, or upon the transgressor. And shall we hesitate? Is it a matter of doubt to which our preference shall be given? Which is best, that sin should die, or that we should die? Will the question allow a moment's consideration? Surely not, unless we are so enamored with sin as calmly and deliberately to choose death rather than life, hell rather than heaven. "The wages of sin is death." Sin unrepented, unforgiven, unpardoned, is the certain prelude to eternal death. Everlasting destruction follows in its turbid wake. There is a present hell in sin, for which the holy shun it; and there is a future hell in sin, for which all should dread it. If, then, we would be among "the pure in heart who shall see God," if we would lift up our faces with joy before the Judge at the last great day, if we would be freed from the final and terrible sentence of condemnation, oh, let us be holy, "denying all ungodliness and worldly lusts, and living righteously, soberly, and godly in this present world." Oh, let us condemn sin, that sin may not condemn us. And let us draw the motive that constrains us, and the power that helps us, from that cross where Jesus "condemned sin in the flesh."

APRIL

APRIL 1

"For if we would judge ourselves, we should not be judged." 1 Cor. 11:31

Self-condemnation averts God's condemnation. When a penitent sinner truly, humbly, graciously sits in judgment upon himself, the Lord will never sit in judgment upon him. The penitent publican, who stood afar off, wrapped in the spirit of self-condemnation, retired from His presence a justified man. The proud, self-righteous Pharisee, who MARCHed boldly to the altar and justified himself, went forth from God's presence a condemned man. When God sees a penitent sinner arraigning, judging, condemning, loathing himself, He exclaims, "I do not condemn you; go and sin no more." He who judges and condemns himself upon God's footstool shall be acquitted and absolved from God's throne. The Lord give unto us this secret spirit of self-judgment. Such was Job's, when in deep contrition he declared, "I abhor myself, and repent in dust and ashes." Such was David's, when he penitentially confessed, "Against You, You only have I sinned, and done this evil in Your sight." Such was Peter's, when he vehemently exclaimed, "Depart from me; for I am a sinful man, O Lord." Such was Isaiah's, when he plaintively cried, "Woe is me, for I am undone; because I am a man of unclean lips." Such was the publican's, when he humbly prayed, "God be merciful to me a sinner." Oh lovely posture! Oh sacred spirit of self-abhorrence, of self condemnation! The Holy Spirit works it in the heart, and this stamps it as so precious, so salutary, and so safe. The great day of the Lord will unveil blessings passing all thought, and glories passing all imagination, to the soul who beneath the cross lies prostrate, in the spirit of self-condemnation. The judgment-day of the self—condemning soul is on this side of eternity; while the judgment-day of the self-justifying soul is on the other side of eternity. And oh, how terrible will that judgment be!

APRIL 2

"There is a friend that sticks closer than a brother." Proverbs 28:24

The power of human sympathy is amazing, if it leads the heart to Christ. It is paralyzed, if it leads only to ourselves. Oh, how feeble and inadequate are we to administer to a diseased mind, to heal a broken heart, to strengthen the feeble hand, and to confirm the trembling knees! Our mute sympathy, our prayerful silence, is often the best exponent of our affection, and the most effectual expression of our aid. But if, taking the object of our solicitude by the hand, we gently lead him to God—if we conduct him to Jesus, portraying to his view the depth of His love, the perfection of His atoning work, the sufficiency of His grace, His readiness to pardon, and His power to save, the exquisite sensibility of His nature, and thus His perfect sympathy with every human sorrow; we have then most truly and most effectually soothed the sorrow, stanched the wound, and strengthened the hand in God.

There is no sympathy—even as there is no love, no gentleness, no tenderness, no patience—like Christ's. Oh how sweet, how encouraging, to know, that in all my afflictions He is afflicted; that in all my temptations He is tempted; that in all my assaults He is assailed; that in all my joys He rejoices—that He weeps when I weep, sighs when I sigh, suffers when I suffer, rejoices when I rejoice. May this truth endear Him to our souls! May it constrain us to unveil our whole heart to Him, in the fullest confidence of the closest, most sacred, and precious friendship. May it urge us to do those things always which are most pleasing in His sight. Beloved, never forget—and let these words linger upon your ear, as the echoes of music that never die—in all your sorrows, in all your trials, in all your needs, in all your assaults, in all your conscious wanderings, in life, in death, and at judgment day—you possess a friend that sticks closer than a brother! That friend is—Jesus!

APRIL 3

"Do not be deceived; God is not mocked: for whatever a man sows, that shall he also reap. For he that sows to his flesh shall of the flesh reap corruption; but he that sows to the Spirit shall of the Spirit reap life everlasting." Gal. 6:7-8

It is a self-evident truth, that there can be no harvest where no seed has been sown. But the fact that there is coming a moral harvest in each individual life—a future reaping of present sowing—is a truth equally demonstrable. The life that now is, is the seed-time of a life that is to come. The future of human destiny derives all its complexion and its form from the present of human character. The spring does not more certainly deepen into summer—nor the summer fade into autumn—nor the autumn pale into winter—nor the winter bloom again into spring, than does our present probation merge into our future destiny, carrying with it its fixed principles, its unchanged habits, and its tremendous account.

And what, my dear reader, are you sowing? I wish this question to have all the earnestness and force of a personal appeal. With what seed, again I ask, are you sowing for the future? If you are unconverted, nothing is more true than that you are sowing to the flesh! You may be rigidly moral, deeply intellectual, profoundly learned, exquisitely refined, outwardly religious, generous, and amiable, and yet all the while you are but sowing to the flesh, and not to the Spirit. "That which is born of the flesh is flesh," and nothing but flesh. "That which is born of the Spirit is spirit," it is spiritual and divine, heavenly and holy; and, what is more, it is imperishable. No lowly seed of divine truth, or grace, love, or service, sown in this present life of suffering and toil, shall ever be lost. All other things shall perish—the world with its loveliness and love, the "lust, of the flesh, and the lust of the eye, and the pride of life," all shall pass away and vanish; but not one seed of grace implanted in the heart of man by the Holy Spirit shall ever perish. The Divine image once restored to the soul shall never more be obliterated. Nothing done by Jesus, or for Jesus—no sin laid down, no cross taken up, no holiness cultivated, no labor wrought, no service done, no cup of cold water given—nothing, the fruit of love to God and of faith in Jesus Christ, shall ever be lost. Oh, who does not earnestly desire that in his heart and life may be sowing the good incorruptible seed, that shall, though long buried and concealed, yield a golden harvest of future joy, bliss, and glory?

APRIL 4

"How are the dead raised up? and with what body do they come?" 1 Cor. 15:35

The identical body that was sown, yet so changed, so spiritualized, so glorified, so immortalized, as to rival in beauty the highest form of spirit, while it shall resemble, in its fashion, the glorious body of Christ Himself. We can form but a faint conception, even from the glowing representations of the apostle, of the glory of the raised body of the just. But this we know, it will be in every respect a structure worthy of the perfected soul that will inhabit it. Now 'the body' is the antagonist, and not the auxiliary of 'the soul'—its clog, its prison, its foe. The moment that Jesus condescends to "grace this mean abode" with His indwelling presence, there commences that fierce and harassing conflict between holiness and sin, which so often wrings the bitter cry from the believer, "Oh wretched man that I am! who shall deliver me from the body of this death?" Oh, what a cumbrance is this body of sin! Its corruptions, its infirmities, its weaknesses, its ailments, its diseases, all conspire to render it the tyrant of the soul, if grace does not keep it under, and bring it into subjection as its slave. How often, when the mind would pursue its favorite study, the wearied and over-tasked body enfeebles it! How often, when the spirit would expatiate and soar in its contemplations of, and in its communings with, God, the inferior nature detains it by its weight, or occupies it with its needs! How often, when the soul thirsts for divine knowledge, and the heart pants for holiness, its highest aspirations and its strongest efforts are discouraged and thwarted by the clinging infirmities of a corrupt and suffering humanity!

Not so will it be in the morning of the resurrection. "Then shall this corruptible put on incorruption, and this mortal shall put on immortality." Mysterious and glorious change! "In a moment, in the twinkling of an eye, at the last trump," the dead in Christ shall awake from their long sleep, and spring from their tombs into a blissful immortality. Oh, how altered! oh, how transformed! oh, how changed! "Sown a natural body, it is raised a spiritual body." "A spiritual body!" Who can imagine, who describe it? What anatomy can explain its mysteries? What pencil can paint its beauties! "A spiritual body!" All the remains, all the vestiges of corrupt matter passed away. "A spiritual body!" So regenerated, so sanctified, so etherealized, so invested with the high and glorious attributes of spirit, yet retaining the "form and pressure" of matter; that now sympathizing and blending with the soul in its high employment of obeying the will and chanting the praises of God, it shall rise with it in its lofty soarings, and accompany and aid it in its deep researches in the hidden and sublime mysteries of eternity.

APRIL 5

"If God be for us, who can be against us?" Romans 8:31

With such a Father, such a Friend, and such a Comforter, who can wage a successful hostility against the saints of God? God Himself cannot be against us, even when the clouds of His providence appear the most lowering, and His strokes are felt to be the most severe. "Though He slay me, yet will I trust in Him." The law cannot be against us; for the Law-fulfiller has, by His obedience, magnified and made it honorable. Divine justice cannot be against us; for Jesus has, in our stead, met its demands, and His resurrection is a full discharge of all its claims. Nor sin, nor Satan, nor men, nor suffering, nor death, can be really or successfully against us, since the condemnation of sin is removed, and Satan is vanquished, and the ungodly are restrained, and suffering works for good, and the sting of death is taken away. "If God be for us, who can be against us?" With such a Being on our side, whom shall we fear? We will fear nothing but the disobedience that grieves, and the sin that offends Him. Fearing this, we need fear nothing else. "God is our refuge and strength, a very present help in trouble. Therefore will not we fear." Listen once more to His wondrous words: "Fear not; for I am with you: do not be dismayed; for I am your God: I will strengthen you; yes, I will help you; yes, I will uphold you with the right hand of my righteousness."

Would we always have God for us? Then let us aim to be for God. God deals with us His creatures by an equitable rule. "The ways of the Lord are equal." "If you walk contrary unto me, their will I walk contrary unto you." Is not God for you? Has He not always, since He manifested Himself to you as your covenant God, been on your side? Has He ever been a wilderness to you, a land of darkness? Has He, in any instance, been unkind, unfriendly, unfaithful? Never. Then be for God—decidedly, wholly, uncompromisingly for God. Your heart for God, your talents for God, your rank for God, your property for God, your influence for God, your all for God; a holy unreserved consecration to Him, all whose love, all whose grace, all whose perfections, all whose heaven of glory is for you. Trembling Christian! God is on your side; and "if God be for us, who can be against us?"

APRIL 6

"But even the very hairs of your head are all numbered." Luke 12:7

You know so little of God, my reader, because you live at such a distance from God; you have so little transaction with Him—so little confession of sin, so little searching of your own conscience, so little probing of your own heart, so little dealing with Him in the blood and righteousness of Christ, so little transaction with Him in the little things of life. You deal with God in great matters; you take great trials to God, great perplexities, great needs; but in the minutiae of each day's history, in what are called the little things of life, you have no dealings with God whatever; and consequently you know so little of the love, so little of the wisdom, so little of the glory, of this glorious covenant God and reconciled Father.

I tell you, the man who lives with God in little matters, who walks with God in the minutiae of his life, is the man who becomes the best acquainted with God—with His character, His faithfulness, His love. To meet God in my daily trials, to take to Him the trials of my calling, the trials of my church, the trials of my family, the trials of my own heart—to take to Him that which brings the shade upon my brow, that rends the sigh from my heart—to remember it is not too trivial to take to God—above all, to take to Him the least taint upon the conscience, the slightest pressure of sin upon the heart, the softest conviction of departure from God—to take it to Him, and confess it at the foot of the cross, with the hand of faith upon the bleeding sacrifice—oh! these are the paths in which a man becomes intimately and closely acquainted with God!

APRIL 7

"I the Lord search the heart." Jeremiah 17:10

Solemn as is this view of the Divine character, the believing mind finds in it sweet and hallowed repose. What more consolatory truth in some of the most trying positions of a child of God than this—the Lord knows the heart. The world condemns, and the saints judge, but God knows the heart. And to those who have been led into deep discoveries of the heart's hidden evil, to whom have been made startling and distressing unveilings, how precious is this character of God—"He that searches the heart!" Is there a single recess of our hearts we would veil from His penetrating glance? Is there a corruption we would hide from His view? Is there an evil of which we would have Him ignorant? Oh no! Mournful and humiliating as is the spectacle, we would throw open every door, and uplift every window, and invite and urge His scrutiny and inspection, making no concealments, and indulging in no reserves, and framing no excuses when dealing with the great Searcher of hearts, exclaiming, "Search me, O God, and know my heart; try me, and know my thoughts; and see if there be any wicked way in me, and lead me in the way everlasting." And while the Lord is thus acquainted with the evil of our hearts, He most graciously conceals that evil from the eyes of others. He seems to say, by His benevolent conduct, "I see my child's infirmity,"—then, covering it with His hand, exclaims—"but no other eye shall see it, but my own!" Oh, the touching tenderness, the loving-kindness of our God! Knowing, as He does, all the evil of our nature, He yet veils that evil from human eye, that others may not despise us as we often despise ourselves. Who but God could know it? who but God would conceal it? And how blessed, too, to remember that while God knows all the evil, He is as intimately acquainted with all the good that is in the hearts of His people! He knows all that His Spirit has implanted, that His grace has wrought. Oh encouraging truth! That spark of love, faint and flickering—that pulsation of life, low and tremulous—that touch of faith, feeble and hesitating—that groan, that sigh, that low thought of self that leads a man to seek the shade—that self-abasement that places his mouth in the dust, oh, not one of these sacred emotions is unseen, unnoticed by God. His eye ever rests with infinite complaisance and delight on His own image in the renewed soul. Listen to His language to David: "Forasmuch as it was in your heart to build a house for my name, you did well, in that it was in your heart."

APRIL 8
"This is my infirmity." Psalm 77:10

The infirmities of the believer are as varied as they are numerous. Some are weak in faith, and are always questioning their interest in Christ. Some, superficial in knowledge, and shallow in experience, are ever exposed to the crudities of error and to the assaults of temptation. Some are slow travelers in the divine life, and are always in the rear; while yet others are often ready to halt altogether. Then there are others who groan beneath the burden of bodily infirmity, exerting a morbid influence upon their spiritual experience. A nervous temperament—a state of perpetual depression and despondency—the constant corrodings of mental disquietude—physical ailment—imaginary forebodings—a facile yielding to temptation—petulance of spirit—unguardedness of speech—gloomy interpretations of providence— an eye that only views the dark hues of the cloud, the somber shadings of the picture. Ah! from this dismal catalogue how many, making their selection, may exclaim, "This is my infirmity." But be that infirmity what it may, let it endear to our hearts the grace and sympathy of Him who for our sake was encompassed with infirmity, that He might have compassion upon those who are alike begirt. All the fulness of grace that is in Jesus is for that single infirmity over which you sigh.

APRIL 9

"He shall take of mine, and shall show it unto you." John 16:15

The Spirit is the Great Conveyancer of Christ to the soul. Placing Himself between the Fountain and the believer, He purposes to convey all blessing, to supply all need, by taking the things of Christ's mediatorial fulness, and bringing them into our blest and holy experience. Having gone before to prepare the soul for the blessing, by discovering its poverty of state, and creating its poverty of spirit, He now takes of the atoning blood and applies it to the conscience; the justifying righteousness, and wraps it around the soul; the sanctifying grace, and conducts it into the heart. In a word, He reveals Jesus to the mind, testifies of Christ to the soul—how divine He is, therefore able to save; how loving He is, therefore as willing as He is able; how gracious He is, therefore stooping to our lowest circumstance; how tender He is, therefore trampling not upon our weak faith, nor despising our little grace; how sympathizing He is, therefore turning not away His ear, and withdrawing not His heart from our tale of sorrow or our burden of grief. Oh, what a Glorifier of Christ is the Divine Spirit! All that we truly know of Jesus, all that we have inwardly experienced of His grace, has been of His teaching and conveyance. He has conducted us to the Fountain—He has led us to the robing-chamber of the King—He has anointed us with the "oil of gladness,"—He has caused our "garments to smell of myrrh, and aloes, and cassia; out of the ivory palaces,"—He has opened the treasury, taking of the precious, glorious things of a precious, glorious Christ, spreading them out in all their vastness, suitableness, and freeness before our longing eye. How often, when the soul has hungered, He has broken up to us the bread that came down from heaven! when it has thirsted, He has smitten the rock, and satiated us with its life-giving stream! How often, when guilt has distressed us, He has sprinkled anew the peace-speaking blood; and when sorrow has oppressed, and difficulties have embarrassed, and dependences have failed, and resources have become exhausted, and creatures most deeply loved have most deeply wounded us, He, the tender, loving Comforter, He, the blessed Teacher, He, the great Glorifier of Jesus, has given to us some new and appropriate and precious view of our Immanuel; and in a moment the storm has passed, the waves have stilled, and peace, serenity, and joy have shed their luster on the soul. One glimpse of Jesus in deep tribulation, one glance in heart-rending bereavement, one discovery of His countenance when all is dark, and dreary, and desolate, one surprisal of His love when the heart sinks into loneliness, one touch of His cross when it is depressed, and bowed, and broken by sin—oh, it is as though heaven had expanded its gates, and we had passed within, where neither tribulation, nor bereavement, nor darkness, nor loneliness, nor sin, is known any more forever!

APRIL 10

"More than conquerors." Romans 8:37

The original word will admit a stronger rendering than our translators have allowed it. The same word is in another place rendered "a far more exceeding and eternal weight of glory." So that in the present instance it might be translated, "far more exceeding conquerors." The phrase seems to imply that it is more than a mere victory which the believer gains. A battle may be won at a severe loss to the conqueror. A great leader may fall at the head of his troops. The flower of an army may be destroyed, and the best

blood of a nation's pride may be shed. But the Christian conquers with no such loss. Nothing whatever essential to His well-being is imperiled. His armor, riveted upon his soul by the Holy Spirit, he cannot lose. His life, hid with Christ in God, cannot be endangered. His Leader and Commander, once dead, is alive and dies no more. Nothing valuable and precious shall he lose. There is not a grace in his soul but shall come out of the battle with sin, and Satan, and the world, purer and brighter for the conflict. The more thoroughly the Lord brings our graces into exercise, the more fully shall they be developed, and the more mightily shall they be invigorated. Not a grain of grace shall perish in the winnowing, not a particle of faith shall be consumed in the refining. Losing nothing, he gains everything! He returns from the battle laden with the spoils of a glorious victory—"more than a conqueror." All his resources are augmented by the result. His armor is brighter, his sword is keener, his courage is more dauntless, for the conflict. Every grace of the Spirit is matured. Faith is strengthened—love is expanded—experience is deepened—knowledge is increased. He comes forth from the trial holier and more valorous than when he entered it. His weakness has taught him wherein his strength lies. His necessity has made him better acquainted with Christ's fulness. His peril has shown him who taught his hands to war and his fingers to fight, and whose shield covered his head in the day of battle. He is "more than conqueror"—he is triumphant!

APRIL 11

"There is no fear in love; but perfect love casts out fear: because fear has torment. He that fears is not made perfect in love." 1 John 4:18

Who that has felt it will deny, that "fear has torment"? The legal fear of death, of judgment, and of condemnation—the fear engendered by a slavish view of the Lord's commandments—a defective view of the believer's relation to God—imperfect conceptions of the finished work of Christ—unsettled apprehensions of the great fact of acceptance—yielding to the power of unbelief—the retaining of guilt upon the conscience, or the influence of any concealed sin, will fill the heart with the torment of fear. Some of the most eminent of God's people have thus been afflicted: this was Job's experience—"I am afraid of all my sorrows." "Even when I remember, I am afraid, and trembling takes hold on my flesh." "When I consider Him, I am afraid of Him." So also David—"What time I am afraid, I will trust in You." "My flesh trembles for fear of You; I am afraid of Your judgments." But "perfect love casts out fear:" he that fears is not perfected in the love of Christ. The design and tendency of the love of Jesus shed abroad in the heart is to lift the soul out of all its "bondage through fear of death," and its ultimate consequences, and soothe it to rest on that glorious declaration, triumphing in which, many have gone to glory, "There is therefore now no condemnation to those who are in Christ Jesus." See the blessed spring from where flows a believer's victory over all bondage-fear—from Jesus: not from his experience of the truth, not from evidence of his acceptance and adoption, not from the work of the Spirit in his heart, blessed as it is—but from out of, and away from, himself—even from Jesus. The blood and righteousness of Christ, based upon the infinite dignity and glory of His person, and wrought into the experience of the believer by the Holy Spirit, expels from the heart all fear of death and of judgment, and fills it with perfect peace. O you of fearful heart! why these anxious doubts, why these tormenting fears, why this shrinking from the thought of death, why these distant, hard, and unkind thoughts of God? Why this prison-house—why this chain? You are not perfected in the love of Jesus, for "perfect love casts out fear:" you are not perfected in that great truth, that Jesus is mighty to save, that He died for a poor sinner, that His death was a perfect satisfaction to Divine justice; and that without a single meritorious work of your own, just as you are, poor, empty, vile, worthless, unworthy, you are welcome to the rich provision of sovereign grace and dying love. The simple belief of this, will perfect your heart in love; and perfected in love, every bondage-fear will vanish away. Oh, seek to be perfected in Christ's love. It is a fathomless ocean, its breadth no mind can scan—its height no thought can scale.

APRIL 12

"Those who are Christ's have crucified the flesh,
with the affections and lusts." Galatians 5:24

True mortification has its foundation in the life of God in the soul. A spiritual, yes, a most spiritual work, it can only spring from a most spiritual principle. It is not a plant indigenous to our fallen nature. It cannot be in the principle of sin to mortify itself. Human nature possesses neither the inclination nor the power by which so holy an achievement can be accomplished. A dead faith, a blind zeal, a superstitious devotion, may prompt severe austerities; but to lay the axe close to the root of indwelling evil, to marshal the forces against the principle of sin in the heart—thus besieging and carrying the very citadel itself—to keep the body under, and bring it into subjection, by a daily and a deadly conflict with its innate and desperately depraved propensities, is a work transcending the utmost reach of the most severe external austerities. It consists, too, in an annulling of the covenant with sin: "Have no fellowship with the unfruitful works of darkness"—enter into no truce, make no agreement, form no union; "but rather reprove them." "Ephraim shall say, What have I to do any more with idols?" The resources of sin must be cut off: "Put on the Lord Jesus Christ, and make no provision for the flesh, to fulfill the lusts thereof." Whatever tends to, and terminates in, the sinful gratification of the flesh is to be relinquished, as frustrating the great aim of the Christian in the mortification of the deeds of the body. Mortification is aptly set forth as a crucifixion: "Those who are Christ's have crucified the flesh." Death by the cross is certain, yet lingering. Our blessed Lord was suspended upon the tree from nine in the morning until three in the afternoon. It was a slow lingering torture, yet terminating in His giving up the spirit. Similar to this is the death of sin in the believer. It is progressive and protracted, yet certain in the issue. Nail after nail must pierce our corruptions, until the entire body of sin, each member thus transfixed, is crucified and slain.

APRIL 13

"If you through the spirit do mortify the deeds
of the body, you shall live." Romans 8:13

"If you." The believer is not a cipher in this work. It is a matter in which he must necessarily possess a deep and personal interest. How many and precious are the considerations that bind him to the duty! His usefulness, his happiness, his sunny hope of heaven, are all included in it. The work of the Spirit is not, and never was designed to be, a substitute for the personal work of the believer. His influence, indispensable and sovereign though it is, does not release from human and individual responsibility. "Work out your own salvation," "Keep yourselves in the love of God," "Building up yourselves," are exhortations which emphatically and distinctly recognize the obligation of personal effort and human responsibility. The reasoning which bids me defer the work of battling with my heart's corruptions, of mortifying the deeds of the body, until the Spirit performs his part, argues an unhealthy Christianity, and betrays a kind of truce with sin, which must on no account for a moment be entertained. As, under the law, the father was compelled to hurl the first missile at the profane child, so under the Gospel—a milder and more benignant economy though it be—the believer is to cast the first stone at his corruptions; he is to take the initiative in the great work of mortifying and slaying the cherished sin. "If you do mortify." Let us, then, be cautious of merging human responsibility in divine influence; of exalting the one by lowering the other; of cloaking the spirit of slothfulness and indolence beneath an apparently jealous regard for the honor of the Holy Spirit. How narrow is the way of truth! How many diverging paths there are, at each turning of which Satan stands, clothed as an angel of light, quoting Scripture with all the aptness and eloquence of an apostle! But God will never release us from the obligation of "striving against sin." "I keep under my body, and bring it into subjection," was Paul's noble declaration. Is no self-effort to be made to escape the gulf of habitual intoxication, by dashing the ensnaring beverage from the lips? Is no self-effort to be made to break away from the thraldom of a companionship, the influence of which is fast hurrying us to ruin and despair? Is no self-effort to be made to dethrone an unlawful habit, to resist a powerful temptation, to dissolve the spell that binds us to a dangerous enchantment, to unwind the chain that makes us the vassal and the slave of a wrong and imperious inclination? Oh, surely, God deals not with us as we deal with a piece of mechanism—but as reasonable, moral, and accountable beings. "I drew you with the bands of a man." Mortification, therefore, is a work to which the believer must address himself, and that with prayerful and resolute earnestness.

APRIL 14
"Somebody has touched me." Luke 8:46

We must acknowledge that the mortification of sin infinitely transcends the mightiest puttings forth of creative power. "If you through the Spirit do mortify." This He does by making us more sensible of the existence of indwelling sin—by deepening our aspirations after holiness—by shedding abroad the love of God in the heart. But, above all, the Spirit mortifies sin in the believer by unfoldings of the Lord Jesus. Leading us to the cross, He would show us that as Christ died for sin, so we must die to sin—and by the self-same instrument too. One real, believing sight of the cross of Jesus!—oh, what a crucifying power it has! Paul, standing beneath its tremendous shadow, and gazing upon its divine victim, exclaimed, "God forbid that I should glory, save in the cross of our Lord Jesus Christ, by which the world is crucified unto me, and I unto the world." Get near the Savior's cross, if you would accomplish anything in this great and necessary work of mortification. The Spirit effects it, but through the instrumentality of the Atonement. There must be a personal contact with Jesus. This only is it that draws forth His grace. When the poor woman in the Gospel touched the Savior, we are told that multitudes thronged Him. And yet, in all that crowd that pressed upon His steps, one only extracted the healing virtue. Thus do multitudes follow Christ externally; they attend His courts, and approach His ordinances, and speak well of His name, who know nothing by faith of personal transaction with the Lord. They crowd His path, and strew their branches in His way, and chant their hosannas; but of how few can Christ say, "Somebody has touched me"! Oh, let us have more personal dealing with the Lord Jesus. He delights in this. It pleases, it glorifies Him. He bids us come and disclose every personal feeling, and make known every need, and unveil every grief, and confide to His bosom each secret of our own. The crowd cannot veil us from His eye. He sees the poor and contrite; He marks the trembling and the lowly; He meets the uplifted glance; He feels the thrill of the gentle, hesitating, yet believing touch. "Somebody has touched me." Who? Is it you, my reader?

APRIL 15

"My son, despise not you the chastening of the Lord, nor faint when you are rebuked of him: For whom the Lord loves he chastens, and scourges every son whom he receives." Hebrews 12:5-6

The rod of your heavenly Father is upon you. In the experience of your sensitive spirit, your feeling heart, the stroke is a heavy, and a sore one. To a keen sense of its severity, is perhaps added the yet keener conviction of the sin that has evoked it—that, but for your wanderings from God, your rebellion against His will, your disobedience of His commands, there would not have come upon you a correction so painful and humiliating. But where in your sorrow will you repair? To the solace and sympathy of whose heart will you betake yourself? Will you flee from that Father? Will you evade His eye, and shun His presence? Eternal love forbids it! What then? You will hasten and throw yourself in His arms, and fall upon His bosom, confessing your sins, and imploring His forgiveness. Thus taking hold of His strength, with that displeased and chastening Father you are in a moment at peace. Blessed is the man, O Lord, whom You chasten, and draw closer within the sacred pavilion of Your loving, sheltering bosom. Oh, what an unveiling of the heart of God may be seen in a loving correction! No truth in experimental religion is more verified than this, that the severest discipline of our heavenly Father springs from His deepest, holiest love. That in His rebukes, however severe, in His corrections, however bitter, there is more love, more tenderness, and more real desire for our well-being, than exists in the fondest affection a human heart ever cherished. And oftentimes, in His providential dealings with His children, there is more of the heart of God unfolded in a dark, overhanging cloud than is ever unveiled and revealed in a bright and glowing sunbeam. But this truth is only learned in God's school.

APRIL 16

"The law was our school-master to bring
us unto Christ." Galatians 3:24

In the school of the law, the first and the grand lesson which the sinner learns is his sin, his curse, and his condemnation. There he is convinced of his vileness, convicted of his guilt, and learns his poverty, helplessness, and hell-deserving. All the fond conceit of his own worthiness, strength, and fitness, vanishes as a vapor, and he sees himself in the power, under the curse, and exposed to the tremendous condemnation of God's righteous, broken, avenging law. Thus convicted in the very act of his rebellion against God, he is brought, like a felon, into the presence of Jesus. There he stands, pale and trembling, his witnesses many and loud, while his own awakened conscience pleads guilty to the charge.

Are you that soul, dear reader? Has the law arrested and brought you within Christ's court? Oh, you never were in such a position before—so new, so strange, so blessed! It may be, you never felt yourself so near hell as now, under the sentence of God's law; but you never were so near heaven as now, in the presence of Jesus. You are now in that court where justice to the fullest is honored, and where mercy to its utmost is extended. You are in Christ's court, at Christ's bar—awaiting the sentence of Him who was made under that law, fulfilled its precepts, and endured its penalty to the uttermost. You are in the presence of Him who came to deliver sinners from its curse and woe, and to raise them far above the reach of all condemnation. Never were you so sensible of your guilt and ruin as now, yet never were you so near the fountain that cleanses from all sin, or so close to Him who was pierced to shelter the vilest of the vile. Your judge is your Savior. He who sits upon that throne is He who hung upon the cross. You are arraigned in the presence and are thrown upon the mercy of Him, the delight of whose heart, and the glory of whose character, it is to save sinners; whose love for them induced Him to screen His glory, and to appear in humiliation—to suffer, bleed, and die. You are in the presence of Him who, though He has ascended on high, and is now glorified with the glory "he had with the Father before the world was," is yet engaged in securing the precious fruits of His soul's travail.

Look up, poor soul! for "your redemption draws near." Never yet did he allow a sin-accused, self-condemned sinner, to go out of this court unblessed, unsaved.

APRIL 17

"If you love me, keep my commandments." John 14:15

As King in Zion, our adorable Lord Jesus delights to reign over a loving and an obedient people. Thus He has made their obedience to His commands a test of their love to His person—"If you love me, keep my commandments." "Teaching them to observe all things whatever I have commanded you," was the last charge given to His disciples. Now it is this keeping of His commandments, this observance of what He has enjoined, that glorifies Him in His saints. Coming to Him in our ignorance glorifies Him as Prophet; coming to Him with our guilt glorifies Him as Priest; and walking obediently to His precepts glorifies Him as King. It places the crown upon the head of His sovereignty, it recognizes the spiritual nature of His kingdom, and it upholds the purity, majesty, and authority of His laws. It becomes, then, the solemn and imperative duty of every believer to search the will and testament of his dying, risen, and exalted Lord, to ascertain all that He has enjoined upon his obedience in the way of precept and command. For how can he be a good and an obedient subject, if he does not understand the laws of Christ's kingdom? Then, when the precept is clearly revealed, and the command is distinctly made known, immediate, self-denying, and cheerful obedience is to follow, as that path which, while it insures the sweetest peace to the soul, brings the highest glory to Christ. Let yours be an obedient walk, dear reader! Let your obedience be the fruit of faith, the dictate of love. Permit no reserve in your obedience; let it be full, honest, and complete. Search the New Testament Scripture, and examine closely your own walk, and ascertain in what particular your obedience to Christ is deficient. Be upright, honest, and sincere in your inquiry. Let your fervent prayer be, "Lord, what will You have me to do? Is there any precept of Your word slighted, any, command disobeyed, any cross not taken up? Is there any desire to withhold my neck from Your, yoke, or to withdraw my shoulder from Your burden, or to mark out a smoother path than that which You have chosen and bade me walk in? Is there any secret framing of excuse for my disobedience, any temporizing, any carnal feeling, any worldly motive, any fear of man, any shrinking from consequences? Lord, You know all things, You know that I love You. You are precious to my soul, for You have borne my sins, endured my curse, carried my cross; and in return do only ask, as an evidence of how much I owe, and how much I love, that I should keep Your commandments, and follow Your example. Now, Lord, take my poor heart, and let it be Your, Your wholly, and Your forever. Let Your sweet love constrain me to run in the way of Your commandments, for this will I do, when You shall enlarge my heart." Then will follow the precious fruits of obedience, even as the bud expands into the blossom, and the blossom ripens into the fruit. There will be a growth, a delightful expansion of the life of God in the soul; and with the increase of the divine life, there will be an increase of all the precious "fruits of the Spirit." See that your Redeemer is glorified in your obedience; that for the happiness of your soul, and for the honor of Christ, you "stand complete in all the will of God."

APRIL 18

"Is not this the carpenter's Son?" Mark 6:3

The attending circumstances of His birth, and the subsequent events of His life, entered deeply into the fact of His abasement. In each step that He took, He did seem to say, "I was born to humiliation and suffering; therefore I came into the world." His parents were poor, of lowly extraction, and humble occupation. Until the age of thirty, He lived a life of entire seclusion from the world; and as He was "subject unto His parents," doubtless His early years were employed in assisting His father in his lowly calling; thus, with His own hands, ministering to His temporal necessities. For, be it remembered, it was a material part of the original curse pronounced by God on man, "In the sweat of your face shall you eat bread." Jesus was made under the law, that He might endure the curse; that curse He fully sustained. There was not a part, the bitterness of which He did not taste, and the tremendousness of which He did not endure; and that for His elect's sake. It were no fanciful idea, therefore, to suppose, that in this feature of the curse our Lord personally entered; that this part of the penalty of human transgression He fully paid; and that, in early life, by the sweat of His brow, He did literally provide for His own temporal sustenance. Oh touching view of the humiliation of the Son of God! How does it dignify the most lowly occupation, sweeten the heaviest trial, and lighten the deepest care, to reflect, "thus lived, and labored, and toiled, the Incarnate God!"

His riper years were marked by corresponding lowliness. The curse tracked His every step, pressing its claims, and exacting its penalties, to the last moment of existence. What were all His excessive privations, but parts of the same? No home sheltered Him—no domestic comforts cheered Him—no smile of fondness greeted Him—no hand of affection welcomed Him—"The Son of man has not where to lay His head," was the heart-rending acknowledgment extracted from His lips. And when a day of exhausting toil had closed upon Him—a day spent in journeying from village to village, and from house to house, preaching the kingdom, healing all manner of diseases, supplying the needs, alleviating the sufferings, and soothing the cares of others—He would retire, lonely and unrefreshed, to the bleak mountain, and spend His long sleepless night in unremitting prayer for His Church! O adorable and adored Jehovah-Jesus! was ever humiliation and love like yours?

APRIL 19

"They shall call his name, Emmanuel, which interpreted is, God with us." Matt. 1:23

Apart from the doctrine of the supreme Godhead of Christ, upon what mere sand do men build their hope of heaven; what dreams, what shadows are all their expectations of eternal life! The Divinity of Jesus denied or rejected, all that is precious and valuable in His death is reduced to a mere negation. What would be His obedience to the law, if reduced to a mere finite obedience? What would be His endurance of its penalty upon the cross, if a 'creature' only were suffering? How could either meet the claims of God's moral government, sustain His holiness, satisfy His justice, and present Him to our view—just to Himself, and yet the justifier of him that believes? Never! If your acceptance as a sinner with this holy Lord God is based on any other righteousness than the "righteousness of God," you are lost, and that to all eternity! A 'created' Savior! Oh, wretched fantasy! A finite Redeemer! Oh awful and malignant scheme of Satan to drown men's souls in perdition!

But to the true believer how glorious, invaluable, and precious is this truth! What a rock does he stand upon, whose faith rests upon the Godhead of Christ! He sees in His blood and righteousness the infinite dignity and worth of the God-Man Mediator. All that he needs as a poor, guilty, undone sinner he finds here. A righteousness that fully acquits him from all the charges of law; a fountain that cleanses him from all the pollution of sin; a Savior, not mighty only, but almighty, to carry his sorrows, bear his burdens, and strengthen him for the conflicts and the difficulties of the pilgrimage. Look up, then, O believer! and fasten the eye of your faith upon the eternal glory of your covenant Head. Your salvation is secured by an Almighty Redeemer, who is able to keep that which you have committed unto Him against the day when He will make up His peculiar treasure.

APRIL 20

"And the angel of the Lord appeared unto him in a flame of fire out of the midst of a bush; and he looked, and behold the bush burned with fire, and the bush was not consumed." Exodus 3:3

This remarkable incident in the history of God's ancient Israel is illustrative of most important truth, bearing upon the experimental and practical experience of each believer in Jesus. It presents a true and beautiful outline of the Church of God. We are reminded of the two opposite natures of the believer—the fallen and the restored, the fleshly and the spiritual. The one low, sinful, unlovely, and of the earth—earthly; the other elevated, holy, glorious, and of heaven—heavenly. "That which is born of the flesh is flesh; that which is born of the Spirit is spirit."

The conflict between these opposite and antagonist natures in the child of God is also presented to view. As the bush in which the Divinity dwelt was surrounded by flame, so the regenerated man, in whom the eternal God deigns to dwell by His spirit, is perpetually encircled by the fire of conflict, trial, and suffering. Nature and grace, sin and holiness, are as contrary the one to the other as any two principles can be. They can no more agree, commingle, or coalesce, than can the opposite and antagonist elements in the natural world. Nor can there ever be a truce between them. They must necessarily and perpetually be at variance, hostile to and at war one with the other. The contest is for supremacy. The great question at issue is, "which shall reign in the believer—sin or holiness; nature or grace; Satan or God?" Oh, what a fiery conflict is this! Hear the confession of an inspired apostle, drawn from his own painful experience: "I am carnal, sold under sin. For that which I do, I allow not; for what I would, that I do not; but what I hate, that do I." Who cannot trace the conflict here? Sin he deeply, inveterately abhorred. The prevailing tendency, the habitual and fixed inclination, of his renewed mind was to holiness—the bent of his desires was towards God. And yet, in consequence of the native depravity of his heart, the influence of sinful propensities, corrupt inclinations and desires, he felt like one chained to a body of death, from which he longed to be delivered. Here was that which defined the two natures, marked the perpetual conflict between both, and which distinguished the holy man from the sinner.

In addition to this spiritual conflict, there are the flames of suffering and trial which encircle a child of God. "He shall baptize you," says John, "with the Holy Spirit, and with fire." God has His "fire in Zion, and his furnace in Jerusalem." But it is not the furnace of justice, nor the fire of wrath. Jesus, the surety, has passed through and sustained all this; He has quenched its flame, and extinguished its embers. But it is the discipline of everlasting love and mercy. And though persecution may be permitted to rage, and the confessor of Christ may ascend, to glory in a chariot of fire—though trials of various kinds may overtake the child of God, his grace and his graces "tried with fire,"—yet both the persecution of the Church and the trial of the believer are but the fruit of eternal and unchangeable love; and will prove purifying, sanctifying, and saving. Nothing will be consumed but the tinsel of the world and the dross of sin, so frequently found allowed with pure gold.

APRIL 21

"I will now turn aside and see this great sight, why the bush is not burned." Exodus 3:3

Contemplate one more surpassing and precious truth—the Church is unconsumed! And why? Because He who dwelt in the bush dwells in the Church. The believer is the temple of the Holy Spirit. The High and Lofty One that inhabits eternity, whose name is Holy, dwells in him. Christ is in him the hope of glory. It is impossible that he can perish. Why has not the poor feeble bush been consumed? why has not grace declined, and faith failed, and love become totally extinguished? why has not the "fiery dart" of Satan prevailed, and the fierce and hot flame of persecution and of trial utterly consumed? Because greater is He that is in the believer than he that is in the world. Believer in Jesus! tell me not only of the sin that dwells in you, often bringing your soul into bondage and distress; tell me also of the grace that dwells in you, which as often gives you the victory, and sends you rejoicing on your way. Tell not only of the burning fiery furnace seven times heated; tell also of Him whose form is like the Son of God, who is with you in the furnace, and who has brought and who yet will bring you through, with not a hair of your head singed, nor the smell of fire passed upon your garments. Tell not only of the "trial of your faith," "though it be tried with fire," but that also, through the ceaseless intercession of Jesus within the veil, that faith never yet has failed. Tell not only of the burden that has oppressed, tell also of the grace that has sustained—not only of the sorrow that has wounded, but also of the divine sympathy, tenderness, and gentleness that have soothed and comforted, bound up and healed that wound. Oh, to hear more frequently the shout of victory and the song of praise breaking in sweet music from the lips of the redeemed! How much more would Jesus be glorified!

APRIL 22

"Surely he has borne our griefs, and carried our sorrows." Isaiah 53:4

In order to the perfection of His character as the High Priest of His people, as the Brother born for adversity, in order to be "touched with the feeling of our infirmities," He must Himself suffer. He must know from painful experience what sorrow meant—what a wounded spirit and a broken bleeding heart, a burdened and a beclouded mind, were. In this school He must be taught, and disciplined, and trained; He must "learn obedience by the things which He suffered;" He must be made "perfect through sufferings." And oh, how deeply has He been taught, and how thoroughly has He been trained, and how well has He learned thus to sympathize with a suffering Church! You have gone, it may be, with your trouble to your earthly friend; you have unfolded your tale of woe, have unveiled every feeling and emotion. But, ah! how have the vacant countenance, the wandering eye, the listless air, the cold response, told you that your friend, with all his love, could not enter into your case! The care that darkened your brow had never shaded his—the sorrow that lacerated your heart had never touched his—the cup you were drinking he had never tasted. What was lacking? Sympathy, growing out of an identity of circumstance. You have gone to another. He has trod that path before you, He has passed through that very trouble, His spirit has been accustomed to grief, His heart schooled in trial, sorrow in some of its acutest forms has been His companion; and now He is prepared to bend upon you a melting eye, to lend an attentive ear and a feeling heart, and to say, "Brother, I have known all, I have felt all, I have passed through all—I can sympathize with all." That Friend of friends, that Brother of brothers, is Jesus. He has gone before you; He has left a fragrance on the brim of that very cup you are now drinking; He has bedewed with tears and left the traces of His blood on that very path along which you are now walking; He has been taught in that very school in which you are now learning. Then what encouragement to take your case, in the sweet simplicity of faith, and lay it before the Lord! to go and tell Jesus, confessing to Him, and over Him, the sin which has called forth the chastisement, and then the grief which that chastisement has occasioned. What a wonderful High Priest is Jesus! As the bleeding Sacrifice, you may lay your hand of faith upon His head, and acknowledge your deepest guilt; and, as the merciful Priest, you may lay your head on His bosom, and disclose your deepest sorrow. O my precious Savior! must You sink to this deep humiliation, and endure this bitter suffering, in order to enter into my lonely sorrow!

APRIL 23

"Little children, keep yourselves from idols." 1 John 5:21

An idolatrous and unsanctified attachment to the creature has again and again crucified love to Christ in the heart. Upon the same principle that no man can love the world and God with a like supreme and kindred affection, so no man can give to Christ and the creature the same intensity of regard. And yet, how often has the creature stolen the heart from its lawful Sovereign! That heart that was once so simply and so supremely the Lord's, those affections that clung to Him with such purity and power of grasp, have now been transferred to another and an inferior object; the piece of clay that God had given but to deepen the obligation, and heighten the soul's love to Himself, has been molded into an idol, before which the heart pours its daily incense; the flower that He has caused to spring forth but to endear His own beauty, and make His own name more fragrant, has supplanted the "Rose of Sharon" in the bosom. Oh! is it thus that we abuse our mercies? is it thus that we convert our blessings into poisons? that we allow the things that were sent to endear the heart of our God, and to make the cross, through which they came, more precious, to allure our affections from their holy and blessed center? Fools that we are, to love the creature more than the Creator!

Dear reader, why has God been disciplining you as it may be, He has? why has He removed your idols, crumbled into dust your piece of clay, and blown witheringly upon your beauteous flower? Why? Because He hates idolatry; and idolatry is essentially the same, whether it be offered to a lifeless, shapeless stock, or to a being of intellect and beauty. And what does His voice speak in every stream that He dries, in every plant that He blows upon, and in every disappointment He writes upon the creature? "My son, give me your heart. I want your love, your pure and supreme affection; I want to be the one and only object of your delight. I gave my Son for you—His life for yours; I sent my Spirit to quicken, to renew, to seal, and possess you for myself; all this I did that I might have your heart. To possess myself of this, I have smitten your gourds, removed your idols, broken your earthly dependences, and have sought to detach your affections from the creature, that they may arise, undivided and unfettered, and entwine around One who loves you with an undying love."

APRIL 24
"Precious faith." 2 Peter 1:1

Truly is faith the crowning grace of all, and a most costly and precious fruit of the renewed mind. From it springs every other grace of a gracious soul. It has been designated the 'queen' grace, because a royal train ever attends it. Faith comes not alone, nor dwells alone, nor works alone. Where faith in Jesus is, there also are love, joy, peace, long-suffering, patience, godly sorrow, and every kindred perfection of the Christian character, all blending in the sweetest harmony, all uniting to celebrate the glory of God's grace, and to crown Jesus Lord of all. Is it, then, surprising that this should be distinguished from all the others by the term "precious faith"? No! that must needs be precious which unfolds the preciousness of everything else. It makes the real gold more precious, and it transmutes everything else into gold. It looks to a "precious Christ" It leads to His "precious blood." It relies upon the "precious promises." And its very trial, though it be by fire, is "precious." It so changes the nature of the painful, the humiliating, and the afflictive, as to turn a Father's frown, rebuke, and correction, into some of the costliest mercies of life. Precious grace, that bids me look upon God in Christ as reconciled; and which, in the absence of all evidence of sight, invites me to rest upon the veracity of God! which takes me in my deepest poverty to Jesus, my true Joseph, having in His hands and at His disposal all the treasures of grace and glory! These are some of the characteristics of this royal grace. "Being justified by faith, we have peace with God, through our Lord Jesus Christ." By faith I can not only say that Jesus died for sinners, but that He died for me. Faith makes the great atonement mine. Faith appropriates to itself all that is in Christ. It lays its hand upon the covenant of grace, and exclaims, "All things are mine." Oh, to see one bowed to the dust under a sense of sin, yet by faith traveling to the blood and righteousness of the Lord Jesus for salvation, and finding it too—to mark the power of this grace in sustaining the soul in deep waters, holding it up in perilous paths—is a spectacle on which God Himself must look down with ineffable delight.

APRIL 25

"Do you believe on the Son of God?" John 9:35

The application of this question, reader, must be to your conscience. Have you "like precious faith" with that which we have attempted to describe? Alas! it may be that you are that tree which brings not forth this good fruit. Yours may be a species of fruit somewhat resembling it; but do not be deceived in a matter so momentous as this. "You believe that there is one God; you do well: the devils also believe, and tremble." That is, you assent to the first proposition of true religion—the being of God; this is well, because your judgment assents to that which is true. And still you have not gone beyond the faith of demons! They believe, and yet horror inconceivable is but the effect of the forced assent of their minds to the truth—they "tremble." Oh, look well to your faith! There must be, in true faith, not only an assent, but also a consent. In believing to the saving of the soul, we not only assent to the truth of the word, but we also consent to take Christ as He is there set forth—the sinner's reconciliation with God. A mere intellectual illumination, or a historical belief of the facts of the Bible, will never place the soul beyond the reach of hell, nor within the region of heaven. There is a "form of knowledge," as well as a "form of godliness;" and both existing apart from vital religion in the soul constitute a "vain religion." Again we press upon you the important inquiry, Have you the "faith of God's elect"? Is it a faith that has stained the glory of self-merit, and laid the pride of intellect in the dust? Is it rooted in Christ? Has it transformed you, in some degree, into the opposite of what you once were? Are any of the "precious fruits" of the Spirit put forth in your life? Is Jesus precious to your soul? And to walk in all circumstances humbly with God—is it the earnest desire of your heart? If there is no sorrow for sin, no going out of yourself to Jesus, no fruits of holiness, in some degree, appearing, then is yours but a "dead faith,"—dead, because it is a part and parcel of a nature "dead in trespasses and in sins,"—dead, because it is not the fruit of the quickening Spirit—dead, because it is inoperative, even as the lifeless root transmits no vitality and moisture to the tree—dead, because it never can bring you to eternal life. Of what value, then, is it? Cut it down! why should it use up the ground? If, then, you have never brought forth the good fruit of prayer, and repentance, and Faith, you are yet in the old nature of sin of rebellion, and of death.

APRIL 26

"For through him we both have access by one
Spirit unto the Father." Ephesians 2:18

What is prayer? It is the communion of the spiritual life in the soul of man with its Divine Author; it is a breathing back the divine life into the bosom of God, from where it came; it is holy, spiritual, humble converse with God. That was a beautiful remark of a converted heathen—"I open my Bible, and God talks with me; I close my Bible, and then I talk with God." Striking definition of true prayer! It is a talking with God as a child talks with his father, as a friend converses with his friend: "And the Lord talked with Moses." Let it be remembered, then, that true prayer is the aspiration of a renewed soul towards God; it is the breathing of the divine life, sometimes in the accents of sorrow, sometimes as the expression of need, and always as the acknowledgment of dependence; it is the looking up of a renewed, afflicted, necessitous, and dependent child to its own loving Father, in all the consciousness of utter weakness, and in all the sweetness of filial trust.

Who is the object of prayer? Jehovah, the Lord of heaven and earth; to Him, as the Three in One, does true prayer only address itself. He alone has an ear to hear our tale of sorrow; an arm than can support in time of need; and a heart that can sympathize with our deep necessity. The high and lofty One, that inhabits eternity, whose name is Holy, who is the Creator and Governor of all worlds, who bears up the pillars of the universe, to whom all the powers in heaven, in earth, and in hell are subject, He is the glorious object to whom we address ourselves in prayer. Not less amazing is the medium of prayer—what is it? Not a creature, dependent as ourselves; but the Lord Jesus Christ, the Son of God, equal in might, majesty, and dominion with the Father, and yet the Elder Brother, the slain Lamb, the Mediator and Surety, the High Priest of His people. Prayer finds acceptance within the veil, only as it is presented in the name of Jesus. The voice that speaks there, in behalf of the lowly suppliant, is the voice of Immanuel's blood; this is the "new and living way,"—this is the plea that prevails, this is the argument that moves Omnipotence itself. He who pleads the blood of Jesus in prayer may have ten thousand tongues all pleading against him, but "the blood of Jesus speaks better things," and drowns their every voice. Oh precious, costly medium of prayer!

Marvellous, too, is the Author of prayer—who is He? The apostle informs us: "Likewise the Spirit also helps our infirmities; for we know not what we should pray for as we ought; but the Spirit itself makes intercession for us, with groanings which cannot be uttered." Thus is it the Holy Spirit who begets the desire, indites the petition, and breathes it forth in prayer through Christ to God. What a sublime exercise, then, is prayer! The outgoing of the divine life in the soul is its nature—Jehovah its object—the Lord Jesus its medium—and the Holy Spirit its author. Thus the blessed Trinity is unity is engaged in the great work of a sinner's approach unto God.

APRIL 27

"Jesus Christ the same yesterday, and
today, and forever." Hebrews 13:8

You will make no advance in the divine life, if your eye is ever upon yourself instead of Christ. What though the experience of today is the opposite of the experience of yesterday—yesterday all brightness, today all cloudiness; yesterday your soul like a well-tuned psalm, today every string loosed and breathing no melody; yesterday, Jesus felt to be so near and precious, today seeming to awaken not a loving emotion in your heart; yesterday, communion with God so sweet, today, none whatever; yesterday, desiring to walk uprightly, holily, and humbly, today detecting so much that is vacillating, weak, and vile. Nevertheless, Jesus is not changed. The work of Christ is the same—your acceptance in Him is the same—His intercession in heaven for you is the same; then, where should you fly to spiritual experiences for support, strength, and consolation—rising when they rise, falling when they fall—when all your standing, joy, peace, and hope are entirely out of yourself, and are solely in Christ? What though you change a thousand times in one day? He never changes. God may vary His dispensations—He may alter His mode of dealing—He may change the nature of His discipline—He may vary the lesson, but His loving-kindness and His truth are as unchangeable as His very being. He may dry up the earthly cistern, but He will never seal up the heavenly fountain!—that will flow on in grace through all time, and in glory through all eternity.

APRIL 28

"For he has made him to be sin for us, who knew no sin; that eve might be made the righteousness of God in him." 2 Corinthians 5:21

My reader, it is your highest honor, as it was His deepest shame; your richest glory, as it was His deepest humiliation; that He literally did bear all the sins of all His Church. As truly as we are "made the righteousness of God in Him," He was "made sin," or a sin-offering, for us. Behold how beautifully has the Holy Spirit brought out the doctrines of substitution and union. Of substitution thus, "He has made Him (who knew no sin) to be sin for us." And of union thus, "that we might be made the righteousness of God in Him." Oh amazing truth! Sinking to our deepest dishonor, He raises us to His highest glory. Sinking Himself with our fallen humanity, He raises us to a union with God. Substituting Himself for us, He makes us one with Himself. An affecting thought! Were all our iniquities, and all our "transgressions in all our sins," laid on Jesus? Yes, all! Before His infinite mind, to whom the past and the future are one eternal now, the sins of all His chosen ones, to the remotest period of time, passed in review, and were made to meet on the head of the atoning Lamb. Here is opened the high source of all real blessed ness to a believing soul. Sweet is the spring, and sweet are the streams that flow from it. Reconciliation with God—His free forgiveness—union with His nature—adoption into His family—acceptance in the Beloved—oneness with a risen Head—access within the veil—filial and perpetual communion—and the "peace of God, which, passes all understanding," are among the costly results of Christ bearing sin. And see how completely He has borne the mighty load. The moment our iniquities touched Him, it would seem as though He flung them to an infinite distance, or sunk them to an infinite depth. Never, in point of law and justice, can they appear against the pardoned soul. Laid upon our Surety, condemned, and punished, and pardoned in Him, "there is now no condemnation" of, or for sin, to "those who are in Christ Jesus." How strong is the language which declares this truth: "I have blotted out as a thick cloud your transgressions, and as a cloud your sins;" "You have cast all my sins behind Your back;" "Thus says the Lord, The iniquity of Israel shall be sought for, and there shall be none; and the sins of Judah, and they shall not be found." And why? "Behold the Lamb of God, that takes away the sin of the world!" And may we not account as among the most precious and costly blessings resulting from this truth, its sanctifying tendency? My beloved, the deepest view you can ever have of God's hatred of sin is in the cross of Calvary; and the deepest sense of the "exceeding sinfulness of sin" you can ever feel is its entire pardon, imprinted on your heart with the atoning blood of Jesus, and witnessed by the power and grace of the Holy Spirit. You hate it because it is forgiven; you abhor it because it is pardoned. Oh, powerful and precious motive to holiness! My soul, yield yourself to its sweet influence, draw your constraints to a life of deeper sanctification from the cross; thirst and pant with more intense desire after Divine conformity, as one all whose iniquities, transgressions, and sins are forever cancelled by the heart's blood of God's dear Son. Oh hateful and hated sin, atoned for so richly, pardoned so freely, blotted out so entirely, how can I admire you? how can I love you? how can I cherish you? and how can I yield to you now? You did burden and bow down to the earth the soul of my blessed Lord. You did mar the beauty, and veil the glory, and humble the spirit of my Beloved. You did crimson His body with the bloody sweat—you did wreath His brow with thorns—you did trouble his soul even unto death; and yet you, my transgressions, are forgiven—you, my sins, are covered—you, my iniquities, are not imputed, and that because Jesus, my surety, was wounded, and bruised, and stricken for me!

APRIL 29

"You are complete in Him." Colossians 2:10

Here is a truth, the vastness of which is only equaled by its unspeakable preciousness. The Lord Jesus is the life of our acceptance with God. We stand as believers in the righteousness of a living Head. Within the veil He has entered, "now to appear in the presence of God for us," presenting all His people each moment complete in Himself. It is a present justification. "You are complete in Him," "accepted in the Beloved," "justified from all things." Perfection in himself the enlightened soul utterly repudiates. Completeness in anything that he is, or has done, he totally rejects. Incomplete his deepest repentance—incomplete his strongest faith—incomplete his best obedience—incomplete his most costly sacrifice—low in the lowest dust does he lay himself. Too wretched he cannot think himself—too little he cannot be in his own eyes. Language fails to express the deep self-loathing and sin-abhorrence of his soul. But lo! a voice is heard—oh, it falls upon his ear like the music of the spheres—"You are complete in Him." In one moment all is peace. The believing soul ceases from his works—the weary spirit enters into rest, because, believing, it enters into Jesus. In Christ he now stands complete. His pardon complete—his justification complete—his adoption complete—his whole person complete before a holy God! Is not this a vast truth? and is it not a glorious one? Where is the doctrine that exceeds it? Where is the declaration that has in it such life as this? Dear reader, it may be you have long been looking at yourself for some one thing complete. Something—in your judgment you may reject the thought, yet in your heart there is that principle which has been looking for something in yourself to commend you to God—something to make you more acceptable to, more welcomed by, Him. But behold where your completeness is found—in, and solely in, Christ. Oh precious truth! A poor, vile sinner, standing before a holy God, complete in righteousness! the object of His infinite love and delight, over whom He rejoices with singing. Oh, how divine, how finished, how glorious must that righteousness be, which so covers your soul as to present you before a God of immaculate purity, "without a spot, or wrinkle, or any such thing!"

APRIL 30

"You have received the Spirit of adoption." Romans 8:15

The Spirit of adoption is the same as the Spirit of God. There are two essential features which identify Him as such. The first is, He imparts the nature of the Father to all the children of the family. In this there is a wide difference between a human and a Divine adoption. Man can only confer his name and his inheritance upon the child he adopts. But in the adoption of God, to the name and inheritance of God is added the Divine nature, imparted in regeneration; so that, in the words of our Lord, we become manifestly the "children of our Father who is in heaven." The second feature is—having begotten the nature of the Father, He then breathes the spirit of the child into the heart. He inspires a filial love. The love which glows in the believer's heart is the affection of a child to its parent. It is not a servile bondage, but a filial and free spirit. Oh sweet and holy emotion! How tender and confiding, how clinging and child-like is it! Such ought to be our love to God. He is our Father—we are His children. Why should not our love to Him be marked by more of the exquisite tenderness, and the unquestioning confidence, and the calm repose of a child reclining upon a parent's breast? A child-like fear of God is another inspiration of the Spirit of adoption. Love and fear are twin graces in the Christian character. The Spirit of God is the Author of both; and both dwell together and cooperate in the same renewed heart. It is not the dread of the servant, but the holy trembling of the child, of which we speak. It is a filial, loving, reverential fear. A child-like trust in God also springs from the Spirit of adoption. The trust of a child is implicit, affectionate, and unquestioning. Upon whose counsel may he so safely rely, in whose affection may he so fully confide, upon whose fidelity may he so confidently trust, as a parent's? God is your Father, O child of a divine adoption, of a heavenly birth!—let your trust in Him be the result of the relationship you sustain. It admits you to the closest intimacy, and invites you to the most perfect confidence. You have not a need, nor an anxiety, nor a grief, which is not all His own. His adoption of your person—an act of His spontaneous and most free grace—pledged Him to transfer all your individual interests to Himself. To these we must add a filial obedience—"If you love me, keep my commandments." Obedience, whether to the Savior's precept, or to the Father's law, is the test of love; and love is the spring of obedience. "All that the Lord God has spoken to us will we do," is the language of that heart where the Spirit of adoption dwells. Such are some of the features of adoption.

MAY

MAY 1

*"This people has a revolting and a rebellious heart;
they are revolted and gone." Jeremiah 5:23*

We look at a believer's lax practice, we mourn and weep over it, and we do well; we trace our own, and still deeper shame and confusion of face cover us: but we forget that the cause of our bitterest sorrow and humiliation should be the concealed principle of evil, from where springs this unholy practice. How few among the called of God are found confessing and mourning over the sin of their nature; the impure fountain from where the stream flows from, the unmortified root from where the branch originates, and from which both are fed and nourished. This is what God looks at—the sin of our fallen, unsanctified nature—and this is what we should look at, and mourn over. Indeed, true mortification of sin consists in a knowledge of our sinful nature; and its subjection to the power of divine grace. The reason why so few believers "through the Spirit mortify the deeds of the body" is, a forgetfulness that the work has to do first and mainly with the root of sin in the soul. "Make the tree good, and the fruit will also be good;" purify the fountain, and the streams will be pure. Oh, were there a deeper acquaintance with the hidden iniquity of our fallen nature—a more thorough learning of the truth, that "in our flesh there dwells no good thing,"—a more heart-felt humiliation on account of it, and more frequent confession of it before God—how much higher than they now are, would be the attainments in holiness of many believers! There is, then, in every child of God, the innate principle of departure. Notwithstanding the wonders of grace God has wrought for the soul—though He has elected, called, renewed, washed, and clothed the believer—yet if He did not check and bridle him in, he would depart, and that forever!—this unsanctified, unmortified principle would bear him away. Is there not in this aspect of our theme something truly heartbreaking?—the subject of God's kind and benevolent government, and yet to be always rebelling against the Sovereign; dwelling under a kind and loving Father's roof, and yet to be perpetually grieving Him and departing from Him; to have received so many costly proofs of His love, and yet rendering the most ungrateful returns—oh, it is enough to sink the soul in the deepest self-abasement before God. Reader, what has the Lord been to you? Come, witness for Him; has He ever been a wilderness to you, a dry and barren land? has there been anything in His dealings, in His conduct, in His way with you, why you should have turned your back upon Him? has there been any harshness in His rebukes, any unkind severity in His corrections, anything judicial and vindictive in His dealings? No, on the contrary, has He not been a fruitful garden, a pleasant land, a fountain of living waters to you? has He not blended kindness with all His rebukes, tenderness with all His chastisements, love with all His dealings, and has not His gentleness made you great? Then why have you departed from Him? What is there in God that you should leave Him, what in Jesus that you should wound Him, what in the blessed Spirit that you should grieve Him? Is not the cause of all your departure, declension, unkindness, unfruitfulness, in yourself, and in yourself alone? But if this has been your conduct towards God, not so has been His conduct towards you.

MAY 2

"I will not let you go, except you bless me." Genesis 32:26

It is the knowledge of his need that gives true eloquence to the petition of the beggar; a sense of destitution, of absolute poverty, of actual starvation, imparts energy to his plea, and perseverance in its attainment; his language is, "I must have bread, or I die." This is just what we want the child of God to feel: what is he but a pensioner on God's daily bounty? what resources has he within himself?—none whatever; and what is he without God?—poor indeed. Now, in proportion as he becomes acquainted with his real case, his utter destitution, he will besiege the throne of grace, and take no denial. He must know his needs, he must know what grace he is deficient in, what besetting sin clings to him, what infirmities encompass him, what portion of the Spirit's work is declining in his soul, where he is the weakest and the most exposed to the attacks of the enemy, and what he yet lacks to perfect him in all the will of God; let him examine himself honestly, and know his real condition. This will endear the throne of grace, will stir up the slumbering spirit of prayer, will supply him with errands to God, and give argument, energy, and perseverance to his suit. It was his deep and pressing sense of need that imparted such boldness and power to the wrestlings of Jacob. "I will not let You go, except You bless me;" and the Lord said, "Your name shall be called no more Jacob, but Israel; for as a prince have you power with God and with men, and have prevailed." Thus imitate the patriarch; begin the day with thinking over what you may possibly need before its close—whether any cross is anticipated, or any temptation is apprehended, or any danger to which you may be exposed; and then go and wrestle for the needed and the promised grace. Oh, it is a great mercy to have an errand that sends us to God; and when we remember what a full heart of love He has, what a readiness to hear, what promptness in all His answers, what entering into the minutest circumstance of a believer's history—how it chides the reluctance and rebukes the unbelief that we perpetually manifest in availing ourselves of this most costly, holy, and precious of all our privileges!

MAY 3

"Those who are whole have no need of the physician,
but those who are sick: I came not to call the
righteous, but sinners to repentance." Mark 2:17

The Spirit glorifies Christ by revealing what Christ is to an emptied, lowly, penitent soul. And this He does by unfolding the great truth of the Bible—that Jesus died for sinners. Not for the righteous, not for the worthy, but for sinners, as sinners; for the unrighteous, for the unworthy, for the guilty, for the lost. Precious moment, when the Eternal Spirit, the great Glorifier of Jesus, brings this truth with power to the heart! "I had believed," exclaims the transported soul, "that Jesus died only for those who were worthy of so rich a sacrifice, of such immense love. I thought to bring some price of merit in my hands, some self-preparation, some previous fitness, something to render my case worthy of His notice, and to propitiate His kind regard. But now I see His salvation is for the vile, the poor, the penniless. I read that 'when we were without strength, Christ died for the ungodly,' that 'while we were yet sinners, Christ died for us,' that 'when we were enemies, we were reconciled to God by the death of His Son,' that 'it is a faithful saying, and worthy of all acceptation, that Christ Jesus came into the world to save sinners,' that it is 'without money and without price,' that it is 'by grace we are saved,' and that it is 'of faith, that it might be by grace.'" This good news, these joyful tidings, this glorious message of free mercy for the vilest of the vile, believed, received, welcomed, in a moment the clouds all vanish, the fogs all disappear, the face of God beams in mild and softened luster, and, amid light and joy, gladness and praise, the jubilee of the soul is ushered in. Oh, what glory now encircles the Redeemer! That soul venturing upon Him with but the faith of reliance, traveling to Him in all weakness, and in the face of all opposition, brings more glory to His name than all the hallelujahs of the heavenly minstrelsy ever brought.

MAY 4

"Why are you so fearful? how is it that you have no faith?" Mark 4:40

The habitual, or even the occasional, doubtful apprehension indulged in of his interest in Christ will tend materially to the enfeebling and decay of a believer's faith; no cause can be more certain in its effects than this. If it be true that the exercise of faith develops its strength, it is equally true that the perpetual indulgence of doubtful apprehensions of pardon and acceptance must necessarily eat as a canker-worm at the root of faith. Every misgiving felt, every doubt cherished, every fear yielded to, every dark providence brooded over, tends to unhinge the soul from God, and dims its near and loving view of Jesus. To doubt the love, the wisdom, and the faithfulness of God, to doubt the perfection of the work of Christ, to doubt the operation of the Spirit on the heart, what can tend more to the weakening and decay of this precious and costly grace? Every time the soul sinks under the pressure of a doubt of its interest in Christ, the effect must be a weakening of the soul's view of the glory, perfection, and all-sufficiency of Christ's work. But imperfectly may the doubting Christian be aware what dishonor is done to Jesus, what reflection is cast upon His great work, by every unbelieving fear he cherishes. It is a secret wounding of Jesus, however the soul might shrink from such an inference; it is a lowering, an undervaluing of Christ's obedience and death—that glorious work of salvation with which the Father has declared Himself well pleased—that work with which divine justice has confessed itself satisfied—that work, on the basis of which every poor, convinced sinner is saved, and on the ground of which millions of redeemed and glorified spirits are now basking around the throne—that work, we say, is dishonored, undervalued, and slighted by every doubt and fear secretly harbored or openly expressed by a child of God. The moment a believer looks at his unworthiness more than at the righteousness of Christ—supposes that there is not a sufficiency of merit in Jesus to supply the absence of all merit in himself before God—what is it but a setting up his sinfulness and unworthiness above the infinite worth, fulness, and sufficiency of Christ's atonement and righteousness? There is much spurious humility among many of the dear saints of God. It is thought by some, that to be always doubting one's pardon and acceptance is the evidence of a humble spirit. It is, allow us to say, the mark of the very opposite of a lowly and humble mind. That is true humility that credits the testimony of God—that believes because He has spoken it—that rests in the blood and righteousness and all-sufficiency of Jesus, because He has declared that "whoever believes in Him shall be saved." This is genuine lowliness—the blessed product of the Eternal Spirit. To go to Jesus just as I am, a poor, lost, helpless sinner—to go without previous preparation—to go glorying in my weakness, infirmity, and poverty, that the free grace, and sovereign pleasure, and infinite merit of Christ might be seen in my full pardon, justification, and eternal glory. There is more of unmortified pride, of self-righteousness, of that principle that would make God a debtor to the creature, in the refusal of a soul fully to accept of Jesus, than is suspected. There is more real, profound humility in a simple, believing venture upon Christ, as a ruined sinner, taking Him as all its righteousness, all its pardon, all its glory, than it is possible for any mortal mind to fathom. Doubt is ever the offspring of pride, humility is ever the handmaid of faith.

MAY 5

"If we believe not, yet he abides faithful; he cannot deny himself." 2 Tim. 2:13

This is the only true and secure anchorage-ground for a poor soul, tossed amid the waves of doubt and perplexity—to know that God cannot alter His word; that it is impossible that He should lie; that were He to deviate from His infinite perfection, He would cease to be a perfect being, and consequently would cease to be God: to know, too, that He is faithful in the midst of the unfaithfulness and perpetual startings aside of His child—faithful in the depth of the deepest affliction—faithful when earthly hopes wither, and human cisterns are broken, and when the soul is led to exclaim, "His faithfulness has failed!"—Oh, what a spring to a tried and drooping faith is this view which God Himself has given of His own glorious and perfect character! It is no small triumph of faith to walk with God, when all is darkness with the soul, and there is no light; to feel amid the roaring of the waves that still He is faithful—that though He slay, yet the soul can trust Him; that though He were to take all else, away He would never remove Himself from His people. Oh glorious triumph of faith! "Who is among you that fears the Lord, that obeys the voice of his servant, that walks in darkness, and has no light? let him trust in the name of the Lord, and stay upon his God."

MAY 6

"You did run well; who did hinder you that you
should not obey the truth?" Galatians 5:7

The apostle Paul, skillful to detect and faithful to reprove any declension in the faith or laxity in the practice of the early Churches, discovered in that of Galatia a departure from the purity of the truth, and a consequent carelessness in their walk. Grieved at the discovery, he addresses to them an affectionate and faithful Epistle, expressive of his astonishment and pain, and proposing a solemn and searching inquiry. "I marvel," he writes, "that you are so soon removed from Him that called you into the grace of Christ. How, after that you have known God, or rather are known of God, how turn you again to the weak and beggarly elements? I am afraid of you, lest I have bestowed upon you labor in vain. Where is the blessedness you spoke of? I stand in doubt of you. You did run well; who did hinder you?" To the reader conscious of secret declension in his soul, we propose the same searching and tender inquiry. You did run well; who hindered you?—what stumbling block has fallen in your way?—what has impeded your onward course?—what has enfeebled your faith, chilled your love, drawn your heart from Jesus, and lured you back to the weak and beggarly elements of a poor world? You set out fair; for a time you did run well; your zeal, and love, and humility gave promise of a useful life, of a glorious race, and of a successful competition for the prize; but something has hindered you. What is it? Is it the world, creature love, covetousness, ambition, presumptuous sin, unmortified corruption, the old leaven unpurged? Search it out. Rest not until it be discovered. Your declension is secret, perhaps the cause is secret—some spiritual duty secretly neglected, or some known sin secretly indulged. Search it out, and bring it to light. It must be a cause adequate to the production of effects so serious. You are not as you once were. Your soul has lost ground; the divine life has declined; the fruit of the Spirit has withered; the heart has lost its softness, the conscience its tenderness, the mind its lowliness, the throne of grace its sweetness, the cross of Jesus its attraction. Oh, how sad and melancholy the change that has passed over you! And have you not the consciousness of it in your soul? Where is the blessedness you spoke of? where is the sunlight countenance of a reconciled Father? where are the rich moments spent before the cross? the hallowed seasons of communion in the closet, shut in with God? where is the voice of the turtledove, the singing of birds, the green pastures where you did feed, the still waters on whose banks you did repose? Is it all gone? Is it winter with your soul? Ah! yes; your soul is made to feel that it is an evil and a bitter thing to depart from the living God.

MAY 7

"For I know that in me (that is, in my flesh) dwells no good thing." Rom. 7:18

The Lord will cause His people to know their total weakness and insufficiency to keep themselves, and that, too, not notionally, not theoretically, nor from what they hear, or from what they read, but from their own deep personal experience of the truth: yes, He is perpetually causing them to learn it. I do not allude merely to that blessed period when the Holy Spirit first lays His axe at the fabric of their self-righteousness—truly they first learn it then—but it is a truth they become growingly acquainted with; it is a lesson they are made daily to learn; and he becomes the most perfectly schooled in it, who watches most narrowly his own heart, is most observant of his own way, and deals most constantly and simply with the cross of Jesus. With regard to the way which the Lord adopts to bring them into the knowledge of it, it is various. Sometimes it is by bringing them into great straits and difficulties, hedging up their path with thorns, or paving it with flints. Sometimes it is in deep adversity after great prosperity, as in the case of Job, stripped of all, and laid in dust and ashes, in order to be brought to the conviction and the confession of deep and utter vileness. Sometimes it is in circumstances of absolute prosperity, when He gives the heart its desire, but sends leanness into the soul. Oh, how does this teach a godly man his own utter nothingness! Sometimes it is by permitting the messenger of Satan to buffet—sending and perpetuating some heavy, lingering, lacerating cross. Sometimes by the removal of some beloved prop, on which we too fondly and securely leaned—putting a worm at the root of our pleasant out-spreading gourd, drying up our refreshing spring, or leading us down deep into the valley of self-abasement and humiliation. But the great school in which we learn this painful yet needed and wholesome lesson, is in the body of sin which we daily bear about with us. It was here Paul learned his lesson, as the seventh chapter of his letter to the Church at Rome shows, and for which Epistle the saints of God will ever have reason to praise and adore the blessed and eternal Spirit. In this school and in this way did the great apostle of the Gentiles learn that the most holy, deeply taught, useful, privileged, and even inspired saint of God was in himself nothing but the most perfect weakness and sin. Do not be cast down, dear reader, if the Lord the Spirit is teaching you the same lesson in the same way; if He is now ploughing up the hidden evil, breaking up the fallow ground, discovering to you more of the evil principle of your heart, the iniquity of your fallen nature, and that, too, it may be, at a time of deep trial, of heavy, heart-breaking affliction. Ah! you are ready to exclaim, "All these things are against me. Am I a child of God ? Can I be a subject of grace, and at the same time be the subject of so much hidden evil, and of such deep, overwhelming trial? Is this the way He deals with His people?"

Yes, dear believer, you are not solitary nor alone; for along this path all the covenant people of God are traveling to their better and brighter home. Here they become acquainted with their own weakness, their perpetual liability to fall; here they renounce their former thoughts of self—power and of self-keeping; and here, too, they learn more of Jesus as their strength, their all—sufficient keeper, more of Him as their "wisdom, righteousness, sanctification, and redemption." Cheer up, then, for the Lord your God is leading you on by a safe and a right way to bring you to a city of rest.

MAY 8

"That the trial of your faith, being much more precious than of gold that perishes, though it be tried with fire, might be found unto praise and honor and glory at the appearing of Jesus Christ." 1 Peter 1:7

The trial of faith is a test of its character; it is the furnace that tries the ore of what kind it is—it may be brass, or iron, or clay, or perhaps precious gold; but the crucible will test it. There is much that passes for real faith, which is no faith; there is much spurious, counterfeit metal; it is the trial that brings out its real character. The true character of Judas was not known until his covetousness was tempted; Simon Magus was not discovered to possess a spurious faith, until he thought to purchase the gift of God with money; Demas did not forsake the apostle, until the world drew him away. But true faith stands the trial; where there is a real work of grace in the heart, no tribulation, or persecution, or power of this world, will ever be able to expel it thence; but if all is chaff, the wind will scatter it; if all is but dross and tinsel, the fire will consume it. Let the humble and tried believer, then, thank God for every test that brings out the real character of his faith, and proves it to be "the faith of God's elect." God will test His own work in the gracious soul; every grace of His own Spirit he will at one time or another place in the crucible; but never will He remove His eye from off it; He will 'sit as a refiner,' and watch that not a grain of the precious metal is consumed; He will be with His child in all and every affliction; not for one moment will He leave him. Let gratitude rather than murmuring, joy rather than sorrow, attend every test which a loving and faithful Father brings to His own gracious work, "that the trial of your faith might be found unto praise and honor and glory at the appearing of Jesus Christ."

MAY 9

"No man has seen God at any time; the only begotten Son, which is in the bosom of the Father, he has declared him." John 1:18

Of the spirituality of the Divine nature we can form no just or definite conception. All our ideas of it must necessarily be unintelligible, vague, and shadowy. Referring to this impossibility, and in language of condescending adaptation to our sensible view of objects, Jesus says of His Father, "You have neither heard His voice at any time, nor seen His shape." Ignorant of this inspired truth, and yet with a quenchless thirst ever desiring such a conception of an infinite spirit as would afford a resting-place for the mind, an object on which faith could repose, and around which the affections could entwine, man has been beguiled into atheism and idolatry of the most debasing and fearful character. Framing his conceptions of spirit after his own low and depraved idea of matter, he has "changed the glory of the incorruptible God into an image made like to corruptible man, and to birds, and four footed beasts, and creeping things."

But God has revealed Himself. He has stooped to our nature, and in the person of His incarnate Son has embodied the spirituality of His being, with all its divine and glorious attributes. All that we clearly, savingly know of God is just the measure of our acquaintance with this truth. Jesus brings God near. "You are near, O Lord." Oh, how near! "They shall call His name Emmanuel, which being interpreted is, God with us." The most stupendous, glorious truth which created mind ever grasped is involved in this wondrous declaration, "Emmanuel, God with us." With what glory does it invest the Bible! what a foundation does it lay for faith! what substance does it impart to salvation! and what a good hope does it place before the believing soul! God is with us in Christ, with us in the character of a reconciled Father, with us every step of our journey to heaven, with us to guide in perplexity, to soothe in sorrow, to comfort in bereavement, to rescue in danger, to shield in temptation, to provide in need, to support in death, and safely to conduct to glory. My soul! fall prostrate in the dust before the majesty of this amazing, this precious truth; adore the wisdom that has revealed it, and admire the grace that makes it yours!

MAY 10

"Set your affection on things above, not on things on the earth." Col. 3:2

How solemn and full of meaning are these words! To set the affections on heavenly things is to realize the ardent desire of the apostle, that he might "know Christ and the power of His resurrection." Oh, there is a mighty, elevating power in the resurrection of Christ! It is the great lever of a child of God, lifting him above earth, heavenward. To know that he is closely and inseparably one with the risen Head of the Church, is to be the subject of a continuous, quickening influence, which in spirit raises him from the dust and darkness and pollutions by which he is surrounded, fixing the affections with greater ardency of devotion and supreme attachment on things above. Oh, nothing will more sanctify and elevate our hearts, than to have them brought under the "power of Christ's resurrection." Following Him by faith, from the dust of earth to the glory of heaven, the affections will ascend with their Beloved. Where He is—the heart's most precious treasure—there it will be also. And oh, to have the heart with Christ in heaven, what an unspeakable mercy! And why should it not be? Has earth more that is attractive and lovely, holy and worthy of its affection, than heaven? Here, we are encircled by, and combat with, spirits of darkness and pollution, principalities and powers; there, is "an innumerable company of angels." Here, we are much separated from the Church of God; there, is the "general assembly and Church of the first-born," from whom nothing shall divide us. Here, the Divine presence is often withdrawn, and we are taunted and accused by our foes; there, is "God the Judge of all," whose presence will be our eternal glory, and who will "bring forth our righteousness as the light, and our judgment as the noon-day." Here, we often hang our heads in sorrow, at the imperfections we mark in the saints; there, are the "spirits of just men made perfect," "without fault before the throne." Here, we often lose sight of our beloved Lord; there, is "Jesus, the Mediator of the new covenant," never more to be veiled from our view. Oh, then, how much richer and more attractive is heaven than earth, to a renewed and holy mind, each moment growing richer and more attractive, by the accession to its happiness of those, the holy and loved ones of the earth, who have for a little while preceded us to that world of perfect bliss! Our treasure in glory, how rapidly it accumulates! Death, which impoverishes us here, by snatching from our embrace the objects of our love, by that same act augments our riches in heaven, into the full possession and enjoyment of which it will, in its appointed time, beneficently translate us. But the sweetest, the most powerful attraction of heaven, let us never forget, is, that Jesus is there. Ah! what would heaven be, were He absent? Could we, at this moment, rush into the fond embrace of the dearest of the glorified ones, and not meet the "Chief among ten thousand, the altogether lovely One," who on earth was more precious to our hearts than life itself, oh, how soon would its glory fade from our eye, and its music pall upon our ear! It would cease to be heaven without Christ. Even on earth His presence and His smile constitute the first dawnings of that better world. And he who lives most in the enjoyment of this—and oh, how much more may be enjoyed than we have the faintest conception of!—has most of the element of heaven in his soul. Aim, then, to cultivate heavenly affections, by a life of high communion with God.

MAY 11

"Being confident of this very thing, that he, which has begun a good work in you, will perform it until the day of Jesus Christ." Philippians 1:6

The doctrine of the Spirit's personal dignity affords a pledge that the work thus commenced shall be carried forward to a final and glorious completion. Because He is God, He will finish what He has begun. And let it not be forgotten, that the growth of the believer in the experience of the truth is as much the work of the eternal Spirit as was the first production of divine life in the soul. The dependence of the believer on the Spirit by no means ceases in conversion. There are after-stages along which it is his office to conduct the believing soul. Deeper views of sin's exceeding sinfulness—a more thorough knowledge of self, more enlarged discoveries of Christ—a more simple and habitual resting upon His finished work, increasing conformity to the Divine image—the daily victory over indwelling sin, and a constant fitting for the inheritance of the saints in light—all these works the one and the self-same Spirit, who first breathed into his soul the breath of spiritual life. Not a step can the believer advance without the Spirit—not a victory can he achieve without the Spirit—not a moment can he exist without the Spirit. As he needed Him at the first, so he needs Him all his journey through. And so he will have Him, until the soul passes over Jordan. To the last ebbing of life, the blessed Spirit will be his Teacher, his Comforter, and his Guide. To the last, He will testify of Jesus; to the last, He will apply the atoning blood; and to the very entrance of the happy saint into glory, the eternal Spirit of God—faithful, loving to the last—will be present to whisper words of pardon, assurance, and peace. Holy Spirit! build us up in the infinite dignity of Your person, and in the surpassing greatness and glory of Your work!

MAY 12

"In whom also, after that you believed, you were sealed with that Holy Spirit of promise." Ephesians 1:13

Although it is most true that the moment a sinner believes in Jesus he becomes actually an "heir of God, and a joint heir with Christ," and enters into the family as an adopted child, yet the clear and undoubted sense of this vast mercy may not be sealed upon his heart until after years. He may long have walked without the sweet sense of God's adopting love in his heart, and the frame of his spirit, and the language of his soul in prayer, has been more that of the "son of the bond-woman" than the "son of the free-woman;"he has known but little of the "free spirit,"—the spirit of an adopted child—and he has seldom gone to God as a kind, loving, tender, and faithful father. But now the Divine Sealer—the eternal Spirit of God—enters afresh, and impresses deeply upon his soul the unutterably sweet and abiding sense of his adoption. Oh, what an impression is then left upon his heart, when all his legal fears are calmed—when all his slavish moanings are hushed, all his bondage spirit is gone—and when, under the drawings of filial love, he approaches the throne of grace, and cries, "My Father!" and his Father responds, "My child! You shall call me, My Father; and shall not turn away from me!"

The sealing of the Spirit does not always imply a rejoicing frame. It is not necessarily accompanied by great spiritual joy. While we cannot forget that it is the believer's privilege to be "always rejoicing," "rejoicing evermore," and that a state of spiritual joy is a holy as it is a happy state, yet we cannot suppose that the "sealed" are always in possession of this "fruit of the Spirit." It is perhaps more a state of rest in God—a state of holy quietude and peace, which, in many cases, seldom rises to that of joy. There is an unclouded hope, a firm and unshaken resting on the finished work, a humble reliance on the stability of the covenant and the immutability of God's love, which is never moved even when there is no sensible enjoyment, and when comfort seems to die. It is a state corresponding to that which David thus expresses—"Although my house do not be so with God; yet He has made with me an everlasting covenant, ordered in all things, and sure: for this is all my salvation, and all my desire, although He make it not to grow." Perhaps more akin to Job's frame of soul when he exclaimed, "Though He slay me, yet will I trust in Him." Sensible comforts may be withdrawn, joy maybe absent—the Sun of Righteousness casting but a faint twilight over the soul—and yet, such is the power of faith grasping the cross of Christ—such the firm resting of the soul upon the stability of the covenant—upon, what God is, and upon what He has promised—that, without one note of joy, or one ray of light, the believer can yet say, "I know in whom I have believed." And why, we ask, this strong and vigorous reliance?—why this buoying up of the soul in the absence of sensible comfort? We reply, because that soul has attained unto the sealing of the Spirit. This forms the great secret.

MAY 13

"The Holy Spirit of God, whereby you are sealed
unto the day of redemption." Eph. 4:30

The believer will never lose the sealing of the Spirit. The impression of God's pardoning love, made upon the heart by the Holy Spirit, is never entirely effaced. We do not say that there are no moments when the "consolations of God are small" with the believer—when he shall have no severe "fightings within, and fears without," when the experience of the Church shall be his, "I opened to my beloved; but my beloved had withdrawn himself, and was gone: my soul failed when he spoke: I sought him, but I could not find him; I called him, but he gave me no answer;"—all this he may experience, and still not lose the sealing of the Spirit. In the midst of it all, yes, in the lowest depth, there shall be the abiding conviction of an interest in God's love, which sustains, animates, and comforts. It will be seen, by reverting to the state of the Church above alluded to, that, although there was the consciousness of her beloved's withdrawment—though he was gone, and she sought him but could not find him, called him but he gave her no answer—yet not for one moment did she lose the impression that He was still her beloved. Here was the glorious triumph of faith, in the hour when all was loneliness, desolation, and joylessness. Here was the sealing of the Spirit which never left her, even though her "beloved had gone." And while not a beam of His beauty glanced upon her soul, nor a note of His voice fell upon her ear, she still could look up and exclaim, "I am my beloved's, and my beloved is mine." Oh mighty power of faith, that can anchor the soul firm on Jesus, in the darkest and wildest tempest! And this is but the sealing of the Spirit. It is the Holy Spirit so deeply impressing on the heart a sense of pardoning love—so firmly establishing it in the faithfulness of God—the finished work of Christ—the stability of the covenant, and the soul's adoption into the one family, that in the gloomiest hour, and under the most trying dispensation, there is that which keeps the soul steady to its center—Jehovah-Jesus. And even should his sun go down behind a mist, he has the sustaining assurance that it will rise upon another world, in peerless, cloudless splendor. O yes! the sealing of the Spirit is a permanent, abiding impression. It is "unto the day of redemption,"—the day when there shall be no more conflict, no more darkness, no more sin. It is not to the day of pardon—for he cannot be more entirely pardoned than he is; it is not to the day of acceptance—for he cannot be more fully accepted than now—no, it is to the glorious "day of redemption"—the day of complete emancipation, longed for by the sons of God, and even sighed for by the "whole creation:" "and not only they, but ourselves also, which have the first-fruits of the Spirit, even we ourselves groan within ourselves, waiting for the adoption, to wit, the redemption of our body." Oh, shout for joy, you sealed of the Lord! You tried and afflicted, tossed with tempest, and not comforted—you who find the wilderness to be but a wilderness, a valley of tears—the way rougher and rougher, narrower and narrower—lift up your heads with joy, the hour of "your redemption draws near," and the "days of your mourning shall be ended." And this is your security—a faithful, covenant-keeping God, "who has also sealed us, and given the earnest of the Spirit in our hearts."

MAY 14

"And suddenly, when they had looked round about, they saw no man any more, save Jesus only with themselves." Mark 9:8

It is possible, my dear reader, that this page may be read by you at a period of painful and entire separation from all public engagements, ordinances, and privileges. The way which it has pleased God to take thus to set you aside may be painful and humbling. The inmate of a sick chamber, or curtained within the house of mourning, or removed far remote from the sanctuary of God and the fellowship of the saints, you are, perhaps, led to inquire, "Lord, why this?" He replies, "Come apart, and rest awhile." Oh the thoughtfulness, the discrimination, the tenderness of Jesus towards His people! He has set you apart from public, for private duties, from communion with others for communion with Himself. Ministers, friends, privileges are withdrawn, and you are—oh enviable state!—alone with Jesus. And now expect the richest and holiest blessing of your life!

Is it sickness? Jesus will make all your bed in your sickness, and your experience shall be, "His left hand is under my head, and His right hand embraces me." Is it bereavement? Jesus will soothe your sorrow and sweeten your loneliness; for He loves to visit the house of mourning, and to accompany us to the grave, to weep with us there. Is it exile from the house of God, from the ordinances of the Church, from a pastor's care, from Christian fellowship? Still it is Jesus who speaks, "There will I be unto you as a little sanctuary." The very circumstances, new and peculiar as they are, in which you are placed, God can convert into new and peculiar mercies, yes, into the richest means of grace with which your soul was ever fed. The very void you feel, the very need you deplore, may be God's way of satiating you with His goodness. Ah! does not God see your grace in your very desire for grace? Does He not mark your sanctification in your very thirsting for holiness? And can He not turn that desire, and convert that thirst, into the very blessing itself? Truly He can, and often does. As one has remarked, God knows how to give the comfort of an ordinance in the desire of an ordinance. And He can now more than supply the absence of others by the presence of Himself. Oh, who can compute the blessings which now may flow into your soul from this season of exile and of solitude? Solitude! no, it is not solitude. Never were you less alone than now. You are alone with God, and He is infinitely better than health, wealth, friends, ministers, or sanctuary, for He is the substance and the sweetness of all. You have perhaps been laboring and watching for the souls of others; the Lord is now showing His tender care for your soul. And oh, if while thus alone with Jesus you are led more deeply to search out the plague of your own heart, and the love of His—to gather up the trailing garment—to burnish the rusted armor—to trim the glimmering lamp—and to cultivate a closer fellowship with your Father, how much soever you may mourn the necessity and the cause, you yet will not regret that the Lord has set you apart from others, that you might rest awhile in His blest embrace—alone with Jesus.

MAY 15

"The throne of grace." Hebrews 4:16

Forget not, dear reader, it is the throne of grace, to which you come in prayer. It is a throne, because God is a Sovereign. He will ever have the suppliant recognize this perfection of His nature. He hears and answers as a Sovereign. He hears whom He will, and answers what and when He will. There must be no dictation to God, no refusing to bow to His sovereignty, no rebelling against His will. If the answer be delayed, or God should seem to withhold it altogether, remember that "He gives no account of any of His matters," and that He has a right to answer or not to answer, as seems good in His sight. Glorious perfection of God, beaming from the mercy-seat!

But it is also a throne of grace. And why? Because a God of grace sits upon it, and the scepter of grace is held out from it, and all the favors bestowed there are the blessings of grace. God has many thrones. There is the throne of creation, the throne of providence, the throne of justice, and the throne of redemption; but this is the throne of grace. Just the throne we need. We are the poor, the needy, the helpless, the vile, the sinful, the unworthy; we have nothing to bring but our deep wretchedness and poverty, nothing but our complaints, our miseries, our crosses, our groanings, our sighs, and tears. But it is the throne of grace. For just such is it erected. It is set up in a world of woe—in the midst of the wilderness—in the very land of the enemy—in the valley of tears, because it is the throne of grace. It is a God of grace who sits upon it, and all the blessings He dispenses from it are the bestowments of grace. Pardon, justification, adoption, peace, comfort, light, direction—all, all is of grace. No worth or worthiness in the creature draws it forth—no price he may bring purchases it—no tears, or complainings, or misery moves the heart of God to compassion—all is of grace. God is so full of compassion, and love, and mercy, He does not need to be stimulated to pour it forth. It gushes from His heart as from a full and overflowing fountain, and flows into the bosom of the poor, the lowly, the humble, and the contrite; enriching, comforting, and sanctifying their souls. Then, dear reader, whatever be your case, you may come. If it is a throne of grace, as it is, then why not you? Why stand afar off? If the poor, the penniless, the disconsolate, the guilty are welcome here—if this throne is crowded by such, why make yourself an exception? Why not come too? What is your case, what is your sorrow, what is your burden? Ah! perhaps you can disclose it to no earthly ear. You can tell it only to God. Then take it to Him. Let me tell you for your encouragement, God has His secret audience-chamber, where He will meet you alone, and where no eye shall see you, and no ear shall hear you, but His; where you may open all your heart, and disclose your real case, and pour all your secrets into His ear. Precious encouragement! It comes from those lips into which grace was poured. "You, when you pray, enter into your closet, and when you have shut your door, pray to your Father which is in secret; and your Father which sees in secret shall reward you openly." Then, upon this promise, go to the throne of grace. Whatever be the need, temporal or spiritual, take it there. God loves your secrets. He delights in your confidence, and will honor the soul that thus honors Him.

MAY 16

"For we are saved by hope." Romans 8:24

The phrase, as employed by the apostle, does not imply the instrument by which we are saved, but the condition in which we are saved. The condition of the renewed creature is one of hope. Salvation by the atonement of Christ—faith, and not hope, being the instrument of its appropriation, is a complete and finished thing. We cannot give this truth a prominence too great, nor enforce it with an earnestness too intense. We cannot keep our eye too exclusively or too intently fixed on Jesus. All salvation is in Him—all salvation proceeds from Him—all salvation leads to Him, and for the assurance and comfort of our salvation we are to repose believingly and entirely on Him. Christ must be all; Christ the beginning—Christ the center—and Christ the end. Oh blessed truth to you who sigh and mourn over the unveiled abominations that crown and darken the chamber of imagery! Oh sweet truth to you who are sensible of your poverty, vileness, and insufficiency, and of the ten thousand flaws and failures of which, perhaps, no one is cognizant but God and your own soul! Oh, to turn and rest in Christ—a full Christ—a loving Christ—a tender Christ, whose heart's love never chills, from whose eye darts no reproof, from whose lips breathes no sentence of condemnation! But, as it regards the complete effects of this salvation in those who are saved, it is yet future. It is the "hope laid up for us in heaven." It would seem utterly incompatible with the present economy that the renewed creature should be in any other condition than one of hopeful expectation. The constitution towards which he tends, the holiness for which he looks, the bliss for which he pants, and the dignity to which he aspires, could not for a moment exist in the atmosphere by which he is here enveloped. His state must of necessity be one of hope, and that hope must of necessity link us with the distant and mysterious future. The idea, "saved by hope," is illustrated by the effects of Christian hope. It is that divine emotion which buoys up the soul amid the conflicts, the trials, and the vicissitudes of the present life. So that we are cheered and sustained, or "saved" from sinking amid the billows, by the hope of certain deliverance and a complete redemption. "In hope of eternal life, which God, who cannot lie, promised before the world began."

MAY 17

"Joint-heirs with Christ." Romans 8:17

This must be understood in a limited though still in a very enlarged sense. In its highest meaning—touching the essential Deity of our Lord—He is the heir of all things. All worlds and all souls are His. All things were created by and for Him. Heaven is His throne, and earth is His footstool. To participation in this heirship we cannot be admitted. Nor can there be any conjointure with Christ in the merit that purchased our redemption. Here again He is alone, no creature aiding the work, or dividing the glory. But, mediatorially, in consequence of the union subsisting between Christ and His people, they become heirs with Him in all the privileges and hopes appertaining to His kingdom. Our union to the Lord Jesus brings us into the possession of vast and untold blessings. On the basis of His atonement we build our claim. He merits all, and we possess all. All the blessings and glories of our present and reversionary inheritance flow to us through Christ. "In whom also we have obtained an inheritance." "If a son, then an heir of God through Christ." We cannot lay too great stress on this truth. We possess nothing—we receive nothing—we expect nothing, but through Christ. All is given to us in consideration of a righteousness which upholds and honors the Divine government. Jesus is the meritorious Recipient, and we receive only through Him. Alluding to our right to, and our possession of, our inheritance, the apostle traces both to the atonement of the Son of God—"And for this cause He is the Mediator of the New Testament, that by means of death, for the redemption of the transgressions that were under the first testament, they which are called might receive the promise of eternal inheritance." Thus it is alone through the "fitness" imparted by Christ, the merit He substitutes in our behalf, and the righteousness He imputes to us, that we become "partakers of the inheritance of the saints in light." Blessed Redeemer! to what dignity and honor, to what privilege and blessing, to what hope and glory, our union with You has advanced us! We were fallen; and you have lifted us up; we were poor, and You have enriched us; we were naked, and You have clothed us; we were aliens, and You have made us children; we were bankrupts, and You have made us heirs: we lost all from fatal union with the first Adam; we receive all, and infinitely more, by our glorious union with You, the second Adam. Oh, for a heart to love You! Oh, for grace to glorify You! Be increasingly precious to us, and may we be increasingly devoted to You!

MAY 18

"You shall love the Lord your God with all your heart, and with all your soul, and with all your mind. This is the first and great commandment." Matthew 22:37-38

Love to God is spoken of in His word as forming the primary and grand requirement of the divine law. Now, it was both infinitely wise and good in God thus to present Himself the proper and lawful object of love. We say it was wise, because, had He placed the object of supreme affection lower than Himself, it had been to have elevated an inferior object above Himself. For whatever other object than God is loved with a sole and supreme affection, it is a deifying of that object, so that it, as God, sits in the temple of God, showing itself that it is God. It was good, because a lesser object of affection could never have met the desires and aspirations of an immortal mind. God has so constituted man, implanting in him such a capacity for happiness, and such boundless and immortal desires for its possession, as can find their full enjoyment only in infinity itself. He never designed that the intelligent and immortal creature should sip its bliss at a lower fountain than Himself. Then, it was infinitely wise and good in God that He should have presented Himself as the sole object of supreme love and worship to His intelligent creatures. His wisdom saw the necessity of having one center of supreme and adoring affection, and one object of supreme and spiritual worship, to angels and to men. His goodness suggested that that center and that object should be Himself, the perfection of infinite excellence, the fountain of infinite good. That, as from Him went forth all the streams of life to all creatures, it was but reasonable and just that to Him should return, and in Him should center, all the streams of love and obedience of all intelligent and immortal creatures: that, as He was the most intelligent, wise, glorious, and beneficent object in the universe, it was fit that the first, strongest, and purest love of the creature should soar towards and find its resting-place in Him. Love to God, then, forms the grand requirement and fundamental precept of the divine law. It is binding upon all intelligent beings. From it no consideration can release the creature. No plea of inability, no claim of inferior objects, no opposition of rival interest, can lessen the obligation of every creature that has breath to "love the Lord his God with all his heart, and with all his soul, and with all his mind." It grows out of the relation of the creature to God, as his Creator, moral Governor, and Preserver; and as being in Himself the only object of infinite excellence, wisdom, holiness, majesty, and grace. This obligation, too, to love God with supreme affection is binding upon the creature, irrespective of any advantage which may result to him from so loving God. It is most true that God has benevolently connected supreme happiness with supreme love, and has threatened supreme misery where supreme affection is withheld; yet, independent of any blessing that may accrue to the creature from its love to God, the infinite excellence of the Divine nature and the eternal relation in which He stands to the intelligent universe, render it irreversibly obligatory on every creature to love Him with a supreme, paramount, holy, and unreserved affection.

MAY 19

"Those who love God." Romans 8:28

Surely it is no small mercy belonging to the Church of Christ, that, composed as it is of all people and tongues, its members as "strangers scattered abroad," its essential unity deeply obscured, and its spiritual beauty sadly disfigured by the numerous divisions which mar and weaken the body of Christ, there yet is an identity of character in all, by which they are not only known to God, but are recognized by each other as members of the one family—"those who love God."

Love to God, then, is the grand distinctive feature of the true Christian. The reverse marks all the unregenerate. Harmonious as their nature, their creed, their Church may be, no love to God is their binding assimilating feature, their broad distinctive character. But the saints are those who love God. Their creeds may differ in minor shades, their ecclesiastical relations may vary in outward forms—as rays of light, the remoter their distances from the center, the more widely they diverge from each other. Yet in this one particular there is an essential unity of character, and a perfect assimilation of spirit. They love one God and Father; and this truth—like those sundered rays of light returning to the sun, approximate to each other—forms the great assimilating principle by which all who hold the Head, and love the same Savior, are drawn to one center, and in which they all harmonize and unite. The regeneration through which they have passed has effected this great change. Once they were the children of wrath, even as others, at enmity with God. Ah! is not this a heart-affecting thought? But now they love Him. The Spirit has supplanted the old principle of enmity by the new principle of love. They love Him as revealed in Christ, and they love Him for the gift of the Revealer—the visible image of the invisible God. Who, as he has surveyed the glory and realized the preciousness of the Savior, has not felt in his bosom the kindling of a fervent love to Him who, when He had no greater gift, commended His love to us by the gift of His dear Son? They love Him, too, in His paternal character. Standing to them in so close and endearing a relation, they address Him as a Father—they confide in Him as a Father—they obey Him as a Father. The spirit of adoption takes captive their hearts, and they love God with a child's fervent, adoring, confiding affection. They love God, too, for all His conduct. It varies, but each variation awakens the deep and holy response of love. They love Him for the wisdom, the faithfulness, the holiness of His procedure; for what He withholds, as for what He grants; when He rebukes, as when He approves. For His frown—they know it to be a Father's frown; for His smile—they feel it to be a Father's smile. They love Him for the rod that disciplines, as for the scepter that governs—for the wound that bleeds, as for the balm that heals. There is nothing in God, and there is nothing from God, for which the saints do not love Him. Of one truth—the source of this feeling—let us not lose sight—"We love Him because He first loved us." Thus the motive of love to God as much springs from Him as the power to love Him.

MAY 20

"I am he that lives, and was dead; and, behold,
I am alive for evermore." Rev. 1:18

Let the Christian reader fully believe this one truth—that Jesus is alive again, and it will afford to his soul greater confirmation of the veracity of God's character, of the truth of His word, and of the perfection and all-sufficiency of Christ's work, than all other truths beside. Is Jesus alive at the right hand of God?—then the debt is paid, and justice is satisfied. Is Jesus alive at the right hand of God?—then the Father is well pleased in the work of His Son, and He "rests in His love, and rejoices over His Church with singing." Is Jesus alive?—then every promise shall be fulfilled, and all the blessings of the everlasting covenant shall be freely bestowed, and I, a poor worthless sinner, yet resting upon His atoning work, shall live also. May the Holy Spirit lead you into the full belief—the belief of the heart as of the judgment—of this glorious truth. It is the keystone of the temple; press it as you will, the more you lean upon it, the stronger you will find it—the more you rest upon it, the firmer will grow your hope. Only receive it in simple faith; Jesus is alive—alive for you—all you need in this valley of tears is here; all your temporal mercies are secured to you here; all your spiritual blessings are laid up for you here. Such is the great charter, such the immense untold blessings it contains, that, come how you will, come when you will, and "ask what you will, it shall be granted to you by the Father," because Jesus is at His right hand. Well may we take up the dauntless challenge of the apostle, "Who is he that condemns? It is Christ that died; yes, rather, that is risen again, who is even at the right hand of God, who also makes intercession for us." Your salvation is complete, your heaven secure, and all victory, happiness, and glory bound up in this one great fact. Then may we not again exclaim with Paul, "Blessed be the God and Father of our Lord Jesus Christ, which, according to His abundant mercy, has begotten us again unto a lively hope, by the resurrection of Jesus Christ from the dead."

MAY 21

"Is there no balm in Gilead? is there no
physician there?" Jeremiah 8:22

There is! The physician is Jesus, the balm is His own most precious blood. He binds up the broken heart, He heals the wounded spirit. All the skill, all the efficacy, all the tenderness and crucial sympathy needed for the office meet and center in Him in the highest degree. Here then, disconsolate soul, bring your wounded heart. Bring it simply to Jesus. One touch of His hand will heal the wound. One whisper of His voice will hush the tempest. One drop of His blood will remove the guilt. Nothing but a faith's application to Him will do for your soul now. Your case is beyond the skill of all other physicians. Your wound is too deep for all other remedies. It is a question of life and death, heaven or hell. It is an emergency, a crisis, a turning point with you. Oh, how solemn, how eventful is this moment! Eternity seems suspended upon it. All the intelligences of the universe, good spirits and bad, seem gazing upon it with intense interest. Decide the question, by closing in immediately with Jesus. Submit to God. All things are ready. The blood is shed, the righteousness is finished, the feast is prepared, God stands ready to pardon, yes, He advances to meet you, His returning child, to fall upon your neck and embrace you, with the assurance of His full and free forgiveness.

Let not the simplicity of the remedy keep you back. Many stumble at this. It is but a look of faith: "Look unto me, and be saved." It is but a touch, even though with a palsied hand "And as many as touched him were made whole." It is but a believing the broad declaration, "that Christ Jesus came into the world to save sinners." You are not called to believe that He came to save you; but that He saves sinners. Then if you inquire, "But will He save me? How do I know that if I come I shall meet a welcome?" Our reply is, only test Him. Settle not down with the conviction that you are too far gone, too vile, too guilty, too unworthy, until you have gone and tried Him. You know not how you wound Him, how you dishonor Him, and grieve the Spirit, by yielding to a doubt, yes, the shadow of a doubt, as to the willingness and the ability of Jesus to save you, until you have gone to Him believingly, and put His readiness and His skill to the test.

Do not let the freeness of the remedy keep you away. This, too, is a stumbling-block to many. Its very freeness holds them back. But it is "without money, and without price." The simple meaning of this is, no worthiness on the part of the applicant, no merit of the creature, no tears, no convictions, no faith, is the ground on which the healing is bestowed. Oh no! It is all of grace—all of God's free gift, irrespective of any worth or worthiness in man. Your strong motive to come to Christ is your very sinfulness. The reason why you go to Him is that your heart is broken, and that He only, can bind it up; your spirit is wounded, and that He only can heal it; your conscience is burdened, and that He only can lighten it; your soul is lost, and that He only, can save it. And that is all you need to recommend you. It is enough for Christ that you are covered with guilt; that you have no plea that springs from yourself; that you have no money to bring in your hand, but have spent your all upon physicians, yet instead of getting better you only grow worse; that you have wasted your substance in riotous living, and now are insolvent; and that you really feel a drawing towards Him, a longing for Him—that you ask, you seek, you crave, you earnestly implore His compassion—that is enough for Him. His heart yearns, His love is moved, His hand is stretched out—come and welcome to Jesus, come.

MAY 22

"Bear you one another's burdens, and so
fulfil the law of Christ." Galatians 6:2

Thank God for an errand to Him. It may be you have felt no heart to pray for yourself—you have been sensible of no peculiar drawings to the throne for your own soul, but you halt gone in behalf of another; the burden, the trial, the affliction, or the immediate need of some member of God's family has pressed upon you, and you have taken his case to the Lord: you have borne him in your arms to the throne of grace, and, while interceding for your brother, the Lord has met you, and blessed your own soul. Perhaps you halt gone and prayed for the Church, for the peace of Jerusalem, for the prosperity of Zion, that the Lord would build up her waste places, and make her a joy and a praise in the whole earth—perhaps it has been to pray for your minister, that the Lord would teach him more deeply and experimentally, and anoint him more plenteously with the rich anointing and unction of the Holy Spirit—perhaps it has been to pray for Christian missions, and for laborious and self-denying missionaries, that the Lord would make them eminently successful in diffusing the knowledge of a precious Savior, and in calling in His people: and thus, while for others you have been besieging the throne of grace, and pouring out your heart before the Lord, the Lord Himself has drawn near to your own soul, and you have been made to experience the blessing that is ever the attendant and the reward of intercessory prayer. Then let every event, every circumstance, every providence be a voice urging you to prayer. If you have no needs, others have—take them to the Lord. If you are borne down by no cross, smitten by no affliction, or suffering from no need, others are—for them go and plead with your heavenly Father, and the petitions you send up to the mercy-seat on their behalf may return into your own bosom freighted with rich covenant blessings. The falls, the weaknesses, the declensions of others make them grounds for prayer. Thus, and thus only, can you expect to grow in grace, and grace to grow in you.

MAY 23

"Above all, taking the shield of faith, with which you shall be able to quench all the fiery darts of the wicked." Ephesians 6:16

Few of the children of God are ignorant, more or less, of Satan's devices. But few are exempt from the "fiery darts " of the adversary; our Lord Himself was not. Many, peculiar, and great are their temptations. They are often those which touch the very vitals of the gospel, which go to undermine the believer's faith in the fundamentals of Christianity, and which affect his own personal interest in the covenant of grace. Satan is the sworn enemy of the believer—his constant, unwearied foe. There is, too, a subtlety, a malignity, which does not mark not the other and numerous enemies of the soul. The Holy Spirit speaks of the "depths of Satan." There are "depths" in his malice, in his subtlety, in his sagacity, which many of the beloved of the Lord are made in some degree to fathom. The Lord may allow them to go down into those "depths," just to convince those who are there are depths in His wisdom, love, power, and grace, which can out-fathom the "depths of Satan."

But what are some of the devices of the wicked one? What are some of his fiery darts? Sometimes he fills the mind of the believer with the most blasphemous and atheistical thoughts, threatening the utter destruction of his peace and confidence. Sometimes he takes advantage of periods of weakness, trial, and perplexity to stir up the corruptions of his nature, bringing the soul back as into captivity to the law of sin and death. Sometimes he suggests unbelieving doubts respecting his adoption, beguiling him into the belief that his professed conversion is all a delusion, that his religion is all hypocrisy, and that what he had thought was the work of grace is but the work of nature. But by far the greatest and most general controversy which Satan has with the saint of God is, to lead him to doubt the ability and the willingness of Christ to save a poor sinner. The anchor of his soul removed from this truth he is driven out upon a rough sea of doubt and anguish, and is at the mercy of every wind of doctrine and every billow of unbelief that may assail his storm-tossed bark. But in the midst of it all, where does the comfort and the victory of the tempted believer come from? From the promise which assures him that "when the enemy shall come in like a flood, the Spirit of the Lord shall lift up a standard against him." And what is the standard which the Spirit, the Comforter, lifts up to stem this flood? A dying, risen, ascended, exalted, and ever-living Savior. This is the standard that strikes terror into the foe; this is the gate that shuts out the flood. So the disciples proved. This is their testimony: "And the seventy returned again with joy, saying, Lord, even the devils are subject unto us through Your name." Immanuel is that name which puts to flight every spiritual foe. And the Comforter, which is the Holy Spirit, leads the tempted soul to this name, to shelter itself beneath it, to plead it with God, and to battle with it against the enemy. Dear reader, are you a target against which the fiery darts of the devil are leveled? Are you sorely tempted? Do not be astonished as though some strange thing had happened unto you. The holiest of God's saints have suffered as you are now suffering; yes, even your blessed Lord, your Master, your Pattern, your Example, and He in whose name you shall be more than conqueror; was once assailed as you are, and by the same enemy. And let the reflection console you, that temptations only leave the traces of guilt upon the conscience, and are only regarded as sins by God, as they are yielded to. The mere suggestion of the adversary, the mere presentation of a temptation, is no sin, so long as, in the strength that is in Christ Jesus, the believer firmly and resolutely resists it. "Resist the devil, and he will flee from you." Jesus has already fought and conquered for you. He knew well what the conflict with Satan was. And He remembers, too, what it is. Lift up your head, dear tempted soul! You shall obtain the victory. The seed of the woman has bruised the serpent's head; yes, has crushed him, never to obtain his supremacy over you again. He may harass, annoy, and distress you; but pluck you from the hollow of the hand that was pierced for you, he never can.

MAY 24

"Jesus said unto them, Verily, verily, I say unto
you, Before Abraham was, I am." John 8:58

Dear reader, what a wondrous declaration is this! What a glorious and precious truth does it involve! Are you a believer in Jesus? Is He all your salvation, your acceptance, your hope, and desire? Then cast the anchor of your faith deeply, firmly here; you shall find it an eternal rock. Weak faith you may have, and doubtful faith numbers have; but here is the ground of faith, respecting which there can be neither weakness nor doubt. Is it an Almighty Savior that you need? Behold Him! "Before Abraham was, I am." Oh, what a foundation for a poor sinful worm of the dust to build upon! What a stable truth for faith in its weakest form to deal with—to have a glorious incarnate 'I Am' for an atoning sacrifice—an 'I Am' for a Redeemer—an 'I Am' for a Surety—an 'I Am' as a Day's-man between God and the soul—an 'I Am' as an Advocate, an unceasing Intercessor at the court of heaven, pleading each moment His own atoning merits—an 'I Am' as the center in whom all the promises are "yes and amen"—an 'I Am' as a "Brother born for adversity"—an 'I Am' as "a very present help in trouble"! This is the answer which faith receives to its trembling and anxious interrogatories. To each and all touching His faithfulness, His tenderness, His long-suffering, His fulness, and His all-sufficiency, Jesus answers, "I Am." "Enough, Lord," replies the believer, "on this I can live, on this I can die."

MAY 25

*"But grow in grace, and in the knowledge of our
Lord and Savior Jesus Christ." 2 Peter 3:18*

There is an idea fatal to all true sanctification, which some believers, especially those who are young in experience, are prone to entertain—that nothing is to be done in the soul after a man has believed, that the work of conversion having taken place, all is accomplished. So far from this being the case, he has but just entered upon the work of sanctification—just started in the race, just buckled on the armor. The conflict can hardly be said to have begun in conversion; and, therefore, to rest composed with the idea that the soul has nothing more to do than to accept of Christ as his salvation—that there are no corruptions to subdue—no sinful habits to cut off no long-existing and deeply imbedded sins to mortify, root and branch—and no high and yet higher degrees in holiness to attain, is to form a most contracted view of the Christian life—such a view as, if persisted in, must necessarily prove detrimental to the spiritual advance of the believer. The work of sanctification, beloved, is a great and a daily work. It commences at the very moment of our translation into the kingdom of Christ on earth, and ceases not until the moment of our translation into the kingdom of God in heaven. The notion, so fondly cherished by some, of perfect sinlessness here, is as fatal to true sanctification as it is contrary to God's word. They know but little of their own heart, who do not know that sin, in the language of Owen, "not only still abides in us, but is still acting, still laboring to bring forth the deeds of the flesh;"—who do not know that in their "flesh there dwells no good thing," that "that which is born of the flesh is flesh," and will retain its fleshly nature and propensities to the very last. Let us not exult "as though we had already attained, or were already perfect,"—let us not be "ignorant of Satan's devices," one of which is to build us up in the belief that, in the present life, a man may cease from the work of mortification. The Lord keep the reader from cherishing so erroneous an idea. The work of sanctification is the work of a man's life. "When sin lets us alone (as has been remarked), we may let sin alone." But when is the day, yes, when is the hour, that sin does not strive for the mastery, and in which the believer can say he has completely slain his enemy? He may "through the Spirit, mortify the deeds of the body," and if he does, "he shall live;" but, as the heart is the natural and luxuriant soil of every noxious weed of sin, and as another springs up as soon as one is cut down, yes, as the same root appears again above the surface, with new life and vigor, it requires a ceaseless care and vigilance, a perpetual mortification of sin in the body, until we throw off this cumbrous clay, and go where sin is known no more.

MAY 26

"For all the promises of God in him are yes, and in him
Amen, unto the glory of God by us." 2 Corinthians 1:20

It pleased a gracious and sin-pardoning God to meet our guilty and conscience-stricken parents, immediately after the fall, with the comforting and gracious promise that the "seed of the woman"—His eternal Son, the everlasting Mediator—should "bruise the serpent's head." On this divine assurance of recovering and saving mercy they rested. Believing in this, as they doubtless did, they were saved, "the first fruits unto God and the Lamb." They rested, let it be emphatically spoken, not upon the bare letter of the promise, but upon its substance; not merely, upon the grace promised; but upon the truth of God in the promise. The bare letter of a promise is no resting-place for a believing soul; it can convey no solid consolation and support. Thus far, and no further, did the Jews get, to whom pertained the promises. This is all that they saw in the types and promises which set forth "God's unspeakable gift." They rested in the mere letter. They saw not Christ in them; and, seeing not Christ to be their substance and glory, to them "the promises of God were made of none effect." Now God has fulfilled His ancient promise. The word He spoke to Adam, He has made good to the letter to us, His posterity. It is true, the vision of grace and glory seemed for a while to tarry, but it tarried only for its appointed time. It is true, the vista was long and dreary, through which patriarchs, seers, and prophets beheld it. The star of hope was often scarcely seen in the dim distance, and frequently seemed for a moment entirely quenched in darkness. Time rolled heavily along—a period of four thousand years elapsed; but, true to His word, faithful to His promise, "when the fulness of the time was come, God sent forth His Son, made of a woman, made under the law, that we might receive the adoption of sons." Oh, how gloriously did the truth of Jehovah shine in the person of the babe of Bethlehem! How did it gather brightness as the holy child Jesus increased in stature and in favor with God and man! And to what meridian splendor did it blaze forth, when on Calvary it united with holiness and justice, in finishing the great work of the Church's redemption! Then was it that "mercy and truth met together, righteousness and peace kissed each other." Jesus is the grand evidence that God is true. Faith needs, faith asks no more. Here, as on a stable foundation, it rests. Its eye ever "looking unto Jesus," it can thread its way—often sunless and starless—through a dreary, and an intricate wilderness. It can travel through trials, endure temptations, bow meekly to disappointments, bear up under cross providences, and sustain the shock of fearful conflicts, trusting in the God of the covenant, resting on His promise and oath, and implicitly believing His word, because it sees in Jesus an ever-living witness that God is true.

MAY 27
"He is faithful that promised." Hebrews 10:23

O you of doubting and fearful heart! looking at the waves rolling at your feet, and well near sinking beneath their swellings, exclaiming, "Will the Lord cast off forever? and will He be favorable no more? Is His mercy clean gone forever? Does His promise fail for evermore? Has God forgotten to be gracious? has He in anger shut up His tender mercies?" Behold the glory of God's truth beaming in the face of Jesus Christ, and doubt no more. So long as Jesus lives—lives as your Advocate, as your High Priest, as your Representative in the court of heaven, all is yours which the covenant promises, and which His mediation secures. "The promises of God are all yes and Amen in Christ Jesus." Never will he break His oath, or falsify His word, or alter the thing that has gone out of His mouth. "Heaven and earth shall pass away, but my word shall not pass away." God says it, and let faith believe it because He says it. So essential is it to your comfort, that I would repeat the caution—in all your dealings with the Divine promises, avoid a Jewish faith. Do not so much look at the grace of the promise, or at the thing promised—precious as both are—as at God in the promise. The promise is the heart of your Father speaking; it is the faithfulness of your Father performing. Rest then not in the blessing promised, but in the veracity of Him who promises it, and then shall your faith have confidence towards God.

MAY 27

"Old things are passed away; behold, all things
are become new." 2 Corinthians 5:17

A believer's experience of the truth of God is no mere fancy. However severely experimental godliness may have been stigmatized by an unrenewed world, as the offspring of a morbid imagination, the product of an enthusiastic mind, "he that believes in the Son of God has the witness in himself," that he has yielded the consent of his judgment and his affections to no "cunningly-devised fable." A sense of sin—brokenness and contrition before God—faith in the atoning blood of Christ—a sweet consciousness of pardon, acceptance, adoption, and joy in the Holy Spirit, are no mere hallucinations of a disordered mind. To read one's pardon, fully, fairly written out—to look up to God as one accepted, adopted, to feel the spirit going out to Him in filial love and confidence, breathing its tender and endearing epithet, "Abba, Father,"—to refer every trial, cross, and dispensation of His providence to His tender and unchangeable love—to have one's will, naturally so rebellious and perverse, completely absorbed in His—to be as a weaned child, simply and unreservedly yielded up to His disposal, and to live in the patient waiting for the glory that is to be revealed—oh, this is reality, sweet, blessed, solemn reality! Holy and happy is that man whose heart is not a stranger to these truths.

MAY 29

"Cast not away therefore your confidence, which has
great recompense of reward." Hebrews 10:35

There is nothing essentially omnipotent in any single grace of the Spirit; to suppose this would be to deify that grace: although regeneration is a spiritual work, and all the graces implanted in the soul are the product of the Spirit, and must necessarily be in their nature spiritual and inde-structible, yet they may so decline in their power, become so enfeebled and impaired in their vigor and tendency, as to be classed among the "things that are ready to die." It is preeminently so with faith; perhaps there is no part of the Spirit's work more constantly and severely assailed, and consequently more exposed to declension, than this. Shall we look at the examples in God's word? We cite the case of Abraham, the father of the faithful; beholding him, at God's command, binding his son upon the altar, and raising the knife for the sacrifice, we unhesitatingly exclaim—"Surely never was faith like this! Here is faith of a giant character; faith, whose sinews no trial scan ever relax, whose luster no temptation can ever dim." And yet, tracing the history of the patriarch still further, we find that very giant faith now trembling and yielding under a trial far less acute and severe; he, who could surrender the life of his promised son—that son through whose lineal descent Jesus was to come—into the hands of God, could not intrust that same God with his own. We look at Job: in the commencement of his deep trial we find him justifying God; messenger follows messenger, with tidings of yet deeper woe, but not a murmur is breathed; and as the cup, now full to the brim, is placed to his lips, how sweetly sounds the voice of holy resignation," The Lord gave, and the Lord has taken away; blessed be the name of the Lord." "In all this did not Job sin with his lips:" and yet the very faith, which thus bowed in meekness to the rod, so declined as to lead him to curse the day of his birth! We see David, whose faith could at one time lead him out to battle with Goliath, now fleeing from a shadow, and exclaiming—"I shall one day perish by the hand of Saul." And mark how the energy of Peter's faith declined, who at one period could walk boldly upon the tempestuous sea, and yet at another could deny his Lord, panic-struck at the voice of a little maid. Who will say that the faith of the holiest man of God may not at one time greatly and sadly decline?

But we need not travel out of ourselves for the evidence and the illustration of this affecting truth: let every believer turn in upon himself. What, reader, is the real state of your faith? is it as lively, vigorous, and active as it was when you first believed? Has it undergone no declension? Is the object of faith as glorious in your eye as He then was? Are you not now looking at second causes in God's dealings with you, instead of lifting your eye and fixing it on Him alone? What is your faith in prayer?—do you come boldly to the throne of grace, asking, nothing doubting? Do you take all your trials, your needs, your infirmities, to God? What is your realization of eternal things—is faith here in constant, holy exercise? Are you living as a pilgrim and a sojourner, "choosing rather to suffer affliction with the people of God," than float along on the summer sea of this world's enjoyments? What is the crucifying power of your faith?—does it deaden you to sin, and wean you from the world, and constrain you to walk humbly with God, and near to Jesus? And when the Lord brings the cross, and says, "Bear this for Me," does your faith promptly and cheerfully acquiesce, "any cross, any suffering, any sacrifice for You, dear Lord"? Thus may you test the nature and the degree of your faith; bring it to the touch-stone of God's truth, and ascertain what its character is, and how it has suffered declension.

MAY 30

*"Whom the Lord loves he corrects; even as a father
the son in whom he delights." Proverbs 3:12*

Hard and harsh thoughts of God will be the effect of wrong interpretations of His dealings: if for one moment we remove the eye from off the heart of God in the hour and depth of our trial, we are prepared to give heed to every dark suggestion of the adversary; that moment we look at the dispensation with a different mind, and to God with an altered affection; we view the chastisement as the effect of displeasure, and the covenant God who sent it, as unkind, unloving, and severe. But let faith's eagle-eye pierce the clouds and darkness that surround the throne, and behold the heart of God as still love, all love, and nothing but love, to His afflicted, bereaved, and sorrow-stricken child; and in a moment every murmur will be hushed, every rebellious feeling will be still, and every unkind thought will be laid in the dust; and, "He has done all things, well—in love and faithfulness has He afflicted me," will be the only sounds uttered by the lips. If then, beloved, you would have your heart always fixed on God, its affections flowing in one unbroken current towards Him, interpret every dispensation that He sends in the light of His love; never allow yourself to be betrayed into the belief that any other feeling prompts the discipline;

do not give place to the suggestion for one moment—banish it from the threshold of your mind the moment it seeks an entrance. And let this be the reflection that hushes and soothes you to repose, even as an infant upon its mother's breast: "My God is love! my Father is unchangeable tenderness and truth! He has done it, and it is well done."

MAY 31

"My people are bent to backsliding from me." Hosea 11:7

The divine life has its dwelling-place in a fallen, fleshly nature. It is encompassed by all the corruptions, weaknesses, infirmities, and assaults of the flesh; there is not a moment that it is not exposed to assaults from within; there is not a natural faculty of the mind, or throb of the heart, that is favorable to its prosperity, but all are contrary to its nature, and hostile to its advance. As there is nothing internal that is favorable to a state of grace, so there is nothing external that assists it forward. It has its many and violent enemies: Satan is ever on the watch to assault it, the world is ever presenting itself in some new form of fascination and power to weaken it—a thousand temptations are perpetually striving to ensnare it; thus its internal and external enemies are leagued against it. Is it then any wonder that faith should sometimes tremble, that grace should sometimes decline, and that the pulse of the divine life should often beat faintly and feebly?

The saints in every age have felt and lamented this. Hence the prayer of David, which is the prayer of all true believers: "Hold me up, and I shall be safe;" implying the greatest weakness in himself, and his perpetual exposure to the greatest falls: "Hold me up, for only as I am upheld by You am I safe." Again he prays "Keep back Your servant also from presumptuous sins; let them not have dominion over me;" implying that a believer, left to the tendencies of his fallen nature, might become a prey to the worst sins. In addressing himself to the converted Hebrews, the apostle seizes the occasion thus to exhort them: "Take heed, brethren, lest there be in any of you an evil heart of unbelief, in departing from the living God." "In departing,"—implying a constant tendency to depart from God. And what does God Himself say of His people? "My people are bent on backsliding from me." And again, "Why is this people of Jerusalem slidden back by a perpetual backsliding?" Yes, it is a perpetual proneness to declension. The sun rises but to set, the clock is wound up but to run down; and not more natural is it for them thus to obey the laws that govern them, than for the heart of a child of God to follow the promptings of its corrupt and wayward nature.

JUNE

JUNE 1

"And the inhabitant shall not say, I am sick: the people that dwell therein shall be forgiven their iniquity." Isaiah 33:24

Let the Christian invalid be cheered with the prospect of before long arriving at this land of light and love, of rest and holiness. The moment the spirit is "absent from the body, and present with, the Lord," it treads those balmy shores, where health breathes in the air, flows in the waters, and sparkles in the sunbeams. There is no sickness in heaven, for "the people that dwell therein shall be forgiven their iniquity;" and this accounts for the absence of all physical malady. There is no sickness in heaven, because there is no sin. But the more full enjoyment of this blessing is reserved for the new earth, upon which the "holy city, New Jerusalem, coming down from God out of heaven, prepared as a bride adorned for her husband," will dwell. Then it is that "God shall wipe away all tears front their eyes; and there shall be no more death, neither sorrow nor crying, neither shall there be any more pain: for the former things are passed away." Christian sufferer! you are nearing this land—a few more days of languishing and pain, a few more nights of weary wakefulness, and you are there! Don't you see, through the chinks of the "earthly house of this tabernacle," "a building of God, a house not made with hands, eternal in the heavens"? Don't you see the "city which has foundations, whose maker and builder is God"? It has "no need of the sun, neither of the moon, to shine on it: for the glory of God does enlighten it, and the Lamb is the light thereof. . . The gates of it shall not be shut at all by day: for there is no night there." Soon you will exchange this hospital for your Father's house, and as you cross the threshold, the last pang is inflicted, the last sigh is heaved, and the last tear is brushed from your eye. Then, at the resurrection of the just, comes the new body. "It is sown in corruption; it is raised in incorruption: it is sown in dishonor; it is raised in glory: it is sown in weakness; it is raised in power. It is sown a natural body, it is raised a spiritual body." All this blessedness and glory Jesus has procured for you. All this blessedness and glory awaits you; and into its full possession and experience Jesus will soon bring you. Animated with such a prospect, and cheered with such a hope, patiently endure the prolonged sickness, the protracted suffering, exclaiming in the spirit and language of Jesus, "O my Father, if this cup may not pass from me, except I drink it, Your will be done!"

JUNE 2
"I have prayed for YOU." Luke 22:32

We must not overlook the individuality of our Lord's intercession. As if forgetting for that moment the whole Church, and regarding Peter as representing in his person each tempted believer, Jesus makes him the especial object of His prayer. How much comfort do we lose in overlooking this truth—in not more distinctly recognizing the personal interest which each believer has in the love of Christ! "My grace is sufficient for you;" "I have prayed for you," are the gracious words with which Jesus would meet each individual case. Think not then, O believer, that you are alone, unloved, uncared for, unthought of—Jesus bears you upon His heart; and if loved, and cared for, and remembered by Him, you can afford to part with some creature stream, however loved and valued that stream may be. Keep your eye intently fixed upon your Lord's intercession.

We too much lose ourselves in the crowd, and merge ourselves in the mass. We forget alike our individual interest in the covenant, and our personal obligation to glorify God in our different walks of life. But it is the especial privilege of the believer to concentrate upon himself, as in focal power, every thought and affection of God, just as the eye of a well-executed portrait may be said to fasten itself exclusively upon each individual in the room. "I have prayed for you." O cheering declaration! Christian reader, lose not sight of it. Come and lay your hand of faith upon the covenant of grace, and say, "the fulness of the covenant is mine." Lay your hand upon the covenant of God, and say, "the God of the covenant is mine; Jesus, its Mediator, is my Savior. He obeyed, suffered, bled, and expired, all for me. 'He has loved me, and has given Himself for me.' Lord! do you think of me? does my case come up before Your notice? do You bear my burden upon Your arm, my sorrow upon Your heart, my name upon Your lips; and do You pray for my poor, assaulted, and trembling faith? Yes, Lord, You do. I believe it, because You have said it, and press the precious truth, so rich in consolation, to my trembling, grateful heart."

JUNE 3
"I have prayed for you that your faith fail not." Luke 22:32

The Lord as its Shepherd goes before His flock. He precedes it every step, not only to map its path, but also to provide for all the circumstances, the most trivial and minute, of its history. To Him nothing can be unforeseen, from Him nothing can be concealed. No event can surprise Him, no contingency can thwart Him, no difficulty can embarrass Him. The entire history of the individual saint of God, from his earliest to his latest breath, is written in His book, when as yet it had no existence, as minutely and as accurately as though it were a record of the past. In anticipation of each developed circumstance, of each temptation and trial, difficulty and need, Jesus prays for His people "I have prayed." It would seem as if the sorrow had reached His heart before it touched our own; as if the assault had fallen upon Him before it fell upon us; and that, knowing what would transpire, seeing in what critical and painful circumstances His child would be placed, He anticipates his case by especial intercession on his behalf: "I have prayed for you."

Can the mind of the tried believer repose upon a truth more sustaining and soothing than this? It had been a glorious unfolding of the love of Jesus, to know that when the sifting came, when faith was actually tried, that then Jesus prayed for the sufferer. But to be assured that before a dart was winged, or a shock was felt, or even a suspicion was awakened that the tempter was approaching, and that danger was near, Jesus, robed in His priestly garments, and bearing the golden censer in His hand, had entered within the veil to make especial intercession for that trial of faith—oh, it is a view of His love, which to the mind of the tempted believer would seem to overtop and outshine all others!

And for what does Jesus pray? That the temptation might not come? that faith may not be tried? Oh no! He does not ask the Father in behalf of His people, for their entire exemption from temptation and trial. Full well does He know that if conformed to Him, their Head, they must through much tribulation enter the kingdom. Pure and sinless though He was, needing no sifting and no refining, He yet passed through each process as if there were in Him the chaff to scatter, and the alloy to consume. How much more needful does Jesus see that His people, in whom there is such an admixture of the precious with the vile, so much indwelling sin, so much powerful corruption perpetually seeking to destroy indwelling grace, should not be exempted from the process which, painful though it be, is absolutely needful and eternally good! But Jesus prays that in the actual trial of faith it might not fail. Now, why, is it, O believing soul, that your tried faith has not failed? Why, have you passed through the sifting with not one precious grain fallen to the ground? Because your great High Priest prayed for you before the trial, and prayed for you in the trial, and has not ceased to pray for you since the trial. All upholding grace, all restraining grace, all restoring grace, all establishing grace, has been meted out to you through the channel of your Lord's perpetual and ever-prevalent intercession. Oh, how should this truth endear the Savior to your heart! With what holy contrition should it fill your spirit, and with what sweet affection should it constrain your soul to a simple and an unreserved surrender to God!

JUNE 4
"Have faith in God." Mark 9:22

Have faith in Him as God. His character justifies it, His word invites it, His promises encourage it, His blessing crowns it. How frequently in the word does God condescend to invite the exercise of faith in Himself by a declaration and on the ground of what He is. Thus to Abraham: "And when Abram was ninety years old and nine, the Lord appeared to Abram, and said unto him, I am the Almighty God: walk before me, and be perfect." And again to His Church: "I am the Lord God, who brought you up out of the land of Egypt; open your mouth wide, and I will fill it." How kind and condescending in God is this mode of asking and encouraging the confidence of His people! How signally does He come down to our weakness and infirmity! What a foundation for faith to build upon does He reveal! what a field for faith to work in does He open! what amplitude, what scope, and what riches amid which it may revel! "I am God all—sufficient. Is anything too hard for me?" Faith needs and asks no more. Less than this would not meet its case more than this it could not have. When faith feels that it has God's word for its warrant in believing, God's command for its rule in obeying, God's promise for its encouragement in suffering, and God Himself as the foundation of its confidence and the center of its rest, it becomes invulnerable, and almost omnipotent. The exact measure of our faith is the extent of our experimental knowledge of God. Acquaintance with God must inspire the mind with confidence in Him. The more truly we know, the more implicitly we trust in Him. It is in this way, among others, that He answers the prayer of His people, "Establish Your word unto Your servant, who is devoted to Your fear." God establishes the truth of His word by enlarging the believer's knowledge of Himself, and this knowledge is mainly attained through the truth. The word reveals God, and an experimental knowledge of God confirms the truth of the word; the one thus establishing the other. Our faith, then, if it be a real principle, must have respect to God as God. "Have faith in God."

JUNE 5

"Speak you comfortably to Jerusalem, and cry unto her, that her warfare is accomplished, that her iniquity is pardoned: for she has received of the Lord's hand double for all her sins." Isaiah 40:2

By sealing a sense of pardon upon the conscience, God comforts the disconsolate. There is no comfort equal to this. As our deepest sorrow flows from a sense of sin, so our deepest joy springs from a sense of its forgiveness. What comfort can there be where this is lacking? what sorrow where this is felt? "When he gives quietness, who then can make trouble?" This was the comfort which God commanded the prophet to speak to His spiritual Jerusalem: "Say unto her, that her sins are forgiven." And this is the message which the Lord sends to His whole Church. This comfort have all His saints. Your sins, O believer, are forgiven. "I have blotted out your sins as a cloud, and your iniquities as a thick cloud," says God. You are not called upon to believe that God will pardon, but that He has pardoned you. Forgiveness is a past act; the sense of it written upon the conscience is a present one. "By one offering Jesus has perfected forever those who are sanctified," has forever put away their sins. Faith in the blood of Jesus brings the soul into the possession of a present forgiveness. And when God the Holy Spirit thus imprints a sense of pardoned sin upon the troubled conscience, all other sorrows in comparison dwindle into insignificance. "Strike, Lord," says Luther, "I bear anything willingly, because my sins are forgiven." Thus, beloved, God comforts his conscience-troubled people. He loves to speak comfortably to their hearts. Is it any delight to Him to see you carrying your burden of conscious sin day after day and week after week? Ah no! He has procured the means of your pardon at a great price—nothing less than the sacrifice of His beloved Son; and will not the same love which procured your forgiveness, speak it to your heart? Oh yes; the sun in the heavens pours not forth its light more freely, light itself speeds not more rapidly, the mountain stream rushes on not more gladsome and unfettered, than the pardon of sin flows from the heart of God to the humble and the contrite mourner. Is sin your trouble? Does conscious guilt cast you down? Look up, disconsolate soul! there is forgiveness with God. It is in His heart to pardon you. Repair to His feet, go you to God's confessional, and over the head of the atoning sacrifice acknowledge your transgression, and He will forgive the iniquity of your sin. And, oh, what will be the joy of your heart, the music of your lips, the grateful surrender of your person, when Jesus says, "Your sins are forgiven; go in peace"!

JUNE 6

"And he that takes not his cross, and follows after
me, is not worthy of me." Matthew 10:38

How few there are, among the many professing Christ, who yet know anything by experience of the great and wondrous life of faith! Only those who are taught by the Spirit the plague of their own hearts can possibly know it. How few there are who appear to possess vital religion in their souls! How few choose Christ with His cross! The great mass of professors are aiming to separate them. They would sincerely bear the name of Christ, and be accounted as the followers of Christ, and do something for the cause of Christ; but they hide His cross, they are ashamed of His cross, they shrink from His cross. Christ and His outward lowliness, Christ and His poverty, Christ and His humiliation, Christ and the world's despising, form no part of their creed nor their religion. But Christ and the world, Christ and the popular opinion, Christ and the slavery of sin, Christ and an unhumbled spirit, Christ and a love of money, and ease, and self—indulgence, make up the religion of vast numbers who yet profess and call themselves Christians. Awful fact! How forcibly does it remind us of the solemn words of Jesus, "Not every one that says unto me, Lord, Lord, shall enter into the kingdom of heaven; but he that does the will of my Father who is in heaven." Let us, in view of this solemn truth, search our hearts, and ask the searching of God's Spirit; and in ascertaining the real state of our souls, let us take nothing for granted, rest not in past experience, nor in gifts, nor usefulness, but be satisfied only with the present, inward witness of the Holy Spirit.

JUNE 7

"Submit yourselves therefore to God." James 4:7

Submission to the Divine will is a great advance in holiness; and this is mainly and effectually attained through sanctified chastisement. In prosperity, how full are we of self-sufficiency! When the Lord asks our obedience, we give Him our counsel. But when He sends the rod, and by the accompanying grace of His Spirit sanctifies its stroke, we learn in what true obedience consists. It was in this school our blessed Lord Himself was taught. "Though He were a Son, yet learned He obedience by the things which He suffered." He learned to obey in suffering—to bring His will in suffering into complete submission to His Father's will. God has not in His family such obedient children as those who, "passing under the rod," are "brought into the bond of the covenant." Oh, what a high Christian attainment is submission to the will of God! The noblest grace attainable upon earth is it. When our Lord taught His disciples to pray to the Father for the spread of holiness, He embodied the petition, in these words, "Your will be done on earth, as it is in heaven." The universal and complete holiness of heaven springs from the universal and complete perfection in which the will of God is done by angels and glorified spirits. In proportion as the Divine will prevails upon earth, holiness will reign. And, oh, what a beauteous earth and what a blissful world would this be, were the will of God done by every creature! In the new earth, in which will dwell righteousness, it will be so. The original harmony of this fallen universe will then be restored, its pristine beauty recovered, and God, in the person of His Son, will once more reign over, and walk in the midst of, a people whose will shall be but the reflection of His own. Thus to approximate to the Divine will is to assimilate with the Divine holiness. What God will, how God will, and when God will, defines the rule which should govern all the conduct and limit all the desires of the child of God. The instant the overwhelmed heart is brought into this state, the afflicted believer has planted his feet upon the Rock that is higher than he. All is peace, all is composure, because all is submission to the will of God. "The Lord reigns" is the truth whose all-commanding yet gentle whisper has stilled the tempest and calmed the waves. In its intense anxiety that the Divine will might be done, the chastened soul is but breathing after deeper holiness; and every fervent desire for the attainment of holiness is holiness already attained. Blessed chastening of love, that produces in this world, so distant and uncongenial, the buds and blossoms and fruits of heaven! A richer fruit grows not within the Paradise of God than Holiness. And yet, in the experience of a chastened believer, bleeding under the rod of his heavenly Father, there may be obtained such victories over sin, such purification of heart, such meekness of spirit, such Christ-like conformity, and such a discipline of the will, as to make him a rich "partaker of the Divine holiness."

JUNE 8

"Now the just shall live by faith." Hebrews 10:38

We cannot too frequently nor too deeply study the profound meaning of these words. God will have his child perpetually looking to, leaning upon, and receiving from Him. At present we are but in an immature state. We are not, therefore, in a condition to be trusted with grace for the future. Improvident and careless, we would soon squander and exhaust our resources; and when the emergency came, we should find our selves unprepared to meet it. The Lord, in wisdom and love, keeps all our grace in His own hands, and deals it out just as our circumstances demand. Oh, who that knows his own heart, and the heart of Christ, would not desire that all his supply should be in God, and not in himself? Who, so to speak, would wish to be his own spiritual treasurer? Who that knows the blessedness of a life of faith, the sweetness of going to God in everything, and for everything, would wish to transfer his mercies from Christ's keeping to his own, or wish to hold in the present the supply of the future? Be satisfied, dear reader, to walk by faith, and not by sight. You have a full Christ to draw from, and a faithful God to look to. You have a "covenant ordered in all things and sure," and the precious promise, "As your days, so shall your strength be," to lean confidently upon all your journey through. Be content, then, to be poor and dependent. Be willing to travel on empty-handed, seeing God's heart opened, and Christ's hand outstretched to supply your daily bread. Oh! it is sweet to be a dependent creature upon God—to hang upon a loving Father—to live as a poor, needy sinner, day by day, moment by moment, upon Jesus—to trace God in ten thousand ways—to mark His wisdom here, His condescension there—now His love, and then His faithfulness, all combining and exerted for our good—truly it is the most holy and blessed life upon earth. Why should we, then, shrink from any trial, or flee from any duty, or turn aside from any cross, since for that trial, and for that duty, and for that cross, Jesus has provided its required and appropriate grace? You are perhaps exclaiming, "Trouble is near!" Well, be it so. So also Divine grace is near—and strength is near—and counsel is near—and deliverance is near—and Jesus is near—and God is near—and a throne of grace is near; therefore, why must you fear, though trouble be near? "God is our refuge and strength, a very present help in trouble."

JUNE 9

"As the Father has loved me, so have I loved
you: continue you in my love." John 15:9

What sweet repose is here for the saints of God. Does God rest in His love? then the believer in Jesus may rest in it too. Does Infinity, find repose here? then may a poor finite creature. Does Immanuel rest in it? then may I, resting in Immanuel. If it is enough for Jehovah, surely, it is enough for the people of Jehovah. Our dear Lord's exhortations harmonize with this truth, "Abide in me;" "Continue in my love." Beloved reader, come and rest in this love—Jesus invites you to its blessed repose. Are you weary, tossed with tempest? Is there sadness in your spirit, sorrow in your heart, a cloud upon your mind? Is some crystal cistern broken, some fragrant flower withered, some fond and pleasant mercy gone? "Come," says Jesus, "and rest in my love—rest in the reality of my love—rest in the depth of my love—rest in the tenderness of my love—rest in the deathlessness of my love." Oh blessed rest! Poor, heart-broken sinner, weeping penitent, weary, laboring soul! what do you need? Mercy? it is in Christ. Forgiveness? it is in Christ. Acceptance? it is in Christ. The silencing power of love? it is in Christ. A reconciled Father, a pacified God? He is in Christ. All that you need is in Christ. Draw near, then, and rest in His love. The Father rests in Jesus, His justice rests in Jesus, His holiness rests in Jesus, His truth rests in Jesus, His power rests in Jesus—and in Jesus you too may rest! God rests in His love towards you, because He rests in the Son of His love. And in the Son of His love your weary, jaded, trembling spirit may find full and eternal repose. And whatever your present circumstances are, be the severity of your Father's dealings what it may, ever remember that He still rests in His love. Judging of Him by providences rather than by promises, your faith may become unhinged from this truth. But the standard by which you are to form your views of God's character is the same by which you are to judge your own—His word. That word declares that He rests in His love, that He now rests in it, that He rests in it at the present time, and, therefore, He rests in it at the moment that His providences in your history are the darkest and most lowering. When to your view all things seem against you—when even God himself seems against you—then is He resting with infinite satisfaction and delight in the love with which He has loved you from everlasting. And when all the mighty wheels of His providence are rapidly revolving, when event follows event, and convulsion succeeds convulsion—when your spirit is agitated, and your heart is alarmed, and your whole soul is awe-struck and appalled at the wonder-workings of His power, then is God calmly, serenely, resting in His love towards you, unmoved, unruffled, unbeclouded by the things which convulse the universe.

JUNE 10
"The Lord has laid on him the iniquity of us all." Isaiah 53:6

How shall we account for the sufferings of Christ, which were intense, and mysterious, if not on the ground of their vicarious character? Those sufferings were intense in the extreme. There was a severity in those who, if not required by Divine justice, would be perfectly unaccountable. Heaven, earth, and hell, all were in league against Him. Survey His eventful history—mark every step which He took from Bethlehem to Calvary; and what do we learn of His sufferings, but that they were of the most extraordinary and intense character. His enemies, like dogs of war, were let loose upon Him. His professed followers themselves stood aghast at the scenes through which their Lord was passing—one betraying Him, another denying Him, and all, in the hour of His extremity, forsaking Him. Is it any wonder that, in the anguish of His soul, His suffering humanity should exclaim, "Father, if it be possible, let this cup pass from me; yet not my will, but yours be done." In that awful moment, all the waves and billows of God's wrath, due to the sins of His people, were passing over Him. The Father, the last resource of sympathy, veiled His face, and withdrew from Him His sensible presence; and on the cross, draining the cup of sorrow, He fulfilled the prophecy, which spoke of Him—"I have trodden the wine press alone; and of the people there were none with me."

His sufferings, too, were mysterious. Why a holy, harmless being, whose whole life had been one act of unparalleled beneficence, should be doomed to persecution so severe, to sufferings so acute, and to a death so painful and ignominious, the denier of the atonement must be embarrassed to account. But the doctrine of a vicarious sacrifice explains it all, and presents the only key to the mystery. "He was made sin for us, who knew no sin, that we might be made the righteousness of God in Him." "Christ has redeemed us from the curse of the law, being made a curse for us." All the mystery now is gone. He was "made sin for us." He was "made a curse for us." He bore the sin, and consequently the penalty of sin. Had we been left, Christian reader, to bear our sins, we must inevitably have borne alone the punishment of our sins. But Jesus took upon Him our sins. For this, He became a party in the covenant of redemption; for this, He assumed our nature; for this, He sorrowed in Gethsemane; for this, the law of God exacted its utmost claim; and for this, the justice of God inflicted the utmost penalty. Oh, what a truth is this! The Son of God offering Himself up a sacrifice for sin! He who knew no sin—who was holy, harmless, and undefiled—not one thought of evil in His heart, yet made sin, or a sin—offering! Oh the greatness of the thought! If God had not Himself declared it, we could not have believed it, though an angel's tongue had announced it. God Himself must proclaim it; and because He has so proclaimed it, we believe it. And God alone can write it upon the heart.

JUNE 11

"Then shall we know, if we follow on to know the Lord." Hosea 6:3

True faith in God supposes him reconciled in Christ. This is the ground-work of all holy, humble converse with God. But here we must be cautious of placing a limit, as too many do. It is a great display of sovereign grace that we should have peace with God. God reconciled to us in Jesus is, of all divine and experimental truths, the greatest. Until this is experienced, we can affirm of no individual that he is safe for eternity. Yet, alas! what numbers reject this truth, and still dream on of heaven! But, great as is this grace, it is not less our mercy to be advancing, on the ground of assured peace, to more matured attainments in universal holiness. We are, at best, but dull scholars in the science of spiritual arithmetic. We have imperfectly learned one of its first rules, that of adding grace to grace. "Giving all diligence," exhorts the apostle, "add to your faith virtue," etc. Peace through the atoning blood being obtained, the movement is to be progressive, the course onward; each day, if possible, augmenting the measure of our grace, and adding to the number of the Spirit's graces. Reconciliation with God is but the starting-post in the divine life, not the finish-line; it is the commencement, and not the end, of our course. In other words, vast numbers rest in their first reception of Christ. They are hopefully converted, they unite themselves with a particular section of the Church of God, and settle down under an attached ministry. But here they seem to abide. There is no advance, no progress, no forgetting of the things that are behind, pressing upwards to higher rounds in the glorious ladder, which a gracious Father has let down out of heaven, by which we may ascend to heaven. Content with having placed the foot upon the first step, there they remain. There is no "following on to know the Lord." And yet why has the Lord removed the burden from the shoulder, but that we might mount upward? Why has He broken the chains from our feet, but that we may go forward? Thus are we constantly forgetting that the cross is our starting-point in our race, and yet ever to be kept in view—while holiness, breathed after upon earth, and in some blessed degree attained, but perfected in heaven, is our bright and certain goal.

JUNE 12

*"Hitherto have you asked nothing in my name: ask, and
you shall receive, that your joy may be full." John 16:24*

A most powerful incentive to prayer is found in a close and realizing view of the atoning blood. What encouragement does it present to this blessed and holy life of communion with God! the atoning blood!—the mercy-seat sprinkled over!—the High Priest before the throne!—the cloud of incense constantly ascending!—the Father well pleased! What can more freely invite the soul that pants for close and holy communion with God? And when the atoning blood is realized upon the conscience, when pardon and acceptance are sealed upon the heart by the Eternal Spirit, oh, then what a persuasion to draw near the throne of grace has the believer in Christ! Then, there is no consciousness of guilt to keep the believer back; no dread of God; no trembling apprehensions of a repulse. God is viewed through the cross as reconciled, and as standing in the endeared relationship, and wearing the inviting smile of a Father. With such an altar, such a High Priest, such atoning blood, and such a reconciled God, what an element should prayer be to a believer in Christ! Let the soul, depressed, burdened, tried, tempted, as it may be, draw near the mercy-seat: God delights to hear, delights to answer. Taking in the hand the atoning blood, pleading the infinite merit of Christ—reminding the Father of what His Son has accomplished, of His own gracious promise to receive and favorably answer the petition endorsed with the name and presented in behalf of that Son—the feeblest child of God, the most disconsolate, the most burdened, may approach and open all the heart to a prayer-hearing and prayer-answering God. Let the atoning blood be strenuously pleaded, let the precious and infinite merit of Christ be fully urged, and the blessing petitioned for will be obtained.

May not this be assigned as a reason why so few of our petitions are answered, why so little blessing is obtained—the faint pleading of the atoning blood? There is so feeble a recognition of the blessed way of access, so little wrestling with the precious blood, so little looking by faith to the cross, the dear name of Immanuel so seldom urged, and when urged so coldly mentioned—oh, is it any marvel that our prayers return to us unanswered, the petition ungranted, the draft on the full treasury of His love unhonored? The Father loves to be reminded of His beloved Son; the very breathing of the name to Him is music; the very waving of the censer of infinite merits to Him is fragrant. He delights to be pressed with this plea; it is a plea at all times prevalent; it is a plea He cannot reject; it glorifies Himself, honors His Son, while it enriches him who urges it. And, oh, in the absence of all other pleas, what a mercy to come with a plea like this! Who can fully estimate it? No plea has the poor believer springing from himself: he searches, but nothing can he find on which to rest a claim; all within is vile, all without is marred by sin; unfaithfulness, ingratitude, departure do but make up the history of the day. But in Christ he sees that which he can urge, and in urging which God will hear and answer.

JUNE 13

"Those who wait upon the Lord shall renew their strength." Isaiah 40:31

We may here meet a question which has often been asked by those who are conscious of a relapsed state of soul—"Am I still to be found in spiritual duties and enjoyments while sensible of a backsliding state of heart from God?" To this we reply—The warrant of a Christian's duty is not the measure of his grace, but the command of his God. If this be so—and we have no reason to question its truth—then, be your state of soul low as it may, you are bound to meet all those obligations and to discharge all those duties which a profession of Christ enjoins, irrespective of the spiritual and mental fluctuations to which the soul is always exposed. Unless aware of his design, Satan will here obtain a great advantage over you. Assuming the form of an angel of light, and with angelic gentleness and plausibility, he will suggest that your frame of soul is too torpid and lifeless and dull to draw near to God; that your affections are too frigid, your love too congealed, your heart too carnal, your mind too groveling, your pursuits too earthly, your backslidings too great, your neglects too many to take to Christ. He will hold up to view the folly, the hypocrisy, and the inconsistency of being found in the employment and use of holy and spiritual duties, while your soul thus cleaves to the dust. But listen not to his false suggestions, and heed not his sophistical reasoning, no, not for a moment. It is only in the way of waiting upon God that you will be recovered from the lapsed state of your soul. In the way of meditation, of confession, of tears, of prayer, you may yet rise from the dust, and with bolder pinion, and richer plumage, and sweeter song, soar to the gate of heaven, and return again, scattering around you its blessings, and reflecting its glory. Oh! go to Jesus, then, however low and discouraging your spiritual state may be, and relax not a single means of grace.

JUNE 14

"Though I walk in the midst of trouble, you will revive me." Psalm 138:7

Contemplate the Psalmist's circumstances "Walking in the midst of trouble." It was no new and untrodden path along which he was pursuing his way to God. The foot-print, sometimes stained with blood, always moistened with tears—of many a suffering pilgrim might be portrayed in that way, from the time that Abel, the primeval martyr, laid the first bleeding brow that ever reposed upon the bosom of Jesus. And yet how often does trial overtake the believer, as "though some strange thing had happened to him"! That at the peculiar nature of an affliction a Christian man should be startled and alarmed, would create no surprise; but that he should be startled at the trial itself, as if he alone—the only one of the family—were exempted from the discipline of the covenant, and had no interest in the Savior's declaration, "In the world you shall have tribulation," might well astonish us.

But David's experience is that of many of the spiritual seed of David. His words seem to imply, continuous trial: "I walk in the midst of trouble." With how many travelers to the celestial city it is thus! They seem never to be without trial. They know no cessation, they obtain no repose, they experience no rest. The foam of one mountain billow has scarcely broken and died upon the shore, before another follows in its wake—"Deep calls unto deep." Is it the trial of sickness? the darkened chamber, scarcely ever illumined with one cheering ray of light, the bed of suffering, seldom offering one moment's real repose, the couch of weariness, rarely left, are vivid pictures of trial, drawn from real life, needing no coloring of the fancy to heighten or exaggerate. Is it domestic trial? What scenes of incessant chafings and anxieties, turmoils and sources of bitterness, do some families present; trouble seems never to absent itself from the little circle. Yes, it is through a series of trials that many of Christ's followers are called to travel. The loss of earthly substance may be followed by the decay of health, and this succeeded perhaps by that which, of all afflictions, the most deeply pierces and lacerates the heart, and for a season covers every scene with the dark pall of woe—the desolation of death. Thus the believer ever journeys along a path paved with sorrow, and hemmed in by trial. Well, be it so! We do not speak of it complainingly; God forbid! We do not arraign the wisdom, nor doubt the mercy, nor impeach the truth of Him who has drawn every line of that path, who has paved every step of that way, and who knows its history from the end to the beginning. Why should our heart fret against the Lord? Why should we weary at the way? It is the ordained way—it is the right way—it is the Lord's way; and it is the way to a city of habitation, where the soul and body—the companions of the weary pilgrimage—will together sweetly and eternally rest. Then all trouble ceases; then all conflict terminates. Emerging from the gloom and labyrinth of the wilderness, the released spirit finds itself at home, the inhabitant of a world of which it is said, "God shall wipe away all tears from their eyes; and there shall be no more death, neither sorrow, nor crying, neither shall there be any more pain; for the former things are passed away."

JUNE 15

"My soul is exceeding sorrowful, even unto death." Matthew 26:38

The spiritual troubles which encompass the Christian are the deepest and the severest of all his trials. What, in comparison, are others? Our Lord keenly felt this when He uttered that affecting exclamation, "Now is my soul troubled; and what shall I say? Father, save me from this hour but for this cause came I unto this hour." What to Him—galling and agonizing as they were—what to Him the smiting, and the scourging, and the spitting, and the excruciating torture, compared with the sword which was now entering His soul—the mental conflict and spiritual sorrow which, in the hour of atonement, amazed, staggered, and overwhelmed Him? Listen again to His affecting cry: "My soul is exceeding sorrowful, even unto death." Then, withdrawing Himself from His disciples—for the human sympathy upon which He had relied in anticipation of the hour of suffering failed Him now—retiring from man, He flung Himself upon the bosom of God, and kneeling down, He prayed, "O my Father, if it be possible, let this cup pass from me!" Such, my soul, was the conflict which your Savior endured for you!

Partakers of Christ's sufferings, all true believers are in a measure acquainted with some of those soul troubles which thus overwhelmed the Son of God. The suspensions of Divine consolation—the hidings of God's countenance—the assaults of Satan—the contact and conflict with sin—are bitter ingredients in that cup of spiritual sorrow of which they are sometimes called deeply to drink.

Are you, beloved, walking in the midst of trouble? Think not that you are alone. May your eye of faith be "anointed with fresh eye-salve," to see One walking side by side with you, the same who walked with the three children through the fiery furnace, "whose form is like the Son of God." Yes! Jesus is with you in your trial. Christ is with you in your trouble. The path, however strait, is not so narrow that your Lord cannot tread it with you, side by side. Your way is not so intricate that He cannot enable you to thread your steps through the labyrinth. There is room enough for you and Christ to walk together. He is with you; though, like the two disciples journeying in mournful communion one with the other to Emmaus, your eyes may be so blurred that you see Him not, yet is He traveling with you along that sad and mournful, that lone and pensive path. Christ is in your adversity—Christ is in your cross—Christ is in your burden—Christ is in your suffering—Christ is in your persecution—Christ is m your sickness—yes, Christ is at your side every step you take, and He will conduct you safely to your Father's house. Though you walk in the midst of trouble, He will revive you.

JUNE 16

"Call upon me in the day of trouble: I will deliver you, and you shall glorify me." Ps. 50:15

It is in the time of trouble that we learn to pray with new power. We become more thoroughly acquainted with the divine nature and the omnipotent energy of prayer. We learn what our resources, as the true sons of Israel, are. Many are then led to pray who never prayed before. "Lord, in trouble have they visited You, they poured out a prayer when

Your chastening was upon them." Then it is the proud spirit yields; the knee, that never bent before, bends now, and the terrified soul cries out unto Him whose chastening is upon it. The slumbering Christian, too, is awakened to call upon God. Then it is he finds at what a distance he had been living from God. Then he discovers his true position—the real state of his soul—touching prayer. Thus aroused, like the slumbering prophet, by a voice, and startled by a rebuke issuing from a quarter he would least have suspected—"What meanest you, O sleeper? arise and call upon your God!"—he awakes, and finds himself in a storm, threatening instant destruction. To what does he then betake himself? David shall answer: "I give myself unto prayer." And oh, how, eloquent is then the voice of the wrestling believer! Never did the fugitive prophet "pray unto the Lord his God" as when walking in the midst of trouble. "I cried by reason of my affliction unto the Lord, and He heard me; out of the belly of hell cried I, and You heard my voice. When my soul fainted within me, I remembered the Lord: and my prayer came in unto You, into Your holy temple." In this way the Lord revives the spirit of prayer within us. And oh, what words can describe the blessedness of prayer in trial!—the preciousness of the privilege of having a God to go to, a Father to flee to in trouble! To bring you more deeply and personally into the experience of this, dear tried Christian, the Lord your God is dealing with you now. O beloved, betake yourself unto prayer! You shall indeed find it the outlet of all sorrow, and the inlet of all joy. Welcome the trouble that thus revives you. Receive with meekness of spirit, yes, with gladness of heart, the discipline, however humbling, that throws you upon God—yes, that severs you from all creatures, and that shuts you up to Him alone. That discipline, painful as it is, springs from love. In love that trouble is sent, in love that cross is permitted, in love that cup is given, in love that rod is used—it is to set you upon the work of prayer. What are these frowns of your Father, what these hidings of your Savior, what these withholdings of the Spirit, but to allure you within the holiest, there to find the throne of grace? "I will go," says the Lord, "and return to my place, until they acknowledge their offence, and seek my face; in their affliction they will seek me early."

JUNE 17

"You meet him that rejoices and works righteousness,
those that remember you in your ways." Isaiah 64:5

Let us not fail to learn the secret of receiving much from Christ—even the free dispensing abroad of what we have already received. Be assured of this, that he will receive the most from God who does the most for God: "The diligent soul shall be made fat. He becomes poor that deals with a slack hand: but the hand of the diligent makes rich. There is that scatters, and yet increases." This is God's law, and He will never repeal it; His promise, and He will ever and in all cases make it good. Go forth, believer in Christ, and let your beams of light irradiate, let your streams of grace be dispersed abroad; live for God, suffer for Christ, witness for the truth, and labor for man. Be such a depository of this living and life-giving treasure, that others, less favored than yourself, instructed, guided, and strengthened by your wisdom, experience, and grace, may proceed on their way, glorifying God for the grace given to you. Oh, to have the word of God dwelling in us so richly, and our hearts so intensely glowing with the love of Christ, as to be ever ready, to open our lips for God—a well always full and running over.

This, then, is the secret of adding to our stores,—by scattering them—of replenishing our resources, even by exhausting them. Who, we repeat the question, has ever become impoverished by giving and laborings for God? Where lives the Christian steward whose fidelity to his Master's interest has compromised the welfare of his own? Where is the Christian man who, with cheerful munificence, has consecrated his intellectual wealth or his temporal wealth to advance the truth and kingdom of Jesus, whom Christ has not reimbursed a thousand—fold? Where is the believer in Jesus who has endured reproach and suffering, patiently and silently, for conscience' sake, for truth's sake, for Christ's sake, who has not infinitely gained in the rest which he has found in God? Where is the active Christian, who, zealously laboring to dispense abroad the life-giving waters, has not felt, in the solemn retirement and calm repose of his closet, when pouring out his sorrow into the bosom of his Savior, or in holding close and holy communion with his God, the springing up into his soul of a hidden well of peace, and joy, and love, which has more than restored the energies he has exhausted, and recompensed him for the sacrifice which he has made? God meets His people in all their works of faith and labors of love. They are never alone. He meets them in the path of duty and of trial—both in doing and in suffering His will. He meets them, when embarrassed; with counsel; He meets them, when assailed, with protection; He meets them, when exhausted, with strength; He meets them, when faint, with cordials. If we take up Christ's cross upon our shoulder, Christ will take both us and our cross up in His arms. If we bow down our neck to His yoke, and bend low our back to His burden, we shall find our rest in both.

JUNE 18

"But the anointing which you have received of him abides in you, and you need not that any man teach you: but as the same anointing teaches you of all things, and is truth, and is no lie, and even as it has taught you, abide in him." 1 John 2:27

"The Lord's anointed" is the expressive and appropriate designation of all the Lord's people. This anointing it is that marks them as a "chosen generation, a royal priesthood, a holy nation, a peculiar people." It is the Lord's peculiar mark upon those who distinguishes and designates them as His own. All who are strangers to this anointing are strangers to the grace of God and the calling of the Holy Spirit. There may be much spiritual light in the judgment, and even an open profession of religion before the world, added to which there shall be something of Jehu's "zeal for the Lord;" and yet that anointing of the Holy Spirit be still lacking, apart from which all intellectual illumination, and outward profession, and party zeal, pass for nothing with a heart searching God. As the proper signification of the endeared name, Christ, is anointed, so the true signification of the honored appellation, Christian, points us to the anointing, of which all who have union with Christ personally share. I believe the remark to be as solemn as it is true, that eternity will only fully unfold the amount of evil that has sprung from calling those Christians who call themselves Christians, without any valid title to the high, holy, and distinguished appellation. How imperfectly are men in general aware of the deep, the significant, the spiritual import of the term! They think not, they know not, that a Christian is one who partakes, in His renewing, sanctifying grace, of that same Divine Holy

Spirit with which Christ was anointed of the Father for His great work. The effects of this anointing are what might be expected from a cause so glorious. It beautifies the soul. It is that anointing spoken of by the Psalmist: "And oil to make his face to shine." Therefore it is called the "beauties of holiness." How does a man's face shine—how is his countenance lighted up—when the joy of the Lord is his strength, when the spirit of adoption is in his soul, when the love of God is shed abroad in his heart! It gladdens too. Therefore it is called the "oil of joy" and "the oil of gladness." It causes the heart to sing in its deep sorrows, imparts the "garment of praise for the spirit of heaviness," and fills the soul with the glory of that "kingdom which consists not in foods and in drinks, but in righteousness and peace and joy in the Holy Spirit." Another effect springing from this anointing is the deep teaching it imparts—"You have an anointing from the Holy One, and you know all things." Such are some of the effects of this holy anointing. It beautifies, gladdens, and teaches.

JUNE 19

"I shall be anointed with fresh oil." Psalm 92:10

That the Lord re-anoints His people, who can doubt? Alas for them, if He did not! The ample provision which He has made for the exigence proves it. There is more of the precious oil in the sacred vessel! Oh blessed, holy, comforting truth to those who, mournfully conscious of their loss, are earnestly desirous for their recovery. In the Lord Jesus Christ all fulness of anointing dwells. "With Him is the fulness of the Spirit." He is prepared to impart more grace to those who have lost grace, or who to their present state desire to add an increase. In the renewed quickening of the Spirit, the re-anointing is received. "Quicken me!" was the reiterated prayer of David. What! was he not already a quickened soul? Undoubtedly. Yet, feeling the need of a renewed quickening, he earnestly importunes for it: "Quicken me in Your truth, through Your judgments, by Your precepts: only quicken me—for this my soul pants." And while the world was asking, "Who will show us any good?" the fervent breathing of this anointed priest of God was, "Quicken me, O Lord, for Your name's sake." Oh, seek this renewed quickening. New supplies of grace from Christ are implied in this fresh anointing. New grace—to subdue new corruptions, perpetually rising to the surface; to meet new temptations, through the ever-shifting ways of the subtle enemy; to overcome new difficulties, perpetually occurring in the path to heaven; and to bear up under new trials, ever transpiring in a world of tribulation. The renewed joys and comforts of the Holy Spirit are also found in the fresh anointing. The joys which had evaporated are replaced by others; the peace which had been interrupted flows back again; consolations, which had fled, are restored; and confidence in God, which seemed shaken, is once more established in the soul. Do not be content with the old anointing. It is essential to a more holy and happy life, it is essential to a peaceful and cloudless death, that you seek to be anointed with fresh oil. Do not be satisfied with past experiences. You may at one time have possessed the clear witness of the Spirit; you may have enjoyed the love of God in your heart; you many have lived so near to Christ as to have found "Wisdom's ways, ways of pleasantness, and her paths, paths of peace:" but the old anointing ceases to afford you now the high delight which you once experienced. Seek, then, the fresh anointing of the Spirit. Seek to have a new revelation of Christ to your soul. Seek the renewed application of His precious blood to your conscience. Oh, seek the fresh oil! There is a fresh supply in Christ; a fresh supply in the Spirit; a fresh supply in the heart of God; a fresh supply in the covenant of grace. Jesus is prepared to pour it upon your soul more abundantly. The Holy Spirit is prepared to lead you to the source where this costly treasure dwells. A vessel of clay though you are—your capacity small—your unworthiness great—yet is the Triune God ready to recognize your exalted dignity and rank as a king and a priest, by shedding more copiously than ever the oil of gladness upon your head. Let aged Christians especially look to the state of their souls, and seek this renewed anointing. In nearing the end of their journey, in looking into their graves, and beyond them, to the meeting with their God and Savior, they will need to be anointed with fresh oil. One drop—oh, how will it insinuate itself through the whole inner life, diffusing energy and might!—the soul thus renewing its strength, and composing its ruffled pinions for its heavenly flight. Come, pilgrim of many a weary stage! come, soldier of many a hard-fought battle! come, voyager of many a storm and tempest, and sit down at the Savior's feet, and receive of the fresh oil! Come, gather up the trailing garments, shake off the gathered dust from your sandals, wipe the sweat from your brow, and rest awhile upon the bosom of your Lord, while with fresh oil He anoints you for your burial. Is it not time for you to give up this poor world's pursuit, and lay aside in some measure its needless anxiety and care, and allow a holy pause, a solemn calm, to intervene—before you unclasp your helmet, lay down your staff, and are gathered to your fathers?

JUNE 20

"For you are all the children of God by faith in Christ Jesus." Gal. 3:26

It is delightful to trace the different exhibitions of faith which the Holy Spirit has presented to our view in His own Word. And he seems to have thus spread them out before us, that the ever varied and varying circumstances of the saints of God may be adequately met. In some sections of His Word, He has presented to our view sturdy characters, impressed with the lineaments of a strong, gigantic faith. For example that was strong faith in the centurion, when he said, "Lord, I am not worthy that You should come under my roof; but speak the word only, and my servant shall be healed." That was great faith exhibited in the case of the woman of Canaan, who, at the apparent repulse of the blessed Lord, would take no denial, but met His seeming objection by saying, "Truth, Lord; yet the dogs eat of the crumbs which fall from their master's table. Then Jesus answered and said unto her, O woman, great is your faith: be it unto you even as you will." That, too, was strong faith in Abraham, who could take his son, his only, son, his son whom he loved, and offer him up at God's bidding. And, to mention no more, that was strong, unwavering faith in Job, who could say, "Though He slay me, yet will I trust in Him." But, on the other hand, the Holy Spirit presents to the view some of the weakest exhibitions of faith, in order that no dear child of God, reposing by simple reliance on Christ, might despair. That was feeble faith which the leper exercised when he said, "Lord, if you will, you can make me clean." Here was no doubting of Christ's ability—the only point He seemed to question was His willingness to cleanse him. That was faith of the same feeble character, exercised by the father who brought his child possessed of a dumb spirit to Jesus, to be dispossessed, with the request thus couched—"If you can do anything, have compassion on us and help us." In this case, Christ's willingness was fully believed, His ability only doubted; and yet, in both cases, the one that doubted His willingness, and the other that doubted His ability, Christ manifested His compassion and answered their requests. Let no anxious, seeking soul, then, hang back from Jesus, because of the weakness of its faith. It may be small faith; it may be small in its degree, and weak in its exhibition; yet it is "precious faith,"—yes, "like precious faith" with Abraham and Job, and all the prophets and apostles. If it be faith, however small, it yet is "the faith of God's elect;" it is of the mighty operation of the Holy Spirit, and though feeble, yet, if it directs its eye out of and off of itself, simply to Jesus, that single glance shall sweep the ocean fulness of His love in the soul.

JUNE 21

"This do in remembrance of me." Luke 22:19

To the soul hungering and thirsting for the Lord Jesus in the ordinance, Jesus presents Himself. He draws back the shutter, opens the window, stands within it, and looks forth upon His people, clustering around His table, desiring to remember His love. "Precious Jesus!" is the meditation of a soul thus looking for its Beloved, "I have come to Your ordinance invited by Your love, drawn by Your Spirit; but what is it to my soul without You? Your minister may open this institution with clearness and power, but if You do not manifest Yourself, to break and heal my heart—if I don't catch one glimpse of You, my Lord, it is no ordinance of grace or sweetness to my soul. I want by faith to see You in the baptism of Your sufferings, to feed upon Your flesh, and to drink of Your blood. I want to enjoy communion with You. You know, Lord, the workings of my heart; You know that this is the great desire of my soul, that I might enjoy fellowship with Christ. Oh, that I might have more of Christ, that I might meet with Christ, that I might have some further manifestation of Christ, and that I might have my soul closer knit to Christ. I come with thirsting after Jesus, knowing my infinite need of Him, and His infinite excellency and fulness to meet my case. My soul does famish and perish without Christ; but in the enjoyment of Christ there is a sufficiency for the satisfying of my soul. That which I have had of Christ, sometimes in the word, and sometimes in prayer, has been sweet unto my taste; but I look for closer communion, for a clearer manifestation of Christ here, for this is the great "communion of the body and blood of Jesus." Behold, Lord, I approach these windows of Your house, a poor, unworthy, backsliding child, tried and tempted; yet just as I am, dear Lord, I come. I dare not, I cannot, stay away from You, Divine loadstone of my heart, precious magnet of my soul! Draw me, and then I will run after You; Show Yourself in the window, and, overcome with Your beauty and Your love, I exclaim, "Turn away Your eyes from me, for they have overcome me." Blessed Spirit! I have been taught to believe that You will take of the things of Jesus, and show them unto me. Open the window of this ordinance, and let me behold my soul's Beloved standing within it. I cannot live, I cannot die, without Him. Living or dying I must have Christ. "I am any Beloved's, and His desire is towards me;" and truly my soul's desire is towards Him. There is to my soul no love like Christ's love. There is no voice like Christ's voice. There is no sympathy like Christ's sympathy. There is no friend like this Friend; there is no Christ like my Christ.

The window is open! "The voice of my Beloved! behold, He comes, leaping upon the mountains, skipping upon the hills." He looks forth at the window; and lively faith and ardent love, sweet contrition and holy joy, possess and overwhelm my soul!

JUNE 23

"The God of peace, that brought again from the dead our Lord Jesus." Heb. 13:20

How beautifully the apostle associates the two blessings! He is now truly the "God of peace"—the pacified God, the reconciled Father; and the evidence of it is His raising up His dear Son from the grave. Thus what a bright view does this truth unfold to us of God! When we retire within ourselves, we see much to engender dark views of, and distrustful feelings towards, Him. But when faith travels to the grave of Jesus, and we see it empty, we have such an overwhelming evidence of the perfect reconciliation of God, of His thoughts of peace towards us, that instantly faith triumphs, and all our gloomy, trembling apprehensions of His character vanish and disappear. He is the "God of peace," because Jesus is a risen Savior. And in proportion as you lay hold by faith of the resurrection-life of Christ, you will have that pillar to sustain you upon which rests the whole fabric of salvation. The peace of God will fill your heart, as you know from experience the power of the Lord's resurrection in your soul. The power of Christ's resurrection, in fact, lies in a sense of pardoned sin, in our apprehension of complete justification, in the living hope of eternal glory. Jesus saves to the uttermost all that come unto God by Him, because he is a risen and a living Savior, and ever lives to make intercession in behalf of all His people. Oh, deal believingly with a risen Christ! The same resurrection-power which brought back to life again the Head of the Church is exerted in effecting the spiritual resurrection of the Church itself. The true believer is already risen. He was once dead in sin, and entombed in the grave of his iniquities. But a power—the same which awoke the death-slumber of Lazarus—has darted from the tomb of Jesus, and has quickened Him to a new and a deathless life. Oh, were we more directly to trace the mighty energy of the Eternal Spirit in our souls, raising us from the region of death to life and immortality, to that stupendous fact of redemption—the resurrection of Christ from the dead—how would it exalt our views of its importance, and fill our souls with its glory! What must be the power of our Lord's resurrection, that can even now awake the profoundest sleep of spiritual death! When the Spirit of God puts forth His own grace to raise a soul from the grave of sin, oh, forget not it is in virtue of a risen, living Savior. Despair not of the spiritual life of any, though they may have laid in the grave so long as well near to have quenched all hope of their conversion, since Christ has risen from the dead, and is alive, to give life in answer to the prayer of faith. "The second Adam is a quickening Spirit."

JUNE 23

"That I may know him, and the power of
his resurrection." Philippians 3:10

Of the downward tendency of our hearts we are, alas! but too conscious. We need an antagonistic principle—something to counteract the overworking influence of an ungodly world. Where shall we meet with it? We answer, in the power of Christ's resurrection, felt, realized, and experienced in the soul. This is the argument of Paul: "You are a risen people, risen in union with Christ. If this be so, then seek after heavenly mindedness, setting your affections on things above." What a heaven-attracting power, then, has this glorious truth! What is Christ? He is alive. Where is Christ? He is in heaven, at the right hand of God, as my head—my representative—my forerunner—my treasure—my all. Then, let me rise! Shall not my affections soar to their best beloved? Shall not my heart be where its treasure is? Shall I set my mind upon things on the earth, when my Lord rose out of the earth, and ascended above the earth, and bids me rise and follow Him in faith, in spirit, and in love, until He calls me to come away to Him entirely, that I may be ever with Him and behold His glory? If I am indeed risen with Christ, then let me evidence it by my increasing spiritual-mindedness. Christ, who is my life, is in heaven—why should I needlessly be buried in the earth? Why allow—as I appear to do—that there is an object upon earth whose claims to my love are paramount, whose beauty to my eye is greater, whose attraction to my soul is stronger, than my risen, ascended, and glorified Lord? Is there upon earth one who loves me as Jesus loves me? Is there one who has done for me what Jesus has done? Is there one who is doing for me now what Jesus is doing? Is there one who is to me such a friend, such a brother, such a counselor as Jesus? No, not one! Then, why should not my thoughts be more with Him? Why should not my heart cling closer to Him? Why this vagrancy of mind, this truancy of affection, this wandering of desire; why this forgetfulness, coldness, and cleaving to earth, when my Lord is risen, and I am professedly risen with Him? Oh, to feel more sensibly, more deeply; more constantly the power of His resurrection! Lord! I detect my heart settling down on creature things—objects of sense and sin. My business is a snare—my domestic blessings are a snare—my friendships are a snare—my position is a snare—the too fond opinion which others entertain of me is a snare—my grace, my gifts, my usefulness, through the corruption of my heart, are snares. Lord, place beneath my soul the mighty lever of Your resurrection, and lift me towards Yourself! Oh, let me feel the earth-severing, the heaven—attracting power of Your resurrection-life! Having been buried with You by baptism into death, sincerely would I now rise with You, like as You were raised up from the dead by the glory of the Father; that I might walk with You in newness of life, until I reach You in the realms of glory.

JUNE 24

"For verily he took not on him the nature of angels; but he took on him the seed of Abraham." Hebrews 2:16.

Who are the people upon whom the heart of Jesus is set? They, are not angels; and yet He loves angels, because they are elect and holy; He loves them as the creatures of His power, and as the ministers of His will. But God loves not angels as He loves man. The Lord Jesus bears not the same affection towards those unfallen and pure spirits as He does towards a poor sinner hiding in His wounded side, cleansing in His blood, and enfolding himself within the robe of His righteousness. He never took part of the nature of angels, nor wept over angels, nor bled for angels—but all this He did for man!

It is His Church, then, which is represented as the object of His love—His own people, the donation of His Father, the creatures of His choice, the subjects of His grace, the treasure of His heart. Is it asked wherein has He loved them? Rather might we ask wherein has He not loved them? Look at His assumption of their nature! What a mighty stoop was this!—the Infinite to the finite. Were it possible for me to save the life of an insect by assuming the form of that insect, I should, by so doing, manifest my great benevolence. But behold the love of our Incarnate God! His heart was bent, His whole soul was set, upon saving man. But He could save man only by becoming man. He could not raise our nature, but as He stooped and assumed that nature. He must not only look upon it, and pity it, and weep over it, but He must take it into the closest and most indissoluble union with Himself. Nor was it the mere exchange or blending together of natures so as to form one new nature. It was not the absorption of the Infinite into the finite, for He ceased not to be God when He became man; He only veiled, He did not extinguish, the glory of His Deity. In this consisted the mightiness of the stoop. I see no humiliation in the Savior's life, but as it springs from this one fact—His condescension in taking up into union with His own Divine our human nature. This was the first and greatest step in the path that conducted Him to the cross. All the acts of abasement and ignominy which follow were ingrafted upon this. And, oh, what humiliation! Look at your nature! Contemplate it in some of its severest forms of degradation, wretchedness, and woe. Are you not often constrained to blush that it is your own? Do you not turn from it at times with loathing and abhorrence, ashamed to confess that you are a man? Above all, what self-loathing, what self-abhorrence, when the Holy Spirit opens the chambers of iniquity in your own heart, and makes you acquainted with the abominations that are there! And yet the Son of God stooped to our nature. "A body have You prepared me." But it was unfallen, sinless humanity that He took into union with His Godhead. Where, then, is His condescension? In stooping to an inferior nature, though in that stoop He received no taint from us. He was made a sin—offering, yet He was "without sin." If this truth, dear reader, has no glory to your eye, nor sweetness to your soul, what is your Christianity? It is the foundation of Christianity, it is the marrow of the Gospel, it is the hope of the soul, it is that truth which takes every ruffle from the pillow of death.

And is not this just the truth we need as a suffering and a tried people? When do we extract the sweetest honey from this bitter of bitters? Is it not when our humanity is wounded, oppressed, and cast down? When do we most value and love the humiliation of the Incarnate God? Is it not when by suffering we are driven to it, then to learn the tenderness and the sympathy that are in Christ? Oh blessed affliction, sweet sorrow, friendly chastisement, that brings my soul into the deeper experience of what God is in my nature!

JUNE 25

"Walk in love, as Christ also has loved us, and has given himself for us an offering and a sacrifice to God for a sweet-smelling savor. Ephesians 5:2

It was an entire sacrifice. It was Himself He offered up. More He could not give; less would not have sufficed. He gave Himself—all that He possessed in heaven, and all that belonged to Him on earth, He gave in behalf of His people. His life of obedience, His death of suffering, He gave as "an offering and is sacrifice to God." It was an entire surrender.

It was a voluntary offering. "He gave Himself." It was not by compulsion or by constraint that He surrendered Himself into the hands of Divine justice—He went not as a reluctant victim to the altar—they dragged Him not to the cross. He went voluntarily. It is true that there existed a solemn necessity, why Jesus should die in behalf of His people. It grew out of His covenant engagement with the Father. Into that engagement He voluntarily entered: His own ineffable love constrained Him: But after the compact had been made, the covenant of redemption ratified, and the bond given to justice, there was a necessity resting upon Jesus why He should finish the work. His word, His honor, His truth, His glory, all were pledged to the entire fulfilment of His suretyship. He had freely given Himself into the power of justice; He was therefore, on His taking upon Him the form of a servant, under obligations to satisfy all its claims; He was legally bound to obey all its commands. And yet it was a voluntary surrender of Himself as a sacrifice for His people. It was a willing offering. If there was a necessity, and we have shown that there was, it grew out of His own voluntary love to His Church. It was, so to speak, a voluntary necessity. See how this blessed view of the death of Jesus is sustained by the Divine word. "He was oppressed, and He was afflicted, yet He opened not His mouth: He is brought as a lamb to the slaughter, and as a sheep before her shearers is dumb, so He opens not His mouth." His own declaration confirms the truth. "Therefore does my Father love me, because I lay down my life, that I might take it again. No man takes it the following is from me, but I lay it down of myself. I have power to lay it down, and I have power to take it again."

JUNE 26

"Jesus therefore, knowing all things that should come upon him, went forth, and said unto them, Whom seek you?" John 18:4

His voluntariness was not founded on ignorance. He well knew what the covenant of redemption involved—what stern justice demanded. The entire scene of His humiliation was before Him, in all its dark and somber hues—the manger—the bloodthirsty king—the scorn and ridicule of His countrymen—the unbelief of His own kinsmen—the mental agony of Gethsemane—the bloody sweat—the bitter cup—the waywardness of His disciples—the betrayal of one, the denial of another, the forsaking of all—the mock trial—the purple robe—the crown of thorns—the infuriated cry, "Away with Him, away with Him! Crucify Him, crucify Him!"—the heavy cross—the painful crucifixion—the cruel taunts—the vinegar and the gall—the hidings of His Father's countenance—the concentrated horrors of the curse—the last cry of anguish—the falling of the head—the giving up the spirit; all, all was before the omniscient mind of the Son of God, with vividness equal to its reality, when He exclaimed, "Save him from going down to the pit: I have found a ransom." And yet He willingly rushed to the rescue of ruined man. He voluntarily, though He knew the price of pardon was His blood, gave Himself up thus to the bitter, bitter agony. And did He regret that He had undertaken the work? Never! It is said that repented God that He had made man; but in no instance is it recorded that it repented Jesus that He had redeemed man. Not an action, not a word, not a look betrayed an emotion like this. Every step He took from Bethlehem to Calvary did but unfold the willingness of Jesus to die. "I have a baptism to be baptized with, and how am I straitened until it be accomplished!"

Oh, how amazing was the love of Jesus! This, this was the secret why He loved not His own life unto the death. He loved sinners too well. He loved us better than Himself. With all our sinfulness, guilt, wretchedness, and poverty; He yet loved us so much as to give Himself an offering and sacrifice unto God for us. Here was the spring-head where flowed these streams of mercy. This was the gushing fountain that was opened when He died. And when they taunted Him and said, "If You are the King of the Jews, save Yourself," oh, what a reply did His silence give "I came not to save myself, but my people—I hang here, not for my own sins, but for theirs—I could save myself, but I came to give my life a ransom for many." They thought the nails alone kept Him to the cross—He knew it was His own love that fastened Him there. Behold the strength of Immanuel's love. Come, fall prostrate, adore and worship Him. Oh, what love was His! Oh the depth! Content not yourself with standing upon the shore of this ocean—enter into it, drink largely from it. It is for you, if you but feel your nothingness, your poverty, your vileness; this ocean is for you. It is not for angels, it is for men. It is not for the righteous, but for sinners. Then drink to the full from the love of Jesus. Do not be satisfied with small supplies. Take a large vessel to the fountain. The larger the demand, the larger the supply. The more needy, the more welcome. The more vile, the more fit.

JUNE 27

"It is good that a man should both hope and quietly
wait for the salvation of the Lord." Lamentations 3:26

A believer may present a right petition in a right way, and yet he may not wait the Lord's answer in His own time. He may appoint a time, and if the Lord does not answer within that period, he turns away, resigning all expectation of an answer. There is such a thing as waiting for the Lord. The apostle alludes to and enjoins this holy patience, when he speaks to the Ephesians of "praying always with all prayer and supplication in the Spirit, and watching thereunto with all perseverance." A believer may present his request—may have some degree of nearness in urging it—may press it with fervency—and yet, forgetting the hoping, quiet, waiting patience which ought invariably to mark a praying soul; he may lose the blessing he has sought. There is such a thing as "waiting upon the Lord." Oh; how long have we made Him to wait for us! For years, it may be, we kept Him knocking, and standing, and waiting at the door of our hearts, until His own Spirit took the work in His own hands, and unlocked the heart, and the Savior entered. The Lord would now often have us wait His time in answering prayer. And, if the vision tarry, still let us wait, and hope, and expect. Let the delay but stimulate hope, and increase desire, exercise faith, and multiply petitions at the mercy-seat. It will come when the Lord sees best.

A believer may lose the answer to his prayer, by dictating to the Lord the mode, as well as the time, of answering. The Lord has His own mode of blessing His people. We may prescribe the way the Lord should answer, but He may send the blessing to us through an opposite channel, in a way we never thought of, and should never have selected. Sovereignty sits regent upon the throne, and in no aspect is its exercise more manifestly seen than in selecting the way and the means by which the prayers of the saints of God are answered. Dictate not to the Lord. If you ask a blessing through a certain channel, or in a prescribed way, let it be with the deepest humility of mind, and with perfect submission to the will of God. Be satisfied to receive the blessing in any way which a good and covenant God may appoint. Be assured, it will be in that way that will most glorify Himself, and secure to you the greatest amount of blessing.

JUNE 28

"The path of the just is as the shining light, that shines
more and more unto the perfect day." Proverbs 4:18

The first light that dawns upon the soul is the daybreak of grace. When that blessed period arrives, when the Sun of Righteousness has risen upon the long-benighted mind, how do the shadows of ignorance and of guilt instantly disappear! What a breaking away of, perhaps, a long night of alienation from God, of direct hostility to God, and of ignorance of the Lord Jesus, then takes place. Not, however, strongly marked is this state always at the first. The beginning of grace in the soul is frequently analogous to the beginning of day in the natural world. The dawn of grace is at first so faint, the daybreak so gentle, that a skillful eye only can observe its earliest tints. The individual himself is, perhaps, ignorant of the extraordinary transition through which his soul is passing. The discovery of darkness which that day-dawn has made, the revelation it has brought to view of the desperate depravity of his heart, the utter corruption of his fallen nature, the number and the turpitude of his sins, it may be, well near overwhelms the individual with despair! But what has led to this discovery? What has revealed all this darkness and sin? Oh! it is the daybreak of grace in the soul! One faint ray, what a change has it produced! And is it real? Ah! just as real as that the first beam, faintly painted on the eastern sky, is a real and an essential part of light. The daybreak, faint and glimmering though it be, is as really day as the meridian is day. And so is it with the day-dawn of grace in the soul. The first serious thought—the first real misgiving—the first conviction of sin—the first downfall of the eye—the first bending of the knee—the first tear—the first prayer—the first touch of faith, is as really and as essentially the daybreak of God's converting grace in the soul as is the utmost perfection to which that grace can arrive. Oh, glorious dawn is this, my reader, if now for the first time in your life the daybreak of grace has come, and the shadows of ignorance and guilt are fleeing away before the advancing light of Jesus in your soul. If now you are seeing how depraved your nature is; if now you are learning the utter worthlessness of your own righteousness; if now you are fleeing as a poor, lost sinner to Christ, relinquishing your hold of everything else, and clinging only to Him; though this be but in weakness, and tremulousness, and hesitancy, yet sing for joy, for the day is breaking—the prelude to the day of eternal glory—and the shadows of unregeneracy are forever fleeing away. And as this day of grace has begun, so it will advance. Nothing shall impede its course, nothing shall arrest its progress. "He which has begun a good work in you will perform it until the day of Jesus Christ." The Sun, now risen upon you with healing in His beams, shall never stand still—shall never go back. "He has set a tabernacle for the sun" in the renewed soul of man; and onward that sun will roll in its glorious orbit, penetrating with its beams every dark recess, until all mental shadows are merged and lost in its unclouded and eternal splendor.

JUNE 29

"For we know in part, and we prophesy in part." 1 Corinthians 13:9

With all our attainments, how little have we really attained! With all our knowledge, how little do we actually know! How superficially and imperfectly are we acquainted with truth; with Jesus who is emphatically "the Truth," with God whom the Truth reveals. "We see through a glass darkly,"—all is yet but as a riddle, compared with what we shall know when the shadows of ignorance have fled. There are, too, the enshrouding shadows of God's dark and painful dispensations. Our dealings are with a God of whom it is said, "Clouds and darkness are round about Him." Who often "covers Himself as with a cloud," and to whom the midnight traveler to the world of light has often occasion to address himself in the language of the Church, "You are a God that hides Yourself." Ah! beloved, what clouds of dark providences may be gathering and thickening around your present path! Through what a gloomy, stormy night of affliction faith may be steering your tempest-tossed barque! That faith eyeing the promise, and not the providence, the "bright light that is in the cloud," and not the lowering cloud itself—will steer that trembling vessel safely through the surge. Remember that in the providences of God the believer is passive, but with regard to the promises of God he is active. In the one case he is to "be still" and know that God reigns, and that the "Judge of all the earth must do right." In the other, his faith, childlike, unquestioning, and unwavering, is to take hold of what God says, and of what God is, believing that what He has promised He is also able and willing to perform. This is to be "strong in faith, giving glory to God."

JUNE 30

"Until the clay break, and the shadows
flee away." Solomon's Song 2:17

The Divine withdrawment is a shadow, often imparting an aspect of dreariness to the path we are treading to the Zion of God. "Why do You hide Yourself?" says Job. "For a small moment," says God to the Church, "have I forsaken you. ... In a little wrath I hid my face from you for a moment." Ah! there are many who have the quenchless light of life in their souls, who yet, like Job, are constrained to take up the lamentation, "I went mourning without the sun." There are no shadows darker to some of God's saints than this. Many professing Christians dwell so perpetually in the region of shadows, they so seldom feel the sunshine of God's presence in their souls, that they scarcely can discern when the light is withdrawn. But there are others, wont to walk so near with God in the rich, personal enjoyment of their pardon, acceptance, and adoption, that if but a vapor floats between their soul and the sun, in an instant they are sensible of it. Oh, blessed are they whose walk is so close, so filial with God, whose home is so hard by the cross, who, like the Apocalyptic angel, dwell so entirely in the sun, as to feel the barometer of their soul affected by the slightest change in their spiritual atmosphere; in other words—who walk so much beneath the light of God's reconciled countenance as to be sensible of His hidings even "for a small moment." Then there comes the last of our shadows, "the valley of the shadow of death." There they terminate. This may be the focus where they all shall meet, but it is to meet only to be entirely and forever scattered. The sentiment is as true as the figure is poetic—"the shadow of death." It is but a "shadow" to the believer; the body of that shadow Jesus, the "Captain of our salvation," met on the cross, fought and overcame. By dying He so completely destroyed death, and him that had the power of death, that the substance of death in the experience of the dying Christian dwindles into a mere shadow, and that shadow melts into eternal glory.

JULY

JULY 1

*"All things work together for good to those
who love God." Romans 8:28*

Observe the unity of operation. They "work together,"–not singly and separately, but conjointly–as adjunct causes and mutual helps. Therefore it is that we often mark a plurality of trial in the calamity which befalls the Christian. Seldom does affliction come solitary and alone; storm rises upon storm, cloud on cloud. One messenger of woe is quickly succeeded by another, burdened with tidings of yet heavier sorrow. Trace the wisdom, nor the wisdom only, but the love of your God, O child of suffering, in ordaining your path to heaven through "much tribulation," and in weaving around you many trials. Single and alone, the good they are charged to convey were but partially accomplished, and the evil they were designed to meet but imperfectly cured. It is the compounding of the ingredients in the recipe that constitutes its sanative power. Extract any one ingredient, and you impair the others, and destroy the whole. We may not understand the chemistry of the process; we do not see how one element acts upon the properties of the others, nor how by the combination of all the cure is effected. Yet, confiding in the skill of the compounder, and submitting our reason to our faith, we take the remedy, and receive the benefit. So with the Divine dispensations, they work, but "work together." How assuredly would the curative process of trial be impaired, if but one of the several sent were lacking! How would the adjustment, harmony, and symmetry of God's arrangement be destroyed, if one dark dispensation were lacking of, perhaps, the many which lower upon our horizon! It is the combination of sound, the harmony of many and often discordant notes, that constitute music. Oh, how imperfectly are we aware, not of the necessity of trial only, but of a plurality of trial, in order to wake from our lips the sweetest, loftiest anthem of praise and thanksgiving to God! Thus it is that the most deeply tried believers are the most skillful and the most melodious choristers in God's Church.

They sing the sweetest on earth, and they sing the loudest in heaven, who are passing through, and who have come out of, "great tribulation." Then, Christian, count it all joy when you fall into diverse trials; do not be terrified if wave responds to wave–if cloud caps cloud–if storm rises on storm–if your Joseph has been taken, and now your Benjamin be demanded. The greater the accumulation of trial, the richer the freight it bears. Then it is that the interposition, the wisdom, and love of our God appear the most conspicuous and wonderful. Having delivered us out of six troubles, we see Him hastening to our rescue in the seventh. Then it is the experience of the sweet singer of Israel awakes an echo in our heart: "He sent from above, He took me, He drew me out of many waters."

And let us not forget that it is a present working. It says not that all things shall work together for good, though this is equally certain. But it says that all things do now work together for good. It is not a past, nor a future, but a present process. They are always working for good. The operation may be as invisible and noiseless as the leaven fomenting in the meal, and yet not less certain and effectual. The kingdom of God comes not into our souls with observation, nor does it grow in our souls with observation. And whether the good thus borne upon the raven-wing of trial, thus embosomed in the lowering cloud of some crushing providence, be immediate or remote, it matters little; sooner or later it will accomplish its benign and heaven-sent mission, and then trial will expand its dark pinions and fly away, and sorrow will roll up its somber drapery and disappear. The painful and inexplicable dispensations, which at the present moment may be thickening and deepening around your path, are but so many problems in God's government, which He is working out to their certain, satisfactory, and happy results.

JULY 2
"We know that all things work together for good." Romans 8:28

Safely may the apostle rest his appeal with us. We know it, because God has said it. We know it, because others have testified to it. Best of all, we know it, because we have experienced it ourselves. We can set our seal to the truth, that all things under the government of an infinitely great, all-wise, righteous, and beneficent Lord God, both in the world and in the Church, and in the history of each member of the Church, work together for good. What that good may be, the shape it may assume, the complexion it may wear, the end to which it may be subservient, we cannot tell. To our dim view it may appear an evil, but to God's far-seeing eye it is a positive good. His glory is secured by it, and that end accomplished, we are sure it must be good. Oh truth most divine! Oh words most consolatory! How many whose eye traces this page, it may be whose tears bedew it, whose sighs breathe over it, whose prayers hallow it, may be wading in deep waters, may be drinking bitter cups, and are ready to exclaim–"All these things are against me"! Oh no, beloved of God, all these things are for you! "The Lord sits upon the flood." "The voice of the Lord is upon the waters." "He makes the clouds His chariot." Be not then afraid. Calmly stay your faith on this divinely assured truth, that "all things work together for good to those who love God." Will it not be a good, if your present adversity results in the dethronement of some worshiped idol–in the endearing of Christ to your soul–in the closer conformity of your mind to God's image–in the purification of your heart–in your more thorough fitness for heaven? Will it not be a real good if it terminates in a revival of God's work within you–in stirring you up to more prayer–in enlarging your heart to all who love the same Savior–in stimulating you to increased activity for the conversion of sinners, for the diffusion of the truth, and for the glory of God? Oh yes! good, real good, permanent good must result from all the Divine dispensations in your history. Bitter repentance shall end in the experienced sweetness of Christ's love. The festering wound shall but elicit the healing balm. The overpowering burden shall but bring you to the tranquil rest. The storm shall but quicken your footsteps to the hiding-place. The north wind and the south wind shall breathe together over your garden, and the spices shall flow out. In a little while–oh, how soon!–you shall pass away from earth to heaven, and in its clearer, serener light shall read the truth,

"Often read with tears before,"
"All things work together for good to those who love God."

JULY 3

"Therefore, thus says the Lord God, Behold, I lay in Zion
for a foundation a stone, a tried stone." Isaiah 28:16

Jesus is fitly compared to a "stone" for strength and durability. He is a "Savior, and a great one"—"mighty to save." "I have laid help upon one that is mighty." If it were probable that the fact of His Deity should be announced in a voice of thunder from the eternal throne, can we suppose it would be uttered in terms more decided and explicit than those which fell upon the ear of the exiled evangelist from the lips of Christ Himself? "I am Alpha and Omega, the beginning and the ending, says the Lord, who is, and who was, and who is to come, the Almighty." And what a needed truth is this! None but an almighty ransom could have saved from going down to the pit. Jesus is our ransom, and Jesus is the Almighty.

The Redeemer is not only a stone, but a "tried stone." The grand experiment has been made–the great test has been applied, and to answer all the ends for which the Lord God laid it in Zion, it has proved completely adequate. Never was a foundation tried as this. In the eternal purpose of redemption, Omnipotence tried it. In the Divine mind there existed no lurking suspicion, no embarrassing uncertainty as to the result. The Father knew all that this foundation was to sustain, and well He knew, too, that it was capable of sustaining all. Stupendous were the consequences. His own glory and the honor of His government were involved; the salvation of His elect was to be secured; death, with all its horrors, was to be abolished; life, with all its immortal, untold glories, was to be revealed; hell was to be closed, and heaven opened to all believers. With such momentous realities pending, with such mighty and glorious results at stake, the Eternal mind, in its purpose of grace and glory, would lay for a foundation a "tried stone." Blessed Emmanuel! how effulgently does Your glory beam from beneath Your prophetical veil! You are that "tried stone,"–tried by the Father, when He laid upon You all His people's sins and transgressions, bruised You, and put You to grief. Tried by the law, when it exacted and received from You Your utmost obedience to its precepts. Tried by Divine justice, when it kindled around You its fiercest flame, yet consumed You not. Tried by the Church, built upon You so securely that the gates of hell shall never prevail against her. Tried by poor sinners, who have brought their burdens of guilt to Your blood, and have found pardon and peace. Tried by believers, who have taken their trials to Your sympathy, their sorrows to Your love, their wounds to Your healing, their weakness to Your strength, their emptiness to Your fullness, their petitions to Your ear, and have never, never been disappointed. Oh yes, You are that "tried stone" to whom I would come moment by moment.

JULY 4

"A precious corner stone." Isaiah 28:16

Of whom does the prophet speak this but of Jesus, compared with whom nothing is precious? He alone is worthy of the term, who alone can smooth life's rugged path, sweeten life's bitter trials, lighten life's heavy burdens, and this by daily and hourly emanations of His own life, grace, and preciousness. Oh, how precious–what language can express?–is this precious stone to him who, conscious of his vileness, poverty, and nothingness, or with a spirit oppressed with deep trial, or bleeding from painful bereavement, wades to it through the billows, exclaiming, "When my heart is overwhelmed, lead me to the Rock that is higher than I." Precious in His all—atoning blood–precious in His all-justifying righteousness–precious in His infinite fullness—precious in every office that He fills, in every work that He performs, in every promise that He makes, is Christ to him who, finding all other foundations but as sliding sand, builds his hope of glory upon the incarnate God. "To you, therefore, who believe, He is precious."

A "corner stone," too, is our glorious Redeemer. The important position which this occupies in the spiritual building–its essential relation to the compactness, strength, and durability of the whole fabric–we fear, is not duly considered by many who are professedly "lively stones" in the "spiritual house." And yet how momentous and how holy is the instruction it conveys! The corner stone is that which unites the parts of the edifice; it is to the building what the key-stone is to the arch; it imparts unity, symmetry, and strength. The Lord Jesus has been the uniting stone of the

Church in all ages. The saints of the Patriarchal, Levitical, and Christian Churches all meet and form, in Him, one glorious temple of the living God. "No more strangers and foreigners, but fellow-citizens with the saints, and of the household of God:" they are "built upon the foundation of the apostles and prophets, Jesus Christ Himself being the chief corner stone; in whom all the building fitly framed together, grows unto an holy temple in the Lord," and thus becomes "a habitation of God through the Spirit." That there are divisions in the Church of God, visible and painful–that the one body is sadly dismembered, the seamless robe rudely torn and disfigured, is a truth too glaring to conceal, and almost too painful and humiliating to acknowledge. Alas, that it should be! Oh, how much is the unity of the Church lost sight of in the din of religious controversy and in the heat of party zeal! How does brother look coldly upon brother, and minister glance suspiciously at minister, and church stand aloof from church! Ought this so to be? And to what may it in a great degree be traced? We believe to a forgetfulness of the truth that all true believers are "one in Christ Jesus;" that the blood of the Lamb is the bond of union of the saints; that He is the "corner stone," uniting all the parts of the one edifice; and that, if built upon Him, we are one with that Church, and that Church is one with Christ.

JULY 5
"A sure foundation." Isaiah 28:16

"A sure foundation" is the last quality of excellence specified of this precious Stone. As if, in so momentous a matter as the salvation of the soul, to remove all lingering doubt from the mind, to annihilate all imaginary and shadowy conceptions of Jesusl; Jehovah, the great Builder of the Church, declares the foundation thus laid to be a real and substantial one. Confidently here may the weary rest, and the sinner build his hope of heaven. All is sure. Sure that the word he credits is true–sure that the invitation that calls him is sincere–sure that the welcome extended to him is cordial. Sure, in coming to Jesus, of free forgiveness, of full justification, of complete and eternal acceptance with a reconciled God. Sure, that in renouncing all self-dependence, and building high his hope of glory on this foundation, he "shall not be ashamed nor confounded, world without end." All, too, is sure to the believer in the covenant of grace, of which Jesus is the Surety and Mediator. Every promise is sure–the full supply of all our need–the daily efficacy of the atoning blood–the answer to our prayers, though long delayed–the hope of being forever with Jesus–all, all is certain and sure, because based on Jesus, and springing from the heart of an unchangeable God, and confirmed by the oath of Him who has said, "Once have I sworn by my holiness that I will not lie unto David."

Precious Jesus! we have been contemplating Your glory as through a glass darkly. And yet we thank and adore You even for this glimpse. Dim and imperfect though it is, it has endeared You–unutterably endeared You–to our hearts. Oh! if this is Your glory beheld through a clouded medium, what will it be seen face to face! Soon, soon shall we gaze upon it. Then, Oh glorious King, we shall exclaim, "It was a true report that I heard of your acts and of your wisdom, and, behold, the half was not told me." Seeing that we look for such things, grant us grace, that being "diligent, we may be found of You in peace, without spot, and blameless." Send to us what You will, withhold from us what You will; only vouchsafe to us a "part in the first resurrection," and a seat at Your right hand when You come to Your kingdom. Low at Your feet we fall! Here may Your Spirit reveal to us more of Your glory! Oh, irradiate, sanctify, and cheer us with its beams! Behold, we cling to You! You are our Emmanuel, or portion, and our all. In darkness we repair to the fountain of Your light. In sorrow, we flee to the asylum of Your bosom. Oppressed, we come to the shelter of Your cross. Oh, take our hearts, and bind them closer and still closer to Yourself! Won by Your beauty and drawn by Your love, let there be a renewed surrender of our whole spirit, and soul, and body. Oh, claim a fresh possession of us. "Your statutes have been our songs in the house of our pilgrimage: You shall guide us with Your counsel, and afterward receive us to glory." Then shall we unite with the Hallelujah Chorus, and sing in strains of surpassing sweetness, gratitude, and love. "Thanks be unto God for His unspeakable gift!"

JULY 6

*"Come unto me, all you who labor and are heavy
laden, and I will give you rest." Matthew 11:28*

With what brightness does the truth appear, written with beams of
heavenly light–Jesus, the Rest of the weary! "Come unto me." The Father
has made His Son the resting-place of His Church. He Himself has vested
His whole glory in Christ. He knew what Christ was capable of sustaining.
He knew that as His fellow–one equal with Himself–He could with safety
embark the honor of His government in the hands of His Son. He confided
therein Himself! His government, and His Church–all in Christ. To this
"tried stone" He would now bring His people. He found it strong enough
for Himself, and He knows it to be strong enough for them, and with
confidence He invites the weary to come and repose upon it. Jesus but
echoes the heart of the Father when he says, "Come unto me–I will give
you rest." Never did the tongue of Jesus utter words more learned, more
eloquent, more persuasive. Just the word we need. By nature, we seek rest
everywhere, and in everything, but in Jesus. We seek it in the sensual
world, we seek it in the moral world, we seek it in the religious world–we
find it not. We seek it in conviction, we seek it in ordinances, we seek it
in doing the works of the law, and still it evades us. We go from place to
place, from means to means, from minister to minister, and still the burden
presses, and the guilt remains, and we find no rest. No; and never will we
find it, until it is sought and found solely, wholly, exclusively, and entirely
in Jesus. Rest for the sin-weary soul is only to be met with in Him who
bore the curse for man's transgression. Here God rests, and here the sinner
must rest. Here the Father rests, and here the child may rest. Jesus is the
great burden-bearer, for God and for man. Listen again to the melody of
His words: "Come unto me–I will give you rest." See, how He invites you,
without one solitary condition. He makes no exception to your guilt and
unworthiness. The word is, "Come unto me;" in other words, believe in
me. To "come" is simply and only to believe. And oh! how can we fully set
forth the "rest" to be found it Jesus? Let those testify who took their guilt
to His blood, their vileness to His righteousness, their sins to His grace,
their burdens to His arm, their sorrows to His heart. Let them tell how,

in a moment, their sense of weariness fled, and rest, sweet, soothing rest to their soul succeeded. Are you, my reader, a sin-weary soul? Then, to you is this invitation addressed: "Come unto me–to me, a Savior whose willingness is equal to my ability. To me, who never rejected a single soul that sought salvation and heaven at my hands. Come unto me–I will give you rest."

JULY 7

"My grace is sufficient for you: for my strength is made perfect in weakness." 2 Corinthians 12:9

In the case of a tried believer, the rest that Jesus gives does not always imply the removal of the burden from where this sense of weariness proceeds. The burden is permitted to remain, and yet rest is experienced. Yes, it would appear from His procedure, that the very existence of the burden were essential to the experience of the rest. He withdraws not the trouble from us, nor us from the trouble; and still the repose we sighed for is given. Wonderful indeed! But how is it explained? That burden takes us to Jesus. It is but the cause of our simply going to Him. But for that sorrow, or that calamity, or that sickness, or that bereavement, we would have stayed away. The pressure compelled us to go. And how does He meet us! Does He open a way of escape from our difficulty, or does He immediately unbind our burden and set us free? No; better than this, He pours strength into our souls, and life into our spirits, and love into our hearts, and so we find rest. Thus are fulfilled in our experience the precious promises, "As your day, so shall your strength be." "My grace is sufficient for you."

The timing of the Lord's promised grace is no small unfolding of His love. Nor less an evidence of His complex person as God-man. How could He so time His supply of strength as to meet the exigency at its very crisis, did not His Deity make Him cognizant of the critical juncture in which His people were placed! And let it be mentioned that this operation is going on in every place and at every moment. And how could He meet that exigency, and speak a word in season to the weary, but as His humanity was touched with the feeling of the infirmity? It is by this process of experience that we are brought into close views of the glory of our incarnate God.

When He speaks through the ministry of the word, or by the word itself, to the believer, wearied with conflict and with trial, it has been just at the moment that its sustaining and consoling power was most needed. The eye that neither slumbers nor sleeps was upon you. He knew in what furnace you were placed, and was there to temper the flame when it seemed the severest. He saw your frail bark struggling through the tempest, and He came to your rescue at the height of the storm. How has He proved this in seasons of difficulty and doubt! How often at a crisis, the most critical of your history, the Lord has appeared for you! Your need has been supplied, your doubt has been solved, and your perplexity has been guided; He has delivered your soul from death, your eyes from tears, and your feet from falling. A word by Jesus, spoken in due season, how good is it!

JULY 8

*"For here have we no continuing city, but
we seek one to come." Hebrews 13:14*

The true believer in Jesus is a traveler. He is journeying to a city of habitation, to the mount of God–and, blessed be God, he will soon be there! The apostle Peter dedicates his pastoral letter to the "strangers scattered" abroad–the people of God dispersed over the face of the earth. Such is the Church of Christ. It is sometimes incorrectly called "the visible Church." The idea is unscriptural. Visible churches there may be, but a visible Church there is none. The saints of God are "strangers and pilgrims" scattered abroad. Here on earth they have no permanent abode, no certain resting-place. The Church is in the wilderness, journeying through it. The present is called the "time of our sojourning." We are but wayfarers at an inn, abiding only for a night. "Here we have no continuing city." We are strangers and sojourners, as all our fathers were. But this, beloved, is the reconciling, animating thought–we are journeying to the dwelling of God. We are on our way to the good land which the Lord our God has promised us; to the kingdom and the mansion which Jesus has gone to take possession of and to prepare for us. In a word–and this image is the climax of the blissful prospect–we are hastening to our "Father's house," the home of the whole family in heaven and in earth, the residence of Christ, the dwelling-place of God.

To this each believer in Jesus is journeying. The road is difficult, the desert is tedious—sometimes perilous from its smoothness, or painful from it roughness; its difficultness now wearying, its intricacy now embarrassing. But who will complain of the path that conducts him to his home? Who would yield to the sensation of fatigue, who is journeying to an eternal rest? Much of the disquietude and repining of spirit peculiar to the pilgrimage of the saints arises from the faint conceptions which the mind forms of the coming glory. We think too faintly and too seldom of heaven. The eye is bent downwards, and seldom do we "lift up our heads" in prospect of the "redemption that draws near."

And yet how much there is in the thought of glory, in the anticipation of heaven–its nature and associations–calculated to stimulate, to cheer, and to allure us onwards! It is the place where we shall be sinless; it is the residence where we shall see God; it is the mansion where we shall be housed with Christ; it is the home where we shall dwell with all the saints; it is the point at which are collecting all the holy of earth, some of whom have already left our embrace for its holier and happier regions, and whom we shall meet again. Why, then, should we be cast down because of the difficulty of the way, or for one moment lose sight of the glory that awaits us, or cease to strive for the fitness essential to its enjoyment? In a little while–oh, how short the journey!–and we shall be there. Then we shall realize, to their fullest extent, the beauty and the sweetness of the description so often read and pondered with tears of hope—"You have come to Mount Zion, to the city of the living God, the heavenly Jerusalem, and to thousands of angels in joyful assembly. You have come to the assembly of God's firstborn children, whose names are written in heaven. You have come to God himself, who is the judge of all people. And you have come to the spirits of the redeemed in heaven who have now been made perfect. You have come to Jesus, the one who mediates the new covenant between God and people, and to the sprinkled blood, which graciously forgives instead of crying out for vengeance as the blood of Abel did." O my soul! will you not stretch every nerve, endure every privation, and relinquish every weight, thus to reach this glorious city of God?

JULY 9

"But my God shall supply all your needs, according to his riches in glory by Christ Jesus." Philippians 4:19

For all the exigencies of the Christian journey God has amply provided. The Lord Jesus being the believer's "way," all nourishment for the pilgrimage of the saints is laid up in Him. All supply of wisdom for the perplexing way, of strength for the wearisome way, of grace for the perilous way, of sympathy for the trying way, is in Jesus. In Him has the Father laid up the provision for the wilderness journey. And what storehouses of nourishment–both testifying of Jesus–are the word of God and the covenant of grace! How full, how rich and ample the supply! All the soul-establishing doctrines, all the sanctifying precepts, and all the precious, comforting promises go to make up the nourishment for the wilderness journey. Sometimes the Lord brings us into the very heart of the wilderness, just to prove to us how easily and how readily He can provide a table for us even there. And when all other resources are exhausted, and all supply is cut off, and every spring of water is dried up, lo! He opens the eye of our faith to see what His heart of love has prepared.

Are you, dear reader, sitting down to weep like Hagar, or to die like Elijah, in the wilderness—desolate, weary, and exhausted? Oh, see what appropriate and ample nourishment your God and Father has provided for you. The Angel of the covenant touches you with the right hand of His love, and bids you rise and eat and drink, yes, to "drink abundantly." In the glorious gospel are "all manner of pleasant fruits, new and old," which the Lord has laid up for His people. "Go your way, eat your bread with joy, and drink your wine with a merry heart," for all this storehouse of nourishment, this table of provision, is for you. All the love that is in God's heart, all the grace that is in the Savior's nature, all the comfort that is in the Spirit's tenderness, all the sanctifying truths, free invitations, and precious promises which cluster in the Gospel of Christ, all are yours–the sacred nourishment provided for the your journey to the mount of God. Listen to the voice of Jesus, saying to you, as of old, "Come and dine."

JULY 10

"Wherefore he is able also to save to the uttermost,
those who come unto God by him." Hebrews 7:25

What a witness is this to the power and readiness of Christ to save!
And this is the testimony of the Holy Spirit to the blessed Son of God.
But He does more than this. He brings home the record with power to the
soul. He writes the testimony on the heart. He converts the believing soul
itself into a witness that "Christ Jesus came into the world to save sinners."

And what a gospel is this for a poor sinner! It speaks of pardon–of
acceptance–of peace–of full redemption here, and unspeakable glory
hereafter. It proclaims a Savior to the lost; a Redeemer to the captive;
a Surety to the insolvent; a Physician to the sick; a Friend to the needy;
an Advocate to the criminal;–all that a self-ruined, sin-accused, law-condemned, justice—threatened, broken-hearted sinner needs, this "glorious
gospel of the blessed God" provides. It reveals to the self-ruined sinner
One in whom is his help, Hosea 13:9. To the sin-accused, One who can
take away all sin, 1 John 1:7. To the law-condemned, One who saves from
all condemnation, Romans 8:1. To the justice-threatened, One who is a
hiding-place from the wind, and a covert from the tempest, Isaiah 32:2.
To the broken-hearted, One who binds up and heals, Isaiah 61:1. That One
is–Jesus. O name ever dear, ever sweet, ever precious, ever fragrant, ever
healing to the "poor in spirit"!

What a witness, then, is this which the Eternal Spirit bears for Jesus!
He assures the believer that all he can possibly need is treasured up in
Christ–that he has no cross but Christ can bear it–no sorrow but Christ
can alleviate it–no corruption but Christ can subdue it–no guilt but Christ
can remove it–no sin but Christ can pardon it–no need but Christ can
supply it. Lift up your heads, you poor, you needy, you disconsolate! Lift
up your heads and rejoice that Christ is all to you–all you need in this
valley of tears–all you need in the deepest sorrow–all you need under the
heaviest affliction–all you need in sickness–all you will need in the hour
of death and in the day of judgment.

Yes, and Christ is in all too. He is in all you salvation–He is in all your
mercies–He is in all your trials–He is in all your consolations, and in all
your afflictions. What more can you want? What more do you desire? A

Father who loves you as the apple of His eye–a full Savior to whom to go, moment by moment–and a blessed indwelling, sanctifying, comforting Spirit, to reveal all to you, and to give you Himself, as the "pledge of your inheritance, until the redemption of the purchased possession." "Happy is that people that is in such a case: yes, happy is that people whose God is the Lord."

JULY 11

"I am crucified with Christ; nevertheless I live; yet not I, but Christ lives in me." Galatians 2:20

The life of Christ and the life of self cannot coexist in the same heart. If the one lives, the other dies. The sentence of death is written upon a man's self, when the Spirit of Christ enters his heart, and quickens his soul with the life of God. "I live," he exclaims, "yet not I." What a striking and beautiful example of this have we in the life and labors of the apostle Paul! Does he speak of his ministry?–what a renunciation of self appears! Lost in the greatness and grandeur of his theme, he exclaims–"We preach not ourselves, but Christ Jesus the Lord." Again–"Unto me who am less than the least of all saints, is this grace given, that I should preach among the Gentiles the unsearchable riches of Christ." Does he refer to his office?–what self-crucifixion! "I magnify my office." In what way? Was it by vaunting proclamations of its grandeur and legitimacy, its Divine institution, or its solemn functions? Never! but he magnified his office by diminishing himself, and exalting his Master. He was nothing–aye, and even his office itself was comparatively nothing–that "Christ might be all in all." Does he speak of his gifts and labors? what absence of self! "I am the least of the apostles, that am not fit to be called an apostle, because I persecuted the Church of God. But by the grace of God I am what I am; and His grace, which was bestowed upon me, was not in vain, but I labored more abundantly than they all: yet not I, but the grace of God which was with me." Such was the religion of Paul. His Christianity was a self-denying, self-crucifying, self-renouncing Christianity. "I live, yet not I. I labored more abundantly than they all, yet not I." Oh what a self-denying spirit was his!

But every truly spiritual man is a self-renouncing man. In the discipline of his own heart, beneath the cross of Jesus, and in the school of trial and temptation, he has been taught in some degree, that if he lives, it is not he that lives, but that it is Christ that lives in him. Upon all his own righteousness, his duties, and doings, he tramples as to the great matter of justification; while, as fruits of the Spirit, as evidences of faith, as pulsations of the inner spiritual life, as, in a word, tending to authenticate and advance his sanctification, he desires to be "careful to maintain good works," that God in all things might be glorified.

JULY 12

"But by the grace of God I am what I am: and his grace which was bestowed upon me was not in vain; but I labored more abundantly than they all: yet not I, but the grace of God which was with me." 1 Corinthians 15:10

We should be always careful to distinguish between the denial of self and the denial of the life of God within us. The most entire renunciation of ourselves, the most humiliating acknowledgment of our personal unworthiness, may harmonize with the strongest assurance and profession of Christ living in us. Self-denial does not necessarily involve grace-denial. It is the profoundest act of humility in a Christian man to acknowledge the grace of God in his soul. Never is there so real a crucifixion, never so entire a renunciation of self, as when the heart, in its lowly but deep and grateful throbbings, acknowledges its indebtedness to sovereign grace, and in the fervor of its adoring love, summons the whole Church to listen to its recital of the great things God has done for it–"Come and hear, all you that fear God, and I will declare what He has done for my soul." Oh yes! it is a self-denying life. Listen to Job–"I abhor myself, and repent in dust and ashes." Listen to Isaiah–"Woe is me! for I am undone; because I am a man of unclean lips, and I dwell in the midst of a people of unclean lips: for my eyes have seen the King, the Lord of hosts." Listen to the penitent publican–"God be merciful to me a sinner!" Listen again to Paul–"I live, yet not I." Thus does a sense of sin, and a believing sight of Christ, lay the soul low before God in self-renunciation and self-abhorrence.

Judge your spiritual condition, dear reader, by this characteristic of the inner life. Is it yours? Has there been this renunciation of your sinful self and of your righteous self? Has the Spirit of God emptied you? has the grace of God humbled you? has the life of God crucified you? Are you as one in whom Christ lives, walking humbly with God! Oh, it is the essence of vital godliness, it is the very life of true religion. If Christ is living in you, you are a humble soul. Pride never existed in the heart of Christ. His whole life was one act of the profoundest self—abasement. In the truest and in the fullest sense of the emphatic declaration, "He humbled Himself." It is impossible, then, that He who was thus "meek and lowly in heart," can dwell in one whom "pride compasses as a chain." "I live, yet not I," are two states of the renewed soul, as inseparable as any cause and effect. A humble and a self-denying Christ dwells only with a humble and a self-denying soul. If your gifts inflate you, if your position exalts you, if your usefulness engenders pride, if the honor and distinction which God or man has placed upon you has turned you aside from the simplicity of your walk, and set you upon the work of self—seeking, self-advancing, so that you are not meek and gentle, child-like, and Christ-like in spirit, be sure of this–you are either not a partaker of the life of Christ, or else that life is at a low ebb in your soul. Which of the two, do you think, is your real state?

JULY 13

"I have glorified you on the earth: I have finished the work which you gave me to do. And now, O Father, glorify me with your own self, with the glory which I had with you before the world was." John 17:4-5

His work being finished, the great atonement made, and salvation eternally secured to all the covenant seed, it was fit that the Son of God should return back to glory. Heaven was His original and proper place. He was but a stranger and a sojourner here. His mission accomplished, earth, which had once attracted Him to its bosom, attracted Him no longer. As the field of His labors, and the scene of His humiliation, and the theater of His conflict, He had willingly bent His steps towards it. His labors now finished, His humiliation now passed, His battle now fought, and His victory won, He as readily hastened from all below. Oh, what stronger ties, what more powerful allurements, had earth than heaven for Jesus? All to Him had been toil and suffering, trial and sorrow. Wearisome had been His pilgrimage, laborious His life, humiliating its every scene, and painful its every incident. Creatures the best and the fondest had disappointed Him, sources of created good the most promising had failed Him, and the hour of His deepest necessity and woe found Him treading the wine-press alone, forsaken by man, deserted by God! An atmosphere of sin had enveloped Him on every side; forms of suffering and pollution each moment flitted before His eye, and sounds of blasphemy and woe fell at each step upon His ear. At whatever point He turned, He saw His Father's name dishonored, His Spirit grieved. His own dignity outraged, His teaching despised, His Gospel rejected, and His authority trampled under-foot, by men swearing allegiance to another and a rival sovereign.

What greater, sweeter, and holier attractions, then, had earth than heaven for Jesus? His resurrection from the dead was His preparative for glory. Leaving the garments of mortality in the forsaken tomb, He wrapped around Him the robe of immortality, and, poised upon the wing, awaited but the signal for His heavenly flight. All that now remained for Him to accomplish was to authenticate the fact of His risen life, place His Church in a position to receive the promised Spirit, breathe His parting blessing, and then ascend to glory. Heaven was His home, loved and longed for! How sweet to Him were its recollections! how hallowed its associations, heightened by their contrast with the scene from which He was now retiring! There, no curse; there, no sorrow; there, no suffering; there, no tears; there, no indignity, awaited Him. All was one expanse of glory, all one pavilion of happiness! Bright was the landscape stretched before His view; redolent the breezes, and soft the music that floated from its fields and bowers.

But far above all the glory suggested by the most splendid material imagery, rose, in spiritual and surpassing grandeur, the seat, the altar, and the throne which, as Prophet, Priest, and King, He sighed to occupy. A more perfect investiture of Him in these offices, a more complete establishment of His mediatorial dominion, awaited Him. All power in heaven and on earth was to be placed in His hands: and all things were to be put in subjection under Him; and all beings, from the loftiest angel in heaven to the lowest creature on earth, were to acknowledge His government, submit to His sovereignty, worship, and "crown Him Lord of all."

JULY 14

*"And if any man sins, we have an advocate with the Father,
Jesus Christ the righteous." 1 John 2:1*

The work of our Lord as Priest was two-fold, atonement and
intercession. The one He accomplished upon the cross, the other He
now transacts upon the throne. "When He had by Himself purged our
sins, He sat down on the right hand of the Majesty on high." The high
priest, under the law, after that he had slain the sacrifice, took the blood,
and, passing within the veil, sprinkled it on the mercy-seat, so making
intercession for the people. "The Holy Spirit this signifying, that the
way into the holiest of all was not yet made manifest, while as the first
tabernacle was yet standing." "But, Christ being come, an high priest of
good things to come, by a greater and more perfect tabernacle, not made
with hands, that is to say, not of this building; neither by the blood of
goats and calves, but by His own blood, He entered in once into the holy
place, having obtained eternal redemption for us."

And what is He now doing? Presenting His own blood each moment
before the mercy-seat on behalf of His redeemed people! "He ever lives to
make intercession for us." Oh, do not forget this, dear saint of God! This is
spoken for the comfort of the mourners in Zion–for those who, knowing
the plague of their own hearts, and deploring its constant tendency to
outbreak, are humbled in the dust with deep godly sorrow. Look up! Does
sin plead loudly against you? the blood of Jesus pleads louder for you. Do
your backslidings, and rebellions, and iniquities, committed against so
much light and love, call for vengeance? the blood of Jesus "speaks better
things." Does Satan stand at your right hand to accuse you? your Advocate
stands at God's right hand to plead for you. All hail! you mourning souls!
you that smite on the breast, you broken—hearted, you contrite ones! "who
is he that condemns! It is Christ who died, yes rather, who is risen again;
who is even at the right hand of God, who also makes intercession for us."

Jesus is a glorious and a successful Advocate. He has never lost a cause
entrusted to His advocacy, and never will. He pleads powerfully, He pleads
eloquently, He pleads prevalently, because He pleads in behalf of a people
unspeakably dear to His heart, for whom He "loved not His own life unto
the death," and presses His suit, on the ground of His own most precious

blood and accepted person, and with His father and their Father, His God and their God.

JULY 15

"This is how God showed his love among us: He sent his one and only Son into the world that we might live through him." 1 John 4:9

"God is love" was the great truth Jesus came to make known. Hence God's love is clearly a revelation to man, rather than a discovery by man. Divine love was the last perfection of Deity to baffle the research of human wisdom. Other attributes might be dimly traced in creation. Some faint glimmerings of God's wisdom, power, and goodness might be seen in the "things which are made;" but how God could love sinners, could redeem and save sinners, was a question to which nature's oracle returned no response. In the exercise of the vast powers with which his Creator has endowed him, man may discover everything, but this. He sweeps the firmament above him with his telescope, and a new constellation of surpassing glory arises before his view. He delves into the earth beneath him, and an ancient and long-lost city is untombed. He works a problem, and science develops some new and startling wonder. But there is one discovery he cannot make–one wonder surpassing all wonders, the most marvelous and stupendous, he cannot unravel. Nature, aiding him in all other researches, affords him no clue to this. The sunbeam paints it not upon the brilliant cloud; the glacier reflects it not from its dazzling brow; the valley's stream murmurs it not in its gentle music; it thunders not in the roar of ocean's billow; it sighs not in the evening's zephyr; it exhales not the opening flower; all nature is profoundly silent upon a theme so divine and strange, so vast and tender, as God's redeeming love to man.

But the Son, leaving the bosom of the Father, in which from eternity He had reposed, and which in the "fullness of time" He relinquished, has descended to our world to correct our apprehensions and to dislodge our doubts, to calm our fears, and to reassure our hopes with the certainty of the wondrous fact, that God is still mindful of man, and takes delight in man; that no revolt or alienation, no enmity or ingratitude, has turned away His heart from man; that He loves him still, and that loving, He "so loved him that He gave His only begotten Son, that whoever believes in Him should not perish, but have everlasting life." Thus did He come,

His Father's representative, to declare Him to man. And as He wrought His brilliant miracles of stupendous power–thus attesting the fact of His Godhead; and as He pronounced His discourses of infinite wisdom–thus unlocking the treasures of His grace; and as He traveled all laden with our sins to the cross–thus unsealing the fountain of His compassion, He could say to all who challenged the Divinity of His mission, or who asked at His hands a vision of the Father, "He that has seen me has seen the Father,"–"I and my Father are one."

Behold the mission of the Savior to our world! He has come to uplift the veil, and reveal the heart of God–that heart all throbbing with a love as infinite as His nature, as deathless as His being. He came not to inspire, but to reveal, the love of God. The atonement did not originate, it expounded the Father's love–the love was already there. Sin had but clouded its existence; rebellion had but arrested its flow. Struggling and panting for a full, unrestrained expression, it could find no adequate outlet, no appropriate channel in its course to man, save in the surrender and sacrifice of its most costly and precious treasure. The Son of the Father must bleed and die, before the love of the Father could embrace its object. And now, O child of God, the veil is withdrawn, the thick cloud is blotted out, and your God stands before you all arrayed in ineffable love, His heart your divine pavilion, His bosom your sacred home. "The only-begotten Son who is in the bosom of the Father, He has declared Him."

JULY 16
"Only believe." Mark 5:36

Precious and significant are the words of Jesus, the very same words that He spoke when on earth. Did those lips, glowing with more than a seraph's hallowed touch–lips into which grace without measure was poured–ever breathe a sentence more touching, more simple, or more significant than this, "Only believe"? Originally addressed to an afflicted parent, who sought His compassion and His help in behalf of a little daughter lying at the point of death, they seem to be especially appropriate to every case of anxiety, of trial, and of need. Alas! how many such will scan this page–how many a sigh will breathe over it, how many a tear will moisten it, how many a mournful glance will light upon it! Be it so;

there comes back a voice of sympathy responsive to each sad heart–not man, but Jesus speaks–"Only believe"–in other words, "only trust." What is faith, but trust? what is believing in Jesus, but trusting in Jesus? When Jesus says, "only believe me," He literally says, "only trust me." And what a natural, beautiful, soothing definition of the word faith is this!

Many a volume has been written to explain the nature and illustrate the operation of faith–the subject and the reader remaining as much mystified and perplexed as ever. But who can fail to comprehend the meaning of the good old Saxon word trust! All can understand what this means. When, therefore, Jesus says–as He does to every individual who reads these words–"only believe me," He literally says, "only trust me." Thus He spoke to the anxious father who besought Him to come and heal his child: "only believe–only trust my power, only trust my compassion, only trust my word; do not be afraid, only trust me." And thus He speaks to you, believer. Oh, for a heart to respond, "Speak, Lord, for your servant hears!"

Trust implies, on our part, mystery and ignorance, danger and helplessness. How wrapped in inscrutability, how shadowy and unreal, is all the future! As we attempt to penetrate the dark clouds, what strange forebodings steal over our spirits. Just at this juncture Jesus approaches, and with address most winning, and in accents most gentle, speaks these words, "Only believe—only trust me! Trust me, who knows the end from the beginning; trust me, who has all resources at my command; trust me, whose love never changes, whose wisdom never misleads, whose word never fails, whose eye never slumbers nor sleeps–only trust me!" Enough, my blessed Lord, my soul replies. I will sit myself down a loving child, a lowly disciple at Your feet, and, indistinct and dreary as my future path may be, will learn from You how and where I may trust You all my journey through.

JULY 17

"He who spared not his own Son, but delivered him up for us all; how shall he not with him also freely give us all things." Romans 8:32

How beautiful and conclusive the reasoning of the apostle! Arguing from the greater to the lesser, he proceeds to assure the believer of God's readiness freely to bestow all needful blessing. To this He stood pledged. The gift of His own Son, so freely and unreservedly bestowed, was the security and the channel of every other mercy. When God gave His Son, the reconciliation had not actually been effected, justice had received no satisfaction, and the broken law no repair. Thus "God demonstrates his own love for us in this: While we were still sinners, Christ died for us." If then, when we were enemies, we were reconciled to God by the death of His Son, much more, being reconciled, will He freely give us all things.

"All things!" How comprehensive and grant! "According as His Divine power has given unto us all things that pertain unto life and godliness," holding the security in the hand of faith, you may repair to your heavenly Father, and ask for all that you need. So to speak, God has bound Himself to withhold no good thing from you. He is pledged, and from that pledge He will never recede, to grant you all you need. What is your demand? Is it the Spirit to seal, to sanctify, to comfort you? Then draw near and ask the gift. "For if you who are evil know how to give good things to your children, how much more shall your heavenly Father give the Holy Spirit to those who ask Him?" Is it pardon? Then ask it. He who provided the sacrifice for sin, will He not freely bestow the forgiveness of sin? Is it grace? Having given you the Reservoir of grace, is He not as willing and "able to make all grace abound toward you, that you, always having all sufficiency in all things, may abound to every good work"? Is it comfort? Having given you the "Consolation of Israel," will He not prove to you the "God of all comfort"? Is your necessity temporal? Are your circumstances adverse? Filled with forebodings of approaching difficulty, the cruse of oil and the barrel of meal wasting, are you anxious and fearful? Take your temporal need to God. What! will He bestow the higher blessings of grace, and withhold the inferior ones of providence? Never! And can you press to your believing heart the priceless, precious, unspeakable gift of His Son, and yet cherish in that heart the gloomy misgiving thought of God's unwillingness and inability to supply all you need?

"Freely give." God's gifts are both rich and gratuitous. He always bestows more, never less, than we ask. It would seem as though He could not open His hand to a poor comer, but it overflowed with a bounty worthy of Himself. Here are met all the objections to our coming which spring from our unworthiness, unfruitfulness, and unfaithfulness. Having nothing to pay, nothing in return is required. "Without money, and without price."

Free as the sunlight–free as the balmy air–free as the mountain-stream–free as the heart of God can make it, is every blessing which He bestows. "He who spared not His own Son, but delivered Him up for us all, how shall He not with Him also freely give us all things?"

JULY 18

"Those who live according to the sinful nature (the flesh) have their minds set on what that nature desires; but those who live in accordance with the Spirit have their minds set on what the Spirit desires." Romans 8:5

By this truth let us test the reality of our religious profession. In this light let us closely examine our Christian character and walk. What, reader, is the habitual and supreme bent of your mind? Is it that which is spiritual, or that which is carnal? Judge of your preparation for death, in the near view of its approaching solemnities. Decide upon your state for eternity, in the rapid progress of its deepening shadows. Ascertain the real state of your case for the judgment, in the certain arrival of its dread scrutiny. You have your mind either set upon the things of the flesh, or upon the things of the Spirit. You are either born again from above, or are groveling in things below. You are either holy, or you are unholy. You are for the Lord, or you are against Him. You are either Satan's slave or Christ's freeman. Which?

You inquire, "How may I know that I am of the Spirit?" We answer–by your producing the fruits of the Spirit. A broken heart for sin–a felt conviction of the hidden plague–a humble and a contrite spirit–an utter rejection of a human righteousness–a simple, believing reception of the Lord Jesus–and a breathing after Divine conformity, are evidences of a renewed and sanctified state. If these are yours in any degree, then you are of the Spirit.

But rest not here. Be exhorted to walk in the Spirit. Do not be satisfied with having the question decided in your favor–with just barely knowing that you have crossed the line that separates the regenerate from the unregenerate–death from life. Remain not where you are: go forward. Do not be content with a low standard. Compare not your church with other churches, nor yourself with other Christians; nor measure yourself by yourself. But fix your eye upon Christ; copy His example, imbibe His mind, and place yourself under the government of His Spirit. Strive to go forward! Endeavor to be always sowing to the Spirit. Be satisfied with the Lord's disposal of you. Study the divine art of contentment. Be convinced that what the Lord ordains is best. Covet but little of earthly good; and, as an old divine exhorts, "sail with a low gale." Lie low. The great secret of a holy and a happy life is contained in a small compass–walking humbly with God. In all failures in duty, in all shortcomings in practice, in all transactions with God, and in all dealings with man–remembering the innumerable traces of imperfection and sin found upon all you do–deal frequently, closely, with the atoning blood. "Wash and be clean."

JULY 19
"We are in him who is true, even in his Son Jesus Christ." 1 John 5:20

"I in them." Thus it is a mutual indwelling–Christ in us, and we in Christ. Here is our security. The believer is in Christ as Jacob was in the garment of the elder brother when Isaac kissed him, and he "smelled the smell of the clothing, and blessed him, and said, See, the smell of my son is as the smell of a field which the Lord has blessed." He is in Christ as the poor homicide was within the city of refuge, when pursued by the avenger of blood, but who could not overtake and slay. He is in Christ as Noah was enclosed within the ark, with the heavens darkening above him, and the waters heaving beneath him, yet with not a drop of the flood penetrating his vessel, nor a blast of the storm disturbing the serenity of his spirit.

How expressive are these Scriptural emblems of the perfect security of a believer in Christ! He is clothed with the garment of the Elder Brother, the righteousness of the Lord Jesus Christ, "which is unto all and upon all those who believe." On that garment the Father's hands are placed; in that robe the person of the believer is accepted; it is to God "as the smell of a field which the Lord has blessed:" the blessing of the heavenly birthright is his–and for him there is no condemnation. Pursued by the avenger of blood, the threatenings of a condemning law, he has reached the city of refuge, the Lord Jesus Christ. Fearful and trembling, yet believing and hoping, he has crossed the sacred threshold, and in an instant he is safe—and for him there is no condemnation. Fleeing from the gathering storm–"the wrath which is to come"–he has availed himself of the open door of the sacred ark–the crucified Savior–has entered, God shutting him in–and for him there is no condemnation.

Yes, Christ Jesus is our sanctuary, beneath whose shadow we are safe. Christ Jesus is our strong tower, within whose embattlements no avenger can threaten. Christ Jesus is our hiding-place from the wind, and covert from the tempest; and not one drop of "the wrath to come" can fall upon the soul that is in Him. Oh, how completely accepted, and how perfectly secure, the sinner who is in Christ Jesus! He feels he is saved on the basis of a law whose honor is vindicated; through the clemency of a righteous Sovereign, whose holiness is secured; and through the mercy of a gracious God, the glory of whose moral government is eternally and illustriously exhibited. And now is his head lifted up above his enemies round about him; for there is no condemnation to those who are in Christ Jesus. Reader, are you in Christ Jesus? Is this your condition?

JULY 20

"Except you repent, you shall all likewise perish." Luke 13:5

This was the doctrine which our Lord preached; and so did His apostles, when they declared, "God now commands all men everywhere to repent." No command, no duty, can be more distinctly, intelligently, and solemnly defined and urged than this. But the inquirer will ask, "What is repentance?" The reply is–it is that secret grace that lays the soul low before God–self loathed; sin abhorred, confessed, and forsaken. It is the abasement and humiliation of a man, because of the sinfulness of his nature and the sins of his life, before the holy, heart-searching Lord God. The more matured believer is wont to look upon a broken and contrite spirit, flowing from a sight of the cross, as the most precious fruit found in his soul. No moments to him are so hallowed, so solemn, or so sweet, as those spent in bathing the Savior's feet with tears.

There is indeed a bitterness in the grief which a sense of sin produces; and this, of all other bitterness, is the greatest. He knows, from experience, that it is an "evil thing and bitter, that he has forsaken the Lord his God." Nevertheless, there is a sweetness, an indescribable sweetness, which must be experienced to be understood, blended with the bitterness of a heart broken for sin, from a sight of the cross of the incarnate God. Oh, precious tears wept beneath that cross!

"For thus says the high and lofty One who inhabits eternity, whose name is Holy; I dwell in the high and holy place, with him also that is of a contrite and humble spirit, to revive the spirit of the humble, and to revive the heart of the contrite ones." But how shall I portray the man who is of a contrite and humble spirit? He is one who truly knows the evil of sin, for he has felt it. He apprehends, in some degree, the holiness of God's character, and the spirituality of His law, for he has seen it. His views of himself have undergone a radical change. He no longer judges of himself as others judge of him. They exalt him; he abases himself. They approve; he condemns. And in that very thing for which they most extol him he is humbling himself in secret. While others are applauding actions, he is searching into motives; while they are extolling virtues, he is sifting principles; while they are weaving the garland for his brow, he, shut in alone with God, is covering himself with sackcloth and with ashes.

Oh precious fruit of a living branch of the true vine! Is it any wonder, then, that God should come and dwell with such a one, in whom is found something so good towards Him? Oh, no! He delights to see us in this posture–to mark a soul walking before Him in a conscious sense of its poverty; the eye drawing from the cross its most persuasive motives to a deep prostration of soul at His feet. Dear reader, to know what a sense of God's reconciling love is–to know how skillfully, tenderly, and effectually Jesus binds up and heals–your spirit must be wounded, and your heart must be broken for sin. Oh, it were worth an ocean of tears to experience the loving gentleness of Christ's hand in drying them. Has God ever said of you, as He said of Ahab, "See how he humbles himself before me?" Search and ascertain if this good fruit is found in your soul.

JULY 21

"Likewise the Spirit also helps our infirmities." Romans 8:26

The word here rendered "helps" properly means to take part with. It implies, not merely sympathy with, but a personal participation in our infirmity. The Spirit helps our infirmities by sharing them with us. Now take the general infirmities of the believer–infirmities which, unaided by another and a superior power, must crush and overwhelm–and trace the help thus afforded by the Spirit. We are taught to adore the love of the Father, from where each rill of mercy has its rise. We delight to dwell upon the love of the Son, through whose channel all redemption-blessing flows. And shall we overlook the love of the Holy Spirit? Shall we forget His comforts, His grace, His succourings? Forbid it, oh eternal and blessed Spirit! Your essential Deity–Your personal subsistence–Your tender love–Your Divine power–Your efficacious grace–Your sovereign mercy–Your infinite patience–Your exquisite sympathy–all demand our deepest love, and awake our loftiest praise.

But how is this sympathy of the Spirit expressed? Seeing the soul bound with an infirmity, all His compassion is awakened. Approaching, He takes hold of the burden. Constrained by a love which no thought can conceive, moved by a tenderness no tongue can describe, He advances, and places the power of His Godhead beneath the pressure–and thus He helps our infirmity. Do you doubt this? We summon you as a witness to its truth. Why are you not a ruin and a wreck? Why has not your infirmity long since dethroned reason, and annihilated faith, and extinguished hope, and clad all the future with the pall of despair? Why have you ridden serene and secure upon the crest of the billow, smiling calmly upon the dark and yawning surges dashing and foaming around you? Why have you, when your heart has been overwhelmed, found relief in a sigh, in a tear, in an uplifted glance, in one thought of God? Oh, it has been because the Spirit, all silent and invisible, was near to you, sympathizing, helping, bearing your infirmities. Because around you the power of His Deity was placed. And when you have staggered and turned pale, and have well near given up all for lost, resigning yourself to the broodings of despair, that Spirit has approached, all-loving and powerful, and helped, by sharing your infirmity. Some appropriate and precious promise has been sealed upon your heart–some clear and soothing view of Christ has been presented to your eye–some gentle whisper of love has breathed upon your ear–and you have been helped. The pressure has been lightened, the grief has been assuaged, the weakness has been strengthened, and you have risen superior to the infirmity that bowed you to the dust. Oh, it was the Spirit who helped you. Grieved, and wounded, and slighted a thousand times over though He has been, receiving at your hands the unkindest requital for the tenderest love, yet when your infirmity bowed you to the earth, and the sword entered your soul, He drew near, forgetting all your base ingratitude, and administered wine to your dejected spirit, and oil to your bleeding wound, and placed beneath you the encircling arms of His everlasting love.

JULY 22

"And the Holy Spirit helps us in our distress. For we don't even know what we should pray for, nor how we should pray. But the Holy Spirit prays for us with groanings that cannot be expressed in words." Romans 8:26

The Holy Spirit is here represented in the character of a pleader or advocate for the saints. To form a vivid conception of this truth, we have but to imagine an anxious and embarrassed client prosecuting some important suit, or, perchance, battling for his life in a court of justice. At his side stands his counselor, thoroughly acquainted with the nature of his case, and deeply versed in the bearings of the law. He is there to instruct his client how to shape his course, with what arguments to support, with what pleas to urge, with what words to clothe his suit. Such is the advocacy and such the aid of the Spirit in the matter of prayer. We stand in the presence of the Lord–it may be to deprecate a deserved punishment, or to plead for a needed blessing.

"We don't even know what we should pray for, nor how we should pray." How shall we order our cause before the Great Judge? With what feelings, with what language, with what arguments shall we unburden our heart, unveil our sorrow, confess our sin, and make known our request? How shall I overcome the remembrance of past ingratitude, and the conviction of present guilt, and the pressure of deep need, and the overwhelming sense of the Divine Majesty? How shall I wake the heart to feeling; rouse the dull, sluggish emotions of the soul; recall the truant affections; and concentrate the mind upon the holy and solemn engagement? But our counselor is there! "The Holy Spirit prays for us." And how does He this?

He indites the prayer. Do not think that that spiritual petition, which breathed from your lips and rose as an incense-cloud before the mercy-seat, was other than the inditing of the Holy Spirit. He inspired that prayer, He created those desires, and He awoke those groanings. The form of your petition may have been ungraceful, your language simple, your sentences broken, your accents tremulous, yet there was an eloquence and a power in that prayer which reached the heart and moved the arm of God. It overcame the Angel of the Covenant. And whose eloquence and whose power was it?–the interceding Spirit's.

He also teaches us what to pray for. Many and urgent as our needs are, we only accurately know them as the Spirit makes them known. Alas! what profound ignorance of ourselves must we cherish, when we know not what we should ask God for as we ought! But the Spirit reveals our deep necessity, convinces us of our emptiness, poverty, and need, and teaches us what blessings to ask, what evils to deprecate, what mercies to implore.

He sympathizes, too, with our infirmity in prayer, by portraying to our view the parental character of God. Sealing on our hearts a sense of adoption, he emboldens us to approach God with filial love and child-like confidence. He leads us to God as a Father. Nor must we overlook the skill with which the Spirit enables us to urge in our approaches to God the sinner's great plea–the atoning blood of Jesus. This is no small part of the Divine aid we receive in our infirmity. Satan, the accuser of the saints, even follows the believer to the throne of grace to confront and confound him there. When Joshua stood before the Angel of the Lord, Satan stood at his right hand to resist him. But the Spirit, too, is there! He is there in the character, and to discharge the office, of the praying soul's Intercessor. He instructs the accused suppliant what arguments to use, what pleas to urge, and how to resist the devil. He strengthens the visual organ of the soul, so that it clearly discerns the blood upon the mercy-seat within the veil, on which it fixes the eye in simple faith. Oh, it is the delight of the Spirit to take of the things of Jesus–His love, His work, His sympathy, His grace, His power–and show them to the soul prostrate in prayer before the throne of grace.

JULY 23

"I lie in the dust, completely discouraged; revive me by your word." Ps. 119:25

Ah! how many whose eye scans this page may take up and breathe David's words. You feel a deadness, a dullness, and an earthliness in spiritual enjoyments, and duties, and privileges, in which your whole soul should be all life, all fervor, all love. You are low where you ought to be elevated; you grovel where you ought to soar; you cleave to the earth where you ought to be embracing the heavens. Your thoughts are low; your affections are low; your feelings are low; your spirits are low; and you seem almost ready to question the existence of the life of God in your soul.

But even in this sad and depressed state may there not be something cheering, encouraging, hopeful? There was evidently in David's–"My soul cleaves unto the dust: quicken me." This was the cheering, encouraging, hopeful feature in the Psalmists's case–his breathing after the requickening of the Divine life of his soul. Here was that which marked him a man of God. It was a living man complaining of his deadness, and breathing after more life. It was a heaven—born soul lamenting its earthliness, and panting after more of heaven. It was a spiritual man mourning over his carnality, and praying for more spirituality. It is not the prayer of one conscious of the low state of His soul, and yet satisfied with that state.

"I lie in the dust, completely discouraged; revive me by your word." Perhaps no expression is more familiar to the ear, and no acknowledgment is more frequently on the lips of religious professors, than this. And yet where is the accompanying effort to rise above it? Where is the putting on of the armor? Where is the conflict? Where is the effort to emerge from the dust, to break away from the enthrallment, and soar into a higher and purer region? Alas! many from whose lips smoothly glides the humiliating confession still embrace the dust, and seem to love the dust, and never stretch their pinions to rise above it. But let us study closely this lesson of David's experience, that while deep lamentation filled his heart, and an honest confession breathed from his lips, there was also a breathing, a panting of soul, after a higher and a better state. He seemed to say–"Lord, I am prostrate, but I long to rise; I am fettered, but I struggle to be free; my soul cleaves to the dust, but quicken me!" Similar to this was the state of the Church, so graphically depicted by Solomon in his Song–"I sleep, but my heart wakes."

JULY 24
"Revive me." Psalm 119:25

This prayer implies what, alas! is so needful in many, a revival of soul. It is a putting of the Lord's hand a second time to the work of grace in the heart. "When you are converted," said our Lord to Peter, "strengthen your brethren." What! had not Peter already been converted? Most truly. But; although a regenerate man, he had so relapsed in grace as to need a re-conversion. Our Lord's meaning, then, obviously is, "When you are restored, recovered, re-quickened, then strengthen your brethren." How many religious professors stand in need of a fresh baptism (filling) of the Holy Spirit! You, perhaps, my reader, are one. Where is the spiritual vigor you once displayed? where the spiritual joy you once possessed? where the unclouded hope you once indulged? where the humble walk with God you once maintained? where the fragrance that once breathed around you? Alas! your soul cleaves to the dust; and you need the re—converting grace, the renewed baptism (filling) of the Spirit. "Revive me" is your prayer.

A clearer manifestation of Divine life in the soul is not the least blessing contained in this prayer for quickening. How little realization enters into the religion of many! There is the full credence of the judgment to the truth; a conversing about religion, the ministry, and the Church. But where is felt the realizing power, the earth-fading, heaven-attracting power, of vital godliness into the soul? Dear reader, the hour that will bring your religious profession, your religious creed, your religious notions, to the test, is at hand; and the great question in that awful moment will be, "Am I ready to die?–have I in my soul the life of God?—am I born of the Spirit?–have I a living Christ in my now failing, dying heart?"

But what a prayer is this in view of a scene and a scrutiny so solemn: "Revive me, Lord, quicken Your work in my soul, and strengthen that which You have wrought in me. The love that congeals, the faith that trembles, the hope that fluctuates, the joy that droops; inspire with new life, new energy, new power! It is of little moment what others think of me; Lord, You know my soul cleaves to the dust. There is in my heart more of earth than of heaven; more of self than of Christ; more of the creature than of God. You know me in secret–how my grace wanes, how my affections chill, how seldom my closet is visited, how much my Bible is neglected, how insipid to my taste the means of grace, and how irksome and vapid are all spiritual duties and privileges. Lord, stir up Yourself to the revivifying of my soul; quicken, oh, revive me in Your ways. Enlarge my heart, that I may run the way of Your commandments."

JULY 25

"I lie in the dust, completely discouraged;
revive me by your word." Psalm 119:25

The argument with which this holy petition is urged is most powerful and prevalent. According to the promise of the word, and the instrumentality of the word. Both are engaged to quicken the soul. The promise is most precious: "I will heal their backslidings, I will love them freely; for my anger is turned away from him. I will be as the dew unto Israel: he shall grow as the lily, and cast forth his roots as Lebanon. Those who dwell under his shadow shall return; they shall revive as the corn, and grow as the vine." This precious promise to quicken and revive you, to shed the dews of His grace upon your soul, thus moistening and nourishing the roots and fibers and fruits of the new and heavenly life within you, God stands ready to fulfill in your holy and happy experience. "I will be to Israel like a refreshing dew from heaven. It will blossom like the lily; it will send roots deep into the soil like the cedars in Lebanon." Christ is our dew: the dew of His love, the dew of His grace, the dew of His Spirit, is prepared, silent and unseen, but effectual and vivifying–to fall upon the renewed powers of your nature–reviving the work of God in your soul.

But by the instrumentality of the word, the Lord quickens the soul. The word of Christ is "spirit and life," therefore it is a quickening word. "This is my comfort in my affliction; for Your word has quickened me." Again, "I will never forget Your precepts; for with them You have quickened me." Therefore did Jesus pray to His Father in behalf of His Church, "Sanctify them through Your truth." Thus does the word quicken. We are here constrained to suggest an inquiry–May not the prevalent decay of spiritual life in the Church of God–the low standard of spirituality–the alarming growth of soul-destroying error–the startling discovery which some modern teachers appear to have stumbled upon, that doctrines which the Church of Christ has always received as revealed truth, which councils have authorized, and which creeds have embodied, and which the sanctified intellects of master-spirits–the Anakims and the Shamgars of polemic divinity and divine philosophy of past ages–have contended for and maintained, are not found in the Bible, but are the visionary dogmata of a by-gone age–we say, may not these prevalent evils be mainly attributable to the contempt thrown upon the word of God? We verily and solemnly believe it to be so.

We need to be constantly reminded that the great regencrator and emancipator of the world is the Bible–that nothing short of this disturbs the spiritual death which universally prevails, and that nothing short of this will free the human mind from the shackles of error and superstition which enslave at this moment nearly two-thirds of the human race. This "sword of the Spirit"—like that of Goliath, "there is none like it"–has overcome popery and infidelity, and, unimpaired by the conflict, it is ready to overcome them yet again. Oh, that in this day of sad departure from the word of God, we may rally round the Bible in closer and more united phalanx! Firm in the belief of its divinity, strong in the conviction of its potency, may we go forth in the great conflict of truth and error, wielding no weapon but the "sword of the Spirit, which is the word of God." In all our spiritual relapses, too, may the word of the Lord quicken us. May it, like a mighty lever, raise our soul from the dust to which it so much cleaves.

JULY 26

"Blessed is the man whom you chasten, O Lord,
and teach him out of your law." Psalm 94:12

That there is a present partial understanding of God's will and ways concerning us we readily concede. We may, now and then, see a needs-be for His conduct. The veil is just sufficiently lifted to reveal a portion of the "end of the Lord." He will make us acquainted with the evil which He corrects, with the backsliding which He chastens, with the temptation which He checks, and with the dangerous path around which He throws his hedge; so that we cannot escape. We see it, and we bless the hand outstretched to save. He will also cause us to be fruitful. We have mourned our leanness, have confessed our barrenness, and lamented the distance of our walk, and the little glory we bring to His dear name–and lo! the dresser of the vineyard has appeared to prune His sickly branch, "that it may bring forth more fruit." "By this therefore shall the iniquity of Jacob be purged; and this is all the fruit to take away his sin." The deeper teaching, too–the result of the Divine chastenings–has revealed to some extent the "end of the Lord" in His mysterious conduct. Oh, there is no school like

God's school; for "who teaches like Him?" And God's highest school is the school of trial. All his true scholars have graduated from this: "Who are these which are arrayed in white robes? and where came they? These are they which came out of great tribulation, and have washed their robes, and made them white in the blood of the Lamb." Ask each spiritually, deeply taught Christian where he attained his knowledge, and he will point you to God's great university–the school of trial.

JULY 27

"Jesus answered and said unto him, What I do you
know not now, but you shall know hereafter." John 8:7

Oh that "hereafter," what a solemn word to the ungodly! Is there, then, a hereafter? Jesus says there is; and I believe it, because He says it. That hereafter will be terrible to the man that dies in his sins. It will be a hereafter whose history will be "written in mourning, lamentation, and woe." It had been better for you, reader, living and dying impenitent and unbelieving, had you never been born, or had there been no hereafter. But there is a hereafter of woe to the sinner, as of bliss to the saint. "These shall go away into everlasting punishment; but the righteous into life eternal."

The position which the Christian shall occupy hereafter will be most favorable to a full and clear comprehension of all the mysteries of the earthly journey. The "clouds and darkness"—emblems in our history of obscurity and distress–which now envelope God's throne, and enshroud His government of the saints, will have passed away; the mist and fog will have vanished, and, breathing a purer atmosphere, and canopied by a brighter sky, the glorified saint will then see every object, circumstance, incident, and step, with an eye unobscured by a vapor, and unmoistened by a tear. "Now we know in part; then shall we know even as we are known." And what shall we know? All the mysteries of providence. Things which had made us greatly grieve, will then be seen to have been causes of the greatest joy. Clouds of threatening, which appeared to us charged with the agent of destruction, will then unveil, and reveal the love which they embosomed and concealed.

All the mysteries of faith, too, will be known. "Now we see through a glass darkly (in a riddle), but then face to face; now I know in part, but then shall I know even as also I am known." The great "mystery of godliness" will develop and unfold its wonders. His everlasting love to His Church–His choice of a people for Himself–His sovereign grace in calling them–all, all, will shine forth with unclouded luster to the eternal praise of His great and holy name. Oh, what a perfect, harmonious, and glorious whole will all His doings in providence and grace appear, from first to last, to the undimmed eye, the ravished gaze of His white-robed, palm-bearing Church.

Many and holy are the lessons we may gather from this subject. The first is the lesson of deep humility. There are three steps in the Christian's life. The first is–humility; the second is—humility; the third is–humility. In veiling His dealings, Jesus would "hide pride" from us. In "leading the blind by a way that they know not," He teaches them to confide in the knowledge, truth, and goodness of their Divine escort–and that confidence is the calm unquestioning repose of faith.

JULY 28

"Showing himself through the lattice." Solomon's Song 2:9

This is a clearer and more glorious discovery of Christ, inasmuch as it is the manifestation of Christ in the revealed word. Our Lord cares not to conceal Himself from His saints. He remembers that all their loveliness is through Him, that all their grace is in Him, that all their happiness is from Him; and therefore He delights to afford them EVERY MEANS and occasion of increasing their knowledge of, and of perfecting their resemblance to, Him. The "lattice" of His house is figurative of the doctrines, precepts, and promises of His Gospel. Through these the Lord Jesus manifests Himself, when we come to the study of the word, not as self-sufficient teachers, but as sincere and humble learners, deeply conscious how little we really know, and thirsting to know more of God in Jesus.

The Lord Jesus often shows Himself through these "lattices,"-perhaps some type, or prophecy, or doctrine, or command–and we are instructed, sanctified, and blest. It is the loss of so many readers of the Bible that they do not search it for Christ. Men will study it with the view of increasing their knowledge of science and of philosophy, of poetry and of painting; but how few search into it for Jesus! And yet in knowing Him the pavilion of all spiritual mystery is unlocked–all that God designed to communicate in the present world. To know God is to comprehend all knowledge; God is only truly known as revealed in Jesus; therefore he who is experimentally acquainted with Jesus, holds in his hand the key that unlocks the vast treasury of God's revealed mind and heart.

Oh, search for Christ in the lattice of the word! The types foreshadow Him, the prophecies unfold Him, the doctrines teach Him, the precepts speak of Him, the promises lead to Him. "Rejoice in the word, but only as the wise men did in the star, as it led them to Christ. The word of Christ is precious, but nothing more precious than Christ Himself and His formation of the soul. Rest not in the word, but look through it to Christ."

Blessed Lord, I would sincerely open this box of precious ointment–Your own word–that the fragrance of Your grace and of Your name might revive me. It is Your word, and not man's word, that can meet my case, and satisfy my soul. Man can only direct me to You; Your word brings me to You. Your servants can at best but bring You in Your Gospel to my heart; but Your Spirit of truth brings You through the gospel into my heart. Oh, show Yourself to me in the gospel "lattice" of Your word, and I shall rejoice as one that has found great spoil–in finding You.

JULY 29

"Who is this that comes up from the wilderness, leaning upon her beloved?" Solomon's Song 8:5

Was ever a poor pilgrim more honored? Was ever a lonely traveler in better company? How can you be solitary or sorrowful, be in peril, or suffer need, while you are journeying homewards in company with and leaning upon Jesus? But for what are you to lean upon your Beloved? You are to lean upon Jesus for your entire salvation. He is "made of God unto you wisdom, righteousness, sanctification, and redemption;" and for each one of these inestimable blessings you are to depend daily upon Christ. Where can you lean for pardon, but upon the atoning blood of Jesus? Where can you lean for acceptance, but upon the justifying righteousness of Jesus? And where can you lean for sanctification, but upon the sin-subduing grace of Jesus? This leaning upon the Beloved, then, is a daily coming up out of ourselves in the great matter of our salvation, and resting in the finished work of Christ–no more, in Christ Himself. You are to lean upon the fullness of your Beloved. He is full to a sufficiency for all the needs of His people. There cannot possibly occur a circumstance in your history, there cannot arise a necessity in your case, in which you may not repair to the infinite fullness which the Father has laid up in Christ for His Church in the wilderness. Why, then, seek in your poverty what can only be found in Christ's riches? why look to your emptiness when you may repair to His fullness? "My grace is sufficient for you" is the cheering declaration with which Jesus meets every turn in your path, every crook in your lot, every need in your journey. Distrust then your own wisdom, look from your own self, and lean your entire weight upon the infinite fullness that is in Christ.

The posture is expressive of conscious weakness and deep self-distrust. Who is more feeble than a child of God? Taught the lesson of his weakness in the region of his own heart, and still learning it in his stumblings, falls, and mistakes, many and painful, in his self-inflicted wounds and dislocations, he is at length brought to feel that all his strength is outside of himself. He has the "sentence of death in himself, that he should not trust in himself." "I am weak, yes, weakness itself," is his language; "I am as a reed shaken of the wind; I stumble at a feather; I tremble at an echo; I recoil at my own shadow; the smallest difficulty impedes me; the least temptation overcomes me. How shall I ever fight my way through this mighty host, and reach in safety the world of bliss?" By leaning daily, hourly, moment by moment, upon your Beloved for strength. Christ is the power of God, and He is the power of the children of God. Who can strengthen the weak hands, and confirm the feeble knees, but Jesus? In those who have no might He increases strength. When they are weak in themselves, then are they strong in Him. His declaration is–"My strength is made perfect in weakness." Lean, then, upon Jesus for strength. He has strength for all your weakness; He can strengthen your faith, and strengthen your hope, and strengthen your courage, and strengthen your patience, and strengthen your heart, for every burden, for every trial, and for every temptation. Lean upon Him; He loves to feel the pressure of your arm; He loves you to link your feebleness to His almightiness, to avail yourself of His grace. Thus leaning off yourself upon Christ, "as your day, so shall your strength be." In all your tremblings and sinkings, you will feel the encircling of His power. "The eternal God is your refuge, and underneath are the everlasting arms."

JULY 30

"And if I go and prepare a place for you, I will come again and receive you unto myself; that where I am, there you may be also." John 14:3

When heart and flesh are fast failing, and the trembling feet descend into the dark valley of the shadow of death, to whom shall we then look but unto Jesus? The world is now receding, and all creatures are fading upon the sight; one object alone remains, arrests and fixes the believer's eye–it is Jesus, the Savior; it is Emmanuel, the Incarnate and now-present God; it is the Captain of our salvation, the Conqueror of death, and the Spoiler of the grave; it is our friend, our brother, our Joseph, our Joshua, loving and faithful, and present to the last. Jesus is there to confront death again, and vanquish him with his own weapons. Jesus is there to remind His departing one that the grave can wear no gloom, and can boast of no victory, since He himself passed through its portal, rose and revived, and lives for evermore.

Sick one! in your languishing, look to Jesus! Departing one! in your death-struggles, look to Jesus! Are you guilty?–Jesus is righteous. Are you a sinner?–Jesus is a Savior. Are you fearful, and do you tremble?–the Shepherd of the flock is with you, and no one shall pluck His sheep out of His hands. How fully, how suitably, does the gospel now meet your case! In your bodily weakness and mental confusion, two truths are, perhaps, all that you can now dwell upon–your sinfulness and Christ's redemption, your emptiness and Christ's sufficiency. Enough! you need no more; God requires no more. In your felt weakness, in your conscious unworthiness, amid the swelling of the cold waters, raise your eye and fix it upon Jesus, and all will be well. Hear the words of your Savior calling you from the bright world of glory to which He bids you come, "Arise, my love, my fair one! and come away." Believer! look to Him–lean upon Him–cleave to Him–labor for Him–suffer for Him–and, if need be, die for Him. Thus loving and trusting, living and dying, for "Jesus only."

JULY 31

"Surely I have behaved and quieted myself, as a child that is weaned of his mother: my soul is even as a weaned child." Psalm 131:2

The first object from which our heavenly Father weans His child is self. Of all idols, he finds self the hardest to abandon. When man in Paradise aspired to be as God, God was dethroned from his soul, and the creature became as a deity to itself. From that moment, the idolatry of self has been the great and universal crime of our race, and will continue to be until Christ comes to restore all things. In the soul of the regenerate, Divine grace has done much to dethrone this idol, and to reinstate God. The work, however, is but partially accomplished. The dishonored and rejected rival is not eager to relinquish his throne, and yield to the supreme control and sway of another. There is much yet to be achieved before this still indwelling and unconquered foe lays down his weapons in entire subjection to the will and the authority of that Savior, whose throne and rights he has usurped.

Thus, much still lingers in the heart which the Spirit has renewed and inhabits, of self-esteem, self-confidence, self-seeking, and self-love. From all this our Father seeks to wean us. From our own wisdom, which is but folly; from our own strength, which is but weakness; from our own wills, which are often as an uncurbed steed; from our own ways, which are crooked; from our own hearts, which are deceitful; from our own judgments, which are dark; from our own ends, which are narrow and selfish, He would wean and detach us, that our souls may get more and more back to their original center of repose–God Himself.

In view of this mournful exhibition of fallen and corrupt self, how necessary the discipline of our heavenly Father that extorts from us the Psalmist's language, "Surely I have behaved and quieted myself as a child that is weaned of this mother"! Self did seem to be our mother–the fruitful parent of so much in our plans and aims and spirit that was dishonoring to our God. From this He would gently and tenderly, but effectually, wean us, that we may learn to rely upon His wisdom, to repose in His strength, to consult His honor, and to seek His glory and smile, supremely and alone. And oh! how effectually is this blessed state attained when God, by setting us aside in the season of solitude and sorrow, teaches us that

He can do without us. We perhaps thought that our rank, or our talents, or our influence, or our very presence were essential to the advancement of His cause, and that some parts of it could not proceed without us! The Lord knew otherwise. And so He laid His hand upon us, and withdrew us from the scene of our labors and duties, engagements and ambition, that He might hide pride from our hearts–the pride of self-importance. And oh, is it no mighty attainment in the Christian life to be thus weaned from ourselves! Beloved, it forms the root of all other blessing. The moment we learn to cease from ourselves–from our own wisdom, and power, and importance–the Lord appears and takes us up. Then His wisdom is displayed, His power is put forth, His glory is developed, and His great name gets to itself all the praise. It was not until God had placed Moses in the cleft of the rock, that His glory passed by. Moses must be hid, that God might be all.

AUGUST

AUGUST 1

"Now I beseech you, brethren, for the Lord Jesus Christ's sake, and for the love of the Spirit, that you strive together with me in your prayers to God for me." Romans 15:30

There are many weighty and solemn considerations which powerfully plead for the prayers of the Church of God, in behalf of her ministers and pastors. The first which may be adduced is—the magnitude of their work. A greater work than theirs was never entrusted to mortal hands. No angel employed in the celestial embassy bears a commission of higher authority, or wings his way to discharge a duty of such extraordinary greatness and responsibility. He is a minister of the Lord Jesus Christ—an ambassador from the court of heaven—a preacher of the glorious gospel of the blessed God—a steward of the mysteries of the kingdom. Properly to fill this high office—giving to the household their portion of food in due season—going down into the mine of God's word, and bringing forth to the view of every understanding its hidden treasures—to set forth the glory of Emmanuel, the fitness of His work, and the fullness of His grace—to be a scribe well instructed, rightly dividing the word of truth—to be wise and skillful to win souls, the grand end of the Christian ministry—oh, who so much needs the sustaining prayers of the Church as he?

Secondly. The painful sense of their insufficiency supplies another affecting plea. Who are ministers of Christ? Are they angels? Are they superhuman beings? Are they inspired? No, they are men in all respects like others. They partake of like infirmities, are the subjects of like assaults, and are estranged from nothing that is human. As the heart knows its own bitterness, so they only are truly aware of the existence and incessant operation of those many and clinging weaknesses of which they partake in sympathy with others. And yet God has devolved upon them a work which would crush an angel's powers, if left to his self-sustaining energy.

Thirdly. The many and peculiar trials of the ministry and the pastorate ask this favor at our hands. These are peculiar to, and inseparable from, the office that he fills. In addition to those of which he partakes alike with other Christians—personal, domestic, and relative—there are trials to which they must necessarily be utter strangers. And as they are unknown to, so are they unrelievable by, the people of their charge. With all the sweetness of affection, tenderness of sympathy, and delicacy of attention which you give to your pastor, there is yet a lack which Jesus only can supply, and which, through the channel of your prayers, he will supply. In addition to his own, he bears the burdens of others. How impossible for an affectionate, sympathizing pastor to separate himself from the circumstances of his flock, be those circumstances what they may. So close and so sympathetic is the bond of union—if they suffer, he mourns; if they are afflicted, he weeps; if they are dishonored, he is reproached; if they rejoice, he is glad. He is one with his Church. How feelingly the apostle expresses this: "Then, besides all this, I have the daily burden of how the churches are getting along. Who is weak without my feeling that weakness? Who is led astray, and I do not burn with anger?" To see a Christian pastor, in addition to his own personal grief, borne often in uncomplaining loneliness and silence, yet bowed down under accumulated sorrows not his own—others looking to him for sympathy, for comfort, and for counsel—is a spectacle which might well arouse in behalf of every Christian minister the slumbering spirit of prayer. We marvel not to hear the chief of the apostles thus pleading, "Brethren, pray for us."

AUGUST 2

"You all are partakers of my grace." Philippians 1:7

Most true is it, that in the grace bestowed by God upon a Christian pastor all the members of the flock share. They partake of that which belongs to him. All the grace with which he is enriched—all the gifts with which he is endowed—all the acquirements with which he is furnished—all the afflictions with which he is visited—all the comforts with which he is soothed—all the strength with which he is upheld—all the distinction and renown with which he is adorned—belong alike to the Church over which God has made him an overseer. There is in the pastoral relation a community of interest. He holds that grace, and he exercises those gifts, not on account of his own personal holiness and happiness merely, but with a view to your holiness and happiness. You are partakers with him.

You are enriched by his "fatness," or are impoverished by his "leanness." The degree of his grace will be the measure of your own; the amount of his intelligence, the extent of yours. As he is taught and blest of Christ, so will you be. The glory which he gathers in communion with God will irradiate you; the grace which he draws from Jesus will sanctify you; the wealth which he collects from the study of the Bible will enrich you. Thus, in all things are you "partakers of his grace." How important, then, that on all occasions he should be a partaker of your prayers! Thus your own best interests are his strongest plea. Your profit by him will be proportioned to your prayer for him.

To the neglect of this important duty much of the barrenness complained of in hearing the word may be traced. You have, perhaps, been wont to retire from God's house caviling at the doctrine, dissecting the sermon in a spirit of captious criticism, sitting in judgment upon the matter or the manner of the preacher, and bitterly complaining of the unprofitableness of the preaching. With all tender faithfulness would we lay the question upon your conscience, "How much do you pray for your minister?" Here, in all probability, lies the secret of the great evil which you deplore. You have complained of your minister to others (alas! how often and how bitterly, to your deep humiliation be it spoken); have you complained of him to the Lord? Have you never seriously reflected how closely allied may be the deficiency in the pulpit, of which you complain, to your own deficiency in the closet, of which you have not been aware? You have restrained prayer in behalf of your pastor. You have neglected to remember in especial, fervent intercession with the Lord, the instrument on whom your advancement in the divine life so much depends. You have looked up to him as a channel of grace, but you have failed to ask at the hands of Jesus that grace of which he is but the channel. You have waited upon his ministrations for instruction and comfort, but you have neglected to beseech for him that teaching and anointing, by which alone he could possibly establish you in truth, or console you in sorrow. You have perhaps observed a poverty of thought, and have been sensible of a lack of power in his ministrations; but you have not traced it in part to your own poverty and lack in the spirit and habit of prayer in his behalf. You have marveled at, and lamented, the absence of sympathy, feeling, and tenderness in the discharge of his pastoral duties, but you have forgotten to sympathize with the high responsibilities, oppressive anxieties, and bewildering engagements inseparable from the office which your pastor fills, and in which he may largely share, often "under great pressure, far beyond our ability to endure, so that we despaired even of life." Thus in a great degree the cause of an unprofitable hearing of the word may be found nearer home than was suspected. There has been a suspension of prayer and sympathy on your part, and God has permitted a suspension of power and sympathy on his.

AUGUST 3

"We wait eagerly for our adoption as sons, the
redemption of our bodies." Romans 8:23

The terms "adoption," "redemption," must here be taken in a restricted sense. Our present adoption into God's family is as perfect as God can make it. We shall not in reality be more the children of God in heaven than we are now. Dwell upon this truth, beloved; press it in faith and gladness to your sighing, groaning heart. Is God's hand uplifted? Oh, tremble not! It is a Father's hand. Say not that it presses heavily upon you—it is the pressure of love. Do not think that there is one throb of affection less towards you in His heart. "Beloved, now are we the sons of God," and all the immunities and blessings of a present sonship are ours.

Equally as complete is our redemption from all that can condemn. When Jesus exclaimed, "It is finished!" by one offering He perfected forever the salvation of His Church. Then did He entirely roll away the curse from His people. Then did He hurl their sins into an infinite depth. Then did He complete the work the Father gave Him to do. For the finishing of that work, thanks be to God, the saints do not "wait."

And still, all believers are the expectants of an "adoption" to be confirmed, and of a "redemption" to be perfected. Their adoption now is concealed; their adoption then will be visible. Their present adoption is limited in its privileges; their future adoption will introduce them to all the riches of their inheritance, and to all the splendors of their Father's house. For this unveiled, this manifest, this full adoption they are "waiting."

And so, too, of "redemption." The ransom-price is paid, but the body is not yet fully redeemed. It still is fettered, and cribbed, and cabined by a thousand clinging corruptions and infirmities. But the day of its complete redemption draws near. In virtue of its ransom it will spring from the dust, its last link of corruption entirely and forever dissolved. "But we are citizens of heaven, where the Lord Jesus Christ lives. And we are eagerly waiting for him to return as our Savior. He will take these weak mortal bodies of ours and change them into glorious bodies like his own, using the same mighty power that he will use to conquer everything, everywhere." Like unto Christ's glorious body! Oh, then, no deformity will mar its symmetry! no infirmity will impair its strength! no sickness, no fainting, no nervousness, no pangs of suffering or throes of death will ever assail and torment it more! For this "redemption of the body" the sons of God are waiting. Our heavenly Father has adopted it. Our Divine Savior has redeemed it. The Holy Spirit, our Comforter, has sealed it. Oh yes! The first-fruits of the "first resurrection" bloom on the grave of the holy dead. This page may arrest the eye of a sufferer, not soothed in his grief or cheered in his loneliness by such prospects as these. But there still is hope. Jesus died for sinners, and there is mercy even for the chief. Blessed suffering, hallowed sorrow, if now, in the agony of your grief, you are led to the Savior to learn, what in the sunny hour of prosperity and gladness you refused to learn, that God only can make you happy, and that God in Christ is prepared to make you happy. O heaven-sent affliction! sweet messenger of love! beautiful in your somber robes, bearing to my soul a blessing so divine, so precious as this!

AUGUST 4

*"And I said, You shall call me, My Father; and
shall not turn away from me." Jeremiah 3:19*

Fellowship with God is the highest, purest, sweetest mercy a saint of God can have on earth. Yes, it is the highest, purest, sweetest bliss the saints of God can have in heaven. What is the enjoyment of heaven? Not merely exemption from trial, and freedom from sorrow, rest from toil, and release from conflict. Oh no! it is the presence—the full unclouded presence of our Father there. To be with Christ—to behold His glory—to gaze upon His face—to hear His voice—to feel the throbbings of His bosom—to bask in the effulgence of God's presence—oh, this is heaven, the heaven of heaven!

The twilight of this glory we have here on earth. "I am not alone," can each sorrowful and banished soul exclaim, "because the Father is with me." Yes, beloved, your own Father! "You shall call me my Father." In Jesus He is your Father—your reconciled, pacified Father—all whose thoughts that He thinks of you are peace, and all whose ways that He takes with you are love. The presence, the voice, the smile of a parent, how precious and soothing! especially when that presence is realized, and that voice is heard, and that smile is seen in the dark, desolate hour of adversity. God is our heavenly Parent. His presence, His care, His smiles are ever with His children. And if there be a solitary child of the one family that shares the richer in the blessing of the Father's presence than another, it is the sick, the suffering, the lone, the chastened child. Yes, your Father is with you ever. He is with you to cheer your loneliness, to sweeten your solitude, to sanctify your sorrow, to strengthen your weakness, to shield your person, to pardon your sins, and to heal all your diseases. Hearken, in your deep solitude, to His own touching words: "Don't be afraid, for I am with you. Do not be dismayed, for I am your God. I will strengthen you. I will help you. I will uphold you with my victorious right hand." Enough, my Father! if thus You are with me, I am not, I cannot be alone; and if such the bliss with which You do sweeten, and such the glory with which You do irradiate the solitude of Your hidden ones, Lord, let me ever be a hidden one—shut out from all others, shut in alone with You!

AUGUST 5

"As one whom his mother comforts, so will I comfort you;
and you shall be comforted in Jerusalem." Isaiah 66:13

Acute is the penitential grief of that child which has strayed from its heavenly Father. Deep and bitter the sorrow when he comes to himself, resolves, and exclaims, "I will arise, and go to my Father." Many the tremblings and doubts as to his reception. "Will He receive back such a wanderer as I have been? Will He take me once more to His love, speak kindly to me again, restore to me the joys of His salvation, give me the blessed assurance of His forgiveness, and once more admit me with His children to His table?" He will, indeed, weeping penitent! God will comfort your present sorrow by the tokens of His forgiving love. He invites, He calls, He beseeches you to return to Him. He is on the watch for you, He advances to meet you, He stretches out His hand to welcome you, He waits to be gracious, He yearns to clasp His penitential, weeping Ephraim to His heart. "When he was yet a great way off, his father saw him, and had compassion, and ran, and fell on his neck, and kissed him."

Will a mother's love live on, warm and changeless, amid all the long years of her child's rebellion, forgetfulness, and ingratitude? Will she, when he returns, and gently knocks at her door, and trembling lifts the latch, and falls, weeping and confessing, upon the bosom he had pierced with so many keen sorrows, press him to a heart that never ceased to throb with an affection which no baseness could lessen, and which no dishonor could quench? And will God our Father, who inspired that mother's love, who gave to it all its tenderness and intensity, and who made it not to change, turn His back upon a poor, returning child, who in penitence and confession seeks restoring, pardoning mercy at His feet? Impossible! utterly impossible!

The love of God to His people is a changeless, quenchless, undying love. No backslidings can lessen it, no ingratitude can impair it, no forgetfulness can extinguish it. A mother may forget, yes, has often forgotten her child; but God, never! "Can a mother forget her nursing child? Can she feel no love for a child she has borne? But even if that were possible, I would not forget you!" How touching, how impressive the figure! It is a woman—that woman is a mother, that mother is a nursing mother—and still she may forget and abandon her little one; "yet will I not forget you," says your God and Father. Touching, heart-melting, heart-winning truth!

Lord! we come unto You in Jesus' name! We have sinned, we have gone astray like lost sheep, we have followed the devices of our own hearts, we have wandered after other lovers, we have wounded our peace, and have grieved Your Spirit: but, behold, we come unto You, we fall down at Your feet, we dare not so much as look unto You, we blush to lift up our faces—receive us graciously, pardon us freely; so will we loathe ourselves, hate the sin You pardon; and love, adore, and serve the God who forgives and remembers it no more forever! As one whom his mother comforts, so do You comfort us!

AUGUST 6

"For to be carnally minded is death; but to be
spiritually minded is life and peace." Romans 8:6

Spiritual-mindedness is life. We fearlessly challenge every believer—
What has been the effect in your soul of a low state of grace? What has
been the effect of carnal indulgence of allowed sin—of needless communion
with the world—of conformity to its policy and its pleasures—of unruly
temper—of a volatile disposition, yes, of any species of carnality whatever:
has it not been "death"? When a process of spiritual relapse has been
allowed to proceed stealthily and unchecked—when the world, and sin, and
self have gained an ascendancy, what has been the consequence? "Death!"

The habit of prayer may not have been totally neglected, but there has
been no communion with God—and so there has been death upon prayer.
The Bible has not been entirely unread, but no light has beamed upon
the sacred page—and so there has been death upon the Bible. The means
of grace have not been utterly forsaken, but no grace has distilled from
these channels—and so there has been death upon the means of grace.
Thus a spiritual deathliness has crept over the soul, the effect and fruit of
indulged and growing carnality.

But "life" is the blessed effect of heavenly-mindedness. It is life springing
from life, or rather, the inner life in its outer actings. What spiritual
mightiness, almost omnipotent, does he possess, whose mind and heart
and faculties are deeply immersed in the Spirit of Christ, closely allied to
the Divine and heavenly! As sin is weakness, so holiness is strength. As
carnality impairs, so spirituality invigorates. The one deadens, the other
vivifies. Close dealing with Essential Life increases the life of spirituality.
Much communion with Jesus draws forth "life more abundantly."

It is impossible to live a life of faith in the Son of God, constantly taking
to His blood every sin, to His heart every care, to His sympathy every
sorrow, to His grace every corruption, to His arm every burden, without
being conscious of new life, of augmented power, of increased heavenliness.
Inquire of the man of prayer what is the effect in his soul of close filial
communion with God? Ask the reflective mind what is the effect upon
his spirit of holy meditation? Ask the conscience much beneath the cross

what is the result of the constant sprinkling of the atoning blood? And, as with one voice, and with one utterance, each believer will answer, "Life!" Oh, there is an energizing influence in spirituality, a quickening of the spiritual life in heavenly-mindedness, which he only can understand whose converse is much with things heavenly, much with God.

There is life in prayer, life in the word, life in ordinances, life in the enjoyment of vital religion, which transmits the thrill of its deep pulsations through the whole soul. Nor life alone in these. But when the storm of adversity blows—when sore affliction comes—when the "noise of the water-spout" is heard, and the tossing waves and the foaming billows roll over the soul—when the shadow of death is settling upon all creature-good; then, even then, the spiritual mind panting after life exclaims, "Though I walk in the midst of trouble, You will revive me." "This is my comfort in my affliction; for Your word has quickened me." And what is all this but the pledge and the prelude of the glorious consummation and crown of all—the life that is to come, even life everlasting?

AUGUST 7

"Peace I leave with you, my peace I give unto you:
not as the world gives give I unto you." John 14:27

Peace also is a fruit of spiritual-mindedness. What peace of conscience does that individual possess whose mind is stayed upon spiritual things! It is as much the reward as it is the effect of his cultivated heavenliness. The existence of this precious blessing, however, supposes the exposure of the spiritual mind to much that has a tendency to ruffle and disturb its equanimity and repose. The Christian is far from being entirely exempt from those chafings and disquietudes which seem inseparable from human life. To the brooding anxieties arising from external things—life's vicissitudes, mutations, and disappointments; there are added, what are peculiar to the child of God, the internal things that distract—the cloudings of guilt, the agitations of doubt, the corrodings of fear, the mourning of penitence, the discipline of love.

But through all this there flows a river, the streams whereof make glad the city of God. It is the peace of the heavenly mind, the peace which Jesus procured, which God imparts, and which the Holy Spirit seals. A heavenly mind soars above a poor dying world, living not upon a creature's love or smile—casting its daily need upon the heart of a kind Providence—anxious for nothing, but with supplication and thanksgiving making known its requests unto God—indifferent to the turmoil, vexations, and chequered scenes of worldly life, and living in simple faith and holy pleasing on Christ. Thus detached from earth, and moving heavenwards by the attractions of its placid coast, it realizes a peace which passes all understanding.

And if this be the present of the heavenly mind, what will be the future of the mind in heaven? Heaven is the abode of perfect peace. There are no cloudings of guilt, no tossings of grief, no agitations of fear, no corrodings of anxiety there. It is the peace of perfect purity—it is the repose of complete satisfaction. It is not so much the entire absence of all sorrow, as it is the actual presence of all holiness, that constitutes the charm and the bliss of future glory.

The season of sorrow is frequently converted into that of secret joy—Christ making our very griefs to sing. But the occasion of sin is always that of bitter grief; our backslidings often, like scorpions, entwined around our hearts. Were there even—as most assuredly there will not be—sadness in heaven, there might still be the accompaniment of happiness; but were there sin in heaven—the shadow of a shade of guilt—it would becloud and embitter all. Thus, then, as heaven is the abode of perfect peace, he who on earth has his conversation most in heaven approximates in his feelings the nearest to the heavenly state. Oh that our hearts were more yielding to the sweet, holy, and powerful attractions of the heavenly world! Then would our conversation be more in heaven.

AUGUST 8

"For what the law could not do, in that it was
weak through the flesh." Romans 8:3

What is it that the law cannot do? The law has no power to place the sinner in a justified state. In other words, it cannot fulfill its own righteousness. "By Him all who believe are justified from all things, from which you could not be justified by the law of Moses." "Therefore by the deeds of the law there shall no flesh be justified in His sight." Nor has it power to give life. "For if there had been a law given which could have given life, verily righteousness should have been by the law."

The law pronounces the unjustified sinner dead—his religion dead—his works dead—his faith dead; but with not one breath of spiritual life has it power to inspire the soul. Oh, the infatuation which prompts men to seek spiritual life from a law powerful only as an instrument of eternal death! Nor has the law power to make anything whatever perfect in the great matter of man's salvation. "For the law made nothing perfect, but the bringing in of a better hope did; by the which we draw near unto God." These things the law fails to achieve. And herein is it weak. Holy in its nature, it is yet incapable of making the sinner holy. Righteous in its precepts, it yet cannot justify the ungodly. Respecting the Divine image, it yet has no power to transfer that image to the soul.

But let us trace this failure to its proper cause. From where, then, this weakness of the law of God? We reply, not from any inherent defect in the law. "The law is holy, just, and good," and of itself powerful enough to take the soul to glory. But the apostle supplies the answer—"weak through the flesh." It was right that he should thus shield the dignity of the law, and maintain that there belonged to it a native force and capacity worthy of Him from whom it emanated, and equal to the accomplishment of the great end for which it was enacted. The weakness of the law, then, is to be traced, not to any inefficiency of the instrument, but to the sinfulness of man; not to the agent, but to the subject.

What an impressive view does this give us of the deep depravity, the utter sinfulness of our nature! So great is the corruption of the flesh, that it opposes and thwarts the law in its great work of imprinting its image upon the mind of man. Oh, what must be the character and power of that sinfulness which can thus sever the locks of its strength, and divert it from its sacred purpose! Sincerely would the law make us holy, but our depravity foils it. Sincerely would it recall our alienated affections, but our heart is so utterly estranged from God that its generous effort fails. Thus the law is weak, through the corrupt and sinful flesh.

Let us be deeply humbled by this truth. How entirely it stains the pride of all our fleshly glory! Where, now, is our native holiness, our boasted pride, and our vaunted worthiness? The law, always on the side of purity and love, yearned to bring us beneath its holy and beneficent influence, but our carnality interposed, and it became weak.

AUGUST 9
"God sending his own Son in the likeness of sinful flesh." Romans 8:3

What words are these—"God sending his own Son!" A person less exalted, less Divine, could not have accomplished what the Divine law failed to do. And since the law, a transcript of Deity, proved too feeble for the purpose, Deity itself undertakes the work. God's own eternal and essential Son embarks in the enterprise, and achieves it. What a Rock of salvation, saint of God, is this! Springing from the lowest depths of your humiliation, see how it towers above your curse—your sin—your condemnation! It is a Rock higher than you. Infinitely removed beyond the reach of hell is that soul whose faith is planted upon this Rock.

"In the likeness of sinful flesh." These words place in the clearest possible light the true humanity of the Son of God. It was not human nature in appearance that He took, as some have taught, but human nature in reality. It was a perfectly organized body, having all the properties, affinities, and functions belonging to our own; bone of our bone, and flesh of our flesh, made in all points like His brethren. Now can He, with a feeling of the most exquisite sympathy, be touched with my infirmity; for this nature which I drag about with me, feeble and bruised, jaded and crushed, was the very nature which He took into mysterious union with His Godhead, wore it here below, and wears it still in heaven!

But with what care and skill does the Holy Spirit guard the perfect sinlessness of our Lord's humanity! Observe, it was not the reality of sinful flesh that the Son of God assumed, but its "likeness" only. He took real flesh, but bearing the resemblance of sinfulness. He was "made like his brethren." "Tempted like we are, yet without sin." And so in the passage before us, "in the likeness of sinful flesh." The words suppose a resemblance to our sinful nature. And, oh! how close that resemblance was! As like a sinner as one could be, who yet in deed and in truth was not one—"who knew no sin," but was "holy, harmless, undefiled, and separate from sinners."

Man is a sinner; our blessed Lord was man—so truly man, that His enemies exclaimed, "We know this man is a sinner." They could not understand how one could be so really human, and yet be untainted with sin. And then, did there not cling to Jesus the infirmities of our fallen nature, which, though sinless in Him, were not the less the effects of sin? He hungered—He thirsted—He wept—He was wearied—He slept—He was afflicted—He sorrowed—He trembled—He suffered—He died. And as we trace these infirmities of our humanity floating upon the transparent surface of His pure life, how forcible do we feel the words—"Made in the likeness of sinful flesh"!

And when we see Him traduced as a sinner by man, and, standing beneath His people's transgressions—dealt with as a sinner by God; by man denounced as "a glutton," "a drunkard," "a friend of publicans and sinners," "an impostor", "a deceiver," a "blasphemer,"—then arraigned, condemned, and executed as a criminal not worthy to live; as an accursed one by God, charged with all the sins of the elect Church, bruised and put to grief, and at last abandoned by Him on the cross, then numbered with transgressors, and making His grave with the wicked in His death—oh! how like sinful flesh was the robe of lowliness and suffering which He wore! And yet, "He was without sin."

It was the resemblance, not the reality. The human nature of the Son of God was as free from sin as the Deity it enshrined. He was the "Lamb of God, without spot." The least taint of moral guilt—a shade of inherent corruption—would have proved fatal to His mission. One leak in the glorious Ark which contained the Church of God would have sunk it to the lowest depths. Oh! this is the glory of His work, and the solace of our hearts, that Christ our Savior "offered Himself without spot unto God." And now we may plead His sinless atonement as the ground of our pardon, and the acceptance of our people. "He has made Him to be sin for us, who knew no sin, that we might be made the righteousness of God in Him." The Lord bless these truths to the comfort and edification of our souls.

AUGUST 10

"Every branch that bears fruit he prunes, that
it may bring forth more fruit." John 15:2

The Lord empties before He fills. He makes room for Himself, for His love, and for His grace. He dethrones the rival, casts down the idol, and seeks to occupy the temple, filled and radiant with His own ineffable glory. Thus does He bring the soul into great straits, lay it low, but to school and discipline it for richer mercies, higher service, and greater glory. Be sure of this, that, when the Lord is about to bless you with some great and peculiar blessing, He may prepare you for it by some great and peculiar trial.

If He is about to advance you to some honor, He may first lay you low that He may exalt you. If He is about to place you in a sphere of great and distinguished usefulness, He may first place you in His school of adversity, that you may know how to teach others. If He is about to bring forth your righteousness as the noon-day, He may cause it to pass under a cloud, that, emerging from its momentary obscuration, it may shine with richer and more enduring luster. Thus does He deal with all His people. Thus He dealt with Joseph. Intending to elevate him to great distinction and influence, He first casts him into a dungeon, and that, too, in the very land in which he was so soon to be the gaze and the astonishment of all men. Thus, too, He dealt with David, and Job, and Nebuchadnezzar; and thus did God deal with His own Son, whom He advanced to His own right hand from the lowest state of humiliation and suffering.

Regard the present suffering as but preparatory to future glory. This will greatly mitigate the sorrow, reconcile the heart to the trial, and tend materially to secure the important end for which it was sent. The life of a believer is but a disciplining for heaven. All the covenant dealings of His God and Father are but to make him a partaker of His holiness here, and thus to fit him for a partaker of His glory hereafter. Here, he is but schooling for a high station in heaven. He is but preparing for a more holy, and, for anything we know, a more active and essential service in the upper world. And every infirmity overcome, every sin subdued, every weight laid aside, every step advanced in holiness, does but strengthen and mature the life of grace below, until it is fitted for, and terminates in, the life of glory above.

Let the suffering believer, then, see that he emerges from every trial of the furnace with some dross consumed, some iniquity purged, and with a deeper impress of the blessed Spirit's seal of love, holiness, and adoption, on his heart. Let him see that he has made some advance towards the state of the glorified; that He is more perfected in love and sanctification—the two great elements of heaven; and that therefore he is fitting for the inheritance of the saints in light. Blessed and holy tendency of all the afflictive dispensations of a covenant God and Father towards a dear and covenant child!

AUGUST 11

"For as many as are led by the Spirit of God,
they are the sons of God." Romans 8:14

It is the office of Jehovah the Spirit in the covenant of redemption, after He has called a people out of the world, to place Himself at their head, and undertake their future guidance. He knows the path to heaven. With all its intricacies and dangers He is acquainted. He is familiar with the sunken rock, the treacherous quicksand, the concealed pit, and the subtle snare. He knows, too, the individual and ordained path of each celestial traveler. All that God has appointed in the everlasting covenant—all the windings, and intricacy, and straitness of the way—He knows. All the future of our history is infinitely more vivid and transparent to His mind than is the past, already trodden, to our eye. It is utterly impossible, then, that He should mislead.

And what is equally as essential to Him as a guide, He knows His own work in the soul. All its light and shade, its depressions and its revivings, its assaults and victories, are vivid to his eye. Dwelling in that heart—His sacred temple—His chosen abode—He reads His own writing inscribed there; understands the meaning of every groan, interprets the language of every sigh, and marks the struggling of every holy desire; He knows where wisely to supply a check, or gently to administer a rebuke, tenderly to whisper a promise, or sympathetically to soothe a sorrow, effectually to aid an incipient resolve, strengthen a wavering purpose, or confirm a fluctuating hope.

But, in less general terms, what is it to be led by the Spirit? The existence of spiritual life in those He leads is an essential point assumed. He does not undertake to lead a spiritual corpse, a soul dead in sins. Many are moved by the Spirit, who are not led by the Spirit. Was not Saul, the king of Israel, a solemn instance of this? And when it is said, "the Spirit of God departed from him," we see how, in an ordinary way, the Spirit may strive with a man's natural conscience, and powerfully work upon his feelings through the word, and even employ him as an agent in the accomplishment of His will, and yet never lead him one step effectually and savingly to Christ and to heaven.

There is, as in Ezekiel's vision of the bones, "a voice, and behold a shaking, and the bones come together, bone to his bone; but there is no breath in them." But there is spiritual life in those whom the Spirit leads. They thus become in a sense voluntary in the movement. They are not forced; it is not by compulsion they follow; they are led—persuasively, gently, willingly led. The leading of the Spirit, then, is His acting upon His own life in the soul.

It supposes, too, entire inability to lead themselves in those who are led by the Spirit: "I will lead the blind by a way they know not." And such are we. Unable to discern a single step before us, and incapable of taking that step even when discerned, we need the guidance of the Holy Spirit. What can we see of truth—what of providence—what of God's mind and will, of ourselves? Absolutely nothing. Oh, what unfoldings of ignorance, what exhibitions of weakness, have marked some of the wisest of God's saints, when left to self-teaching and to self-guidance! Thus there is a strong and absolute necessity that wisdom, and strength, and grace, infinitely transcending our own, should go before us in our homeward journey.

AUGUST 12

"For we who worship God in the Spirit are the only ones who are truly circumcised. We put no confidence in human effort. Instead, we boast about what Christ Jesus has done for us." Philippians 3:3

The first step the Spirit takes in this great work is to lead us from ourselves—from all reliance on our own righteousness, and from all dependence upon our native strength. But let us not suppose that this divorce from the principle of self entirely takes place when we are "married to another, even to Christ." It is the work of a life. Alas! Christ has at best but a portion of our affections. Our heart is divided. It is true, there are moments, bright and blissful, when we sincerely and ardently desire the full, unreserved surrender. But the ensnaring power of some rival object soon discovers to us how partial and imperfect that surrender has been. This severing from ourselves—from all our idols—is a perpetual, unceasing work of the Spirit. And who but this Divine Spirit could so lead us away from self, in all its forms, as to constrain us to trample all our own glory in the dust, and acknowledge with Paul that we are "less than the least of all saints."

But more than this, He leads from an opposite extreme of self—from a despairing view of our personal sinfulness. How often, when the eye has been intently bent within, gazing as it were upon the gloom and confusion of a moral chaos, the Spirit has gently and graciously led us from ourselves to an object, the sight of which has at once raised us from the region of despair! How many walk in painful and humiliating bondage, from not having thus been sufficiently led out of themselves! Always contemplating their imperfect repentance, or their weak faith, or their little fruitfulness, they seem ever to be moving in a circle, and to know nothing of what it is to walk in a large place. Thus from sinful self, as from righteous self, the Spirit of God leads us.

To what does He lead? He leads us to Christ. To whom else would we, in our deep necessity, wish to be led? Now that we know something exper-imentally of Jesus, to whom would we go but to Him? Having severed us in some degree from ourselves, He would bring us into a closer realization of our union with the Savior. "He will bring glory to me by taking from what is mine and making it known to you."

And this promise is fulfilled when, in all our need, He leads us to Christ. Are we guilty? the Spirit leads us to the blood of Jesus. Are we weary? the Spirit leads us to abide in Jesus. Are we sorrowful? the Spirit leads us to the sympathy of Jesus. Are we tempted? the Spirit leads us to the protection of Jesus. Are we sad and desolate? the Spirit leads us to the tender love of Jesus. Are we poor, empty, and helpless? the Spirit leads us to the fullness of Jesus. And still it is to the Savior He conducts us. The Holy Spirit is our comforter, but the holy Jesus is our comfort. And to

Jesus—to His person, to His offices, and to His work, in life and in death, the Divine Guide ever leads us.

AUGUST 13

"Furthermore then we beseech you, brethren, and exhort you by the Lord Jesus, that as you have received of us how you ought to walk, and to please God, so you would abound more and more." 1 Thessalonians 4:1

What are some of the footprints of this walk? How may we trace it? Unreserved obedience is an undoubted mark of pleasing God. An obedience that asks no abatement of the precept, but that follows the Lord fully in its observance, not from an enlightened judgment, but from a love—constrained heart—walking, as did the primitive saints, in all the commandments and ordinances of the Lord blamelessly—is indeed well-pleasing to God. Oh! let there be no reserves in our obedience! Let us withhold from Christ no part of His purchased inheritance, but surrender all at His feet, whose heart's blood was the purchase price of all.

"Lord, however strait be the path, painful the cross, and self-denying the precept, sincerely would I walk uprightly in all Your ways, and fully follow You in all Your commands, leaving the consequences of my simple and implicit obedience to Your control. I can endure the repulsion of the world, the alienation of friends, the coldness of relatives, and can take the spoiling of my earthly goods joyfully, if You, my Lord, sustain me with Your grace, cheer me with Your presence, and solace me with Your love."

Another footprint may be described in the walk of faith by which the Christian journeys to His heavenly home. As unbelief is most dishonoring, so faith is most honoring to the Lord Jesus. What a revenue of praise accrues from it to His name! To repair to His sufficiency—with our anxiety, the moment it occurs; with our corruptions, the moment they are discovered; to His grace—with our sorrow, the moment it is felt; to His sympathy—with our wound, the moment it is inflicted; to His love—with our guilt, the moment it is detected; to His blood—oh! do you do not think that this walk of faith is most pleasing to the Lord?

Let us beware of that which impairs the simplicity of this our walk, and causes us to stumble or turn aside. We must be cautious, in the varied circumstances of our history, of applying first to a human arm for support, or to a human bosom for sympathy. With this the Lord cannot be well pleased. But let us not hesitate to bear them at once to the one-appointed source of all our supply; disclosing our needs to the full Savior; our wanderings to our heavenly Father; our griefs and burdens to our elder Brother and Friend; and in thus walking by faith, we shall have the divine assurance in our souls, our rejoicing this—the testimony of our conscience that we please the Lord.

Oh, let us seek closely to resemble the two illustrious examples set before us in the word, of this high and holy walk. The minor one—because purely human—of Enoch, who "before he was taken up had this testimony, that he pleased God." The higher one—because the human was blended with the Divine—of Jesus, who could say, "I always do those things which please Him."

AUGUST 14

*"For your name's sake, O Lord, pardon my
iniquity; for it is great." Psalm 25:11*

The knowledge of indwelling sin, its existence and power, is often exceedingly defective at conversion, and this ignorance may continue for years after. We just see sin enough to alarm the conscience, awaken conviction, and take us to Christ. As a thing against God, we hate it, mourn over it, and seek its pardon through the atoning blood. This is followed by a sweet and lively sense of its blotting out, and a growing desire after Divine conformity.

But, oh, the unknown depths of sin! These we have never explored. What infinite wisdom and love are seen in hiding these depths at first from our knowledge! Were the Lord fully to have revealed the hidden evils of the heart at the period when grace was yet in the bud, and faith was feeble, our views of the Lord Jesus dim, and the "new creature" yet in its infancy, deep and dark despair would have gathered around the soul.

With, perhaps, just knowledge enough of Christ to go to Him as a Savior; with just faith enough to touch the hem of His garment; the Eternal Spirit just disclosed to us the existence and the guilt of sin; a full disclosure might have shut us up in hopeless despair. It is sweet, beloved, to remember the tender love of God in our espousals; to trace the gentleness of His first dealings with us in conversion; and to bear in mind that what He then was, He is at this moment.

But trace the work of the Spirit in the after days of our experience. He comes, in accordance with the design of the covenant of grace, to sanctify, having called and quickened us. He is about to enlarge the "kingdom of God within" us; to stamp more deeply, and bring out more vividly and broadly on the soul, the varied lineaments of the Divine image. He is about to purify the temple more thoroughly; to take a fresh possession for God; to expel every rival that by slow and imperceptible degrees may have insinuated itself there; in a word, He is about to sanctify us.

And how does He commence the work? By leading us into the chamber of imagery; by disclosing the depths of indwelling sin; sin, whose existence we had never imagined, He shows to have its principal dwelling in the heart! Iniquity, that we had never thought of, He reveals as lurking in secret ambush within. Oh, what darkness, what evil, and what baneful principles are found to have so long existed, where we thought all was light, holiness, and rectitude! We startle, we shudder, and we shrink away, aghast at the discovery!

"What!" says the alarmed soul, "does all this evil dwell in me? Have I borne about with me so long these vile affections? Have I dwelling in me the seeds of such deep and dark depravity? Wonder of wonders is it, that the flood has not long since carried me away; that these deep evils have not broken out, to the wounding of my peace, and to the dishonoring of my God and Savior."

Thus made acquainted with his own heart, almost a stranger to him before, the Holy Spirit awakens in his soul an ardent panting for holiness. In view of such a discovery, where can he fly but to the throne of grace? There, then, he goes, weeping, mourning, confessing; and his prayer is, "Lord, subdue these evils of my heart. I am whelmed with astonishment; yes, 'I lie down in shame, and my confusion covers me,' that I should have harbored so long these treacherous foes against You, O God of holiness and love. 'Save me, O God, for the floodwaters are up to my neck. Deeper and deeper I sink into the mire; I can't find a foothold to stand on. I am in deep water, and the floods overwhelm me.' 'Search me, O God, and know my heart; test me and know my thoughts. Point out anything in me that offends you, and lead me along the path of everlasting life.'"

And now the Spirit deepens and strengthens this panting for sanctification; the believer is set upon earnestly seeking holiness of heart; he sees such an iniquity in sin as he never saw before, and seeing it, he abhors it, and abhorring it, he takes it to the Spirit of holiness, that he might overcome and subdue it. Thus, in leading the believer into a deeper acquaintance with the existence and power of indwelling sin, does the blessed Spirit sanctify the soul, by making it the occasion of stirring up his desires for holiness.

Do not be cast down, beloved, at the discovery of the hidden evil of our heart. Sweet is the evidence it affords to the fact that the Holy Spirit is working there. Whatever be the sin that is brought to light; pride, deceit, carnality, inordinate affection, evil thoughts, unbelief, impatience, whatever it be, He is revealing it to you, not unnecessarily to wound and grieve you; oh no, He is a living and a gentle Spirit; but to beget this desire in your heart, "Lord, conform me to Your image; make me holy, as You are holy."

AUGUST 15

*"My wayward children," says the Lord, "come back to me, and
I will heal your wayward hearts." "Yes, we will come," the
people reply, "for you are the Lord our God." Jeremiah 3:22*

Do not stay away from the throne of grace because of an unfavorable frame of mind. If God is ready to receive you just as you are; if no questions are asked, and no examination is instituted, and no exceptions are made on account of the badness of the state; then count it your mercy to go to God with your worst feelings. To linger away from the throne of grace because of unfitness and unpreparedness to approach it, is to alter its character from a throne of grace to a throne of merit.

If the Lord's ears are only open to the cry of the righteous when they seek Him in certain good and acceptable frames of mind, then He hears them for their frames, and not because He is a God of grace. But He can never alter His character, or change the foundation of His throne. It is the mercy-seat; the throne of grace; and not for any frame, either good or bad, in the suppliant does He bow His ear, but for His own mercy's sake. Yield not, then, to this device of your adversary, to keep you from prayer.

It is the privilege of a poor soul to go to Jesus in his worst frame; to go in darkness, to go in weak faith, to go when everything says, "Stay away," to go in the face of opposition, to hope against hope; to go in the consciousness of having walked at a distance, to press through the crowd to the throne of grace, to take the hard, the cold, the reluctant heart, and lay it before the Lord. Oh what a triumph is this of the power and the grace of the blessed Spirit in a poor believer!

Dear reader, what is your state? Are you feeble in prayer? Are you tried in prayer? And yet, is there anything of real need, of real desire in the heart? Is it so? Then, draw near to God. Your disposition will not be more favorable tomorrow than it is today. You will not be more acceptable or more welcome at any future period than at this moment. Give yourself unto prayer.

I will suppose your state to be the worst that can be; your frame of mind the most unfavorable, your cross the heaviest, your corruption the strongest, your heart the hardest; yet betaking yourself to the throne of grace, and, with groanings that cannot be uttered, opening your case to the Lord, you shall adopt the song of David, who could say in the worst of frames, and in most pressing times, "But I give myself unto prayer." "Come, let us tell of the Lord's greatness; let us exalt his name together. I prayed to the Lord, and he answered me, freeing me from all my fears. Those who look to him for help will be radiant with joy; no shadow of shame will darken their faces. I cried out to the Lord in my suffering, and he heard me. He set me free from all my fears." Psalm 34:3-6

AUGUST 16

*"Beloved, I wish above all things that you may prosper
and be in health, even as your soul prospers." 3 John 2*

Is it true that God, by setting you aside from active engagements, has set you aside from all duty and labor? We do not think so. Is it too much to say, that He is now summoning you, though to a more limited and obscure, yet to a higher and holier, because more self-denying and God-glorifying, sphere of duty? Your present loss of health has brought with it its high and appropriate duties, obligations, and employments. It bears an especial message from God to you, and through you to others. Contemplate the work to be done in your own soul, and the testimony through this which you are to bear to the power of Divine grace, to the sustaining energy of the Gospel, and to the character of God; and I ask if the lone chamber of sickness has not its special and appropriate duties, responsibilities, and work, equally as difficult, as honorable, and as remunerative as any which attach to the sphere of activity or to the season of health?

You are called upon now to glorify God in a passive, rather than in an active consecration to His service. Graces hitherto perhaps dormant, or but feebly brought into play, are now to be developed and exercised to their utmost capacity. Patience is to be cultivated, resignation is to be exhibited, faith is to be exercised, love is to be tried, and example is to be set; and are not these great, holy, and sublime achievements? Who will affirm that there is no sermon to be preached from that languid couch, that sick-bed; yes, and it may be more solemn, more searching, more full of Christ and the power of the Holy Spirit, than the pulpit ever preached.

The Church and the world have now the testimony of one passing through the present and personal experience of what he speaks. A sick-room is not the place for theorizing upon truth and eternity. All transpiring there is stern reality. The dust of human applause is laid aside, the breath of adulation is hushed, the flush of excitement has faded, and the delirium of an admiring throng has passed away; the artificial gives place to the true. All is as real and solemn as eternity.

Deem not yourself a useless cumberer, because sickness has incapacitated you for active labor. God has but changed your sphere of duty, transferring you, doubtless, to one more glorifying to Himself. Receive, then, with meekness your Heavenly Father's dispensation, which, while it has set you apart from the Lord's work, has set you apart more exclusively and entirely for the Lord Himself. Your great desire has been to glorify Him: leave Him to select the means which may best advance it.

You have thought of health and activity, of life and usefulness; of being a champion for the truth, a herald of salvation to the ignorant and the lost, a leader in some high and laborious path of Christian enterprise; but He has ordained it otherwise. And now by sickness and suffering, by silence and solitude, He is giving you other work to perform, which shall not the less secure your usefulness, and promote His glory.

AUGUST 17

"And the Lord said, Simon, Simon, behold, Satan has desired to have you, that he may sift you as wheat." Luke 22:31

That faith should be more frequently and severely assailed than any other grace of the Holy Spirit, will cease to create surprise as we become acquainted with the rank and position it occupies in the renewed soul. Placed in the very front of the battle, itself the strongest, the most determined and successful foe of the assailing powers of darkness and of sin, in effecting its overthrow all their force, skill, and malignity are marshaled and directed.

But who is its chief and most formidable assailant? It is Satan, the accuser of the brethren, the tempter, the sworn enemy of God and man. It is he, the master-spirit of darkness and woe, who, without possessing a single attribute of Deity, yet approaches so near in resemblance to the Divine, that in every place and at each moment of time He is present, closely watching, closely studying, and incessantly working to deceive, and to overthrow, were it possible, the faith of the very elect.

By what power or agency he is enabled to prosecute the dark designs of his gloomy intellect, and to effect the malignant purposes of his depraved heart, we cannot now venture at any length to premise. Whether with the subtlety and velocity which belong to the light, there is an incessant expansion of thought, imparting a kind of personal omnipresence, to the ruling mind of the infernal empire; or, whether, without being personally present, we may account for the extent of his agency, operating alike in every place, and at the same moment, by supposing intelligence communicated to, and commands issued from, him through the medium of the innumerable host of myrmidons who compose those "principalities and powers," over which Jesus triumphed, "making a show of them openly," must, however strong the presumption, still remain points involved in much doubt and obscurity.

But there is one fact respecting which we are not left to conjecture. I allude to the eager and restless machinations of Satan, to weaken, dishonor, and destroy the faith of God's elect. "Satan has desired to have you." Observe here the limitation of Satanic power in reference to the believer. This is its utmost extent. He has no power or control over the redeemed, but that which God permits. He can but desire, and long, and plot; not a hand can He lay upon them, by not a single temptation can He assail them, not a hair of their head can he touch, until God bids Him. "Satan has desired to have you"; there stood the arch-foe waiting permission, as in the case of Job, to destroy the apostle of Christ.

Dear reader, how consolatory is this truth to the believing mind. You have often trembled at the power of Satan, and perhaps well-near as often have been the involuntary object of his implacable hatred and deep devices. But press now this animating thought to your trembling heart—he has no control nor influence nor power over a redeemed soul but that which God permits, and which Christ allows. "Thus far shall you go, and no further," are words which reveal His inferiority, prescribe his limits, and arrest the progress of the proud fiend.

AUGUST 18

"For we wrestle not against flesh and blood, but against principalities, against powers, against the rulers of the darkness of this world, against spiritual wickedness in high places." Ephesians 6:12

Let us inquire what is that which Satan desires to assault? It is the work of God in the soul. Against his own kingdom not a weapon is raised. It is his aim and his policy to keep all there undisturbed and peaceful. But against the work of the Holy Spirit in the renewed mind, his artillery is brought to bear; not a part of this work escapes him. Every grace comes in for its share of malignant attack; but especially the grace of faith. When, for example, a repentant and believing soul approaches Christ with lowliness and hesitancy, and with the tremulous hand of faith attempts to touch the border of His garment, or with a tearful eye looks up to His cross, then comes the assault upon faith in the form of a suggestive doubt of Christ's power and willingness to save. "Is Jesus able to save me? Has He power to rescue my soul from hell? Can He blot out my transgressions, and redeem my life from destruction? Will He receive a sinner, so vile, so unworthy, so poor as I? Has He compassion, has He love, has He mercy sufficient to meet my case?"

In this way Satan assails the earliest and the feeblest exercises of faith in the soul. Does this page address itself to any such? It is Satan's great effort to keep you from Jesus. By holding up to your view a false picture of His character, from which everything loving, winning, inviting, and attractive is excluded, by suggesting wrong views of His work, in which everything gloomy, contracted, and repulsive is foisted upon the mind; by assailing the atonement, questioning the compassion, and limiting the grace of Christ, he would persuade you that in that heart which bled on Calvary there is no room for you, and that upon that work which received the Father's seal there is not breadth sufficient for you to stand. All his endeavors are directed, and all his assaults are shaped, with a view to keep your soul back from Christ. It is thus he seeks to vent his wrath upon the Savior, and his malignity upon you.

Nor does he less assail the more matured faith of the believer. Not infrequently the sharpest attacks and the fiercest onsets are made, and made successfully, upon the strongest believers. Seizing upon powerful corruptions, taking advantage of dark providences, and sometimes of bright ones, and never allowing any position of influence, any usefulness, gift, or grace, that would give force, success, and brilliance to his exploit, to escape his notice, he is perpetually on the alert to sift and winnow God's precious wheat.

His implacable hatred of God, the deep revenge he cherishes against Jesus, his malignant opposition to the Holy Spirit, fit him for any dark design and work implicating the holiness and happiness of the believer. Therefore we find that the histories of the most eminent saints of God, as written by the faithful pen of the Holy Spirit, are histories of the severest temptations of faith, in the most of which there was a temporary triumph of the enemy; the giant oak bending before the storm. And even in instances where there was no defeat of faith, there yet was the sharp trial of faith.

The case of Joseph, and that of his illustrious antitype, the Lord Jesus, present examples of this. Fearful was the assault upon the faith of both, sharp the conflict through which both passed, yet both left the battlefield victorious. But still faith was not the less really or severely sifted.

AUGUST 19

"The life I live in the body, I live by faith in the Son of God, who loved me and gave himself for me." Galatians 2:20

The spiritual life is above human nature, and therefore all the power of nature cannot inspire it. Nature, we admit, can go far in imitating some of its characteristics, but nature cannot create the essential property or principle of this life. Nature can produce a semblance of faith, as in the case of Simon Magus; a semblance of repentance, as in the case of Judas; a semblance of hearing the word with joy, as in the case of Herod. It can even appear to taste the heavenly gift, and feel the powers of the world to come. All this, and much more, can human nature do, and yet be human nature still.

Here its power stops. There is something which it cannot do. It cannot counterfeit the indwelling of Christ in the sinner's soul. It cannot enable a man to say, "I live, and Christ lives in me." This infinitely transcends its mightiest power. Spiritual life, then, springs not from human nature, and is therefore produced by no natural cause or means. It is from God. He it is who calls this new creation into being, who pencils its wonders, who enkindles its glories, and who breathes over it the breath of life. It is God's life in man's soul.

Thus the true Christian is one who can adopt the expressive and emphatic language of Paul; "I live." Amplifying the words, he can exclaim, "I live; as a quickened soul. I live; as a regenerate soul. I live; as a pardoned sinner. I live; as a justified sinner. I live; as an adopted child. I live; as an heir of glory. I live; and I have never lived before! My whole existence until now has been but as a blank. I never truly, really lived, until I died! I lived, if life it may be called, to the world, to sin, to the creature, to myself; but I never lived by Christ, and I never lived to God."

Oh tremendous truth! Oh solemn thought! for a soul to pass away into eternity without having answered the great end of its creation; without having ever really lived! With what feelings, with what emotions, with what plea, will it meet the God who created it? "I created you," that God will say, "for myself, for my glory. I endowed you with gifts, and ennobled you with faculties, and clothed you with powers second only to my own. I sent you into the world to expend those gifts, and to employ those faculties, and to exert those powers, for my glory, and with a view to the enjoyment of me forever. But you buried those gifts, you abused those faculties, you wasted those powers, and you lived to yourself, and not unto me; and now to yourself, and in everlasting banishment from my presence, you shall continue to live through eternity."

Come from the four winds, O breath of the living God, and breathe upon the dead, that they may live! Avert from the reader so dire a doom, so fearful a catastrophe! And permit none, whose eye lights upon this solemn page, any longer to live to themselves, but from this moment and forever, gracious Savior! may they live for You; their solemn determination and their sublime motto this, "For me to live is Christ."

AUGUST 20

"The church of God, which he has purchased
with his own blood." Acts 20:28

The Deity of the Son of God imparted a Divine vitality and value to the blood which flowed from His human nature. So close and intimate was the mysterious union, that while the Deity effected the atonement by the humanity, the humanity derived all its power and virtue to atone from the Deity. There was Deity in the blood of Jesus; a Divine vitality which stamped its infinite value, dignity, and virtue.

Observe in two instances how strikingly the Holy Spirit has coupled these two truths; the Deity and the atonement of Jesus: "Who being the brightness of His glory, and the express image of His person, and upholding all things by the word of His power, when He had by Himself purged our sins." "Awake, O sword, against my shepherd, against the man that is my fellow, says the Lord; smite the shepherd." Here are brought out in the strongest light, and in the most beautiful and intimate relation, Deity and atonement. It was not so much that our Lord was the Priest, as that He was the Sacrifice; not so much that He was the Offerer, as that He was the Offering; in which consisted the value of His blood. "When He had by Himself purged our sins." "Who gave Himself for us." "When He offered Himself." "What did He offer in offering Himself? He offered up

His life; His twofold life. There was on Calvary the sacrifice of Deity with the humanity. The Deity not suffering, for it was incapable of suffering; nor of dying, for essential life could not die; but Deity with the humanity constituted the one offering which has perfected forever the salvation of those who are sanctified.

Profoundly and awfully mysterious as is this truth, faith can receive it. It towers above my reason, and yet it does not contradict my reason. While it transcends and baffles it, it does not oppose nor supersede it. Christian reader, the blood upon which you depend for your salvation is not ordinary blood; the blood of a mere human being, however pure and sinless; but it is the blood of the incarnate God, "God manifest in the flesh." It is the blood of Him who is Essential Life; the Fountain of Life the "Resurrection and the Life;" and because of the Divine life of Jesus, from thence springs the vitality of His atoning blood.

Oh, that is a Divine principle that vivifies the blood of Christ! This it is that makes it sacrificial, expiatory, and cleansing. This it is that enables it to prevail with God's justice for pardon and acceptance; this it is that renders it so efficacious that one drop of it falling upon the conscience, crushed beneath the weight of sin, will melt the mountain of guilt and lift the soul to God. Hold fast the confidence of your faith in the essential Deity of the Son of God, for this it is which gives to His Atonement all its glory, dignity, and virtue.

AUGUST 21

"When Jesus therefore had received the vinegar, he said, It is finished; and he bowed his head, and gave up the spirit." John 19:30

A jar of sour wine was sitting there, so they soaked a sponge in it, put it on a hyssop branch, and held it up to his lips. When Jesus had tasted it, he said, "It is finished!" Then he bowed his head and gave up his spirit. John 19:29-30

Believer in Jesus! remember, all your confidence, all your hope, all your comfort flows from the finished work of your Savior. See that you unwittingly add nothing to the perfection of this work. You may be betrayed into this sin and this folly by looking within yourself, rather than to the person of Jesus; by attaching an importance too great to repentance and faith, and your own doings and strivings, rather than ceasing from your own works altogether, and resting for your peace, and joy, and hope; simply, entirely, and exclusively in the work of Jesus. Remember, that whatever we unintentionally add to the finished work of Christ mars the perfection and obscures the beauty of that work. "If you lift up your tool upon it, you have polluted it."

We have nothing to do, but in our moral pollution and nakedness to plunge beneath the fountain, and wrap ourselves within the robe of that Savior's blood and righteousness, who, when He expired on the tree, so completed our redemption, as to leave us nothing to do but to believe and be saved.

"It is finished!" Oh words pregnant of the deepest meaning! Oh words rich in the richest consolation! Salvation is finished! Look away from your fluctuating frames, and fitful feelings, and changing clouds, to "Jesus only." Look away from sins and guilt, from emptiness and poverty, to "Jesus only." "It is finished!" Let devils hear it, and tremble! Let sinners hear it, and believe! Let saints hear it, and rejoice! All is finished!

"Then, Lord, I flee to You, just as I am! I have stayed away from You too long, and am 'yet instead of getting better, I grew worse.' Too exclusively have I looked at my unworthiness, too absorbed have I been with my impoverishment, too bitterly have I mourned having nothing to pay. Upon Your own finished work I now cast myself. Save, Lord, and I shall be saved!"

Before this stupendous truth, let all creature merit sink, let all human glory pale, let all man's boasting vanish, and let Jesus be all in all. Perish, forms and ceremonies; perish, rites and rituals; perish, creeds and churches; perish, utterly and forever perish, whatever would be a substitute for the finished work of Jesus, whatever would tend to neutralize the finished work of Jesus, whatever would obscure with a cloud, or dim with a vapor; the beauty, the luster, and the glory of the finished work of Jesus!

It was "Jesus only" in the councils of eternity; it was "Jesus only" in the everlasting covenant of grace; it was "Jesus only" in the manger of Bethlehem; it was "Jesus only" in the garden of Gethsemane; it was "Jesus only" upon the cross of Calvary; it was "Jesus only" in the tomb of Joseph; it was "Jesus only" who, "when He had by Himself purged our sins, sat down on the right hand of the Majesty on high." And it shall be "Jesus only"; the joy of our hearts, the object of our glory, the theme of our song, the Beloved of our adoration, our service, and our praise, through the endless ages of eternity. Oh, stand fast, in life and in death, by the finished work of Jesus.

AUGUST 22

"He that covers his sins shall not prosper; but whoever confesses and forsakes them shall have mercy." Proverbs 28:13

A sense of guilt upon the conscience invariably occasions distant views of God. The moment Adam became conscious of having sinned, He hid himself from God's eye. He sought concealment from the endearing presence of Him who had been used to walk in the cool of the evening through the bowers of Paradise, in sweet and confiding communion. It is so now! Guilt upon the conscience, sin unconfessed, imparts misty, gloomy, distorted views of God. We lose that clear endearing view of His character which we once had. We dare not look up with holy, humble boldness. We misinterpret His dealings; think harshly of His ways; and if providences are dark, and afflictions come, in a moment we exclaim, "I have sinned, and God is angry." And so we seek concealment from God. We sink the Father in the Judge, and the child in the slave.

Another evil that results from sin unconfessed is the hardening tendency it produces upon the conscience. To a child of God, who has felt and mourned over the power of sin, we need not stay to prove how hardening is the tendency of sin; how it crusts the heart with a callousness which no human power can soften, and which often requires heavy affliction to remove. Where a child of God, then, neglects the habit of a daily confession of sin, by slow and almost imperceptible degrees, the conscience loses its tenderness, and becomes, by this gradual process, so hardened as at length to think nothing of a sin, which at a previous period would have filled the soul with horror and remorse.

One more evil we may mention, and that is, that a neglect of this most important duty causes a fearful forgetfulness of sin, without the sweet sense of its forgiveness. The believer loses sight of his sin, not because he knows it to be pardoned, afresh blotted out, but from a mere carnal forgetfulness of the sin. The child of God, on whose conscience the atoning blood has been afresh sprinkled, cannot soon forget his sin. Oh no! Freed from a sense of its condemnation, delivered from its guilt, and looking up to the unclouded face of a reconciled God, yet He remembers how far he could depart from the God that so loved him, and so readily and freely forgave him. The very pardon of his sin stamps it upon his memory. He thinks of it only to admire the love, adore the grace, and extol the blood that blotted it out; and thus he is led to go softly all his days. "My soul has them still in remembrance, and is humbled in me."

But the believer who neglects the duty and the privilege of confession loses the remembrance of his sin, until brought under the rod of the covenant. Then some deep and heavy chastisement recalls it to his memory, and fills him with shame, humiliation, and contrition. In this state, the Eternal Spirit comes into the soul with His restoring mercies, leads the abased and humbled believer afresh to the "fountain opened,"; and God; the God of all comfort; speaks in words of comfort to his broken heart.

AUGUST 23
"God is love." 1 John 4:8

God in Christ is no longer a "consuming fire," but a God of love, of peace; a reconciled God. God in Christ holds out His hand all the day long to poor sinners. He receives all; He welcomes all; He rejects, He refuses, He casts out none. It is His glory to pardon a sinner. It is the glory of His power, it is the glory of His love, it is the glory of His wisdom, it is the glory of His grace, to take the prey from the mighty, to deliver the lawful captive, to pluck the brand from the burning, to lower the golden chain of His mercy to the greatest depth of human wretchedness and guilt, to lift the needy and place him among the princes.

Behold Christ upon that cross! Every pang that He endures, every stroke that He receives, every groan that He utters, every drop of blood that He sheds, proclaims that God is love, and that He stands pledged and is ready to pardon the vilest of the vile. Justice, sheathing its sword, and retiring satisfied from the scene, leaves Mercy gloriously triumphant. And "God delights in mercy."

Having at such an infinite cost opened a channel; even through the smitten heart of His beloved Son; through which His mercy may flow boundless and free, venture near, nothing doubting. No feature of your case is discouraging, or can possibly arrest the pardon. Your age, your protracted rebellion against God, your long life of indifference to the concerns of your soul, the turpitude and number of your sins, your lack of deep convictions or of stronger faith, nor worth or worthiness to recommend you to His favor; are no true impediments to your approach, are no pleas why you should not draw near and touch the outstretched scepter, bathe in the open fountain, put on the spotless robe, welcome the gracious pardon, and press it with gratitude and transport to your adoring heart.

In the light of this truth, cultivate loving and kindly views of God. Ever view Him, ever approach Him, and ever transact your soul's affairs with Him, in and through Jesus. He is the one Mediator between God and your soul. God your Father may now be leading you through deep and dark waters. His voice may sound roughly to you. His dim outline is, perhaps, all that you can see of Him. His face seems veiled and averted; yet deal with Him now in Christ, and all your hard thoughts, trembling fears, and unbelieving doubts shall vanish.

In Jesus every perfection of God dissolves into grace and love. With your eye upon the cross, and looking at God through that cross, all the dark letters of His providence will in a moment become radiant with light and glory. That God, who has so revealed Himself in Jesus, must be love, all love, and nothing but love, even in the most dark, painful, and afflictive dealings with His beloved people!

AUGUST 24

"And for their sakes I sanctify myself, that they also might be sanctified through the truth." John 17:19

Christ is glorified in the progressive holiness of His people. "The kingdom of God is within you," says our Lord. The increase of this kingdom is just the measure and extent of the believer's advance in sanctification. This is that internal righteousness, the work of God the Holy Spirit, which consists in the subjugation of the mind, the will, the affections, the desires, yes, the whole soul; to the government and supremacy of Jesus; "bringing into captivity," says the apostle, "every thought to the obedience of Christ."

O you who are "striving against sin." Longing to be "conformed to the image of God's Son," panting to be more "pure in heart," "hungering and thirsting for righteousness," think that in every step which you take in the path of holiness; in every corruption subdued; in every besetting sin laid aside; in every holy desire begotten; Christ is glorified in you! But you perhaps reply, "The more I strive for the mastery, the more I seem to be conquered. The stronger I oppose my sins, the stronger my sins seem to be."

But what does this prove? It proves that "God is working in you both to will and to do of His good pleasure"; that the kingdom of God is invading the kingdom of Satan; that the Spirit dwelling in the heart is warring with the flesh. It is truly remarked by Owen, that "if a believer lets his sins alone, his sins will let him alone." But let him search them as with candles, let him bring them to the light, oppose, mortify, and crucify them; they will to the last struggle for the victory. And this inward warfare undeniably marks the inhabitation of God the Holy Spirit in the soul.

To see one advancing in holiness; thirsting for God; the heart fixed in its solemn purpose of entire surrender; cultivating higher views; and aiming for a loftier standard; to behold him, perhaps, carving his way to his throne through mighty opposition, "fightings without; fears within;" striving for the mastery of some besetting sin; sometimes foiling and sometimes foiled; sometimes with the shout of victory on the lip, and sometimes with the painful consciousness of defeat bowing down the heart; yet still onward; the needle of the soul, with slow and tremulous, but true and certain movement, still pointing to its glorious attraction—God; faith that can never fail; and hope that can never die; and love that can never be quenched; hanging amid their warfare and in all their weakness upon the "nail fastened in a sure place"; how is Christ, our sanctification, glorified in such a saint!

Oh, to be like Jesus! meek and lowly, gentle, kind, and forgiving, without duplicity, without deceit, without malice, without revenge, without one temper, or thought, or feeling, or look, that is unlike Him!

Beloved, mistake not the nature and the evidence of growth in sanctification. In all your self—denial in this great work, be cautious of grace-denial. You will need much holy wisdom here, lest you overlook the work of the Spirit within you. You have thought, it may be, of the glory that Christ receives from brilliant genius and profound talent, from splendid gifts and glowing zeal, from costly sacrifices, and even extensive usefulness. But have you ever thought of the glory, the far greater, richer glory, that flows to Him from a contrite spirit, a broken heart, a lowly mind, a humble walk; from the tear of godly repentance that falls when seen by no human eye, and the sigh of godly sorrow that is breathed when heard by no human ear; from the sin—abhorrence and self-loathing, the deep sense of vileness, poverty, and infirmity that takes you to Jesus with the prayer—"Lord, here I am; I have brought to You my rebellious will, my wandering heart, my worldly affections, my peculiar infirmity, my besetting and constantly overpowering sin. Receive me graciously; put forth the mighty power of Your grace in my soul, subdue all, rule all, and subjugate all to Yourself. Will it not be for Your glory, the glory of Your great name, if this strong corruption were subdued by Your grace, if this powerful sin were nailed to Your cross, if this temper so sensitive, this heart so impure, these affections so truant, this mind so dark, these desires so earthly, these pursuits so carnal, and these aims so selfish, were all entirely renewed by Your Spirit, sanctified by Your grace, and made each to reflect Your image? Yes, Lord, it would be for Your glory, through time and through eternity."

AUGUST 25

"What is the exceeding greatness of his power to us who believe, according to the working of his mighty power." Ephesians 1:19

Divine power, not less than love, is a perfection we shall require at every step of our yet untried and unknown path. We shall have needs which none but the power that multiplied the five loaves to supply the hunger of the five thousand can meet; difficulties, which none but the power that asks, "Is anything too hard for me? says the Lord," can overcome; enemies, with whom none but the power that resisted Satan, vanquished death, and broke from the grave, can cope. All this power is on our side, if our trust is in the Lord. "All power is given unto me in heaven and in earth," exclaims Jesus. This power which the Lord exerts on our behalf, and in which He invites us to trust, is made perfect in weakness.

Hence, we learn the same lesson that teaches us the utter lack of strength in ourselves. And when the Lord has reduced our confidence, and weakened our strength, as in the case of Gideon, whose army He reduced from thirty-two thousand men to three hundred, He then puts forth His power, perfects it in our weakness, gives us the victory, and secures to Himself all the praise. Go forward, relying upon the power of Jesus to do all in us, and accomplish all for us: power to subdue our sins; power to keep our hearts; power to uphold our steps; power gently to lead us over rough places, firmly to keep us in smooth places, skillfully to guide us through crooked paths, and safely to conduct us through all perils, fully to vindicate us from all assaults, and completely to cover our heads in the day of battle. Invincible is that soul thus clad in the panoply of Christ's power.

The power which belongs to Him as God, and the power which He possesses as Mediator, is all exerted in the behalf of those who put their trust in Him. "You have given Him power," are His own words, "over all flesh, that He should give eternal life to as many as You have given Him." Child of God! gird yourself for duties, toils, and trials, "strong in the grace that is in Christ Jesus." And when the stone of difficulty confronts you; lying, perhaps, heavily upon some buried mercy; hear Him ask you, before he rolls it quite away; "Do you believe that I am able to do this?" Oh, that your trusting heart may instantly respond, "Yes, Lord, I believe, I trust; for with You all things are possible."

AUGUST 26

"And I will pray the Father, and he shall give you another Comforter, that he may abide with you forever." John 14:16

He dwells in the believer as an abiding Spirit. It is a permanent indwelling. Our dear Lord laid especial stress upon this feature. When on the eve of leaving His disciples to return to His kingdom, He promised them "another Comforter," whose spiritual presence should more than repair the loss of his bodily absence. And, lest there should be any painful apprehensions as to the time of His dwelling with them, He assures those who the Spirit should abide with them forever. Overlook not this truth. Let no spiritual darkness, no workings of unbelief, nor sense of indwelling sin, rob you of the comfort and consolation which a believing view of it will impart.

There may be periods when you are not sensible of the indwelling of the Spirit; clouds and darkness may be around this doctrine; there may be severe trials, gloomy providences, foreboding fears; the way rough and intricate; the sky dark and wintry; faith small; unbelief powerful; and your soul, from its low depths, led to exclaim, "All these things are against me. Will the Lord cast me off forever? and will he be favorable no more? Is his mercy clean gone forever? does his promise fail for evermore? Has God forgotten to be gracious? has he in anger shut up his tender mercies?"

Oh, do not forget that even then, dejected saint of God; then, when all is dark within, and all is desolate without; then the Holy Spirit, the Sanctifier, the Comforter, the Glorifier of Jesus, dwells in you, and shall be with you forever. True, you may be assailed by powerful corruptions, the "consolations of God" may be small with you, and your prayer like David's "Cast me not away from Your presence, and take not Your Holy Spirit from me;" yet He, the blessed Indweller, is there, and His still, small, and soothing voice shall before long be heard amid the roaring of the tempest, hushing it to a peaceful calm.

He shall "abide with you forever." No wanderings, no neglect, no unkindness, no unworthiness, no unfaithfulness shall ever force Him from our bosom. He may withdraw His sensible presence; He may withhold His comforting influence; He may be so grieved by a careless walk as to suspend for a while His witnessing and sanctifying power, permitting indwelling corruptions for a moment to triumph; but He restores the soul; He brings it back again; breaks the heart, then binds it up; wounds, then heals it; fills it with godly grief, then tunes it with thanksgiving and the voice of melody.

AUGUST 27

"And if we know that he hears us in whatever we ask, we know that we have the petitions that we desired of him." 1 John 5:15

Believing prayer is prevailing, successful prayer. It assails the kingdom of heaven with holy violence, and carries it as by storm. It believes that God has both the heart and the arm; both the love that moves Him, and the power that enables Him; to do all and to grant all that His pleading child requests of Him. We may mention a few of the attributes of believing prayer.

It is real prayer, because it is the expression of need. It springs from a felt necessity of the mercy which it craves. It is sincere prayer, welling up from a soul schooled in the knowledge of its deep poverty and need. Oh, how much passes for real prayer which is not prayer; which is not the breathing of the soul, nor the language of the heart, nor the expression of need. There is in it no true approach to God, no thirsting for Christ, no desire for holiness. Were God to bestow the things which had been so thoughtlessly and heartlessly asked, the individual would be taken by surprise.

The prayer of faith is importunate and persevering. It will not take a refusal. It will not be put off with a denial. Thus Jacob wrestled with the Angel of the covenant until he prevailed; "I will not let you go until you bless me." Thus the woman of Canaan would not release the Savior from her hold until He had granted her suit; "If I am a dog, satisfy me with the crumbs." And thus, too, the man who besieged the house of his friend at midnight for bread, and did not go away until he obtained it; and the oppressed widow, who sought justice at the hands of the unrighteous and reluctant judge until he righted her; illustrate the nature of that prayer; even earnest, persevering prayer, which prevails with God, and obtains the blessing.

Believing prayer is humble. How low in the dust the truly importunate suppliant lies before God! There is nothing of bold ruffianism, of unholy freedom, in the cases of earnest prayer which we have cited. There is no irreverence of manner, nor brashness of speech, nor rushing into God's holy presence as if He were an equal. But rather that awful consciousness of the Divine presence, that profound spirit of self-abasement which seems to say, "How dreadful is this place!" "Behold, I am vile; what shall I answer you? I will lay my hand upon my mouth." Oh, how lowly is the heart from where arises the incense of believing prayer! How utterly unworthy it feels of the least of all the Lord's mercies; how unfit to be a channel of grace to others; and with what trembling it lies prostrate upon the spot where God, the Triune God, is passing by! "Do not be rash with your mouth, and let not your heart be hasty to utter anything before God; for God is in heaven, and you upon earth; therefore let your words be few."

Submission is another attribute of the prayer of faith. Its utmost range of request is bounded, and its deepest fervor of spirit is chastened, by submission to the Divine will. It presumes neither to dictate to God, nor to counsel Him. It leaves the mode of answering its petitions; the time, the place, the way; with God. Trained, perhaps, in the school of bitter disappointment, it has learned to see as much love in God's heart in withholding as in granting its requests; as much wisdom in delaying as in promptly bestowing the blessing. And, seeing that delays in prayer are not denials of prayer, he who believes will not make haste to anticipate the Divine mind, or to antedate the Divine blessing. "Your will, not mine, be done," ever breathes from the praying lip of faith.

Yet another and the crowning attribute of believing prayer is; that it is presented in the name of Jesus. As it is life from God through Christ, so through Christ it is life breathed back again to God. It approaches the Divine Majesty by the "new and living way"; its mighty argument, and its one prevailing plea, is the atoning blood of Jesus. This is the ground of its boldness, this the reason of its nearness, and this the secret of its power and success. "Whatever you shall ask in my name," observes Christ, "that will I do, that the Father may be glorified in the Son."

AUGUST 28

"Blessed are those who mourn, for they
shall be comforted." Matthew 5:4

You feel yourself to be the very chief of sinners. You seem to stand out from the great mass, a lone and solitary being; more vile, polluted, guilty, and lost than all. Your sentiments in reference to yourself, to the world, to sin, to God, and to Christ, have undergone a rapid, total, and surprising change. Yourself you see to be guilty and condemned; the world you feel to be a worthless portion, a cheat, and a lie; sin you see to be the blackest and most hateful of all other things; God you regard in a light of holiness, justice, and truth you never did before; and Christ, as possessing an interest entirely new and overpowering.

Your views in relation to the law of God are reversed. You now see it to be immaculately holy, strictly just, infinitely wise. Your best attempts to obey its precepts you now see are not only utterly powerless, but in themselves are so polluted by sin that you cannot look at them without the deepest self-loathing. The justice of God shines with a glory unseen and unknown before. You feel that in now bringing the condemnatory sentence of the law into your conscience He is strictly holy, and were He now to send you to eternal woe He would be strictly just.

But ah! what seems to form the greatest burden? What is that which is more bitter to you than wormwood or gall? Oh, it is the thought that ever you should have lifted your arm of rebellion against so good, so holy, so just a God as He is. That ever you should have cherished one treasonous thought, or harbored one unkind feeling. That your whole life, thus far, should have been spent in bitter hostility to Him, His law, His Son, His people; and that yet in the midst of it, yes, all day long, He has stretched out His hand to you, and you did not regard it!

Oh, the guilt that rests upon your conscience! Oh, the burden that presses your soul! Oh, the sorrow that wrings your heart! Oh, the pang that wounds your spirit! Is there a posture of lowliness more lowly than all others? You would assume it. Is there a place in the dust more humiliating than all others? You would lie in it. And now you are looking wistfully around you for a refuge, a resting-place, a balm, a quietness for the tossing of the soul.

Beloved, is this your real state? Are these your true feelings? Blessed are you of the Lord! "Blessed, do you say?" Yes! Those tears are blessed! Those humbling, lowly views are blessed! That broken heart, that contrite spirit, that awakened, convinced, and wounded conscience, even with all its guilt, is blessed! Why? because the Spirit, who convinces men of sin, of righteousness, and of judgment, has entered your soul, and wrought this change in you. He has opened your eyes, to see yourself lost and wretched. He has broken the spell which the world had woven round you. He has dissolved the enchantment, discovered the delusion, and made you to feel the powers of the world to come. Then you are blessed.

AUGUST 29

"But he that received the seed into stony places, the same is he that hears the word, and anon with joy receives it; yet has he no root in himself, but endures for awhile: for when tribulation or persecution arises because of the word, by and by he is offended. He also that received seed among the thorns is he that hears the word; and the care of this world, and the deceitfulness of riches, choke the word, and he becomes unfruitful. Matthew 13:20-22

"The rocky soil represents those who hear the message and receive it with joy. But like young plants in such soil, their roots don't go very deep. At first they get along fine, but they wilt as soon as they have problems or are persecuted because they believe the word. The thorny ground represents those who hear and accept the Good News, but all too quickly the message is crowded out by the cares of this life and the lure of wealth, so no crop is produced." Matthew 13:20-22

A season of prosperity often proves fatal to a profession of Godliness. Divine providence smiles, riches increase, and with them the temptations and the snares, the luxury, indulgence, and worldly show which are inseparable from the accumulation of unsanctified and unconsecrated wealth. And what are the results? In most cases, the entire relinquishment of the outward garb of a religious costume. Found to be in the way of the full indulgence of the carnal mind, it is laid aside altogether; and thus freed from all the restraints which consistency imposed, the heart at once plunges deep into the world it all the while secretly loved, sighed for, and worshiped. Oh, what a severe but true test of religious principle is this! How soon it detects the spurious and the false! How soon does the verdure wither away! "The prosperity of fools shall destroy them."

But if a professing man passes through this trial, and still retains his integrity; still walks closely and humbly with God; still adheres to the lowly cross-bearing path of Jesus; is still found as diligent in waiting upon God in public and private means of grace; is still as meek, condescending, and kind, increasing in devotedness, liberality, and love, with the increase of God's providential goodness around him, such a man has the "root of the matter in him;" and "he shall be like a tree planted by the rivers of water, that brings forth his fruit in his season; his leaf also shall not wither; and whatever he does shall prosper." His prosperity has not destroyed him.

A time of adversity is often equally as fatal to a profession of religion, founded upon no true Christian principle. If in the smooth path we are apt to slide, in the rough path we may stumble. Periods of great revolution in the history of the Christian Church, when God tries the principles, the conscience, the love, and the faith of His people, are test-periods. What numbers make shipwreck then of their high profession! And when God enters the pleasant garden of a man's domestic blessings, and blows upon the lovely blossom, or blights the fair flower, or severs the pleasant bough, or scatters the hard-earned wealth of years, or wastes the body's vigor, or frustrates the fond scheme; how does an unrenewed man behave himself?

Is his carriage humble, submissive, child-like? Does stern Christian principle now exhibit itself, in beautiful contrast with the trial that has called it forth? Does divine grace, like the aromatic flower, now appear the sweeter and more precious for its being crushed? Does not every feeling of the heart rise in maddened rebellion against God and against His government? Ah, yes! how accurately does Christ describe his case: "he has not root in himself, but endures for a while; for when tribulation or persecution arises because of the word, by and by he is offended."

AUGUST 30

*"Now no chastening for the present seems to
be joyous, but grievous." Hebrews 12:11*

There is often a severity, a grievousness in the chastisements of our covenant God, which it is important and essential for the end for which they were sent, not to overlook. He who sent the chastisement appointed its character—He intended that it should be felt. There is as much danger in underrating as in overrating the chastisements of God. It is not uncommon to hear some of God's saints remark, in the very midst of His dealings with them, "I feel it to be no cross at all; I do not feel it an affliction; I am not conscious of any peculiar burden."

Is it not painful to hear such expressions from the lips of a dear child of God? It betrays a lack, so to speak, of spiritual sensitiveness; a deficiency of that tender, acute feeling which ought ever to belong to him who professes to have reposed on Jesus' bosom. Now we solemnly believe that it is the

Lord's holy will that His child should feel the chastisement to be grievous; that the smartings of the rod should be felt. Moses, Jacob, Job, David, Paul, all were made to exclaim, "The Lord has sorely chastened me."

When it is remembered that our chastisements often grow out of our sin; that to subdue some strong indwelling corruption, or to correct for some outward departure, the rod is sent; this should ever humble the soul; this should ever cause the rebuke to be rightly viewed; that were it not for some strong indwelling corruption, or some step taken in departure from God, the affliction would have been withheld; oh how should every stroke of the rod lay the soul in the dust before God! "If God had not seen sin in my heart, and sin in my outward conduct, He would not have dealt thus heavily with me." And where the grievousness of the chastisement is not felt, is there not reason to suspect that the cause of the chastisement has not been discovered and mourned over?

There is the consideration, too, that the stroke comes from the Father who loves us; loves us so well, that if the chastisement were not needed, there would not be a feather's weight laid on the heart of his child. Dear to Him as the apple of His eye, would He inflict those strokes, if there were not an absolute necessity for them? "What! Is it the Father who loves me that now afflicts me? Does this stroke come from His heart? What! Does my Father see all this necessity for this grievous chastening? Does He discover in me so much evil, so much perverseness, so much that He hates and that grieves Him, that this severe discipline is sent?" Oh how does this thought, that the chastisement proceeds from the Father who loves him, impart a keenness to the stroke!

And then there is often something in the very nature of the chastisement itself that causes its grievousness to be felt. The wound may be in the tenderest part; the rebuke may come through some idol of the heart; God may convert some of our choicest blessings into sources of the keenest sorrow. How often does He, in the wisdom and sovereignty of His dealings, adopt this method! Abraham's most valued blessing became the cause of his acutest sorrow. The chastisement may come through the beloved Isaac. The very mercy we clasp to our warm hearts so fondly may be God's voice to us, speaking in the tone of severe yet tender rebuke. Samuel, dear to the heart of Eli, was God's solemn voice to His erring yet beloved servant.

Let no afflicted believer, then, think lightly of his chastisements—it is the Lord's will that he should feel them. They were sent for this purpose. If I did not feel the cross, if I was not conscious of the burden, if the wound were not painful, I should never take it to the mercy-seat, there to seek all needed grace, support, and strength. The burden must first be felt, before it is cast upon the Lord; the chastisement must be felt to be grievous, before the tenderness and sympathy of Jesus will be sought.

There is equal danger of overrating our afflictions. When they are allowed too deeply to absorb us in grief; when they unfit us for duty; keep us from walking in the path God has marked out for us; hold us back from prayer and from the means of grace; when they lead us to think harshly and speak severely of God; then we overrate God's chastisements, and prevent the good they were so kindly sent to convey.

AUGUST 31

"Nevertheless, afterward it yields the peaceable fruit of righteousness unto those who are exercised thereby." Hebrews 12:11

The very wisdom seen in this method of instruction—the sanctified discipline of the covenant, proves its divine origin. Had the believer been left to form his own school, adopt his own plan of instruction, choose his own discipline, and even select his own teacher, how different would it have been from God's plan! We would never have conceived the idea of such a mode of instruction, so unlikely, according to our poor wisdom, to secure the end in view. We would have thought that the smooth path, the sunny path, the joyous path, would the soonest conduct us into the glories of the kingdom of grace; would more fully develop the wisdom, the love, the tenderness, the sympathy of our blessed Lord, and tend more decidedly to our weanedness from the world, our crucifixion of sin, and our spiritual and unreserved devotedness to His service. But "my thoughts are not your thoughts, neither are your ways my ways, says the Lord. For as the heavens are higher than the earth, so are my ways higher than your ways, and my thoughts than your thoughts."

Nor is the believer fully convinced of the wisdom of God's method of procedure until he has been brought, in a measure, through the discipline; until the rod has been removed, the angry waves have subsided, and the tempest cloud has passed away. Then, reviewing the chastisement, minutely examining its nature and its causes; the steps that led to it; the chain of providences in which it formed a most important link; and most of all, surveying the rich covenant blessings it brought with it—the weanedness from the world, the gentleness, the meekness, the patience, the spirituality, the prayerfulness, the love, the joy; he is led to exclaim, "I now see the infinite wisdom and tender mercy of my Father in this affliction. While in the furnace I saw it not; the rising of inbred corruption, unbelief, and hard thoughts of God darkened my view, veiled from the eye of my faith the reason of the discipline; but now I see why and wherefore my covenant God and Father has dealt with me thus: I see the wisdom and adore the love of His merciful procedure."

Other discipline may mortify, but not humble the pride of the heart; it may wound, but not crucify it. Affliction, sanctified by the Spirit of God, lays the soul in the dust; gives it low thoughts of itself. Gifts, attainments, successful labors, the applause of men, all conspire the ruin of a child of God; and, but for the prompt and often severe discipline of an ever-watchful, ever-faithful God, would accomplish their end. But the affliction comes; the needed cross; the required medicine; and in this way are brought out "the peaceable fruits of righteousness;" the most beautiful and precious of which is a humble, lowly view of self.

SEPTEMBER

SEPTEMBER 1

"He restores my soul." Psalm 23:3

THE first point we would look at is the love of the Lord Jesus in restoring a wandering believer. Nothing but infinite, tender, unchanging love could prompt Him to such an act. There is so much of black ingratitude, so much of deep turpitude, in the sin of a believer's departure from the Lord, that, but for the nature of Christ's love, there could be no possible hope of His return. Now this costly love of Christ is principally seen in His taking the first step in the restoring of the soul: the first advance is on the part of the Lord. There is no more self-recovery after, than there is before, conversion; it is entirely the Lord's work. The same state of mind, the same principle, that led to the first step in declension from God, leads on to each successive one; until, but for restraining and restoring grace, the soul would take an everlasting farewell of God. But mark the expression of David—"He restores my soul." Who? He of whom he speaks in the first verse as his Shepherd—"The Lord is my Shepherd." It is the Shepherd that takes the first step in the recovery of the wandering sheep. If there is one aspect in the view of this subject more touching than another, it is this—that such should be the tender, unchanging love of Jesus towards His wandering child, He should take the first step in restoring him. Shall an offended, insulted Sovereign make the first move towards conciliating a rebellious people?—that Sovereign is Jesus: shall an outraged Father seek His wandering child, and restore him to His affections and His house?—that Father is God. Oh, what love is that which leads Jesus in search of His wandering child! love that will not let him quite depart; love that yearns after him, and seeks after him, and follows after him through all his devious way, his intricate wanderings, and far-off departures; love that no unkindness has been able to cool, no forgetfulness has been able to weaken, no distance has been able to destroy!

Not less conspicuous is the power of Jesus in the restoring of the soul. "He restores my soul,"— He, the omnipotent Shepherd. We want omnipotence to bring us back when we have wandered; nothing less can accomplish it. We want the same power that converted to re-convert; the power that created, to re-create us: this power Jesus possesses. It was essential to the full salvation of His Church that He should have it; therefore, when praying to His Father, He says, "As You have given Him power over all flesh,"—why this power?—"that He should give eternal life to as many as You have given Him." It was necessary that He should have power over all flesh, yes, over all the powers leagued against the Church, that He should bring to glory all that were given to Him in the covenant of grace.

Now this power is gloriously exerted in the restoring of the soul. Jesus works in the believer, in order to his recovery. He breaks down the hard heart, arrests the soul in its onward progress of departure, places upon it some powerful check, lays it low, humbles, abases it, and then draws from it the blessed acknowledgment, "Behold, I am vile; but he restores my soul."

SEPTEMBER 2

"Before I was afflicted I went astray: but now have I kept your word." Psalm 119:67

THERE is infinite wisdom in the Lord's restorings. This perfection of Jesus is clearly revealed here: in the way He adopts to restore, we see it. That He should make, as He frequently does, our very afflictions the means of restoration to our souls, unfolds the profound depth of His wisdom. This was David's prayer—"Quicken me according to Your judgments:" and this was his testimony—"Before I was afflicted I went astray, but now have I kept Your word." The season of trial is not infrequently the sanctified season of revival. Who that has passed through the furnace has not found it so? Then the declension of the soul has been discovered—then the hidden cause of that declension has been brought to light—then the spirit has bowed in contrition before the Lord—then grace has been stirred up in the heart, a new sweetness has been given to prayer, a new impulse to faith, a new radiance to hope, and from the flame the gold and the silver have emerged, purified from their tin and dross. But for the production of effects like these, why the many peculiar and heavy afflictions that we sometimes see overtaking the child of God? Do not think that our Heavenly Father takes pleasure in chastening us; do not think that it delights Him to behold the writhings, the throes, and the anguish of a wounded spirit; do not think that He loves to see our tears, and hear our sighs and our groans, under the pressure of keen and crushing trial. No: He is a tender, loving Father; so tender and so loving that not one stroke, nor one cross, nor one trial more does He lay upon us than is absolutely needful for our good—not a single ingredient does He put in our bitter cup, that is not essential to the perfection of the remedy. It is for our profit that He chastens, not for His pleasure; and that often to rouse us from our spiritual sleep, to recover us from our deep declension, and to impart new vigor, healthiness, and growth to His own life in the soul.

SEPTEMBER 3

"My sheep hear my voice, and I know them, and they follow me: and I give unto them eternal life; and they shall never perish, neither shall any man pluck them out of my hand." John 10:27-28

As God-man Mediator, Christ is able to keep His people. As the covenant Head and Preserver of His Church, "it pleased the Father that in Him should all fullness dwell." The Father knew what His beloved family would need. He knew what corruptions would threaten them, what temptations would beguile them, what foes would assail them, what infirmities would encompass them, and what trials would depress them; therefore it pleased Him, it was His own good and gracious pleasure, that in His Son, the Mediator of His beloved people, should all fullness dwell—a fullness of merit, a fullness of pardon, a fullness of righteousness, a fullness of grace, wisdom, and strength, commensurate with the varied, multiplied, and diversified circumstances of His family. It is "all fullness."

As the Mediator, then, of His people, He keeps them in perfect safety night and day. No man, no power, can pluck them out of His hands; He has undertaken their full salvation. To die for their sins, and to rise again for their justification, and yet not to provide for their security while traveling through a world of sin and temptation—to leave them to their own guardianship, an unprotected prey to their own heart's corruptions, the machinations of Satan, and the power of worldly entanglement—would have been but a partial salvation of His people. Opposed by a threefold enemy—Satan and the world in league with their own imperfectly renewed and sanctified hearts, that treacherous foe dwelling within the camp, ever ready to betray the soul into the hands of its enemies—how could a poor weak child of God bear up and breast this powerful phalanx? But He, who was mighty to save, is mighty to keep; in Him provision is made for all the trying, intricate, perilous circumstances in which the believer may be placed. Grace is laid up for the subjection of every inbred corruption—an armor is provided for every assault of the foe; wisdom, strength, consolation, sympathy, kindness—all, all that a poor believing sinner can possibly require, is richly stored in Jesus, the covenant Head of all the fullness of God to His people.

But how is the child of God to avail himself of this provision? The simple but glorious life of faith exhibits itself here. By faith the believer travels up to this rich and ample supply; by faith he takes his nothingness to Christ's all-sufficiency; by faith he takes his unworthiness to Christ's infinite merit; by faith he takes his weakness to Christ's strength, his folly to Christ's wisdom; his fearful heart, his timid spirit, his nervous frame, his doubtful mind, his beclouded evidences, his rebellious will, his painful cross—his peculiar case, of whatever nature it may be—in the way of believing, in the exercise of simple faith, he goes with it to Jesus, and as an empty vessel hangs himself upon that "nail fastened in a sure place," the glorious Eliakim on whom is hung "all the glory of His Father's house, the offspring and the issue, all vessels of small quantity, from the vessels of cups even to all the vessels of flagons." Thus may the weakest believer, the most severely assailed, the most deeply tried, the most painfully tempted, lay his Goliath dead at his feet, by a simple faith's dealing with the fullness that is in Christ Jesus. Oh, how mighty is the believer who, in deep distrust of his own power, casting off from him all spirit of self—dependence, looks simply and fully at Jesus, and goes forth to meet his enemy, only as he is "strong in the strength that is in Christ."

SEPTEMBER 4

"And declared to be the Son of God with power, according to the Spirit of holiness, by the resurrection from the dead." Romans 1:4

THE resurrection of the Redeemer established the truth of His Deity. His miracles had already proved the truth of His Divine Sonship. Yet there remained one other evidence, the crowning one of all—the resurrection. This one evidence would put the final seal upon the truth of His Godhood. If not, then all that He had previously said, predicted, and done would prove but to have been, as His enemies would have asserted, the stratagem of a designing man, attempting to deceive a few devoted but deluded followers. But this return to life on the exact day which He had predicted, breaking from the cold embrace of death and the imprisonment of the grave, by the exercise of His divine power, put to rest forever the question of His Deity, and declared Him to be the Son of God. Oh, how truly and properly Divine did He now appear! August and convincing as had been all the previous attestations of His Godhead—His life one succession of the most astonishing and brilliant achievements of Divine power and goodness—diseases healed, sight restored, demons ejected, the dead raised, tempests hushed, and winds stilled—His death marked by prodigies of terrible and surpassing wonder and sublimity—the earth heaving beneath His feet, the sun darkening above Him, the graves opening around Him—yet never had His Godhead shone forth with such demonstrative power and resplendent glory, as when He broke forth from the tomb, and rose triumphant over hell, death, and the grave. Then did He fulfil this prediction and pledge—"Destroy this temple, and in three days I will raise it again." Receding for a while from communion with life—as if to create a pause in nature, which would awaken the interest and fix the gaze of the intelligent universe upon one stupendous event—He disappeared within the very domain of the "king of terrors," wrapped around Him its shroud and darkness, and laid Himself down, Essential Life locked in the embrace of death, immortality slumbering in the tomb! But he rose again; bursting from the cold embrace, and awaking from the mysterious slumber, He came back to life all radiant, immortal, and divine! Saint!—want you further and stronger evidence that your faith is in no cunningly devised fable? That He to whose guardianship you have committed your precious soul is able to keep it until the morning of our own resurrection-glory? Behold it in the risen life of the incarnate God! He has come up from the grave, to make good all His previous claims to Deity, thus to encourage and confirm your belief in the truth, dignity, and glory of His person, and to assure you that he that "believes in Him shall not be ashamed." Now may you take up the triumphant strain, as it falls from the lips of the departing apostle, prolonging it until another shall catch it from your expiring tongue, "I know whom I have believed, and am persuaded that He is able to keep that which I have committed unto Him against that day."

SEPTEMBER 5

*"Therefore, brethren, we are debtors, not to the
flesh, to live after the flesh." Rom. 8:12*

THAT there should be no ambiguity surrounding so vital a matter, that could misguide the judgment, the apostle most distinctly and emphatically affirms, that the flesh has no valid claim whatever upon the believer; and that, consequently, he is under no obligation to yield compliance with its feigned exactions. We are debtors, but the flesh in not our creditor. What are its demands with which it is incumbent upon us to comply? Do we owe anything to sin, the parent of all our woe? Nothing. To Satan, who plotted our temptation, and accomplished our downfall? Nothing. To the world—ensnaring, deceitful, and ruinous? Nothing. No; to these, the auxiliaries of allies of the flesh, we owe nothing but the deepest hatred and the most determined opposition.

And yet the saints of God are "debtors." To whom? What debtors are they to the Father, for His electing love, for the covenant of grace, for His unspeakable gift, for having blessed us with all spiritual blessings in Christ Jesus! We but imperfectly estimate the debt of love, gratitude, and service which we owe to Him whose mind the Eternal Son came to reveal, whose will He came to do, and whose heart He came to unveil. It was the Father who sent the Son. With Him originated the wondrous expedient of our redemption. He it was who laid all our sins on Jesus. It was His sword of Justice that smote the Shepherd, while His hand of love and protection was laid upon the little ones. We have too much supposed that the Atonement of Jesus was intended to inspire the mercy, rather than to propitiate the justice of God; to awaken in His heart a love that did not previously exist. Thus we have overlooked the source from where originated our salvation, and have lost sight of the truth, that the mediation of Jesus was not the cause, but rather the effect, of God's love to man. "Herein is love, not that we loved God, but that He loved us, and gave His Son to be a propitiation for our sins." Oh, for the spirit to understand, and for grace to feel, and for love to exemplify, our deep obligation to God for the everlasting love that gave us His Son!

Equal debtors are we to the Son. He was the active agent in our redemption. He it was who undertook and accomplished all that our salvation required. He left no path untrodden, no portion of the curse unborne, no sin unatoned, no part of the law uncancelled—nothing for us in the matter of our salvation to do, but simply to believe and be saved. Oh, to raise the eye to Him—strong in faith, beaming with love, moist with contrition, and exclaim, "You have borne my sin, endured my curse, extinguished my hell, secured my heaven. Your Spirit was wounded for me; Your heart bled for me; Your body was bruise for me; for me Your soul was stricken—for me, a sinner, the chief of sinners. I am Your debtor—a debtor to Your dying love, to Your eternal, discriminating mercy. Surely an eternity of love, of service, and of praise, can never repay You what I owe You, You blessed Jesus." Oh, how deep the obligation we are under to Christ!

And not less indebted are we to the Holy Spirit. What do we not owe Him of love and obedience, who awoke the first thrill of life in our soul; who showed to us our guilt, and sealed to us our pardon? What do we not owe Him for leading us to Christ; for dwelling in our hearts; for His healing, sanctifying, comforting, and restoring grace; for His influence, which no ingratitude has quenched; for His patience, which no backsliding has exhausted; for His love, which no sin has annihilated? Yes, we are the Spirit's lasting debtors. We owe Him the intellect He has renewed, the heart He has sanctified, the body He inhabits, every breath of life He has inspired, and every pulse of love He has awakened. Thus are all real believers debtors to the Triune God—debtors to the Father's everlasting love, to the Son's redeeming grace, and to the Spirit's quickening mercy. To the flesh we owe nothing but uncompromising hatred; to Jehovah we owe undivided and supreme affection.

SEPTEMBER 6

"If any man defile the temple of God, him shall God destroy; for the temple of God is holy, which temple you are." 1 Corinthians. 3:17

How holy should the temple of the Spirit be! Reader, are you a temple of God the Holy Spirit? Then dedicate yourself unreservedly to God. You are not your own; your body, your spirit, your family, substance, time, talents, influence, all, all belong to God. He dwells in you; walks in you, rules in you, and calls you His dwelling-place. "Know you not that your body is the temple of the Holy Spirit which is in you?" Then, what a separation should there be between you and the world that lies in wickedness! How should you guard against every unnecessary entanglement with it! how cautious and prayerful, lest, by contracting an unholy alliance with it in any form or degree, you should defile the temple of God, "which temple you are"! Oh, what heavenly wisdom, and holy circumspection, and ceaseless prayer, do you need, that you might walk with unspotted garments—that no rival should enter your heart—that no lofty views of self, no spirit of worldly conformity, no temporizing policy, no known sin, no creature idolatry should enter there!—that, like the heavenly temple, nothing that defiles, neither whatever works abomination, should be cherished or entertained in the abode and in the presence of the Holy Spirit! for "what agreement has the temple of God with idols? for you are the temple of the living God; as God has said, I will dwell in them, and walk in them: and I will be their God, and they shall be my people." Reader, whose temple are you? Solemn question! Does God or Satan dwell in you? Christ or Belial? light or darkness? Either the one or the other has, at this moment, entire possession. You cannot serve two contrary masters; you cannot entertain two opposite guests. You are living either for God or for Satan. You are traveling either to heaven or to hell. Which? On your bended knees before God, decide; and may the Lord the Spirit renew you by His grace, and if renewed, make you "a vessel unto honor, sanctified and meet for the Master's use, and prepared unto every good work."

SEPTEMBER 7

"Have you received the Holy Spirit since you believed?"

WHAT the Church of God needs as a Church we equally need as individual Christians—the deeper baptism of the Holy Spirit. Reader, why is it that you are not more settled in the truth— your feet more firm upon the Rock? Why are you not more rejoicing in Christ Jesus, the pardoning blood more sensibly applied to the conscience, the seal of adoption more deeply impressed upon your heart, "Abba, Father" more frequently, and with stronger, sweeter accent, on your lips? Why are you, perhaps, so yielding in temptation, so irresolute in purpose, so feeble in action, so vacillating in pursuit, so faint in the day of adversity? Why is the glory of Jesus so dimly seen, His preciousness so little felt, His love so imperfectly experienced? Why is there so little close, secret transaction between God and your soul?—so little searching of heart, confession of sin, dealing with the atoning blood? Why does the conscience so much lack tenderness, and the heart brokenness, and the spirit contrition? And why is the throne of grace so seldom resorted to, and prayer itself felt to be so much a duty, and so little a privilege, and, when engaged in, so faintly characterized with the humble brokenness of a penitent sinner, the filial boldness of an adopted child, the rich anointing of a royal priest? Ah! let the small measure in which you have received the Holy Spirit's influence supply the answer. "Have you received the Holy Spirit since you believed?"—have you received Him as a Witness, as a Sealer, as a Teacher, as an Indweller, as a Comforter, as the Spirit of adoption? But, rather, have you not forgotten that your Lord was alive, and upon the throne exalted, to give you the Holy Spirit, and that more readily than a father is to give good gifts to his child? That He is prepared now to throw back the windows of heaven, and pour down upon you such a blessing as shall confirm your faith, resolve your doubts, annihilate your fears, arm you for the fight, strengthen you for the trial, give you an unclouded view of your acceptance in the Beloved, and assure you that your "name is written among the living in Jerusalem"? Then, as you value the light of God's countenance, as you desire to grow in a knowledge of Christ, as you long to be more "steadfast, unmoveable, always abounding in the work of the Lord," oh, seek to enjoy, in a larger degree, the presence, the love, the anointing of the Holy Spirit. Christ has gone up on high to give to you this invaluable blessing, and says for your encouragement, "Hitherto have you asked nothing in my name: ask, and you shall receive, that your joy may be full."

SEPTEMBER 8

"But the natural man receives not the things of the Spirit of God: for they are foolishness unto him: neither can he know them, because they are spiritually discerned." 1 Corinthians 2:14

THE mere presentation of truth to the unrenewed mind, either in the form of threatening, or promise, or motive, can never produce any saving or sanctifying effect. The soul of man, in its unrenewed state, is represented as spiritually dead; insensible to all holy, spiritual motion. Now, upon such a mind what impression is to be produced by the mere holding up of truth before its eye? What life, what emotion, what effect will be accomplished?

As well might we spread out the pictured canvas before the glazed eye of a corpse, and expect that by the beauty of the design, the brilliancy of the coloring, and the genius of the execution, we would animate the body with life, heave the bosom with emotion, and cause the eye to swim with delight, as to look for similar moral effects to result from the mere holding up to view divine truth before a carnal mind, "dead in trespasses and sins." And yet there are those who maintain the doctrine, that divine truth, unaccompanied by any extraneous power, can effect all these wonders! Against such a theory we would simply place one passage from the sacred word: "Except a man be born again, he cannot see the kingdom of God." The sacred word, inspired though it be, is but a dead letter, unclothed with the life-giving power of the Holy Spirit. Awful as are the truths it unfolds, solemn as are the revelations it discloses, touching as are the scenes it portrays, and persuasive as are the motives it supplies, yet, when left to its own unaided operation, divine truth is utterly impotent to the production of spiritual life, love, and holiness in the soul of man. Its influence must necessarily be passive, possessing, as it does, no actual power of its own, and depending upon a divine influence extraneous from itself, to render its teaching efficacious. The three thousand who were converted on the day of Pentecost were doubtless awakened under one sermon, and some would declare it was the power of the truth which wrought those wonders of grace. With this we perfectly agree, only adding, that it was truth in the mighty hand of God which pricked them to the heart, and wrung from them the cry, "Men and brethren, what shall we do?" The Eternal Spirit was the efficient cause, and the preached truth but the instrument employed to produce the effect; but for His accompanying and effectual power, they would, as multitudes do now, have turned their backs upon the sermon of Peter, though it was full of Christ crucified, deriding the truth, and rejecting the Savior of whom it spoke. But it pleased God, in the sovereignty of His will, to call them by His grace, and this He did by the effectual, omnipotent power of the Holy Spirit, through the instrumentality of a preached gospel.

Thus, then, we plead for a personal experimental acquaintance with, and reception of, the truth, before it can produce anything like holiness in the soul. That it has found an entrance to the judgment merely will not do; advancing not further—arresting not the will, touching not the heart, renewing not the whole soul—it can never erect the empire of holiness in man; the reign of sanctification cannot have commenced. The mental eye may be clear, the moral eye closed; the mind all light, the heart all dark; the creed orthodox, and the whole life a variance with the creed. Such is the discordant effect of divine truth, simply settled in the human understanding, unaccompanied by the power of the Holy Spirit in the heart. But let a man receive the truth in the his heart by the power of God Himself; let it enter there, disarming and dethroning the strong man; let Jesus enter, and the Holy Spirit take possession, renewing, sealing, and sanctifying the soul; and then we may look for the "fruits of holiness, which are unto eternal life."

SEPTEMBER 9

"Testifying both to the Jews, and also to the Greeks, repentance toward God, and faith toward our Lord Jesus Christ." Acts 20:21

THERE is an order, as well as a harmony, in the operations of the Spirit, which it is highly important should be observed. An ignorance or an oversight of this has led to great and fatal perversions of the gospel. All the self-righteousness of the Pharisee, and all the self-devotion of the deluded disciple of the Papal superstition, have their origin here. Now, the order of the Spirit is this—regeneration of the heart first—then its sanctification. Reverse this, and we derange every part of His work, and, as far as our individual benefit extends, render it entirely useless. Sanctification is not the first and immediate duty of an unrenewed person. Indeed, it were utterly impossible that it should be so. Sanctification has its commencement and its daily growth in a principle of life implanted in the soul by the Eternal Spirit; and to look for holiness in an individual still dead in sins is to look for fruit where no seed was sown—for the actings of life where no vitality exists—it is to expect, in the language of our Lord, to "gather grapes from thorns, and figs from thistles." The first and imperious duty of an unrenewed man is to prostrate himself in deep abasement and true repentance before God; the lofty look must be brought low, the rebellious will must be humbled; and in the posture of one overwhelmed with a sense of guilt. He is to look by faith to a crucified Savior, and draw from thence life, pardon, and acceptance. True, most solemnly true it is, that "without holiness no man shall see the Lord;" yet all attempts towards the attainment of holiness, before "repentance towards God, and faith in the Lord Jesus Christ," will but disappoint the soul that looks for it.

This work of renewal done, sanctification is comparatively an easy and a delightful employ. Motives and exhortations to a life of holiness now find a ready response in the heart, already the temple of the Holy Spirit. The "incorruptible seed" there sown germinates into the plant, blossoms and ripens into the fruits of holiness, and the "living water" there welled springs up, and pours forth its stream of life and purity, adorning and fertilizing the garden of the Lord. Let us, then, be careful how we disturb the arrangement and reverse the order of the blessed Spirit in His work. Great errors have in consequence arisen, and souls have gone into eternity fearfully and fatally deceived. Especially cautious should they be in this matter, who are appointed to the office of spiritual instruction—to whose care immortal souls are intrusted— lest, in a matter involving interests so precious and so lasting, any should pass from beneath their teaching into eternity ignorant of the one a true method of salvation.

SEPTEMBER 10

"For my people have committed two evils; they have forsaken
me, the fountain of living waters, and hewed them out cisterns,
broken cisterns, that can hold no water." Jeremiah 2:13

GOD speaks of it as involving two evils—the evil of forsaking Him, and the evil of substituting a false object of happiness for Him. Dear reader, the true painfulness of this subject consists not in the sorrow which your heart may have felt in seeing your cisterns broken. Ah no! the true agony should be, that you have, in your wanderings and creature idolatry, sinned, deeply sinned, against the Lord your God. This, and not your loss, ought to lay you low before Him. This, and not your broken scheme of earthly happiness, ought to fill you with the bitterness of sorrow, and clothe you with the drapery of woe. Oh! to have turned your back upon such a God, upon such a Father, upon such a Friend, and to have supposed that even a universe of creatures could have made you happy without Him, ought to bring you to His feet exclaiming, "God be merciful to me, the chief of sinners!" Is it no sin to have said to God, as you have a thousand times over—"I prefer myself to You—my family to You—my estate to You—my pleasure to You—my honor to You"? Is it no sin to have taken the gifts with which He endowed you, or the wealth with which He intrusted you, and forming them into a golden image, to have fallen down before it, exclaiming, "This is your god, O my soul?" Oh yes, it is a sin, the guilt and the greatness of which no language can describe. And is it no sin, O believer in Jesus, to have turned away, in your unbelief and inconstancy, from the glorious redemption which the Lord has obtained for you at such a price, and to have sought the assurance and the joy of your salvation from other sources than it? What! is not the atoning work of Jesus sufficient to give your believing soul solid rest, and peace, and hope, but that you should have turned your eye from Him, and have sought it in the polluted and broken cistern of yourself? Oh, slight not the precious blood, the glorious righteousness, the infinite fullness, and the tender love of Jesus. No, you dishonor this precious Jesus Himself! Shall He have wrought such an obedience, shall He have made such an atonement, shall He have died such a death, shall He have risen from the grave and have ascended on high, all to secure your full salvation and certain glory, and will you derive the evidence and the comfort of your acceptance from any other than this one precious source—"looking unto Jesus!" Look away, then, from everything to Jesus. No matter what you are, look away from yourself—to Jesus. The more vile, the more empty, the more unworthy, the greater reason and the stronger argument why you should look entirely off yourself—to Jesus. His atoning work is finished by Him, and is sealed by the Father. It is impossible that God can reject you, entirely renouncing yourself and fleeing into Christ. Coming to Him in the name of Jesus, God cannot deny you. He has pledged Himself that whatever is asked in that name He will grant. Take Him at His word!

Ask Him for a sense of His reconciled love—ask Him for the Spirit of adoption—ask Him for a filial, loving, and obedient heart—ask Him for a meek, lowly, and submissive will. Yes, pour out your heart before Him: God waits to grant your utmost desire breathed out to Him in the name of Jesus. He has given you His beloved Son—oh largess worthy of a God!—oh gift of gifts, priceless and precious beyond all thought!—what inferior blessing will He then, withhold?

SEPTEMBER 11

*"There is therefore now no condemnation to
those who are in Christ Jesus." Romans 8:1*

HOW strong the consolation flowing from this truth to the believer
in Jesus! No condemnation is the ground of all comfort to the suffering
Christian. What a mighty breakwater is this condition to the rolling surge
of sorrow, which else might flow in upon and immerse the soul! Let it be
your aim to improve it on every occasion of suffering and trial. God may
afflict, but He will never condemn you. Chastisements are not judgments;
afflictions are not condemnations. Sickness, bereavement, and low estate,
based upon a condition of non-condemnation, you can welcome and
patiently bear, since they are not the forecastings of a coming storm, but
the distillings of a mercy-cloud sailing athwart the azure sky of a soul in
Christ. The fiery trials which purify our faith have not a spark in them of
that "unquenchable fire" that will consume the condemned hereafter. Oh,
what are crosses and the discomforts of this present world, if at last we are
kept out of hell! and oh, what are the riches, and honors, and comforts of
this life, if at last we are shut out of heaven! At the bottom of that cup of
sinful pleasure which sparkles in the worldling's hand, and which with such
zest and glee he quaffs, there lies eternal condemnation; the death-worm
feeds at the root of all his good. But at the bottom of this cup of sorrow,
now trembling and dark in the hand of the suffering Christian, bitter and
forbidding as it is, there is no condemnation; eternal glory is at the root of
all his evil. And in this will you not rejoice? It is not only your holy duty,
but it is your high privilege to rejoice. Your whole life not only may be, but
ought to be, a sweetly-tuned psalm, a continual anthem of thanksgiving
and praise, pouring forth its swelling notes to the God of your salvation;
since beyond the cloudy scene of your present pilgrimage there unveils
the light and bliss of celestial glory, on whose portal you read as you pass
within—No Condemnation. Unless, then, you either distrust or disparage
this, your joyous condition and blessed hope, you must, in the gloomiest
hour, and from the innermost depths of your soul, exultingly exclaim—"He
is near that justifies me; who will contend with me? Let us stand together.
Who is mine adversary? let him come near to me. Behold, the Lord God
will help me! who is he that shall condemn me?"

SEPTEMBER 12

"And if children, then heirs; heirs of God." Romans 7:17

NOT only are they begotten by God as His children, and by a sovereign act of His most free mercy have become the heirs of an inheritance; but, subjectively, they are made the heirs of Himself. "Heirs of God." Not only are all things in the covenant theirs, but the God of the covenant is theirs. This is their greatest mercy. "I am your part and your inheritance" are His words, addressed to all His spiritual Levites. Not only are they put in possession of all that God has—a boundless wealth—but they are in present possession of all that God is—an infinite portion. And what an immense truth is this, "I will be their God, and they shall be my people"! Take out this truth from the covenant of grace, were it possible, and what remains? It is the chief wealth and the great glory of that covenant, that God is our God. This it is that gives substance to its blessings, and security to its foundation. So long as faith can retain its hold upon the God of the covenant, as our God, it can repose with perfect security in expectation of the full bestowment of all the rest. Here lies our vast, infinite, and incomputable wealth. What constitutes the abject poverty of an ungodly man? His being without God in the world. Be you, my reader, rich or poor, high or low in this world, without God, you are undone to all eternity. It is but of trivial moment whether you pass in rags and lowliness, or move in ermine and pomp, to the torments of the lost; those torments will be your changeless inheritance, living and dying without God, and without Christ, and without hope. But contrast this with the state of the poorest child of God. The universe is not only his—"for all things are yours"—but the God of the universe is his: "The Lord is my portion, says my soul, therefore will I hope in Him." We have a deathless interest in every perfection of the Divine nature. Is it Wisdom? it counsels us. Is it Power? it shields us. Is it Love? it soothes us. Is it Mercy? it upholds us. Is it truth? it cleaves to us. "As the mountains are round about Jerusalem, so the Lord is round about His people, from henceforth, even for evermore." What more can we ask than this? If God be ours, we possess the substance and the security of every other blessing. He would bring us to an absolute trust in an absolute God. Winning us to an entire relinquishment of all expectation from any other source, He would allure us to His feet with the language of the Church breathing from our lips—"Behold, we come unto You, for You are the Lord our God. Truly in vain is salvation hoped for from the hills, and from the multitude of mountains: truly in the Lord our God is the salvation of Israel." It is in the heart of our God to give us the chief and the best. Had there been a greater, a better, a sweeter, and a more satisfying portion than Himself, then that portion had been ours. But since there is not, nor can be, a greater than He, the love, the everlasting, changeless love that He bears to us constrains Him to give Himself as our God, our portion, our all. And have we not experienced Him to be God all-sufficient? Have we ever found a want or a lack in Him? May He not justly challenge us, and ask, "Have I been a wilderness unto Israel? a land of darkness?" Oh no! God is all-sufficient, and no arid wilderness, no dreary land, have we experienced Him to be. There is in Him an all-sufficiency of love to comfort us; an all-sufficiency of strength to uphold us; an all-sufficiency of power to protect us; and all-sufficiency of good to satisfy us; an all-sufficiency of wisdom to guide us; an all-sufficiency of glory to reward us; and an all-sufficiency of bliss to make us happy here, and happy to all eternity. Such is the inheritance to which, as children of God, we are the heirs.

SEPTEMBER 13

"Behold what manner of love the Father has bestowed upon us, that we should be called the sons of God: therefore the world knows us not, because it knew him not." 1 John 3:1

IT is not strange that the fact of his adoption should meet with much misgiving in the Christian's mind, seeing that it is a truth so spiritual, flows from a source so concealed, and has its seat in the profound recesses of the soul. The very stupendousness of the relationship staggers our belief. To be fully assured of our divine adoption demands other than the testimony either of our own feelings, or the opinion of men. Our feelings—sometimes excited and visionary—may mislead; the opinion of others—often fond and partial—may deceive us. The grand, the divine, and only safe testimony is "the Spirit itself bears witness with our spirit." There exists a strong combination of evil, tending to shake the Christian's confidence in the belief of his sonship. Satan is ever on the watch to insinuate the doubt. He tried the experiment with our Lord: "If You be the Son of God." In no instance would it appear that he actually denied the truth of Christ's Divine Sonship; the utmost that his temerity permitted was the suggestion to the mind of a doubt; leaving it there to its own working. Our blessed Lord thus assailed, it is no marvel that His disciples should be exposed to a like assault. The world, too, presumes to call it in question. "The world knows us not, because it knew Him not." Ignorant of the Divine Original, how can it recognize the Divine lineaments in the faint and imperfect copy? It has no vocabulary by which it can decipher the "new name written in the white stone." The sons of God are in the midst of a crooked and perverse nation, illumining it with their light, and preserving it by their grace, yet disguised from its knowledge, and hidden from its view. But the strongest doubts touching the validity of his adoption are those engender in the believer's own mind. Oh! there is much there to generate and foster the painful misgiving. We have said that the very greatness of the favor, the stupendousness of the relationship, startles the mind, and staggers our faith. "What! to be a child of God! God my Father! can I be the subject of a change so great, of a relationship so exalted? Who am I, O Lord God, and what is my house, that You should exalt me to be a King's son? Is this the manner of men, O Lord God?" And then, there crowd upon the believer's mind thoughts of his own sinfulness and unworthiness of so distinguished a blessing. "Can it be? with such a depravity of heart, such carnality of mind, such rebellion of will, such a propensity to evil each moment, and in everything such backslidings and flaws, does there yet exist within me a nature that links me with the Divine? It seems impossible!" And when to all this are added the varied dispensations of his Heavenly Father, often wearing a rough garb, assuming an aspect somber, threatening, and crushing, oh, it is no marvel that, staggered by a discipline so severe, the fact of God's love to him, and of his close and tender relation to God, should sometimes be a matter of painful doubt; that thus he should reason—"If His child, reposing in His heart, and sealed upon His arm, why is it thus? Would He not have spared me this heavy stroke? Would not this cup have passed my lips? Would He have asked me to slay my Isaac, to resign my Benjamin? All these things are against me." And thus are the children of God constantly tempted to question the fact of their adoption.

SEPTEMBER 14

*"The Spirit itself bears witness with our spirit, that
we are the children of God." Romans 8:16*

AS to the great truth thus witnessed to by the Spirit, we are not to
suppose that the testimony is intended to make the fact itself more sure;
but simply to confirm our own minds in the comfortable assurance of it.
Our actual adoption cannot be more certain than it is. It is secured to us
by the predestinating love of God and the everlasting covenant of grace;
is confirmed by our union with the Lord Jesus, and is sealed by the Holy
Spirit of promise, "Having predestinated us unto the adoption of children
by Jesus Christ to Himself, according to the good pleasure of His will." It
is not for the benefit of our fellow-creatures, still less for the satisfaction
of God Himself, but for the assurance and comfort of our own hearts,
that the Spirit bears witness with our spirits that we are the children of
God. The testimony is for the confirmation of our own faith, and the
consolation of our own hearts.

But the question arises, What is the mode of His testimony? In
attempting to supply an answer, we must acknowledge that we have no
certain data to guide us. Sufficient light, however, beams from His work
in general, to assist us in forming an intelligent and correct idea of His
operations. How, then, may we suppose the Spirit witnesses with our spirit?
Not by visions and voices; not by heats and fancies; nor by any direct
inspiration, or new revelation of truth. Far different from this is the mode
of His testimony. We may gather from the measure of light vouchsafed,
that He first implants within the soul the germ of spiritual life, which,
beneath His culture, produces the "fruits of love, joy, peace, long-suffering,
gentleness, goodness, faith, meekness, temperance." From these we are left
to draw the rational deduction of our adoption. If, for example, a child
of God, with all lowliness of spirit, and after much prayerful inquiry,
discover that, more or less, some of these effects of the Spirit's operation are
developed in his experience, then it is no presumption in that individual,
honestly and humbly to conclude that he is a child of God. This is the
Spirit's witness, and he cannot gainsay it without wilful blindness, nor reject
it without positive sin. The breathing of the renewed heart after holiness
supplies another illustration of the mode of the Spirit's testimony. The

panting after Divine conformity is the Spirit's inspiration. Where, therefore, it exists, the deduction is that the individual is a child of God. Thus, be begetting in us the Divine nature, by producing in us spiritual fruits, and by breathing in our souls a desire for holiness, the Spirit conducts us to the rational conclusion that we are born of God. By shedding abroad God's love in the soul—by sprinkling the conscience with the atoning blood—by endearing the Savior to our hearts—by leading us more simply to rest in His finished work, yes, to rest in Himself—by creating and increasing love to the members of the one family, and fellowship with whatever is holy, heavenly, and useful, He thus testifies to our Divine relationship.

SEPTEMBER 15

"That by two immutable things, in which it was impossible for God to lie, we might have a strong consolation, who have fled for refuge to lay hold upon the hope set before us: which hope we have as an anchor of the soul, both sure and steadfast, and which enters into that within the veil; where the forerunner is for us entered, even Jesus." Hebrews 6:17-19

THE hope of heaven fostered by an unrenewed mind is baseless and illusory. There exists not a single element of goodness in its nature. It is the conception of a mind at enmity with God. It is the delusion of a heart in covenant with death, and in agreement with hell. It is the treacherous beacon that decoys the too confiding but deluded voyager to the rock-bound shore. Unscriptural, unreal, and baseless, it must eventually cover its possessor with shame and confusion of face. But not such is the believer's hope. Begotten with his second nature—the in—breathing of the Spirit of God—an element of renewed mind, and based upon the atonement of the Savior, it must be essentially a good hope. Cleansed from moral impurity, not in the laver of baptism, but with the blood of Christ; justified, not by the ritual of Moses, but by the righteousness of the incarnate God; sanctified, not by sacramental grace, falsely so called, but by the in-being of the Holy Spirit—the believer's hope of heaven is as well founded as the throne of the Eternal. Moreover it is "a good hope through grace." The first and the last lesson we learn in our Christian course is, that "by grace we are saved." Lord! do You require of me one thought of stainless purity, one throb of perfect love, one deed of unsullied holiness, upon which shall hinge my everlasting happiness?

Then am I lost forever! But since You have provided a righteousness that justifies me from all things, that frees me from all condemnation—and since this righteousness is Your free, unpurchased gift, the bestowment of sovereign grace—I clasp to my trembling yet believing heart the joyous hope this truth inspires. It is a blessed hope. "Looking for that blessed hope." Its object is most blessed. The heaven it compasses is that blissful place where the holy ones who have fled from our embrace are reposing in the bosom of the Savior. They are the blessed dead. The day of their death was to them better than the day of their birth. The one was the introduction to all sorrow, the other is a translation to all joy. Blessed hope! the hope of being forever with the Lord. No more to grieve the Spirit that so often and so soothingly comforted our hearts; no more to wound the gentle bosom that so often pillowed our head. No more to journey in darkness, nor bend as a bruised reed before each blast of temptation. To be a pillar in the temple of God, to go no more out forever. And what a sanctifying hope is it! This, to the spiritual mind, is its most acceptable and elevating feature. "Every man that has this hope in him purifies himself even as He is pure." It detaches from earth, and allures to heaven. Never does it glow more brightly in the soul, nor kindle around the path a luster more heavenly, than when it strengthens in the believer a growing conformity of character to that heaven towards which it soars. It is, in a word, a sure hope. Shall the worm undermine it? shall the tempest shake it? shall the waters extinguish it? Never. It saves us. It keeps, preserves, and sustains us amid the perils and depressions of our earthly pilgrimage. And having borne us through the flood, it will not fail us when the last surge lands us upon the shore of eternity.

SEPTEMBER 16

"The body is dead because of sin." Romans 8:10

WHAT body is referred to here? Certainly not, as some have supposed, the body of sin. Who can with truth affirm of it that it is dead? The individual who claims as his attainment a state of sinless perfection, an entire victory over the evil propensities and actings of his fallen nature, has yet to learn the alphabet of experimental Christianity. Pride is the baneful root, and a fall is often the fatal consequence of such an error. Oh no! the body of sin yet lives, and dies not but with death itself. We part not with innate and indwelling sin but with the parting breath of life, and then we part with it forever. But it is the natural body to which the apostle refers. And what an affecting fact is this! Redeemed by the sacrifice, and inhabited by the Spirit of Christ, though it be, yet this material fabric, this body of our humiliation, tends to disease, decay, and death; and, sooner or later, wrapped in its shroud, must make its home in the grave, and mingle once more with its kindred dust. "The body is dead because of sin." Our redemption by Christ exempts us not from the conflict and the victory of the last enemy. We must confront the grim foe, must succumb to his dread power, and wear his pale trophies upon our brow. We must die—are dying men—because of sin. "Death has passed upon all men, for that all have sinned." And this law remains unrepealed, though Christ has delivered us from the curse. From this humiliating necessity of our nature even the non-condemned find no avenue of escape; from this terrible conflict, no retreat. One event happens to the wicked and the righteous—they both leave the world by the same dismal process of dissolution. But the character of death is essentially changed; and herein lies the great difference. In the one case death is armed with all its terrors; in the other, it is invested with all its charms—for death has an indescribable charm to the believer in Jesus. Christ did not die to exempt us from the process of death; but He died to exempt us from the sting of death. If, because of original and indwelling sin in the regenerate, they must taste of death; yet, because of pardoned sin in the regenerate, the "bitterness of death is passed." If, because there exists a virus in the body, the body must dissolve; yet, because there exists an infallible antidote, the redeemed soul does not see death as it passes through the gloomy portal, and enters into its own life, light, and immortality. How changed the character of death! If the body of the redeemed is under the sentence, and has within it the seeds of death, and must be destroyed, yet that death is to him the epoch of glory. It is then that the life within germinates and expands; it is then that he really begins to live. His death is the birthday of his immortality. Thus, in the inventory of the covenant, death ranks among the chief of its blessings, and becomes a covenant mercy. "Death is gain." "What!" exclaims the astonished believer, "death a blessing—a covenant blessing! I have been used to contemplate it as my direst curse, to dread it as my greatest foe." Yes; if death is the sad necessity, it is also the precious privilege of our being. In the case of those who are in Christ Jesus, it is not the execution of a judicial sentence, but the realization of a covenant mercy. And, as the Christian marks the symptoms of his approaching and inevitable dissolution—watching the slow but unmistakable advances of the fell destroyer—he can exclaim, as he realizes that there is now no condemnation to those who are in Christ Jesus—"Come, Death, shake hands; I'll kiss your bands— 'It is happiness for me to die. What! do you think that I will shrink?—I go to immortality."

"Because of sin." Ah! it is this truth whose dark shadow flits across the brightness of the Christian's condition. To what are all our ailments, calamities, and sorrows traceable, but to sin? And why do we die? "Because of sin." The immediate and proximate causes of death are but secondary agents. Had we not transgressed, we then had not died. Deathlessness would have been our natural and inalienable birthright. And were we more spiritually-minded than we are, while we looked onward with steady faith to a signal and glorious triumph over the King of Terrors, we should blend with the bright anticipation of the coming victory, the humbling conviction that we have sinned, and that therefore "the body is dead.

SEPTEMBER 17

"This is life eternal, that they might know you, the only true God, and Jesus Christ, whom you have sent." John 17:3

WHEN does this acquaintance between God and man commence? It commences in reconciliation—it commences at the time of man's peace with God. I can form no acquaintance with an individual against whom my heart cherishes deep, inveterate, and deadly enmity; my very hatred, my very dislike to that individual prevents me from studying his character, from analyzing his heart, and from knowing what are his feelings towards me. But bring me into a state of amity with that individual—remove my enmity, take away my dislike, propitiate his feelings towards me, and then I am in a position for studying and becoming acquainted with his character. The Holy Spirit does this in man; He takes away the enmity of the sinner's heart, humbles his spirit, and bows it in penitence; constrains the sinner to lay down the weapons of his hostility against God—brings him to see that the God against whom he has been battling and fighting all his life is a God of love, a God who draws sinners to Himself, a God who is reconciled in Jesus Christ. That soul, disarmed of its rebellion and enmity, is now brought into a position for the study of God's character. Looking at God now, not through the law, but through the gospel, not in creation, but in Christ, he is in a position for becoming acquainted with God. And oh what an acquaintance he now forms! All his dark and shadowy conceptions vanish away; all his distorted views are rectified; and the God that he thought was a God so hateful, a God whose law was so repulsive, a God who was so harsh and tyrannical, he sees now to be a God of infinite mercy and love in Jesus Christ: now he becomes acquainted with Him as a sin—pardoning God, blotting out the utmost remnant of his transgressions; he becomes acquainted with Him as a God reconciled in Christ, and therefore a Father pacified towards him. Oh! what a discovery is made to him of that God, with whom before his soul lived in the darkest and deepest alienation! Thus he becomes acquainted with God, when his heart becomes reconciled to God. A closer and more simple view of Jesus, a daily study of Jesus, must deepen my acquaintance with God. As I know more of the heart of Christ, I know more of the heart of the Father; as I know more of the love of the Savior, I know more of the love of Him who gave me that Savior; as I know more of His travail of soul, to work out my redemption—as I know more of the tears of blood He shed—as I know more of the groans of agony He breathed—as I know more of the convulsions through which He passed—as I know more of the death-throes of the spotless soul of His—I know more of the heart of God, more of the character of God, and more of the love of God. Want you to see more of the glory of God? See it in the face of Jesus. Learn it in the "brightness of the Father's glory," learn it in "the express image of His person," as it stands revealed to you in the person and in the work of Jesus Christ.

SEPTEMBER 18

"But we all with open face, beholding as in a glass the glory of the Lord, are changed into the same image from glory to glory, even as by the Spirit of the Lord." 2 Corinthians 3:18

Is your knowledge of God a transforming knowledge? Have you so become acquainted with God as to receive the impress (as it were) of what God is?—for a true knowledge of God is a transforming knowledge. As I look upon the glory of God I am changed into that glory; and as my acquaintance with God deepens, I become more like God. There is a transfer of God's moral image to my soul. Is your knowledge then transforming? Does your acquaintance with God make you more like God—more holy, more divine, more heavenly, more spiritual? Does it prompt you to pant after conformity to God's mind, desiring in all things to walk so as to please God, and to have, as it were, a transfer of the nature of God to your soul? Examine, therefore, your professed acquaintance with God, and see whether it is that acquaintance which will bring you to heaven, and will go on increasing through the countless ages of eternity.

And I would say to God's saints—trace the cause of much of our uneven walking, of our little holiness, and, consequently, of our little happiness, to our imperfect acquaintance with what God is. Did I know more of what God is to me in Christ—how He loves me, what a deep interest He takes in all my concerns—did I know that He never withdraws His eye from me for one moment, that His heart of love never grows cold—oh! did I but know this, would I not walk more as one acquainted with God? Would I not desire to consult Him in all that interests me, to acknowledge Him in all my ways, to look up to Him in all things, and to deal with Him in all matters? Would I not desire to be more like Him, more holy, more divine, more Christ-like? Yes, beloved; it is because we know Him so little, that we walk so much in uneven ways. We consult man rather than God; we flee to the asylum of a creature-bosom, rather than to the bosom of the Father; we go to the sympathy of man, rather than to the sympathy of God in Christ, because we are so imperfectly acquainted with God. But did I know more clearly what God is to me in the Son of His love, I should say—I have not a trial but I may take that trial to my Father; I am not in a perplexity but I may go to God for counsel; I am in no difficulty, I have no want, but it is my privilege to spread it before my Father—to unveil my heart of sin, my heart of wretchedness, my heart of poverty, to Him who has unveiled His heart of love, His heart of grace, His heart of tenderness to me in Christ. As I become more acquainted with God, my character and my Christian walk will be more even, more circumspect, more holy, and consequently more happy.

SEPTEMBER 19

"And Jonathan Saul's son arose, and went to David into the wood, and strengthened his hand in God." 1 Samuel 23:16

THE Lord's vineyard is a large one, and the departments of labor are many and varied. And if, in this world of activity—where so many agencies, evil and good, are at work, where so many influences, for weal and for woe, are in constant and untiring operation—there is one class which demands our warmest interest, our most fervent prayers, and our most affectionate sympathy and support, it is those who are actively and devotedly employed in the kingdom and service of Jesus. It is needless to enumerate or specify them: those who are preaching Christ's gospel; those who are teaching the little ones; those who are instructing and training the young about to enter upon life; those who disseminate God's holy word, and promote religious literature; those who visit the sick and the dying, the stranger, and the prisoner, and especial and strong claims upon our Christian sympathy. A little expression of kind interest in their self—denying labors, oh, how often has it inspirited, cheered, and encouraged them! What a privilege to repair to the scene of their toil, anxiety, and discouragement, and by a visit, a word, a donation, "strengthen their hand in God"—that hand often so feeble, tremulous, and ready to fall. And is there not a lamentable lack of sympathy for the Christian missionary? Who so much demands, and who so worthy of the support, the prayers, the sympathy of the Christian Church, as those who are her messengers and almoners to the far distant heathen? How much do they need that by our petitions, our zealous cooperation, and our consecrated substance, we strengthen their hand in God! Let us, then, cheer all Christ's true laborers, remembering that thus, indirectly, we are urging forward His truth and kingdom in the world. Nor let us withhold our sympathy from any case of sorrow, Christian effort, or individual labor, on the plea that its expression and its source are feeble, uncostly, and obscure. Ah! from many a darkened chamber, from many a sleepless pillow, from many a couch of languor, there has gone up the secret, silent, but fervent and believing wrestle with

the Angel of the covenant in behalf of some Christian laborer, or some
Christian enterprise, that has brought down from heaven the grace and
might, and smile of Omnipotence, to support, strengthen, and bless. Thus
sympathy has its home in every holy heart and in every lowly dwelling;
and there is no individual, however straitened by poverty, or veiled by
obscurity, oppressed by trial, or enfeebled by sickness, form the altar of
whose heart there my not ascent the sweetest, holiest, most precious and
powerful of all human offerings—the offering and the incense of a true
and prayerful sympathy.

SEPTEMBER 20

*"Then was Jesus led up of the Spirit into the wilderness
to be tempted of the devil." Matthew 4:1*

IMAGINE yourself, my Christian reader, shut in for a single day with
one of the vilest and most degraded of our species. During that period,
his whole conversation shall be an attempt to tamper with your allegiance
to Christ, to undermine your principles, to pollute your mind, to infuse
blasphemous thoughts, to wound your conscience, and destroy your peace.
What mental suffering, what grief, what torture would your soul endure in
the period of time! Yet all this, and infinitely more, did Jesus pass through.
For forty days and nights was He enclosed in the wilderness with Satan.
Never were the assaults of the prince of darkness more fearful, never were
his fiery darts more surely aimed and powerfully winged, and never had
so shining a mark presented itself as the object of his attack as now.

Our Lord's exposure to temptation, and His consequent capability of
yielding to its solicitations, has its foundation in His perfect humanity.
It surely requires not an argument to show that, as God, He could not
be tempted, but that, as man, He could. His inferior nature was finite
and created; it was not angelic, it was human. It was perfectly identical
with our own, its entire exemption from all taint of sin only excepted. A
human body and a human mind were His, with all their essential and
peculiar properties. He was "bone of our bone, and flesh and our flesh;" He
traveled up through the stages of infancy, boyhood, and manhood; He was
encompassed with all the weaknesses, surrounded by all the circumstances,

exposed to all the inconveniences, that belong to our nature. He breathed our air, trod our earth, ate our food. The higher attributes of our being were His also. Reason, conscience, memory, will, affections, were essential appendages of that human soul which the Son of God took into union with His Divinity. As such, then, our Lord was tempted. As such, too, He was capable of yielding. His finite nature, though pure and sinless, was yet necessarily limited in its resources, and weak in its own powers. Touching His inferior nature, He was but man. The Godhead was not humanized, nor was the humanity deified, by the blending together of the two natures. Each retained its essential characters, properties, and attributes, distinct, unchanged, and unchangeable.

But let no one suppose that a liability in Jesus to yield to Satan's temptation necessarily implies the existence of the same sinful and corrupt nature which we possess. Far from it. To deny His capability of succumbing to temptation were to neutralize the force, beauty, and instruction of the eventful part of His history altogether. It were to reduce a splendid fact to an empty fable, a blessed reality to a vague supposition; it were to rob Jesus of the great glory which covered Him when left alone, the victor on this battlefield. And yet that He must necessarily be sinful, in order to be thus capable of yielding, does not follow; it is an error of judgment to suppose that the force of a temptation always depends upon the inherent sinfulness of the person who is tempted. The case of the first Adam disproves this supposition, and in some of its essential features strikingly illustrates the case of the second Adam. In what consisted the strength of the assault before whose fearful onset Adam yielded? Surely not in any indwelling sin, for he was pure and upright. There was no appeal to the existence of an corrupt principles or propensities; no working upon any fallen desires and tendencies in his nature; for, until the moment that the blast swept him to the earth, no angel in heaven stood before the throne purer or more faultless than he. But God left him to the necessary weakness and poverty of his own nature, and thus withdrawing His Divine support and restraint, that instant he fell! That our adorable Lord did not fall, and was not overcome in His fearful conflict with the same foe, was owing solely to the upholding of the Deity, and the indwelling and restraining power of the Holy Spirit, which He possessed without measure.

SEPTEMBER 21

"For in that he himself has suffered being tempted, he is able to support those who are tempted." Hebrews 2:18

DO YOU THINK, my reader, was it no humiliation for the Son of God to be thus assailed by the prince of darkness? Was it no degradation, that His dignity should be questioned, His authority disputed, His reverence for and allegiance to, His Father assailed, and His very purity tampered with by a fallen and corrupt spirit whom He had ejected from heaven? Ah! how deeply and keenly He must have felt it to be so, the first moment He was brought in contact with this arch-fiend and subtle foe of God and man! But, oh, what glory beams from beneath this dark veil of Christ's humiliation! How lovely and precious an object does He appear to saints and angels in this wondrous transaction! What holy sympathies and fond affections are kindled in the heart, and rise towards Him, as the eye surveys each particular—the appalling nature of the onset—the shock which His humanity sustained—the mighty power by which He was upheld—the signal victory which He achieved—the Divine consolation and comfort which flowed into His soul as His vanquished enemy retired from the conflict, leaving Him more than conqueror—and above all, the close and tender sympathy into which He was now brought with a tempted Church! These are features replete with thrilling interest and rich instruction, on which the renewed mind delights to dwell.

But our Lord's humiliation went deeper still than this! The clouds now gathering around Him grew darker and more portentous as He advanced towards the final conflict. We must consider the first step of His bearing sin, the painful consciousness of which increased as the hour of its atonement drew on, as forming one of the most overwhelming demonstrations of that voluntary abasement to which He had stooped, and through which He was now passing. In the following passages this great truth of the Gospel is explicitly and emphatically stated. And let it be borne in mind, that when the Holy Spirit represents our Lord as bearing sin, the statement is not to receive a figurative, but a perfectly literal interpretation, as asserting a solemn and momentous fact. He bore not the appearance of sin, or the punishment merely of sin, but the sin itself.

Thus does the Holy Spirit declare it: "He was wounded for our transgressions, He was bruised for our iniquities." "The Lord has laid on Him the iniquity of us all." "He shall bear their iniquities." "He bare the sin of many." "Who His own self bare our sins in His own body on the tree." "He has made Him to be sin for us, who knew no sin." There stood the eternal God, in the closest proximity to the evil one. Never did two extremes, so opposite to each other, meet in such near contiguity and collision. Essential sin, essential holiness; essential darkness, essential light; essential hatred, essential love; man's deadliest foe, man's dearest friend. What an hour of seeming power and triumph was this to the grand adversary of God and man! what an hour of deepening gloom and humiliation and defeat to God's beloved Son! How would this Lucifer of the morning exult, as with the swellings of pride he placed his foot upon incarnate Deity! And how keenly and powerfully conscious would Jesus be, at that moment, of the deep abasement and degradation to which He had now sunk!

But behold how this great transaction contributed to the deep humiliation of the Son of God. What must have been the revulsion of moral feeling, what the shrinking of His holy soul, the first instant it came in personal contact with sin! What a mighty convulsion must have rocked His human nature, pure and sinless as it was! Saint of God! what composes your bitterest cup, and what constitutes your keenest, deepest sorrow? Has a tender Father blown upon your blessings, removed your mercies, lessened your comforts, darkened your bright landscape, dried up your sweet spring? Is this the cause of your shaded brow, your anxious look, your tearful eye, your troubled and disconsolate spirit? "Ah, no!" you perhaps exclaim; "rid me of this body of sin, and you chase the cloud from my brow, the tear from my eye, and the sorrow from my heart. It is the sin that dwells in me." Do you think, then, what the spotless Lamb of God must have felt, and how deeply must it have entered into His humiliation—the existence of an all-absorbing, ever present, and ever painful and humiliating consciousness of bearing upon His holy soul iniquity, transgression, and sin!

SEPTEMBER 22

"A little while and you shall not see me: and again, a little while, and you shall see me, because I go to the Father."

THE sacred friendships we form in our present state enter deeply into our future happiness. A bosom friend—and we now speak only of the sympathy which a mutual hope in Christ inspires—we feel to be a part of our own existence, an essential element of our intellectual and moral being. Such a friend is identified with our immortality. The affection inspired, the communion maintained, the communion enjoyed here, surely form but the embryo, the germ, of that friendship which, in its fullness and perfection, awaits us on high. The very character of earth's sacred friendships points us to a fuller development. Is the communion, the communion, the reciprocation of feeling springing from a warm confidential and exclusive friendship, at all commensurate with the depth and intensity of the affection that inspires it? Alas! not so. How little and how imperfect here the communion of kindred hearts! Places, oceans, circumstances separate, and it is but now and then that we sip the sweets of a full and unalloyed communion. And then, how frequently does death step in, and cast its shadow and its blight over the heart's fondest treasure! the thread is broken, and our bosom friend is gone! "A little while, and you shall not see me," gently whispers each holy, precious friendship of the heart. It is but "a little while" we enjoy the friends God gives us, and then, disappearing within the veil of eternity, we see them no more. But are they lost? Oh no! Another voice is heard—it is as a voice from heaven speaking—"And again a little while, and you shall see me, because I go to the Father." Yes! it is but a "little while," and we shall see them again; because they are safe in the house and reposing in the bosom of their Father.

And what is heaven? It is not a place of solitude and loneliness. There is society there—there is companionship there. And the life of the blessed will be a life of the closest personal communion and of the highest social enjoyment. And what beings in the Father's house will be more likely to participate with us, and, by participation, heighten, the joys of heaven?

Surely those who, in this lower world, were more closely than all others endeared and assimilated to us, by affection, providence, communion, and time. And when we have passed through the portal of death, and find ourselves in glory, who, amid the bright throng of redeemed spirits, will be the first objects of our eager search? Will it not be those who on earth we knew and loved better than others, and whose associations were so interwoven with our earthly and former life, that not to renew the same peculiar friendship, freed from all the imperfections of sin, and not to enjoy again the same hallowed communion, would be like the destruction of our consciousness and memory? Yes! a little while, and we shall see them again! Oh blessed reunion and of the holy dead! Beloved, in a little while we shall see them all again, because they are with the Father. Let us comfort one another with these words.

SEPTEMBER 23

*"For I reckon that the sufferings of this present
time are not worthy to be compared with the glory
which shall be revealed in us." Romans 8:18*

THE world, where not a spot is found unscathed by the curse, must be a world of suffering. The world, where sin holds its universal empire, tainting every object, and beclouding every scene, must be a world of suffering. The world, where the spirit is wounded, and the heart is broken, where reason is dethroned, and hope languishes, where the eye weeps, and the nerve trembles, where sickness wastes, and death reigns, must needs be a world of suffering. From none of these forms of woe does Christianity exempt its believers. But with this truth, on the other hand, it soothes and reconciles—they are the sufferings of the present time. They are but momentary, will soon be over—and forever. We live in a dying world—a world that is passing away. Time is short—is ever on the wing; and we are ever on the wing of time, borne each moment by its sweeping pinion nearer and still nearer our Father's house; of whose occupants it is said, "God shall wipe away all tears from their eyes; and there shall be no more death, neither sorrow, nor crying, neither shall there be any more pain: for the former things are passed away." Oh, how gentle is the admonition—"Arise you, and depart; for this is not your rest: because it is polluted"! Then comes the glory—"the glory which shall be revealed in us." What word could more appropriately express the future condition of the saints? The world claims the title, but has no claim to the reality. What is the glory of science—of learning—of rank—of wealth, but a tinseled pageant, a meteor blazing for a moment, and then disappearing in eternal night? But the glory that awaits the suffering Christian is a real, a substantial glory. At present it is veiled. The world sees it not; the believer only beholds it through faith's telescope. But the day of its full, unclouded revelation awaits us. It draws near. It will be a glory revealed in us. This truth may be startling to some. "What!" they exclaim, "a glory to be revealed in me! In me, who can scarcely reflect a solitary ray of light! In me, so dark, so sinful, living at so remote a distance from communion with the Father of lights! Can it be that in me this glory will be revealed?" So affirms the word of our God. If a child of the light, dwelling, it may be, in the world's shade, and often called to walk in great darkness, you shall one day outshine the brightness of the firmament and the stars forever and ever.

SEPTEMBER 24

"For our light affliction, which is but for a moment, works for us a
far more exceeding and eternal weight of glory." 2 Corinthians 4:17

IN what respects will it be a glory revealed in us? It will be the glory of perfect knowledge. "Now we see through a glass darkly; but then face to face: now I know in part; but then shall I know even as also I am known." Oh, what an orb of intellectual light will be each glorified mind! What capacity of understanding will it develop—what range of thought will it compass—what perfection of knowledge will it attain! How will all mysteries then be unraveled, and all problems then be solved, and all discrepancies then be reconciled; and every truth of God's revelation, every event of God's providence, every decision of God's government, stand out more transparent and resplendent than ten thousand suns. Do you, in your present search for spiritual knowledge, deplore the darkness of your mind, the feebleness of your memory—the energy of your mental faculties impaired, dimmed, and exhausted? Oh, rejoice in hope of the glory that is to be revealed in you, when all your intellectual powers will be renewed as the eagle's strength; developed, sanctified, and perfected, to a degree outvying the mightiest angel in heaven. Then shall we know God and Christ, and truth, and providence, and ourselves, even as now we are known. It will also be a glory in us of perfect holiness. The kingdom within us will then be complete; the good work of grace will then be perfected. It will be the consummation of holiness, the perfection of purity. No more sin! The conscience no more sullied—the thoughts no more defiled—the affections no more ensnared—but a glory of holiness, dazzling and resplendent, beyond an angel's, revealed in us. "It does not yet appear what we shall be: but we know that when He shall appear, we shall be like Him."

The glory of perfect happiness will be the certain effect of perfect sanctity. The completeness of Christ is the completeness of moral purity. With reverence be it spoken, God Himself could not be a perfectly happy, were He not a perfectly holy Being. The radiance of the glorified countenance of the saints will be the reflection of holy thoughts and holy feelings glowing within. Joy and peace and full satisfaction will beam in every feature, because every faculty and feeling and emotion of the soul will be in perfect unison with the will, and in perfect assimilation to the image, of God. Who can paint the happiness of that world from where everything is banished that could sully its purity, disturb its harmony, and ruffle its repose?— where everything is included that comports with its sanctity, harmonizes with its grandeur, and heightens its bliss. Oh, yes! it will be a glory revealed in us. The glory of the Father's adoption—the glory of Christ's atonement—the glory of the Spirit's regeneration, radiating from a poor fallen son of Adam—a sinner redeemed, renewed, and saved. And what is each present ray of heavenly light, each thrill of divine love, each victory of indwelling grace, and each glimpse of the upper world, but the foreshadowings of the glory yet to be revealed in us? Suffering and glory thus placed side by side, thus contrasted and weighed, to what conclusion does our apostle arrive? "I reckon that the sufferings of this present time are not worthy to be compared with the glory which shall be revealed in us." No, not worthy of a comparison. Do we measure their relative duration? "Then, our light affliction is but for a moment," while our glory is a "far more exceeding and eternal weight." Before long all suffering and sorrow will forever have passed away—a thing of history and of memory only—while glory will deepen and expand as eternity rolls on its endless ages. Do we weight them? What comparison has the weight of the cross with the weight of the crown? Place in the scales the present "light affliction" and the future "exceeding and eternal weight of glory," which is the lightest? Are they worthy to be compared? Oh, no! One second of glory will extinguish a life-time of suffering. What were long years of toil, of sickness, of battle with poverty, persecution, and sorrow in every form, and closing even with a martyr's death, weighted with one draught of the river of pleasure at Christ's right hand—with one breath of Paradise—with one wave of heaven's glory—with one embrace of Jesus—with one sight of God? Oh, what are the pangs of present separation, in comparison with the joy of future reunion? What the pinchings of poverty now, with the untold riches then? What the suffering, and gloom, and contempt of the present time, with the glory that is to be revealed in us? We can go no further. Tell us, you spirits of just men made perfect, if it be lawful, if it be possible, what the glory that awaits us is! Tell us what it is to be an unclothed spirit—to dwell in the bosom of Jesus—to see God—to be perfectly holy—to be supremely happy! Wait, my soul! before long it will be all revealed!

SEPTEMBER 25

"And do not be conformed to this world: but be you transformed by the renewing of your mind, that you may prove what is that good, and acceptable, and perfect will of God." Romans 12:2

THE world, and the love of it, and conformity to it, may please and assist the life of sense, but it is opposed to, and will retard, the life of faith. Not more opposed in their natures are the flesh and the Spirit, darkness and light, sin and holiness, than are a vigorous life of faith and a sinful love of the world. Professor of the gospel! guard against the world; it is your great bane: watch against conformity to it in your dress, in your mode of living, in the education of your children, in the principles, motives, and policy that govern you. Grieve not, then, the Holy Spirit of God by any known inconsistency of conduct, any sinful conformity to the world, any inordinate pursuit of its wealth, its honors, its pleasures, its friendships, and its great things. Pray against the sin of covetousness, that canker-worm that feeds at the root of so many souls; pray against the love of dress, that sin that diverts the mind of so many professors from the simplicity of Christ, and takes the eye off from the true adornment; pray against a thirst for light and trifling reading, that strange and sinful inconsistency of so many, the certain tendency of which is to starve the life of God in the soul, to engender a distaste for spiritual aliment, for the word of God, for holy meditation, and for Divine communion and fellowship—yes, pray against the spirit of worldly, sinful conformity in everything, that the Holy Spirit do not be grieved, and that Christ do not be dishonored and crucified afresh in and through you. It is to be feared that much of the professed Christianity of the day is of a compromising character. The spirit that marks so many is, "What will you give me, and I will deliver him unto you?" There is a betraying of Christ before the world—a bartering of Christianity for its good opinion, its places of honor, and influence, and emolument. The world, the flesh, and Satan are ever on the alert to frame a bargain with a Christian professor for his religion. "What will you give me in return?" is the eager inquiry of many. Oh, awful state! oh, fearful deception! oh, fatal delusion! Reader! are you a professing Christian? Then guard against the least compromise of your principles, the least betrayal of Jesus, the first step in an inconsistency of walk; above all, pray and watch against a worldly Christianity—a Christianity that wears a fair exterior, so far as it is composed of attendance upon sanctuary services and sacraments and religious institutions, but which excludes from it the cross of the meek and lowly Lamb of God—a Christianity which loves the world and the things of the world, "makes a fair show in the flesh," speaks well of Christ, and yet betrays Him with a kiss. Let not this be the model of your religion. The world is the sworn enemy of your Savior; let it not be your friend. No; come out of it, and be you separate.

SEPTEMBER 26

"I know your works, that you are neither old nor hot: I would you were cold or hot. So then, because you are lukewarm, and neither cold nor not, I will spue you out of my mouth." Revelation 3:15-16

OF all spiritual states, lukewarmness is most abhorrent to God, and grieving to the Holy Spirit; and thus has God declared His utter detestation of this state. And yet, who contemplates it in this awful light? who pauses to examine himself, to ascertain what real progress his soul is making— what grace is enfeebled—what part of the Spirit's work is decayed—what spot of his soul is barren and unfruitful, and how far he is secretly and effectually grieving the Holy Spirit by a known, allowed, and cherished state of spiritual declension? If, after all his skill, it must be affecting to the architect to witness the decay of his building—if so to the parent, after his costly expenditure of means in education, to witness the fond hopes he cherished of his child blasted—how infinitely more is the Spirit affected and grieved to behold the temple He had erected at such a cost falling to decay; the soul He had taught with such care and solicitude receding into a state of coldness and formality in its spiritual duties and affections! "The heart of the Spirit," beautifully remarks Dr. Owen, "is infinitely more tender towards us than that of the most affectionate parent can be towards an only child. And when He with cost and care has nourished and brought us up into some growth and progress in spiritual affections, wherein all His concerns in us do lie, for us to grow cold, dull, earthly-minded, to cleave unto the pleasures and lusts of this world, how is He grieved, how is He provoked!" See, then, that your spiritual state is such as occasions joy rather than grief to the Holy Spirit of God. Nothing can fill His loving heart with greater and more holy delight than to witness the deepening character and expanding influence of His own work in the believer. To behold the glimmering light, which He created, "shining more and more,"—the gentle plant emitting its fragrance, and putting forth its fruit—the well-spring in the heart rising heavenward, God-ward—such a picture must be grateful to the Spirit. If the enthroned Redeemer looks down with satisfaction upon the travail of His soul in the calling in of His redeemed, equally joyous must it be to the Eternal Spirit to behold the widening of His kingdom in the saints—the maturing of the soul for the inheritance and the companionship of "just men made perfect." To mark a growing conformity to the image of Christ—holiness expanding its root—each grace in active exercise—every weight cast aside—every sin mortified, and the whole body, soul, and spirit a rising temple to God, must indeed fill all heaven with joy. Christian reader, see well to your state, that the Holy Spirit of God is not grieved at any known and cherished declension of His work in the soul.

SEPTEMBER 27

"Trust you in the Lord forever: for in the Lord Jehovah is everlasting strength." Isaiah 26:4

THERE is no act of the soul more acceptable to God, because there is none that brings more glory to His great name, than this. Wherever we trace in the Scriptures of truth a trust in the Lord, there we find especial and remarkable deliverance. It is recorded of the children of Israel that the Lord delivered their enemies into their hand, "for they cried to God in the battle, and He was entreated of them; because they put their trust in Him." Again, we read of God's wondrous message sent by Jeremiah to Abed-melech, the Ethiopian, "I will surely deliver you, and you shall not fall by the sword, but your life shall be for a prey unto you; because you have put your trust in me, says the Lord." The experience, too, of God's people confirms the blessedness of trusting in the Lord. "In God I have put my trust; I will not fear what flesh can do unto me." "It is better to trust in the Lord than to put confidence in man." "The Lord is my strength and my shield; my heart trusted in Him, and I am helped." The promises connected with trusting in the Lord are equally rich and encouraging. "You will keep him in perfect peace whose mind is stayed on You; because he trusts in You." "None of those who trust in Him shall be desolate." "The Lord knows those who trust in Him." "Oh, how great is Your goodness, which You have laid up for those who fear You; which You have wrought for those who trust in You before the sons of men. You shall hide them in the secret of Your presence." What a marvelous and precious cluster of Divine encouragements to those who trust in the Lord with all their heart, under all circumstances, and at all times! "Only trust," is Jesus' word. "This is all I ask of you, the utmost thing I require at your hand. I demand no costly sacrifice—no wearisome pilgrimage—no personal worthiness—no strength, or wisdom, or self-endeavors of your own. Only trust me. Only believe that I wait to answer prayer—that I am gracious—that I have all power at my command—that I have your interest at heart—that there is no good thing I am willing to withhold—that I, and I alone, can guide your present steps, can unravel the web of your difficulties, guide your perplexities, extricate you from the snares that have woven their net—work around your feet, and bring you through fire and through water into a wealthy place. Only trust me!" Beloved, is this too hard? Is the request unreasonable and impracticable? What! only to trust Jesus? Only to trust your needs to His ear—your burdens to His arm—your sorrows to His heart? Is this too hard? Is it beyond your power? Then tell Jesus so. Remind Him of His own words, "Without me you can do nothing." Ask Him for the faith to trust, the heart to trust, the courage to trust, and the power to trust all your interests, temporal and spiritual, for time and for eternity, into His hands.

SEPTEMBER 28

"Jesus answered and said unto her, Whoever drinks of this water shall thirst again; but whoever drinks of the water that I shall give him shall never thirst; but the water that I shall give him shall be in him a well of water springing up into everlasting life." John 4:13-14

SELECT your choicest, sweetest temporal mercy, and say, is it satisfying to your soul? Does it, in its fullest enjoyment, leave no want unsupplied, no desire unmet, no void unfilled? Does it meet the cravings of the mind? Go into the garden of creature-blessing, and pluck the loveliest flower, and taste the sweetest fruit; repair to the cabinet of friendship, and select from thence its choicest pearl; pass round the wide circle of earth-born joy, and place your hand upon the chief and the best—is it the feeling of your heart and the language of your lips, "I am satisfied, I want no more"? Does it quench the spirit's thirst; does it soothe the heart's sorrow; does it meet the mind's cravings; does it quiet the troubled conscience, and lift the burden from the aching heart? Oh no! the height, the depth, the length, the breadth exclaim, "It is not in me: am I in God's stead?" But how blessed is that which truly satisfies! Listen to the gracious words of the Savior. "Whoever drinks of the water that I shall give him shall never thirst." Did language ever utter a sentiment more true than this? Jesus is an all-satisfying portion. They who have tried Him can testify that it is so. His is not a satisfaction in name, but in reality and in truth. There is a felt, a realized sense of holy satiety. The mind is content. The believer wanders no more in quest of happiness or of rest. He has found them both in Jesus. He is satisfied to stake his eternal all upon the finished work of Immanuel—to live upon His smile, to abide in His love, to draw upon His grace, to submit to His will, to bear His cross, to be guided by His counsel, and afterwards to be received by Him into glory. The Lord Jesus imparts contentment to the soul in which He enters and dwells. Vast as were those desires before, urgent as were those necessities, insatiable as were those cravings, and restless as was that mind, Jesus has met and satisfied them all. The magnetic power of His love has attracted to, and fixed the mind upon, Himself. "He satisfies the longing soul, and fills the hungry soul with goodness." The believer is satisfied that God should possess Him fully, govern him supremely, and guide him entirely, and be the sole Fountain from where he draws his happiness, gratefully acknowledging, "All my springs are in You." Thus is he content to be just what, and just where, his Father would have him. He is satisfied that he possesses God, and that, possessing God, he has all good in God. He knows that his Father cares for him; that He has undertaken to guide all his steps, and to provide for all his needs. The only anxiety which he feels as to the present is how he may the most glorify his dearest, his only Friend, casting the future on Him in the simplicity of child-like faith. Nor is the satisfaction thus felt limited to the present state. It passes on with the believer to eternity. It enters with him into the mansions of bliss. There, in unruffled serenity, in unalloyed joy, in unmingled bliss, it is perfect and complete. "You will show me the path of life: in Your presence is fullness of joy; at Your right hand there are pleasures for evermore." Happy saint! who have found your all in Jesus! Glorified spirit! would we recall you to these scenes of sin, of suffering, and of death? No! the needle of your soul no longer varies and trembles, diverted from its center by other and treacherous objects—Jesus fixes it now, and fixes it forever.

SEPTEMBER 29

"For I have given you an example, that you
should do as I have done to you." John 13:15

EVERY soul re-cast into this model, every mind conformed to this pattern, and every life reflecting this image, is an exalting and a glorifying of the Son of God. There is no single practical truth in the word of God on which the Spirit is more emphatic than the example which Christ has set for the imitation of His followers. The Church needed a perfect pattern, a flawless model. It wanted an impersonation, a living embodiment of those precepts of the gospel so strictly enjoined upon every believer, and God has graciously set before us our true model. "Whom He did foreknow, He also did predestinate to be conformed to the image of His Son." And what says Christ Himself? "My sheep follow me." We allow that there are points in which we cannot and are not required literally and strictly to follow Christ. We cannot lay claim to His infallibility. He who sets himself up as infallible in his judgment, spotlessly pure in his heart, and perfect in his attainments in holiness, deceives his own soul. Jesus did many things, too, as our Surety, which we cannot do. We cannot drink of the cup of Divine trembling which He drank; nor can we be baptized with the baptism of blood with which He was baptized. He did many things as a Jew—was circumcised, kept the passover &christian.—which are not obligatory upon us. And yet, in all that is essential to our sanctification, to our holy, obedient, God-glorifying walk, He has "left us an example, that we should follow His steps." In His lowly spirit, meek, humble deportment, and patient endurance of suffering: "Learn of me, for I am meek and lowly in heart." In the disinterestedness of His love, His pure benevolence, the unselfishness of His religion: "Look not every man on his own things, but every man also on the things of others: let this mind be you which was also in Christ Jesus." "For even Christ pleased not Himself." Look not every man on his own circle, his own family, his own gifts, his own interests, comfort, and happiness; upon his own Church, his own community, his own minister. Let him not look upon these exclusively. Let him not prefer his own advantage to the public good. Let him not be self-willed in matters involving the peace and comfort of others. Let him not form favorite theories, or individual opinions, to the hazard of a Church's prosperity or of a family's happiness. Let him yield, sacrifice, and give place, rather than carry a point to the detriment of others. Let him, with a generous, magnanimous, disinterested spirit, in all things imitate Jesus, who "pleased not Himself." Let him seek the good of others, honoring their gifts, respecting their opinions, nobly yielding when they correct and overrule his own. Let him promote the peace of the Church, consult the honor of Christ, and seek the glory of God, above and beyond all private and selfish ends. This is to be conformed to the image of God's dear Son, to which high calling we are predestinated; and in any feature of resemblance which the Holy Spirit brings out in the holy life of a follower of the Lamb, Christ is thereby glorified before men and angels.

SEPTEMBER 30

"And because you are sons, God has sent forth the Spirit
of his Son into your hearts, crying, Abba, Father."

THE apostle employs in the original two different languages. It may not be improper to infer, that in using both the Syriac and Greek form—the one being familiar to the Jew, and the other to the Gentile—he would denote that both the Christian Jew and the believing Gentile were children of one family, and were alike privileged to approach God as a Father. Christ, our peace, has broken down the middle wall of partition that was between them; and now, at the same mercy-seat, the Christian Jew and the believing Gentile, both one in Christ Jesus, meet, as rays of light converge and blend in one common center, at the feet of their reconciled Father. The expressions, too, set forth the peculiarity and intensity of the affection. Literally, "Abba, Father," signifies "My Father." No bond-servant was permitted thus to address the master of the family; it was a privilege peculiar and sacred to the child. And when our blessed Lord would teach His disciples to pray, he led them to the mercy-seat, and sealed these precious words upon their lips—"Our father, which are in heaven." And after His resurrection, with increased emphasis and intensity did He give utterance to the same truth. Previously to His death, His words were, "I go to the Father." But when He came back from the grave, every truth He had before enunciated seemed quickened as with new life. How tender and touching were His words—"I ascend unto my Father, and your Father; and to my God, and your God." No longer a bondslave, but a son, oh, claim the dignity and privilege of your birthright! Approach God as your father. "Abba, Father!" How tender the relation! how intense the affection! what power it imparts to prayer! What may you not ask, and what can God refuse, with "Abba, Father," breathing in lowliness and love from your lips? Remember, it is an inalienable, unchangeable relation. Never, in any instance, or under any circumstance the most aggravated, does God forget it. He is as much our Father when He chastises as when He approves; as much so when He frowns as when He smiles; as much so when He brims the cup of adversity as when He bids us drink the cup of salvation. Behold the touching display of it in His gracious restorings: "But when he was yet a great way off, his father saw him, and had compassion, and ran, and fell on his neck and kissed him." In all his wanderings that father's love had never lost sight of his wayward child. It tracked him along all his windings, and waited and welcomed his return. We may doubt, and debase, and deny our divine relationship, yet God will never disown us as His children, nor disinherit us as His heirs. We may cease to act as a child, He will never cease to love as a Father. To Him, then, as to a Father, at all times repair.

OCTOBER

OCTOBER 1

"Let your light so shine before men, that they may see your good works, and glorify your Father which is in heaven." Matthew 5:16

LET your life be a clear reflection of the glory of the Redeemer. The saints of God are the only witnesses to this glory—the only reflectors the Lord has in this dark and Christ-denying world. Holiness, springing from the fount of the Spirit's indwelling grace, cherished and matured by close views of the cross, and imparting a character of sanctity of beauty to every act of your life, will be the highest testimony you can bear to the Redeemer's glory. That glory is entrusted to your hands. It is committed to your guardianship. Seeing, then, that it is so, "what manner of people ought you to be, in all holy conversation and godliness!" How exact in principles, and upright in conduct—how watchful over temper, and how vigilant where most assailed—how broad awake to the wiles of the devil, and how sleepless against the encroachments of sin—how strict in all transactions with the world, and how tender, charitable, meek, and forgiving, in all our conduct with the saints! Alas! we are at best but dim reflectors of this great glory of our Lord. We are unworthy and unfaithful depositories of so rich a treasure! How much of clinging infirmity, on unmortified sin, of carelessness of spirit, of unsanctified temper, of tampering with temptation, of a lack of strict integrity of uprightness, dims our light, neutralizes our testimony for God, and weakens, if not entirely destroys, our moral influence! We are not more eminently useful, because we are not more eminently holy. We bring so little glory to Christ, because we seek so much our own. We reflect so faint and flickering a beam, because our posture is so seldom that of the apocalyptic angel. "standing in the sun." We realize so imperfectly our oneness with, and standing in, Christ; and this will ever foster a feeble, fruitless, and drooping profession of Christianity. "As the branch cannot bear fruit of itself, except it abide in the vine, no more can you, except you abide in me." Oh, to know more of this abiding in Christ! See how Jesus invites His saints to it. Are they fallen? He bids them take hold of His strength. Are they burdened? He bids them cast that burden on His arm. Are they wearied? He bids them recline on Him for rest. Does the world persecute them—do the "daughters of Jerusalem" smite them— does the watchman treat them unkindly? He bids them take refuge within the hallowed sanctuary of His own pierced and loving heart. Do they need grace? He bids them sink their empty vessel beneath the depths of His ocean fullness, and draw freely "more grace." Whatever corruptions distress them, whatever temptations assail them, whatever adversity grieves them, whatever cloud darkens them, whatever necessity presses upon them, as a watchful Shepherd, as a tender Brother, as a faithful Friend, as a great High Priest, He bids His saints draw near, and repose in His love. Oh, He has a capacious bosom; there is room, there is a chamber in that heart for you, my Christian reader. Do not think your lot is desolate, lonely, and friendless. Do not think that all have forsaken you, and that in sadness and in solitude you are treading your way through an intricate desert. There is One that loves you, that thinks of you, that has His eye upon you, and is at this moment guiding, upholding, and caring for you; that one is—Jesus! Oh that you could but look into His heart, and see how He loves you; oh that you could but hear Him say so gently, so earnestly, "Abide in my love." Cheer up! you are in Christ's heart, and Christ is in your heart. You are not alone; your God and your Father is with you. Your Shepherd guides you; the Comforter spreads around you His wings, and heaven is bright before you. Soon you will be there. The pilgrim will repose his weary limbs; the voyager will be moored in his harbor of rest; the warrior will put off his armor, and shout his song of triumph. Then look up! Christ is your, God is your, heaven is your. If God is for you, who can be against you? And if you find disappointment in created good, it will but endear Jesus; if you know more of the inward plague, it will but drive you to the atoning blood; if you have storms and tempests, they will but shorten the voyage, and waft you the quicker to glory.

OCTOBER 2

"My soul, wait only upon God; for my expectation is from him." Ps. 62:5

THIS trust implies a ceasing from self, and from all confidence in the arm of flesh, and from all reliance in unbelieving, carnal plans and schemes to obtain deliverance from the pressure of present trial, and supplies for present need. It involves a constant, prayerful, and believing leaning on the Lord; a quiet, patient waiting for the Lord; a peaceful, childlike, passive resting in the Lord; and a holy, filial walking with the Lord. Recollect, a leaning upon Christ—a waiting for Christ—a resting in Christ—and a walking with Christ. Only do this, in all your trials and temptations, needs and sorrows. Only trust Him to lead you by a right way to bring you to heaven. Only trust Him to appear in His own good time to deliver you from a present cross, to remove a present burden, to supply a present need, and to conduct you into the green pastures and beside the sweet flowing waters of His truth and love. So delightsome to Him will be this calm submissive trust—so honoring of His faithfulness and so glorifying to His name this full implicit confidence—He will honor and bless you by granting the desires of your heart, and bestowing from the plenitude of His resources every blessing that you ask and need.

Above all other trusts, trust to Jesus your priceless soul. Relax your grasp upon everything else but Jesus. Let go your religious duties and doings, your sacraments and prayers, your works and righteousness and Babel-built hopes of heaven—and only trust, and trust only, in the Lord Jesus Christ, and you shall be saved. No poor penitent sinner did He ever reject—none was He ever known to cast away. And if you come and trust in His righteousness alone to justify you, and to give you acceptance with God, and a title to eternal glory, you will be the first that ever perished at His feet—if you perish there! Hear the Father and your God say—"As your day, so shall your strength be." "As your day." Each new burden shall bring its support; each new difficulty, its guidance; each new sorrow, its soothing; and each new day, its strength. Be it your only care to deny all ungodliness, and to walk worthy of your high vocation; to separate yourself more widely and distinctly from the world, its practices and its spirit; more closely to resemble Christ in His gentle, charitable, forgiving temper; and yielding yourself more entirely to the disposal of the Lord, to do as seems Him good. And when called to meet death—to hear the summons that bids you rise—then, when all other things are receding from your view, and all other voices are dying upon your ear, Jesus will approach, and amid the gloom and steadiness of the shadowy valley you shall see His person, and hear Him say—"Do not be afraid—only trust me!"

OCTOBER 3

*"Now unto him that is able to keep you from falling, and
to present you faultless before the presence of his glory
with exceeding joy, to the only wise God our Savior, be
glory and majesty, dominion and power, both now and
ever. Amen." Jude 24, 25*

WHAT is the great evil of which the true saints of God most stand in
jeopardy, and which their timid, fearful hearts most dread? Is it not secret
and outward backsliding from God after conversion? Surely it is, as the
experience of every honest, upright, God-fearing man will testify. It is his
consolation, then, to know that Jesus is "able to keep him from falling." This
is the most overwhelming evil that stares the believer in the face. Some, but
imperfectly taught in the word, are dreading awful apostasy from the faith
here, and final condemnation from the presence of God hereafter—believing
that though Christ has made full satisfaction for their sins to Divine justice,
has cancelled the mighty debt, has imputed to them His righteousness, has
blotted out their iniquities, has called, renewed, sanctified, and taken full
possession of them by His Spirit, and has ascended up on high, to plead their
cause with the Father—that yet, after all this stupendous exercise of power,
and this matchless display of free grace, they may be left to utter apostasy
from God, and be finally and eternally lost. If there is one doctrine more
awful in it nature, distressing in its consequences, and directly opposed to
the glory of God and the honor of Christ, than another, methinks it is this.
Others, again, more clearly taught my the Spirit, are heard to say, "I believe
in the stability of the covenant, in the unchangeableness of God's love, and
in the faithfulness of my heavenly Father; but I fear lest some day under
some sharp temptation—some burst of indwelling sin, when the enemy shall
come in as a flood—I shall fall, to the wounding of my peace, to the shame
of my brethren, and to the dishonoring of Christ." Dear believer, truly you
would fall, were He to leave you to your own keeping for one moment; but
Jesus is able to keep you from falling. Read the promises, believe them, rest
upon them. A simple glance will present to the believer's eye a threefold cord,
by which he is kept from falling. In the first place, God the Father keeps
him—"kept by the power of God;" the power that created and upholds the
world keeps the believer. The eternal purpose, love, and grace of the Father

keeps him: this is the first cord. Again, God the Son keeps him: "My sheep hear my voice, and I know them, and they follow me; and I give unto them eternal life; and they shall never perish, neither shall any man pluck them out of my hand." The covenant engagements, the perfect obedience, the atoning death of Immanuel, keep the believer: this is the second cord. Yet again, God the Holy Spirit keeps him: "When the enemy shall come in like a flood, the Spirit of the Lord shall lift up a standard against him and put him to flight). The tender love, the covenant faithfulness, and the omnipotent power of the Eternal Spirit keep the believer: this is the third cord. And "a threefold cord is not quickly broken." But with these promises of the triune God to keep His people from falling, He has wisely and graciously connected the diligent, prayerful use of all the means which He has appointed for this end.

OCTOBER 4

"But you, beloved, building up yourselves on your most holy faith, praying in the Holy Spirit, keep yourselves in the love of God, looking for the mercy of our Lord Jesus Christ unto eternal life." Jude 20, 21

THE believer is nowhere in the Bible spoken of or addressed as a lifeless machine, a mere automaton; but as one "alive unto God,"—as "created in Christ Jesus,"—as a "partaker of the Divine nature." As such he is commanded to "work out his own salvation with fear and trembling,"—to "give diligence to make his calling and election sure,"—to "watch and pray, lest he enter into temptation." Thus does God throw a measure of the responsibility of his own standing upon the believer himself, that he might not be slothful, unwatchful, and prayerless, but be ever sensible to his solemn obligations to "deny ungodliness and worldly lusts, and to live soberly, righteously, and godly in this present world," remembering that he is "not his own, but is bought with a price."

If the power of God is the efficient cause of the eternal security of the believer, yet, as auxiliaries which God has appointed, and by which He instrumentally works, the believer is to use diligently all holy means of keeping himself from falling; as a temple of the Holy Spirit, as the subject of the divine life, as a pardoned, justified man, he is called to labor perseveringly, to pray ceaselessly, and to watch vigilantly. He is not to run willfully into temptation, to expose himself needlessly to the power of the enemy, to surround himself with unholy and hostile influences, and then take refuge in the truth, that the Lord will keep him from falling. God forbid! This were most awfully to abuse the "doctrine that is after godliness," to "hold the truth in unrighteousness," and to make "Christ the minister of sin." Dear reader, watch and pray against this!

Let the cheering prospect of that glory unto which you are kept stimulate you to all diligent perseverance in holy duty, and constrain you to all patient endurance of suffering. In all your conflicts with indwelling sin, under the pressure of all outward trial, let this precious truth comfort you—that your heavenly Father has "begotten you again unto a lively hope, by the resurrection of Jesus Christ from the dead, to an inheritance incorruptible and undefiled, and that fades not away, reserved in heaven for you who are kept by the power of God through faith unto salvation;" oh, how soon!—all that now loads the heart with care, and wrings it with sorrow—all that dims the eye with tears, and renders the day anxious and the night sleepless, will be as though it had never been. Emerging from the entanglement, the dreariness, the solitude, the loneliness and the temptations of the wilderness, you shall enter upon your everlasting rest, your unfading inheritance, where there is no sorrow, no declension, no sin; where there is no sunset, no twilight, no evening shades, no midnight darkness, but all is one perfect, cloudless, eternal day; for Jesus is the joy, the light, and the glory thereof.

OCTOBER 5

"He that is unjust, let him be unjust still; and he which is filthy, let him be filthy still; and he that is righteous, let him be righteous still; and he that is holy, let him be holy still. And, behold, I come quickly; and my reward is with me, to give every man according as his work shall be." Rev. 22:11, 12

IT would seem to be the cherished delusion of many, that a kind of moral transformation transpires in death; that because death itself is a change of relation, around which gather new sensations, new feelings, new thoughts, new solemnities, new prospects, that therefore the soul passes through a kind of spiritual preparedness to meet its approaching destiny. But such is not the case. The character which time has for years been shaping, it yields to the demands of eternity in the precise mold in which it was formed. Death hands over the soul to the scrutiny and the decisions of the judgment exactly as life relinquished it. The "king of terrors" has received no commission and possesses no power to effect a moral change in the transit of the spirit to the God who gave it. Its office is to unlock the cell, and conduct the prisoner into court. It can furnish no plea, it can suggest no argument, it can correct no error, it can whisper no hope, to the pale and trembling being on his way to the bar. The turnkey must present the criminal to the Judge, precisely as the officer delivered him to the turnkey—with all the marks and evidences of criminality and guilt clinging to him as at the moment of arrest. The supposition of the multitudes seems to be, just what we have stated, that when the strange and mysterious but unmistakable signs of death are stealing upon them—when the summons to appear before the Judge admits of not a doubt, allows of no delay, that then what has been held as truth, and now, in the mighty illumination of an unveiling eternity, is found to be error, may be with ease abandoned; and that however negligent they who have lived all their lifetime without God may have been of religion, while the last day appeared distant—and however careless they who had made a Christian profession may have been of the ground of their confidence, and the reason of their hope, under an indefinite expectation of appearing in the presence of God—yet now that the footfall of death is heart approaching, and the invisible world becomes visible through the opening chinks of the earthly house of their tabernacle, they will be enabled to summon all the remainder of strength, and with the utmost strenuousness turn their undivided attention to the business of saving the soul. But is it really so? Is not the whole course of experience against a supposition so false as this? Do not men die mostly as they have lived? The infidel dies in infidelity, the profligate dies in profligacy, and atheist dies in atheism, the careless die in indifference, and the formalist dies in formality. There are exceptions to this, undoubtedly, but the exceptions confirm rather than disprove the general fact, that men die as they lived. In view, then, of this solemn statement, deeply affecting it must be to the Christian professor—if it be thus that our death will derive much of its character and complexion from the present tenor of our life—that in proportion to the lack of spirituality and the undue influence which the world has had upon the mind—to the habitual distance of the walk with God, and the gradual separation from us of those holy, sanctifying influences which go to form the matured, influential, and useful Christian—will be the lack of that bright evidence, and full assured hope in death, which will give to the departing soul an "abundant entrance into the everlasting kingdom,"—then, of what great moment is it that every individual professing godliness should know the exact state of his soul before God!

OCTOBER 6

"And the angel of the Lord came again the second time, and touched him, and said, Arise and eat; because the journey is too great for you. And he arose, and did eat and drink, and went in the strength of that food forty days and forty nights unto Horeb the mount of God." 1 Kings 14:7-8

WE have here an illustration of one of the greatest principles in the divine life—one of the most wonderful, precious, and influential—the principle of faith: "The just shall live by faith." It is in this way the Lord prepares His people for what He has prepared for them in the future of their history. That history is to them wisely and graciously concealed. The path of the future is to them all unknown, a veil of impenetrable mystery enshrouding it from view. In all this we trace the love of our heavenly Father. There may be, for anything that we know, a long season of abstinence before us; many a weary stage is yet untraveled, many a new path is yet untrodden, many a battle is yet unfought, and many a temptation and trial are yet unmet. But faith, living upon the nourishment received, in the strength and sustaining power of some view of God which the Spirit has presented, of some especial grace which Christ has meted out, of some higher attainment in truth and experience and holiness, of some profounder lesson learned, of some especial mercy experienced, of some bright realizing view of glory caught, the believer may travel many a long a toilsome stage of his journey to the "rest that remains for the people of God." Ah! how often has the Lord by His present dealings anticipated the future events of your life! For what circumstances of danger, of trial, and of want has Jesus provided! He well knew—for He had appointed every step and every incident of your journey—the deep and dark waters through which you were to wade, the sands you were to cross, the mountains you were to climb, and the valleys into which you were to descend. That cup of sorrow was not mixed, nor that fiery dart winged, nor that heavy cross sent, before all the necessities it would create, and all the supplies it would demand, had been thought of and provided for by Him who knew the end from the beginning. And when the voice of love gently awoke you as from the stupor of your grief, you marveled at the table spread, and wondered at the supply sent; and you could not define the reason why so much love took possession of your heart, and so much grace flowed into your soul, why so much nerve clothed your spirit, and so much hope and joy bathed you in their heavenly sunlight, and shed their radiance upon your onward way—little thinking that this was the Lord's mode of providing nourishment for the journey. And when the period and event of your life, thus anticipated, arrived, then the recollection of God's preparatory dealings rushed upon your memory, and in an instant you saw how for the "forty days and the forty nights" solitary travel, your God and Savior had been graciously and amply providing. But all this mystery the life of faith, by which the justified live, fully explains.

OCTOBER 7

"For I am with you, says the Lord, to save you: though I make
a full end of all nations where I have scattered you, yet will I
not make a full end of you: but I will correct you in measure,
and will not leave you altogether unpunished." Jeremiah 30:11

THE Lord's love appears in appointing the rebuke, and in tempering the chastisement. That rebuke might have been heavier, that chastisement might have been severer. The deep and dark waters might have engulfed the soul. Thus, perhaps, your prayer has been answered, "O Lord, correct me, but with judgment; not in your anger, lest you bring me to nothing." And then has followed the pleasant psalm of grateful acknowledgment and praise: "The Lord is merciful and gracious, slow to anger, and plenteous in mercy. He will not always chide; neither will He keep His anger forever. He has not dealt with us after our sins; nor rewarded us according to our iniquities." Oh, could we always analyze the cup, how astonished should we be to find that in the bitterest draught that ever touched our lips the principal ingredient was love! That love saw the discipline needful, and love selected the chastisement sent, and love appointed the instrument by which it should come, and love arranged the circumstances by which it should take place, and love fixed the time when it should transpire, and love heard the sigh, and saw the tear, and marked the anguish, and never for one moment withdrew its beaming eye from the sufferer. Alas! how much is this truth overlooked by the disciplined believer! Think, suffering child of God, of the many consoling, alleviating, and soothing circumstances connected with your chastisement. How much worse your position might be, how much more aggravated the nature of your sorrow, and how much heavier the stroke of the rod. Think of the disproportion of the chastisement to the sin, for "know that God exacts of you less than your iniquity deserves." Think of the many divine supports, the precious promises, the tenderness of God, the gentleness of Christ, the sympathy and affection dwelling in the hearts of the saints—and all this will demonstrate to you that the chastisement of the saints is the chastening of love.

OCTOBER 8

"Giving thanks unto the Father, which has made us fit to be
partakers of the inheritance of the saints in light." Colossians 1:12

BEAUTIFUL is the order of the Holy Spirit here. Observe to whom this grateful acknowledgment is made—"unto the Father." Then the sweet truth stands revealed—luminous in its own celestial light—that heaven is a Father's gift. And oh, how sweet, to trace all our mercies to a Father's love, to a Parent's heart—to look to Jesus, whose righteousness gives us a title—to look to the Holy Spirit, whose sanctifying grace gives us a fitness, as the precious gifts of a Father's love; then to rise through these up to the Father Himself, and trace the gift of heaven—the consummation of the inner life—to the heart of the First Person of the glorious Trinity. Who, after reading this passage, will any longer rest entirely and exclusively in Jesus— precious as He is? Who will not, through Jesus as the Mediator, rise to the Father, and trace up all the blessings of redemption, and all His hope of glory, to the part which the Father took in the great and wondrous work? Oh, how unutterable blessed is it to see the Father engaged, equally with the Son and the Spirit, in preparing for us, and in preparing us for, "the inheritance of the saints in light!" "Giving thanks unto the Father." Upon what grounds, beloved? Oh! it was the Father who provided the Savior, His beloved Son. It is from the Father that the Spirit emanates who renews and sanctifies. It is the Father who has prepared the inheritance, and who, by His upholding power, will at last bring us safely there. All thanks, then, all adoration and praise unto the Father, "who has made us fit to be partakers of the inheritance of the saints in light."

Let me affectionately ask you, my reader, in what does your fitness for heaven consist? Put not the question from you—transfer it not to another; let it come home to your own conscience: for in a little while your destiny will be fixed—eternally, irrevocably fixed; and one half-second of hell's torment will fill your soul with remorse, terror, and unavailing regret, that in the land of hope and in the day of grace your turned your back upon both, refused the mercy of God in Christ, rejected His dear Son, and died in your sins. In what does your fitness for heaven, then, consist? If it is only the fitness of a mere profession—if it is but the fitness of a mere notional reception of truth—if it is the fitness merely of an external waiting upon the sanctuary, the public means of grace—it is a fitness not for heaven, but for banishment from heaven! Are you born again of the Spirit of God? Have you fled to the Lord Jesus Christ for salvation? Have you the "earnest," the pledge of heaven, in the indwelling of the Holy Spirit of God—in the life of God in your soul? Have you the first sheaf of the harvest bound up in your bosom? Have you been sealed by God's Spirit as an heir of glory?

To God's saints I would say—cultivate an habitual, a growing fitness for heaven. Do not be satisfied with past attainments, with your present measure of grace and standard of holiness; but, beloved, since heaven is a holy place, cultivate holiness—an habitual growing fitness for "the inheritance of the saints in light." Be advancing, be progressing, be pressing onwards; "putting on the whole armor of God," "laying aside the weight that so easily besets you," the garment that trails upon the earth, pressing onward and heavenward, until you reach the confines of bliss, and enter within the portals of glory.

OCTOBER 9

"In hope of eternal life, which God, that cannot lie,
promised before the world began." Titus 1:2

LOOK upon all the Lord's covenant dealings with you as but preparatory to your approaching emancipation from all sin, suffering, and sorrow. Welcome your trials—they are sent by your Father. Welcome the stroke of His rod—it is a Parent smiting. Welcome whatever detaches you from earth, and wings your spirit heavenward. Welcome the furnace that consumes the dross and the tin, and brings out the precious gold and silver, to reflect in your soul, even now, the dawnings of future glory. Oh! be submissive, meek, and quiet, under God's chastening and afflicting hand, and receive all His dispensations as only tending to fit you more perfectly for "the inheritance of the saints in light." Let his "hope of eternal life" cheer and comfort the bereaved of the Lord, from whose hearts have fled the loved and sanctified ones of earth, to the eternal heaven. Oh! how full of consolation is this prospect! Where have the departed fled, who sleep in Jesus? They have but exchanged the region of darkness and shadow for the regions of light and glory. They have gone from the scene of impurity, defilement, and sin, to the place of perfect holiness, complete sanctification, and eternal love. Then dry your tears—then press the consolations of the gospel to your sorrowing heart, and look up with that eye of faith that pierces the penetrates the dark clouds that intervene between them and you, and behold them now "partakers of the inheritance of the saints in light." And oh! yourselves anticipate the blessed moment when the Savior shall send, not an enemy, but a friend—for such is death to the Christian—to open the cage that imprisons your spirit, and let you escape to the abodes of eternal glory. Oh! anticipate and, by anticipating, be preparing, day by day, for its realization; anticipate the happy moment which releases you from "the body of sin and death," and ushers you into the full enjoyment of "eternal life." Such is heaven, and such is the consummation of the inner life. As that life descended from God so to God it shall ultimately and finally return. It shall never, never die. Not a spark shall be quenched, nor shall a pulse cease to beat—not a thought that it has conceived, nor a desire it has cherished, nor a prayer it has breathed, nor a work it has accomplished, nor a victory it has won, shall die; all, all shall survive in ever—growing, ever-enduring glory.

The babe in grace shall be there! The young man, strong in overcoming the wicked one, shall be there! The father, matured in experience, and laden with the golden fruits of age, shall be there! All, all shall reach heaven at last—the end and the consummation of the life of God in their souls. Oh, to have this heaven in our hearts now! Heaven is love—the place of love—the perfection of love. And what is God's love in our hearts but the foretaste of heaven—the foretaste of heaven—the first gatherings of the vintage—the pledge and earnest of all that is to come?

OCTOBER 10

"Forasmuch as you know that you were not redeemed with corruptible things, as silver and gold, from your vain conversation received by tradition from your father; but with the precious blood of Christ, as of a lamb without blemish and without spot." 1 Peter 1:18, 19

WHAT a powerful motive does this truth supply to a daily and unreserved consecration of ourselves to the Lord! If, under the old economy, the utensil or the garment touched with blood was sacred and solemn, how much more the soul washed in the heart's blood of Christ! When the king of Israel, in the heat of battle, and in the agony of thirst, cried for water, and some of his attendants procured it for him at the hazard of their lives, the God-fearing and magnanimous monarch refused to taste it, because it was the price of blood! but "poured it out before the Lord." Christian soldier! it was not at the risk of His life, but more—it was by the sacrifice of His life that your Lord and Savior procured your redemption, and brought the waters of salvation, all living and sparkling from the throne of God, to your lips. You are the price of blood! "bought with a price." Will you not, then, glorify God in our soul, body, and substance, which are His? will you not pour it all out before the Lord—presenting it as a living sacrifice upon the altar flowing with the life-blood of God's own Son?

If there be a vital, and therefore a deathless, principle in the atoning blood of Jesus, then it will avail to the salvation of the chief of sinners to the latest period of time. Ages have rolled by since it was shed, and millions have gone to heaven in virtue of its merits, and yet it still avails! Listen, lowly penitent, to these glad tidings. Approach the blood of Jesus, simply believing in its divine appointment and sovereign efficacy, and the pardon it conveys and the peace it gives will be yours. Behold the sacred stream, as vital, as efficacious, and as free as when, eighteen hundred years ago, all nature was convulsed at the sight of this blood starting from the pierced heart of its Incarnate Creator, and when the expiring malefactor bathed in it as was saved! No, more; if the virtue of the Savior's blood before it was shed extended back to the time of Adam and of Abel, for He was "the Lamb slain from the foundation of the world," surely since that it has actually been offered, it will continue its virtue through all the revolutions of time to the remotest age of the world, and to the last sinner who may believe. If Jesus is a "Priest forever," the virtue of His sacrifice must abide forever, for He cannot officiate as a priest without a sacrifice. And as His gospel is to be preached to all nations, even to the end of the world, so the saving efficacy of His blood, upon which the gospel depends for its power and its success, must be as lasting as time.

OCTOBER 11

"Who is among you that fears the Lord, that obeys the voice of his servant, that walks in darkness, and has no light? let him trust in the name of the Lord, and stay upon his God." Isaiah 50:10

HOW prone is the believer to attach an undue importance to the mere article of comfort! to give place to the feeling that when comfort vanishes, all other good vanishes with it—thus, in fact, making the real standing of the soul to depend upon an ever-fluctuating emotion. But let it be remembered that the comfort of grace may be suspended, and yet the existence of grace may remain; that the glory of faith may be beclouded, and yet the principle of faith continue. Contemplate, as affording an illustrious example of this, our adorable Lord upon the cross. Was there ever sorrow like His sorrow? Was there ever desertion like His desertion? Every spring of consolation was dried up. Every beam of light was beclouded. All sensible joy was withdrawn. His human soul was now passing through its strange, its total eclipse. And still His faith hung upon God. Hear Him exclaim,

"My God! my God!" My strong One! my strong One! His soul was in the storm—and oh, what a storm was that!—but it was securely anchored upon His Father. There was in His case the absence of all consolation, the suspension of every stream of comfort; and yet in this, the darkest cloud that ever enshrouded the soul, and the deepest sorrow that ever broke the heart, He stayed His soul upon God.

And why should the believer, the follower of Christ, when sensible comfort is withdrawn, "cast away his confidence, which has great recompense of reward"? Of what use is the anchor but to keep the vessel in the tempest? What folly were it in the mariner to weigh his anchor, or to slip his cable, when the clouds gather blackness and the waves swell high! Then it is he most needs them both. It is true he has cast his anchor into the deep, and the depth hides it from his view; but though he cannot discern it through the foaming waves, still he knows that it is firmly fastened, and will keep his storm-tossed vessel from stranding upon a lee shore. And why should the believer, when "trouble is near," and sensible comfort is withdrawn, resign his heart a prey to unbelieving fears, and cherish in his bosom the dark suspicion of God? Were not this to part with the anchor of his hope at the very moment that he the most needed it? I may not be able to pierce the clouds and look within the veil with an eye beaming with an undimmed and assured joy, but I know that the Forerunner is there; that the Priest is upon His throne; that Jesus is alive, and is at the right hand of God—then all is safe: faith demands, hope expects, and love desires no more.

OCTOBER 12

"And if any man sin, we have an advocate with the
Father, Jesus Christ the righteous." 1 John 2:1

WE are used to read in the Bible of one Intercessor, and of one advocacy. But the believer has two courts with which prayer has to do. In the court below, where prayer is offered, the Spirit is his Intercessor. In the court above, where prayer is presented, Jesus is his Intercessor. Then, what an honored, what a privileged man, is the praying man! On earth—the lower court—he has a Counselor instructing him for what he should pray, and how he should order his suit. In heaven—the higher court—he has an Advocate presenting to God each petition as it ascends, separating from it all that is ignorant, sinful, and weak, and pleading for its gracious acceptance, and asking for its full bestowment. Here, then, is our vast encouragement in prayer. The inditings of the Spirit—the Intercessor of earth—are always in agreement with the mind of God. In prayer we need just such a Divine counselor. Is it temporal blessing that we crave? We need to be taught how to graduate our request to our necessity, and how to shape our necessity to our heavenly calling. Supplication for temporal good is, we think, limited. And this is the limit, "Having food and clothing, let us be therewith content." What child of God is warranted in asking worldly wealth, or distinction, or rank? And what child of God, in a healthy state of soul, would ask them? "But," says the apostle, "my God shall supply all your need, according to His riches in glory by Christ Jesus." Should God, in His providence, send either of these temporal things undesired, unasked, and unexpected, receive it as from Him, and use it as to Him. But with regard to spiritual blessings, our grant is illimitable, our requests may be boundless. "Ask what you will," is the broad, unrestricted warrant. When we ask to be perfected in the love of God, we ask for that which is in accordance with the will of God—for "God is love." When we ask for an increase of faith, we ask for that which is in accordance with the will of God; for "without faith it is impossible to please him." When we ask for more divine conformity, we ask for that which is in harmony with God's will; for He has said, "Be you holy, for I am holy." And when we ask for comfort, we plead for that which it is in His heart to give—for He is the "God of all comfort." Oh, to possess a Divine counselor, dwelling in our hearts, who will never indite a wrong prayer, nor suggest a weak argument, nor mislead us in any one particular, in the solemn, the important, the holy engagement of prayer; who is acquainted with the purpose of God; who knows the mind of God; who understands the will of God; who reads the heart of God; yes, who is God Himself. What encouragement is this to more real prayer! Are you moved to pray? While you muse, does the fire burn? Is your heart stirred up to ask of God some especial blessing for yourself, or for others? Are you afflicted? Oh, then, rise and pray—the Spirit prompts you—the Savior invites you—your heavenly Father waits to answer you.

With such an Intercessor in the court on earth—so divine, so loving, and so sympathizing—and with such an Intercessor in the court in heaven—so powerful, so eloquent, and so successful, "let us come boldly unto the throne of grace, that we may obtain mercy, and find grace to help in time of need."

OCTOBER 13

"But the end of all things is at hand: be you therefore
sober, and watch unto prayer." 1 Peter 4:7

WATCH unto prayer, with all diligence and perseverance. Expect an answer to your prayer, a promise to your request, a compliance with your suit. Be as much assured that God will answer, as that you have asked, or that He has promised. Ask in faith; only believe; watch daily at the posts and at the gates of the return; look for it at any moment, and through any providence; expect it not in your own way, but in the Lord's; do not be astonished if He should answer your prayer in the very opposite way to that you had anticipated, and it may be dictated. With this view, watch every providence, even the smallest. You know not when the answer my come—at what hour, or in what way. Therefore watch. The Lord may answer in a great and strong wind, in an earthquake, in a fire, or in a still small voice; therefore watch every providence, to know which will be the voice of God to you. Do not pray as if you asked for or expected a refusal. God delights in your holy fervency, your humble boldness, and your persevering importunity. "The effectual fervent prayer of a righteous man avails much." Pray submissively, expect hopefully, watch vigilantly, and wait patiently.

Behold then the throne of grace! Was ever resting-place so sacred and so sweet? Could God himself invest it with richer, with greater attraction? There are dispensed all the blessings of sovereign grace—pardon, justification, adoption, sanctification, and all that connects the present state of the believer with eternal glory. There is dispensed grace itself—grace to guide, to support, to comfort, and to help in time of need. There sits the God of grace, proclaiming Himself "the Lord God, merciful and gracious, long-suffering, and abundant in goodness and truth; keep mercy for thousands, forgiving iniquity, transgression, and sin." There is extended the scepter of grace, bidding welcome the sons of daughters of want, the weary and the heavy laden, the guilty, the broken in heart, the poor, the friendless, the bereaved. There stands Jesus the High Priest and Mediator, full of grace and truth, waving to and fro His golden censer, from which pours forth the fragrant incense of His atoning merits, wreathing in one offering, as it ascends, the name, the needs, and the prayer of the lowly worshiper. And there, too, is the Spirit of grace, breathing in the soul, discovering the want, inditing the petition, and making intercession for the saints according to the will of God. Behold, then, the throne of grace, and draw near! You are welcome. Come with your cross, come with your infirmity, come with your guilt, come with your want, come with your wounded spirit, come with your broken heart, come and welcome to the throne of grace! Come without price, come without worthiness, come without preparation, come without fitness, come with your hard heart, come and welcome to the throne of grace! God, your Father, bids you welcome. Jesus, your Advocate, bids you welcome. The Spirit, the Author of prayer, bids you welcome. All the happy and the blessed who cluster around it, bid you welcome. The spirits of just men made perfect in glory, bid you welcome. The ministering spirits, "sent forth to minister for them who shall be heirs of salvation," bid you welcome. All the holy below, and all the glorified above, all, all bid you, poor trembling soul, welcome, thrice welcome, to the throne of grace!

OCTOBER 14

"Praying always with all prayer and supplication in the Spirit, and watching thereunto with all perseverance and supplication for all saints; and for me, that utterance may be given unto me, that I may open my mouth boldly, as I ought to speak." Ephesians 6:18, 19

THE two blessings which Paul craved through the prayers of his flock were, utterance and boldness. He knew that He who made man's mouth could only open his lips to proclaim the unsearchable riches of Christ. Great as were his natural endowments, rich and varied as were his intellectual acquirements, he felt their inadequacy when working alone. We should never fail to distinguish between the natural eloquence of man and the holy utterance which the Spirit gives. Paul had splendid gifts and commanding powers of elocution. But what were they? He needed more—he asked for more. Dear reader, if the ministry of reconciliation comes to your soul with any power or sweetness, remember whose it is. Give not to man but to God the glory. Be very jealous for the honor of the Spirit in the ministry of the word. It is "spirit and life" to you only as He gives utterance to him that speaks. It is mournful to observe to what extent the idolatry of human talent and eloquence is carried, and how little glory is given to the Holy Spirit in the gospel ministry.

But there was yet another ministerial qualification which Paul sought. He desired to be unshackled from the fear of man. "That I may open my mouth boldly." Had we heard him utter this request, we might have been constrained to reply, "Do you desire boldness? You are the most courageous and intrepid of the apostles. You fear no man!" Ah! we forget that when God stirs up the heart of a believer deeply to feel his need, and earnestly to desire any particular grace of the Spirit, that grace will be the distinguishing trait of his Christian character. The very possession and exercise of a grace strengthens the desire for its increase. The more we have of Christ, the more we desire of Christ. The heart is never satiated. Do we see a man earnest and importunate in prayer for faith? faith will be his distinguishing grace. See we another wrestling with God for deep views of the evil of sin? that man will be marked for his humble walk with God. Is it love that He desires? His will be a loving spirit. Be sure of this—the more you know of the value and the sweetness of any single grace of the Spirit, the more ardently will your heart be led out after an increase of that grace. The reason why our desires for grace are so faint, may be traced to the small measure of grace that we already possess. The very feebleness of the desire proves the deficiency of the supply. As all holy desire springs from grace, so the deeper the grace, the more fervent will be the desire. The Lord rouse us from our slothful seeking of Him upon our beds.

OCTOBER 15

"Be watchful, and strengthen the things which remain, that are ready to die: for I have not found your works perfect before God." Revelation 3:2

AN incipient state of declension does not involve any alteration in the essential character of divine grace, but is a secret decay of the health, vigor, and exercise of that grace in the soul. As in the animal frame, the heart loses nothing of its natural function, when, through disease, it sends but a faint and languid pulsation through the system; so in the spiritual constitution of the believer, divine grace may be sickly, feeble, and inoperative, and yet retain its character and its properties. The pulse may beat faintly, but still it beats; the seed may not be fruitful, but it "lives and abides forever;" the divine nature may be languid, but it can never assimilate or coalesce with any other, and must always retain its divinity untainted and unchanged. And yet, without changing its nature, divine grace may decline to an alarming extent in its power and exercise. It may be sickly, drooping, and ready to die; it may become so enfeebled through its decay, as to present an ineffectual resistance to the inroads of strong corruption; so low that the enemy may ride roughshod over it at his will; so inoperative and yielding, that sloth, worldliness, pride, carnality, and their kindred vices, may obtain an easy and unresisted conquest. This decay of grace may be advancing, too, without any marked decline in the spiritual perception of the judgment, as to the beauty and fitness of spiritual truth. The loss of spiritual enjoyment, not of a spiritual perception, of the loveliness and harmony of the truth shall be the symptom that betrays the true condition of the soul. The judgment shall lose none of its light, but the heart much of its fervor; the truths of revelation, especially the doctrines of grace, shall occupy the same prominent position as to their value and beauty, and yet the influence of these truths may be scarcely felt. The Word of God shall be assented to; but as the instrument of sanctification, of abasement, of nourishment, the believer may be an almost utter stranger to it; yes, he must necessarily be so, while this process of secret declension is going forward in his soul.

This incipient state of declension may not involve any lowering of the standard of holiness, and yet there shall be no ascending of the heart, no reaching forth of the mind, towards a practical conformity to that standard. The judgment shall acknowledge the divine law, as embodied in the life of Christ, to be the rule of the believer's walk; and yet to so low and feeble a state may vital godliness have declined in the soul, there shall be no panting after conformity to Christ, no breathing after holiness, no "resistance unto blood, striving against sin." Oh, it is an alarming condition for a Christian man, when the heart contradicts the judgment, and the life belies the profession!—when there is more knowledge of the truth than experience of its power—more light in the understanding than grace in the affections—more pretension in the profession than holiness and spirituality in the walk! And yet to this sad and melancholy state it is possible for a Christian professor to be reduced. How should it lead the man of empty notions, of mere creed, of lofty pretension, of cold and lifeless orthodoxy, to pause, search his heart, examine his conscience, and ascertain the true state of his soul before God!

OCTOBER 16

"If I regard iniquity in my heart, the Lord will not hear me." Psalm 64:18

THE true spiritual mortification of indwelling sin, and the entire forsaking of the known cause, whatever it is found to be, of the heart's declension, constitute the true elements of a believer's restoration to the joys of God's salvation. There cannot possibly be any true, spiritual, and abiding revival of grace, while secret sin remains undiscovered and unmortified in the heart. True and spiritual mortification of sin is not a surface-work: it consists not merely in pruning the dead tendrils that hang here and there upon the branch; it is not the lopping off of outward sins, and an external observance of spiritual duties; it includes essentially far more than this: it is a laying the axe at the root of sin in the believer; it aims at nothing less than the complete subjection of the principle of sin; and until this is effectually done, there can be no true return of the heart to God. Christian reader, what is the cause of your soul's secret declension? What is it that at this moment feeds upon the precious plant of grace, destroying its vigor, its beauty, and its fruitfulness? Is it an inordinate attachment to the creature? mortify it;—the love of self? mortify it;—the love of the world? mortify it;—some sinful habit secretly indulged? mortify it. It must be mortified, root as well as branch, if you would experience a thorough return to God. Dear though it be, as a right hand, or as a right eye, if yet it comes between your soul and God, if it crucifies Christ in you, if it weakens faith, enfeebles grace, destroys the spirituality of the soul, rendering it barren and unfruitful, rest not short of its utter mortification. Nor must this great work be undertaken in your own strength. It is preeminently the result of God the Holy Spirit working in and blessing the self-efforts of the believer: "If you through the Spirit do mortify the deeds of the body, you shall live." Here is a recognition of the believer's own exertions, in connection with the power of the Holy Spirit: "If you" (believers, you saints of God) "through the Spirit do mortify the deeds." It is the work of the believer himself, but the power is of the Spirit of God. Take, then, your discovered sin to the Spirit: that Spirit bringing the cross of Jesus, with a killing, crucifying power, into your soul, giving you such a view of a Savior suffering for sin, as it may be you never had before, will in a moment lay your enemy slain at your feet. Oh yield not to despair, distressed soul! Are you longing for a gracious revival of God's work within you?—are you mourning in secret over your heart-declension?— have you searched and discovered the hidden cause of your decay?—and is your real desire for its mortification? Then look up, and hear the consolatory words of your Lord: "I am the Lord that heals you." The Lord is your healer; His love can restore you; His blood can heal you; His grace can subdue your sin.

"Take with you words, and turn to the Lord; say unto him, Take away all iniquity, and receive us graciously:" and the Lord will answer, "I will heal their backslidings, I will love them freely; for mine anger is turned away from him."

OCTOBER 17

"To declare, I say, at this time his righteousness: that he might be just, and the justifier of him which believes in Jesus." Romans 3:26

IN Jesus shines the awful glory of Divine Justice. Justice is but another term for holiness. It is holiness in strict and awful exercise; and yet it is a distinct perfection of Jehovah, in the revelation of acknowledgment of which He will be glorified. The basis of the Atonement is righteousness, or justice. So the apostle argues, "Whom God has set forth to be a propitiation through faith in His blood, to declare His righteousness for the remission of sins." Anterior to the apostasy of man, the only revelation of God's justice was the threatening annexed to the law: "In the day that you eat thereof, you shall surely die." Subsequent to the fall, the appointment of a sanguinary ritual—the institution of expiatory sacrifices, not only recognized the existence, but illustrated the nature, of this awful attribute. There are those who madly dream of acceptance with a holy God, at the expense of this perfection of His nature. In vain do they acknowledge Him in some of His perfections if they deny Him in others, tramping them with indifference beneath their feet. Such was Cain in the offering which he presented to the Lord; there was an acknowledgment of His dominion and goodness, but no distinct recognition of His holiness, no solemn apprehension of His Justice, no conviction of guilt, no confession of sin. The claims of God's moral government were entirely set aside, and, by consequence, the necessity of a Mediator totally denied. Not so Abel; his offering honored God in that in which He most delights to be honored, in His spotless purity, His inflexible justice, and His infinite grace in the appointment of a Savior for the pardon of iniquity, transgression, and sin. Therefore it is recorded, and we do well deeply to ponder it, the "he offered unto God a more excellent sacrifice than Cain."

But this was a prefigurement only of God's justice—the mere type and shadow. The great Antitype and embodiment are seen in Jesus offering Himself up a whole burned-offering to God amid the fearful blaze which was beheld ascending from the summit of Mount Calvary. Then did this perfection appear in its most fearful form—Jesus bearing sin—Jesus enduring the curse of the law—Jesus sustaining the wrath of His father— Jesus surrendering His holy soul a sacrifice for man's transgression. Oh, never, never did Divine justice so imperatively assert its claims, and so loudly demand its rights—never did it so strictly exact its penalty, and so fearfully grapple with its victim, as now; and never before or since had such a sacrifice been bound to its altar; never did Jehovah appear so just, as at the moment the fire descended and consumed His only-begotten and well-beloved Son.

OCTOBER 18

"Lord, behold, he whom you loves is sick."

THIS is the truth, dear invalid reader, upon which the Lord would pillow and sustain your soul—that you are the sick one whom He loves. Doubtless the enemy, ever on the watch to distress the saints of God, eager to avail himself of every circumstance in their history favorable to the accomplishment of His malignant designs, has taken advantage of your illness to suggest hard and distrustful thoughts of the Lord's love to you. "Does He love you? Can He love you, and afflict you thus? What! this hectic fever, these night-sweats, these faintings and swoonings, these insufferable tortures, this long wasting, this low insidious disease—and yet loved by God! Impossible!" Such has been the false reasoning of Satan, and such the echo of unbelief. But Lazarus was loved of Jesus, and so are you! That darkened room, that curtained bed, contains one for whom the Son of God came down to earth—to live, to labor, and to die! That room is often radiant with His presence, and that bed is often made with His hands. Jesus is never absent from that spot! The affectionate husband, the tender wife, the fond parent, the devoted sister, the faithful nurse, are not in more constant attendance at that solemn post of observation than is Jesus. They must be absent; He never is, for one moment, away from that couch. Sleep must overcome them; but He who guards that suffering patient "neither slumbers nor sleeps." Long-continued watching must exhaust the prostrate them; but He, the Divine watcher, "faints not, neither is weary." Yes, Jesus loves you, nor loves you the less, no, but loves you the more, now that you are prostrate upon that bed of languishing, a weak one hanging upon Him. Again I repeat, this is the only truth that will now soothe and sustain your soul. Not the thought of our love to Jesus, but of Jesus' love to you, is the truth upon which your agitated mind is to rest. In the multitude of your thoughts within you, this is the comfort that will delight your soul—"Jesus loves me." Your love to Christ affords you now no plea, no encouragement, no hope. You can extract no sweetness from the thought of your affection to the Savior. It has been so feeble and fluctuating a feeling, an emotion so irregular and fickle in its expression, the spark so often obscured, and to appearance lost, that the recollection and the review of it now only tends to depress and perplex you. But oh, the thought of the Lord's love! to fix the mind upon His eternal, unpurchased, and deathless affection to you—to be enabled to resolve this painful illness, this protracted suffering this "pining sickness," into love—divine, tender, unwearied, inextinguishable love—will renew the inward man, while the outward is decaying day by day, and will strengthen the soul in its heavenly soarings, while its tenement of dust is crumbling and falling from around it. All is love in the heart of God towards you. This sickness may indeed be a correction—and correction always supposes sin—but it is a loving correction, and designed to "increase your greatness." Not one thought dwells in the mind of God, nor one feeling throbs in His heart, but is love. And your sickness is sent to testify that God is love, and that you, afflicted though you are, are one of its favored objects. The depression of sickness may throw a shade of obscurity over this truth, but the very obscuration may result in your good, and unfold God's love, by bringing you to a more simple reliance of faith. Oh, trace your present sickness, dear invalid reader, to His love who "Himself took our infirmities, and carried our sickness." If He could have accomplished the important end for which it is sent by exempting you from its infliction, you then had not known one sleepless hour, nor a solitary day; not a drop of sweat had moistened your brow, nor one moment's fever had flushed your cheek. He, your loving Savior, your tender Friend, the redeeming God, had borne it all for you Himself, even as He bore its tremendous curse—your curse and sin in His own body on the tree. Yield your depressed heart to the soothing, healing influence of this precious truth, and it will light up the pallid hue of sickness with a radiance and a glow—the reflection of the soul's health—heavenly and divine. "Lord, behold, he whom You loves is sick."

OCTOBER 19

"The Lord God has given me the tongue of the learned, that I should know how to speak a word in season to him that is weary." Isaiah 50:4

THE Lord Jesus gives His people the tongue of the learned, the they may sometimes speak a word in season to His weary ones. Have you not a word for Christ? May you not go to that tried believer in sickness, in poverty, in adversity, or in prison, and tell of the balm that has often healed your spirit, and of the cordial that has often cheered your heart? "A word spoken in due season, how good is it!" A text quoted, a sentiment repeated, an observation made, a hint dropped, a kind caution suggested, a gentle rebuke given, a tender admonition left—oh! the blessing that has flowed from it! It was a word spoken in season! Say not with Moses, "I am slow of speech, and of a slow tongue;" or with Jeremiah, "Ah! Lord God! behold, I cannot speak; for I am a child." Hear the answer of the Lord: "Who has made man's mouth? have not I, the Lord? Now therefore go: I will be with your mouth, and teach you what you shall say." And oh! how frequently and effectually does the Lord speak to His weary ones, even through the weary. All, perhaps, was conflict within, and darkness without; but one word falling from the lips of a man of God has been the voice of God to the soul. And what an honor conferred, thus to be the channel conveying consolation from the loving heart of the Father to the disconsolate heart of the child! to go and smooth a ruffled pillow, lift the pressure from off a burdened spirit, and light up the gloomy chamber of sorrow, of sickness, and of death, as with the first dawnings of the coming glory! Go, Christian reader, and ask the Lord so to clothe your tongue with holy, heavenly eloquence, that you may know how to speak a word in season to him that is weary. Ah! it is impossible to speak of the preciousness of Christ to another, and not, while we speak, feel Him precious to our own souls. It is impossible to lead another to the cross, and not find ourselves overshadowed by its glory. It is impossible to establish another in the being, character, and truth of God, and not feel our own minds fortified and confirmed. It is impossible to quote the promises and unfold the consolations of the gospel to another, and not be sensible of a tranquillizing and soothing influence stealing softly over our own hearts. It is impossible to break the alabaster box, and not fill the house with the odor of the ointment.

In contending for the faith, remember that the Lord Jesus can give you the tongue of the learned. Listen to His promises—"I will give you a mouth and wisdom, which all your adversaries shall not be able to gainsay nor resist." Thus the most unlearned and the most weak may be so deeply taught, and be so skillfully armed in Christ's school, as to be able valiantly to defend and successfully to preach the truth, putting to "silence the ignorance of foolish men."

OCTOBER 20

"O Lord, truly I am your servant; I am your servant, and the son of your handmaid: you have loosed my bonds." Psalm 116:16

IT is a circumstance worthy of remark, and important in the instruction which it conveys, that, among all the examples of deep humility, self-abasement, consciousness and confession of sin, recorded of the saints in the word, not one appears to a afford an instance of a denial or undervaluing of the Spirit's work in the heart. Keen as appears to have been the sense of unworthiness felt by Jacob, David, Job, Isaiah, Peter, Paul, and others—deep as was their conviction, and humiliating as were their confessions of sin's exceeding sinfulness, not one expression seems to betray a denial of the work of the Holy Spirit in their souls: they felt and mourned, they wept

and confessed, as men called of God, pardoned, justified, adopted; not ,
men who had never tasted that the Lord was gracious, and who therefore
were utter strangers to the operation of the Spirit upon their hearts: they
acknowledged their sinfulness and their backslidings as converted men,
always ready and forward to crown the Spirit in His work. But what can
grieve the tender loving heart of the Spirit more deeply than a denial of
His work in the soul? And yet there is a perpetual tendency to this, in
the unbelieving doubts, legal fears, and gloomy forebodings which those
saints yield to, who, at every discovery of the sin that dwells in them
resign themselves to the painful conviction, that they have been given
over of God to believe a lie! To such we would earnestly say, Grieve not
thus the Holy Spirit of God. Deep self-abasement, the consciousness of
utter worthlessness, need not necessarily involve a denial of the indwelling
grace in the heart; yes, this blessed state is perfectly consistent with the
most elevated hope of eternal life. He that can confess himself the "chief
of sinners" and "the least of saints," is most likely to acknowledge, "I know
in whom I have believed,"—"He has loved me, and given Himself for me."
What! is it all fabulous that you have believed? is it all a delusion that you
have experienced? have you been grasping at a shadow, believing a lie, and
fighting as one that beats the air? are you willing to yield your hope, and
cast away your confidence? What! have you never known the plague of your
own heart, the sweetness of godly sorrow at the foot of the cross? have you
never felt your heart beat one throb of love to Jesus? has His dear name
never broken in sweet cadence on your ear? are you willing to admit that all
the grief you have felt, all the joy you have experienced, and all the blessed
anticipations you have known, were but as a "cunningly devised fable," a
device of the wicked one, a moral hallucination of the mind? Oh, grieve
not thus the Holy Spirit of God! deny not, undervalue not, His blessed
work within you! What if you have been led into deeper discoveries of
your fallen nature, your unworthiness, vileness, insufficiency, declensions,
and backsliding from God, we ask, Whose work is this? whose, but that
same blessed, loving Spirit whom thus you are wounding, quenching,
grieving, denying? How many whose eye may trace this page are in this
very state—not merely writing hard and bitter things against themselves,
but also against the blessed, loving, faithful Spirit of God—calling grace

nature, denying His work in them, and, in a sense most painful to His tender heart, "speaking words against the Holy Spirit."

OCTOBER 21

"I do not frustrate the grace of God." Galatians 2:21

THERE is much spurious humility among many saints of God, and this is one of its common forms. It is not pride gratefully to acknowledge what great things the Lord has done for us—it is pride that refuses to acknowledge them; it is not true humility to doubt and underrate, until it becomes easy to deny altogether, the work of the Holy Spirit within us—it is true humility and lowliness to confess His work, bear testimony to His operation, and ascribe to Him all the power, praise, and glory. See then, dear reader, that you cherish not this false humility, which is but another name for deep unmortified pride of heart; remember that as Satan may transform himself into an angel of light, so may his agencies assume the disguise of the most holy and lovely graces; thus pride, one of his master-agents of evil in the heart, may appear in the shape of the profoundest humility. And I would have you bear in mind, too, that though the work of the Spirit in your heart may, to your imperfect knowledge and dim eye, be feeble—the outline scarcely visible amid so much indwelling sin—the spark almost hid amid so much abounding corruption, yet, to the Spirit's eye, that work appears in all its distinctness and glory. "The Lord knows those who are His." This declaration will apply with equal truth to the knowledge which the Holy Spirit has of His own work in the believer. His eye is upon the gentlest buddings of indwelling grace; the faintest spark of love, the softest whisper of holy desire, the most feeble yearnings of the heart towards Jesus—all, all is known to, and loved by, the Spirit; it is His own work, and strange should He not recognize it. Suffer this consideration to have its proper weight in hushing those murmurings, soothing those fears, and neutralizing those doubts that so deeply grieve the Holy Spirit of God: yield yourself up unto Him; humbly acknowledge what He has done in you; follow the little light He has given you, call into constant and active exercise the small degree of grace and faith which He has imparted, and seek, "with all prayer and supplication," an enlarged degree of His holy, anointing, sanctifying, and sealing influence.

OCTOBER 22

"Blessed are those who have not seen, and
yet have believed." John 20:29

THE circumstances of the Savior's resurrection were in harmony with its lonely and solemn grandeur. No human witness was privileged to behold it. The mysterious reunion of the human soul with the body of Christ was an illustrious event, upon which no mortal eye was permitted to gaze. There is a moral grandeur of surpassing character in the resurrection of Christ unseen. The fact is not an object with which sense has so much to do, as faith. And that no human eye was permitted to witness the stupendous event, doubtless, was designed to teach man that it was with the spiritual, and not with the fleshly, apprehension of this truth that He had especially to do. What eye but that of faith could see the illustrious Conqueror come forth, binding with adamantine chains hell, death, and the grave? What principle but the spiritual and mighty principle of faith could enter into the revealed mind of God, sympathize with the design of the Savior, and interpret the sublime mystery of this stupendous event? It was proper, therefore, no it was worthy of God, and in harmony with the character and the design of the resurrection of our Lord, that a veil should conceal its actual accomplishment from the eye of His Church; and that the great evidence they should have of the truth of the fact should be the power of His resurrection felt and experienced in their souls. Oh yes! the only power of the Savior's resurrection which we desire to know is that which comes to us through the energy of an all—seeing, all-conquering, all-believing faith. Oh, give me this, rather than to have witnessed with these eyes the celestial attendants clustering around the tomb—the rolling away of the stone that was upon the sepulcher—the breaking of the seal—and the emerging form of the Son of God, bearing in His hands the emblems and the tokens of His victory. The spiritual so infinitely transcends the carnal—the eye of faith is so much more glorious than the eye of sense, that our Lord Himself has sanctified and sealed it with His own precious blessing—"Jesus says unto him, Thomas, because you have seen me you have believed: blessed are those who have not seen, and yet have believed." Blessed Jesus! in faith would I then follow You each step of Your journey through this valley of tears; in faith would I visit the manger, the cross, and the tomb; for You have pronounced him blessed above all, who, though he sees not, yet believes in You. "Lord, I believe: help You mine unbelief."

OCTOBER 23

"The just shall live by faith." Hebrews 10:38

THE experience of every believer is, in a limited degree, the experience of the great apostle of the Gentiles, the tip of whose soaring pinion we, who so much skim the earth's surface, can scarcely touch—"The life which I now live in the flesh, I live by the faith of the Son of God." "Like precious faith" with his dwells in the hearts of all the regenerate. Along this royal highway it is ordained of God that all His people should travel. It is the way their Lord traveled before them; it is the way they are to follow after Him. The first step they take out of the path of sense is into the path of faith. And what a mighty grace do they find it, as they journey on! Do they live? it is by faith. Hebrews 10:38. Do they stand? it is by faith. Romans 11:20. Do they walk? it is by faith. 2 Corinthians 5:7. Do they fight? it is by faith. 1 Timothy 6:12. Do they overcome? it is by faith. 1 John 5:4. Do they see what is invisible? it is by faith. Hebrews 6:27. Do they receive what is incredible? it is by faith. Romans 4:20. Do they achieve what is impossible? it is by faith. Mark 9:23. Glorious achievements of faith!

And, oh, how eminently is Jesus thus glorified in His saints! Was it no glory to Joseph, that, having the riches of Egypt in his hands, all the people were made, as it were, to live daily and hourly upon him? Was no fresh accession of glory brought to his exaltation, by every fresh acknowledgment of his authority, and every renewed application to his wealth? And is not Jesus glorified in His exaltation and in His fullness, in His love and in His grace, by that faith, in the exercise of which "a poor and afflicted people," a needy and a tried Church, are made to travel to, and live upon, Him each moment? Ah, yes! every corruption taken to His sanctifying grace, every burden taken to his omnipotent arm, every sorrow taken to His sympathizing heart, every want taken to His overflowing fullness, every wound taken to His healing hand, every sin taken to His cleansing blood, and every deformity taken to His all-covering righteousness, swells the revenue of glory which each second of time ascends to our adorable Redeemer from His Church. You may have imagined—for I will now suppose myself addressing a seeking soul— that Christ has been more glorified by your hanging back from Him—doubting the efficacy of His blood to cancel your guilt, the power of His grace to mortify your corruption, the sufficiency of His fullness to supply your need, the sympathy of His nature to soothe your grief, and the loving willingness of His heart to receive and welcome you as you are, empty, vile, and worthless; little thinking, on the contrary, how much He has been grieved and wounded, dishonored and robbed of His glory, by this doubting of His love, and this distrusting of His grace, after all the melting exhibitions of the one, and all the convincing evidences of the other. But, is it the desire of your inmost soul that Christ should be glorified by you? Then do not forget the grand, luminous truth of the Bible, that He is the Savior of sinners, and of sinners as sinners—that, in the great matter of the soul's salvation, He recognizes nothing of worthiness in the creature; and that whatever human merit is brought to Him with a view of commending the case to His notice—whatever—be it even the incipient work of His own Spirit in the heart—is appended to His finished work, as a ground of acceptance with God, is so much detraction from His glory as a Redeemer—than which, of nothing is He more jealous—and consequently, places the soul at a great remove from His grace. But like Bartimeus, casting the garment from you, be that garment what it may—pride of merit, pride of intellect, pride of learning, pride of family, pride of place, yes, whatever hinders your entering the narrow way, and prevents your receiving the kingdom of God "as a little child," and coming to Jesus to be saved by Him alone—brings more real glory to Him than imagination can conceive, or words can describe.

OCTOBER 24

"Furthermore, we have had fathers of our flesh which corrected us, and we gave them reverence: shall we not much rather be in subjection unto the Father of spirits, and live?" Hebrews 12:9

IT is the revealed will of God that His child should meekly and silently bow to His chastening hand. And when the tried and afflicted believer "hears the rod, and who has appointed it," and with a humble and filial acquiescence justifies the wisdom, the love, and even the tenderness that sent it—surely such a soul is a rich partaker of God's holiness. In all these particulars, there is a surrender of the will to God, and consequently a close approximation to the holiness of His nature. Dear reader, the point we are now upon is one of the great moment. It involves as much your holy and happy walk, as it does the glory of God. We put the simple questions—can there be any advance of sanctification in the soul, when the will is running counter to the Divine will?—and can that believer walk happily, when there is a constant opposition in his mind to all the dealings of his God and Father? Oh no! Holiness and happiness are closely allied; and both are the offspring of a humble, filial, and complete surrender of the will in all things to God. I speak not of this as an attainment in holiness soon or easily gained. Far from it. In many, it is the work of years—in all, of painful discipline. It is not on the high mount of joy, but in the low valley of humiliation, that this precious and holy surrender is learned. It is not in the summer day, when all things smile and wear a sunny aspect—then it were easy, to say, "Your will be done;" but, when a cloudy and a wintry sky looks down upon you—when the chill blast of adversity blows—when health fails, when friends die—when wealth departs—when the heart's fondest endearments are yielded—when the Isaac is called for—when the world turns its back—when all is gone, and you are like a tree of the desert, over which the tempest has swept, stripping it of every branch—when you are brought so low, that it would seem to you lower you could not be—then to look up with filial love and exclaim, "My Father, Your will be done!"—oh, this is holiness, this is happiness indeed. It may be God, your God and Father, is dealing thus with you now. Has He taken from you health? has He asked for the surrender of your Isaac? have riches taken to themselves wings? does the world frown? Ah! little do you think how God is now about to unfold to you the depths of His love, and to cause your will sweetly, filially, and entirely to flow into His. Let me repeat the observation—a higher degree of sanctification there cannot be, than a will entirely swallowed up in God's. Earnestly pray for it, diligently seek it. Be jealous of the slightest opposition of your mind, watch against the least rebellion of the will, wrestle for an entire surrender—to be where, and to be what, your covenant God and Father would have you; and so shall you be made a partaker of His holiness.

OCTOBER 25

"For they verily for a few days chastened us after their own pleasure; but he for our profit, that we might be partakers of his holiness." Hebrews 12:10

BELOVED reader, have you long asked for the removal of some secret, heavy, painful cross? Perhaps you are still urging your request; and yet the Lord seems not to answer you. And why? Because the request may not be in itself wise. Were He now to remove that cross, He may, in taking away the cross, close up a channel of mercy which you would never cease to regret. Oh, what secret and immense blessing may that painful cross be the means of conveying into your soul! Is it health you have long petitioned for? And is the request denied you? It is wisdom that denies. It is love, too, tender, unchangeable love to your soul, that refuses a petition which a wise and gracious God knows, if granted, would not be for your real good and His glory. Do you not think that there is love and tenderness enough in the heart of Jesus to grant you what you desire, and ten thousand times more, did He see that it would promote your true holiness and happiness? Could He resist that request, that desire, that sigh, that tear, that beseeching look, if infinite wisdom did not guide Him in all His dealing with your soul? Oh no! But He gives you an equivalent to the denied request. He gives you Himself. Can He give you more? His grace sustains you—His arm supports you—His love soothes you—His Spirit comforts you; and your chamber of solitude, though it may not be the scene of health and buoyancy and joyousness, may yet be the secret place where a covenant God and Father puts His grace into your soul—where Jesus seeks to meet you with the choicest unfoldings of His love. Could He not, would He not, heal you in a moment, were it for your good? Then, ask for a submissive spirit, a will swallowed up in God the Father's. And it may be, when the lesson of secret and filial submission is learned, so that health shall no longer be desired but as a means of glorifying God, He may put forth His healing power, and grant you your request. But, forget not, the Lord best knows what will most promote His own glory! You may have thought that health of body would better enable you to glorify Him. He may think that the chamber of solitude of the bed of languishing are most productive of glory to His name. The patience, resignation, meek submission, child-like acquiescence, which His blessed Spirit through this means works in your soul, may more glorify Him than all the active graces that ever were brought into exercise.

OCTOBER 26

"The sacrifices of God are a broken spirit: a broken and a contrite heart, O God, you will not despise." Psalm 49:17

THERE is a sense in which the history of the world is the history of broken hearts. Were the epitaph of many over whose graves—those "mountain-peaks of a new and distant world"—we thoughtlessly pass, faithfully inscribed upon the marble tablet that rears above them so proudly its beautifully chiseled form, it would be this—"Died of a broken heart." Worldly adversity, blighted hope, the iron heel of oppression, or the acid tongue of slander, crushed the sensitive spirit, and it fled where the rude winds blow not, and "where the wicked cease from troubling, and the weary are at rest." Passing beyond the limit of time, we visit in imagination the gloomy precincts of the lost, and lo! we find that the abodes of the finally impenitent are crowded with weeping, mourning, despairing souls. Yes! there are broken hearts there, and there are tears there, and there is repentance there, such as the betrayer of his Lord felt, before he "went to his own place,"—but, alas! it is the "sorrow of the world, which works death." In all this grief there enters nothing of that element which gives its character and complexion to the sorrow of David—the broken and contrite heart, the sacrifice of God which He despises not. A man may weep, and a lost soul may despair, from the consequences of sin; but in that sorrow and in that despair there shall be no real heartfelt grief for sin itself, as a thing against a holy and a righteous God. But we are now to contemplate, not the broken spirit merely, but the contrite heart also—the sorrow of sincere repentance and deep contrition springing up in the soul for sin—its exceeding sinfulness and abomination in the sight of God.

This state defines the first stage in conversion. The repentance which is enkindled in the heart at the commencement of the divine life may be legal and tending to bondage; nevertheless it is a spiritual, godly sorrow for sin, and is "unto life." The newly awakened and aroused sinner may at first see nothing of Christ, he may see nothing of the blood of atonement, and of God's great method of reconciliation with him, he may know nothing of faith in Jesus as the way of peace to his soul—yet he is a true and sincere spiritual penitent. The tear of holy grief is in his eye— ah! we do not forget with what ease some can weep; there are those the fountain of whose sensibility lies near the surface; an arousing discourse, an affecting book, a thrilling story, will quickly moisten the eye; but still we must acknowledge that the religion of Jesus is the religion of sensibility; that there is no godly repentance without feeling, and no spiritual contrition apart from deep emotion. Yes! the tear of holy grief is in his eye; and if ever it is manly to weep, surely it is now, when for the first time the soul that had long resisted every appeal to its moral consciousness is now smitten to the dust, the heart of adamant broken, and the lofty spirit laid low before the cross of Jesus. Oh, it is a holy and a lovely spectacle, upon which angels, and the Lord of angels Himself, must look with ineffable delight. Reader, have you reached this, the primary stage in the great change of conversion? Have you taken this, the first step in the soul's travel towards heaven? It is the knowledge of the disease which precedes the application to the remedy; it is the consciousness of the wound which brings you into contact with the Healer and the healing.

Oh who, once having experienced the truth, would wish to escape this painful and humiliating process? who would refuse to drink the wormwood and the gall, if only along this path he could reach the sunlight spot where the smiles of a sin-pardoning God fill the heart with joy and gladness? Who would not bare his bosom to the stroke, when the hand that plucks the dart and heals the wound is the hand through whose palm the rough nail was driven—when "wounded for our transgressions, and bruised for our iniquities"? Who would not endure the uneasiness of sin, but to feel the rest that Jesus gives to the weary? and who would not experience the mourning for transgression, but to know the comfort which flows from the loving heart of Christ? Again the question is put—has the Spirit of God revealed to you the inward plague, has He brought you just as you are to Jesus, to take your stand upon the doctrine of His unmerited, unpurchased mercy—asking for pardon as a beggar, praying for your discharge as a bankrupt, and beseeching Him to take you as a homeless wanderer into the asylum of His loving and parental heart?

OCTOBER 27

"And all the churches shall know that I am he which searches the reins and hearts: and I will give unto every one of you according to your works." Revelation 2:23

WHOSE prerogative is it to search the heart? who can fathom this fathomless sea of iniquity? who can follow it in all its serpentine windings? who can detect its deep subtlety?—who? "I, the Lord, search the heart: I try the reins." A mere creature—such as the denier of Christ's proper Deity would make Him—cannot know the heart. It is a perfection peculiar to God, and must in its own nature be incommunicable; for were it communicable to a creature, it could not be peculiar to God Himself. Were it possible, we say, that God should delegate the power and prerogative of searching the heart and trying the reins of the children of men to a mere created being, then it could with no propriety be said of Him, the He only searches the heart. And yet to Jesus does this attribute belong. Is not, then, the evidence of His Deity most conclusive? Who can resist it? From this attribute of Christ what blessedness flows to the believing soul! It is at all times a consolation to him to remember that Jesus knows and searches the heart. Its iniquity He sees and subdues; for the promise is, "He will subdue our iniquities." He detects some lurking evil, some latent corruption, and before it develops itself in the outward departure, the overt act, He checks and conquers it. "Cheering thought," may the believer say, "that all my inbred evil, the hidden corruption of my heart, is known to my Savior God. Lord, I would not conceal a thought; but would cry, 'search me, O God, and know my heart; try me, and know my thoughts; and see if there be any wicked way in me, and lead me in the way everlasting.'" He sees, too, His own gracious work in the soul. The little spiritual life that He has breathed there—the little grace that He has implanted there—the little spark of love that He has kindled there—the faint and feeble longings after Him—the inward strugglings with sin—the hungering and thirsting for holiness—the panting for divine conformity—all is known to Jesus. The Lord Jesus knows and recognizes His own work: the counterfeit He soon detects. The outward garb and the unhumbled spirit, the external profession and the unbroken heart, escape not His piercing glance. Man may be deceived—the Lord Jesus, never. We may not be able to discern between the righteous and the wicked—between nature and grace—between the outward profession and the inward reality; but Jesus knows what is genuine and what is base—what is the mere effect of an enlightened judgment and an alarmed conscience.

OCTOBER 28

"Lord, you know all things; you know that I love you." John 21:17

DEAR reader, this is His own solemn declaration of Himself—"I, the Lord, search the heart." Can you open all your heart to Him? Can you admit Him within its most secret places? are you willing to have no concealments? Are you willing that He should search and prove it? Oh, be honest with God!—keep nothing back—tell Him all that you detect within you. He loves the full, honest disclosure: He delights in this confiding surrender of the whole heart. Are you honest in your desires that He might sanctify your heart, and subdue all its iniquity?—then confess all to Him— tell Him all. You would not conceal from your physician a single symptom of your disease—you would not hide any part of the wound; but you would, if anxious for a complete cure, disclose to him all. Be you as honest with the Great Physician—the Physician of your soul. It is true, He knows your case; it is true, He anticipates every want; yet He will have, and delights in having, His child approach Him with a full and honest disclosure. Let David's example encourage you: "I acknowledged my sin unto You, and mine iniquity have I not hid; I said, I will confess my transgressions unto the Lord; and You forgave the iniquity of my sin." And while the heart is thus pouring itself out in a full and minute confession, let the eye of faith be fixed on Christ. It is only in this posture that the soul shall be kept from despondency. Faith must rest itself upon the atoning blood. And oh, in this posture, fully and freely, beloved reader, may you pour out your heart to God! Disclosures you dare not make to your tenderest friend, you may make to Him: sins you would not confess, corruption your would not acknowledge as existing within you, you are privileged thus, "looking unto Jesus," to pour into the ear of your Father and God. And oh, how the heart will become unburdened, and the conscience purified, and peace and joy flow into the soul, by this opening of the heart to God! Try it, dear reader: let no consciousness of guilt keep you back; let no unbelieving suggestion of Satan, that such confessions are inappropriate for the ear of God, restrain you. Come at once—come now—to your Father's feet, and bringing in your hands the precious blood of Christ make a full and free disclosure. Thus from the attribute of Christ's omniscience may a humble believer extract much consolation at all times permitted to appeal to it, and say with Peter, "Lord, You know all things, You know that I love You."

OCTOBER 29

"Lo, I am with you always, even unto the
end of the world." Matthew 28:20

OMNIPRESENCE is an attribute of Deity ascribed to Christ. We would refer the reader to two portions of Scripture for proof; they both run in parallel lines with each other. In Matthew 18:20, we have this encouraging declaration from Christ, "Where two or three are gathered together in my name, there am I in the midst of them." Compare this with Exodus 20:24, "In all places where I record my name, I will come unto you and will bless you." Thus the reader will perceive that the identical promise which God gave to His ancient church, when He established her in the wilderness, when He gave to her the law, built for her the tabernacle, and instituted for her a sacrifice, the Lord Jesus makes of Himself. Consoling thought! Jesus is with His saints at all times, in all places, and under all circumstances. He is "God with us." He is with them to comfort them in the hour of sorrow, to enlighten them in the hour of darkness, to guide them in the hour of doubt and perplexity, to deliver them in the time of conflict, to support them in the hour of death. Oh for faith to realize this! He was with His three faithful servants in the fiery furnace; He was with Daniel in the lions' den; He was with Jacob in his wrestlings at Bethel; He was with John in his exile at Patmos. Jesus is at all times, in all places, and under all circumstances, with His dear people. Reader, are you a child of sorrow?—perhaps you are a son of a daughter of affliction: you may now be passing through the furnace—you may now be draining adversity's bitter cup; the rod of the covenant may be heavy upon you; friends unkind, the world empty, everything earthly changing, faith weak, corruptions strong, and, what embitters the cup, and deepens the shade, your Father hiding from you His dear reconciled face. Is it so? Still is your omnipresent Jesus with you. Do not be cast down; this furnace is but to consume the tin and burnish the gold, this draught is but to work your inward good: these painful dispensations, by which you are learning the changeableness of everything earthly, are but to wean you from a poor, unsatisfying world, and to draw you near and yet nearer to Jesus. Then be of good cheer, for He has promised never to leave or forsake you. So that you may boldly say, "The Lord is my helper."

OCTOBER 30

"Our lamps are gone out." Matthew 25:8

THERE are two periods of awful solemnity, which will be found utterly to extinguish the mere lamp of a Christian profession. Will you follow me, reader, to the dying-bed of a false professor. It is an awful place! It is an affecting spectacle! No hope of glory sheds its brightness around his pillow. There is no anchor within the veil, to which the soul now clings in its wrenchings from the body. No Divine voice whispers, in cheering, soothing accents, "Fear not, for I am with you." No light is thrown in upon the dark valley as its gate opens, and the spirit enters. Coldness is on his brow, earth recedes, eternity nears, the vault damps ascend and thicken around the parting spirit, and the last wail of despair breaks from the quivering lip, "My lamp is going out." And so will it be when the Son of man comes. This great event will fix unchangeably the destiny of each individual of the human race. It will break like the loud artillery of heaven upon a slumbering Church and a careless world. It will find the true saints with "oil in their vessels with their lamps," though in an unwatchful state. It will come upon the nominal professor, grasping firmly his lamp of profession, but utterly destitute of the oil of grace, and in a state of as little expectation of, as preparedness for, the advent of the Lord. And it will overtake and surprise the ungodly world as the flood did in the days of Noah, and the fire in the days of Lot—"They were eating and drinking, marrying and giving in marriage; they bought, they sold, they planted, they built; until the day that Noah entered into the ark, and until the same day that Lot went out of Sodom." "Even thus shall it be in the day when the Son of man is revealed." The true saints will arouse from their slumber—the spirit of slothfulness and lethargy into which they had fallen—and trimming their lamps by a fresh exercise of faith in Jesus, will go forth as the "children of the light," to welcome their approaching Lord. False professors, too, startled by the cry which breaks upon the awful stillness of midnight—solemn as the archangel's trumpet—will eagerly feel for their lamps—their evidences of acceptance based upon an outward profession of the gospel—when lo! to their surprise and consternation, they find themselves destitute of one drop of oil with which to feed the flickering, waning flame, and they exclaim in despair, "Our lamps are going out!" And now the intellectual light goes out, and the moral light goes out, and the professing light goes out, and the official light goes out; and while they have fled to human sources to procure the grace they needed—their backs being thus then turned upon Christ—the "Bridegroom comes; and those who are ready go in with Him to the marriage, and the door is shut." They return with what they suppose the needed evidences, but now they learn—oh that they should have learned it too late!—that to have had a professing name to live—to have outwardly put on Christ by baptism—to have united externally with the Church of God—to have partaken of the Lord's Supper—to have promoted His truth, and to have furthered His cause—to have preached His gospel, and even to have won converts to the faith, will avail nothing—alone and apart from union to Jesus by the Spirit—in obtaining admittance to the marriage supper of the Lamb. "Afterward came also the other virgins, saying, Lord, Lord, open to us. But He answered and said, Verily I say unto you, I know you not." In view of such a catastrophe, oh, how poor, contemptible, and insignificant appears everything, however splendid in intellect, beautiful in morals, or costly in sacrifice, save the humble consciousness of having Christ in the heart the hope of glory.

OCTOBER 31

"Arise, shine; for your light is come, and the glory
of the Lord is risen upon you." Isaiah 40:1

THERE are those whose lamps of Christian profession will not go out when the Lord appears. They are His own chosen, redeemed, and called people. Their light, by reason of manifold infirmities, may often have burned but dimly through life; but there is vital religion in the soul—the golden precious oil of grace, flowing from Jesus into their hearts; and this can never be extinguished. Many were the hostile influences against which their weak grace had to contend, many were the trials of their feeble faith, but the light never quite went out. The waves of sorrow threatened to extinguish it; the floods of inbred evil threatened to extinguish it; the cold blasts of adversity threatened to extinguish it; and the stumbling of the walk, the inconstancy of the heart, the declension of the soul, often for a while, weakened and obscured it; but there it is, living, burning, and brightening, as inextinguishable and as deathless as the source from where it came. The grace of God in the heart is as imperishable, and the life of God in the soul is as immortal, as God Himself. That light of knowledge enkindled in the mind, and of love glowing in the heart, and of holiness shining in the life, will burn in the upper temple in increasing effulgence of glory through eternity. The divine light of Christian profession, which holy grief for sin has enkindled, which love to God has enkindled, which the in-being of the Holy Spirit has enkindled, will outshine and outlive the sun in the firmament of heaven. That sun shall be extinguished, those stars shall fall, and that moon shall be turned into blood, but the feeblest spark of grace in the soul shall live forever. The Lord watches His own work with sleepless vigilance. When the vessel is exhausted, He stands by and replenishes it; when the light burns dimly, He is near to revive it; when the cold winds blow rudely, and the rough waves swell high, He is riding upon those winds, and walking upon those waves, to protect this the spark of His own kindling. The light that is in you is light flowing from Jesus, the "Fountain of light." And can an infinite fountain be exhausted? When the sun is extinguished, then all the lesser lights, deriving their faint effulgence from Him, will be extinguished too—but not until then. Who is it that has often fanned the smoking flax? Even He who will never quench the faintest spark of living light in the soul. "You will light my candle." And if the Lord light it, what power can put it out? Is not His love the sunshine of your soul? Is He not Himself your morning star? Is it not in His light that you see light, even the "light of the glory of God, in the face of Jesus Christ"? Oh, then, "Arise and shine; for your light is come, and the glory of the Lord is risen upon you."

NOVEMBER

NOVEMBER 1

"Now if any man have not the Spirit of Christ,
he is none of his." Romans 8:9

THE Spirit of Christ is the great convincer of sin. "He shall convince the world of sin." Have you thus received Him? Has He discovered to you the moral leprosy of your nature, the exceeding sinfulness of sin? Do you know anything of the conflict of which the apostle speaks in the seventh chapter of this Epistle to the Romans—the law of the mind in battle with the law of the members? And has this discovery led you to self-condemnation, to self-renunciation, to lay your mouth in the dust before God? If this be so, then the Spirit of Christ is a Spirit of conviction in you, and by this you may know that you are Christ's.

The Spirit of Christ leads to Christ. He is to the sinner what John was to the Messiah—He goes before as the Forerunner of the Lord's salvation. He prepares the way, and heralds the coming of Jesus into the soul. This was one specific object for which He was sent, and which entered essentially into His mission—to lead men to Christ. Has He led you to Christ? Can you say, "Christ is made unto me wisdom, and righteousness, and sanctification, and redemption"? What do you think of Christ? Is His blood precious? Does His righteousness give you peace? Does His grace subdue your sins? Do you in sorrow travel to His sympathy, in weakness take hold of His strength, in perplexity seek His counsel, in all your steps acknowledge and wait for Him? Is Christ thus all in all to you? Then you have the Spirit of Christ. This we venture to assert for your encouragement. You may resort to Christ, and there may be no sensible apprehension, no realizing touch, no manifested presence; yet, if your heart goes out after Jesus, if your spirit travels alone to Him, praying for His sympathy, panting for His grace, thirsting for His love, and you are led to say, "Lord, the desire of my heart is to Your name, and to the remembrance of You; I seem not to see You, to touch You, to apprehend You; yet I come, and I find a heaven in coming; and for ten thousand worlds I dare not, I could not, stay away"—then, dear reader, you have the Spirit of Christ, and are Christ's.

Not only does the Spirit lead to Christ, but He also conforms those thus
led to the image of Christ. He guides us to Christ, not for consolation
and instruction only, but also for assimilation. If we are humble, we have
the Spirit of Christ— for He was humble. If we are meek, we have the
Spirit of Christ—for He was meek. If we believe, we have the Spirit of
Christ—for He lived a life of faith. If we love God, we have the Spirit of
Christ—for He was the incarnation of love. If we are holy, we have the
Spirit of Christ—for He was without sin. If we are obedient, meek, and
self-denying in suffering, silent in provocation, submissive in chastisement,
patient in tribulation, and rejoicing in hope, then have we the Spirit of
Christ, for He was all this. Thus the possession of this immense, this
indispensable blessing, comprises two grand things—first, to become the
subject of an actual and permanent in-being of the Spirit; and second, to
be assimilated in character and disposition to the Savior. And while it is
most certain, that if the first-mentioned blessing is attained, the second
follows, yet it is to the second we are to look as the fruit and evidence of
the first. The question, "Am I Christ's?" hinges upon the answer to the
question, "Have I the Spirit of Christ?"

NOVEMBER 2

*"If you endure chastening, God deals with you as with sons; for
what son is he whom the Father chastens not?" Hebrews 12:7*

AS our chastenings are marks of our sonship, equally so are our
consolations. The kindly view the Spirit gives of our Father's dispensations—the meek submission of the will, the cordial acquiescence of the
heart, and the entire surrender of the soul to God, which He creates,
supplies us with indisputable ground for drawing a conclusion favorable to
the reality of our being the children of God. There is a depth of sympathy
and a degree of tenderness in God's comforts, which could only flow from
the heart of a father—that Father, God Himself. "As a father pities his
children, so the Lord pities those who fear Him." Sweet to know that the
correction and the consolation, the wounding and the healing, flow from
the same heart, come from the same hand, and bears each a message of
love and a token of sonship. Is the God of all comfort sustaining, soothing,
and quieting your oppressed, chafed, and sorrowful heart? Oh, it is the

Spirit's witness to your adoption. Bending to your grief, and associating Himself with every circumstance of your sorrow, He seeks to seal on your softened heart the deeper, clearer impress of your filial interest in God's love. And oh, if this overwhelming bereavement—if this crushing stroke—if the bitterness and gloom of this hour, be the occasion of the Spirit's gentle, gracious lifting you from the region of doubt and distress, as to your sonship, into the serene sunlight of your Father's love, so that you shall question, and doubt, and deny no more your acceptance in the Beloved, and your adoption into His family, will you not kiss the rod, and love the hand, and bless the heart that has smitten? Do not forget that the inward seal of adoption is testified by the outward seal of sanctification, and that if the Spirit of Christ is in your heart, the fruits of the Spirit will be exhibited in your life. Then, thus meek, and gently, and lowly, like the Savior, separated from the world, that you live not, and joy not, as the world does—in the secret chamber of your soul you shall often hear the voice of God, saying, "I will be a Father unto you, and you shall be my sons and daughters, says the Lord Almighty."

NOVEMBER 3

"Sanctify them through your truth: your word is truth." John 17:17

"HOW may I know," is the anxious inquiry of many, "that sin is being mortified in me?" We reply—by a weakening of its power. When Christ subdues our iniquities, He does not eradicate them, but weakens the strength of their root. The principle of sin remains, but it is impaired. See it in the case of Peter. Before he fell, his easily besetting sin was self-confidence: "Although all shall be offended, yet will not I." Behold him after his recovery, taking the low place at the feet of Jesus, and at the feet of the disciples too, meekly saying, "Lord, You know all things; You know that I love You." No more self-vaunting, no more self-confidence: his sin was mortified through the Spirit, and he became as another man. Thus often the very outbreak of our sins may become the occasion of their deeper discovery and their more thorough subjection. Nor let us overlook the power of the truth, by the instrumentality of which the Spirit mortifies sin in us: "Sanctify them through Your truth." The truth as it is in Jesus, revealed more clearly to the mind, and impressed more deeply on the heart, transforms the soul into its own divine and holy nature. Our spiritual and experimental acquaintance, therefore, with the truth—with Him who is essential truth—will be the measure of the Spirit's mortification of sin in our hearts. Is the Lord Jesus becoming increasingly precious to your soul? Are you growing in poverty of spirit, in a deeper sense of your vileness, weakness, and unworthiness? Is pride more abased, and self more crucified, and God's glory more simply sought? Does the heart more quickly shrink from sin, and is the conscience more sensitive to the touch of guilt, and do confession and cleansing become a more frequent habit? Are you growing in more love to all the saints—to those, who, though they adopt not your entire creed, yet love and serve your Lord and Master? If so, then you may be assured the Spirit is mortifying sin in you. But oh, look from everything to Christ. Look not within for sanctification; look up for it from Christ. He is as much our "sanctification" as He is our "righteousness." Your evidences, your comfort, your hope, do not spring from your fruitfulness, your mortification, or anything within you; but solely and entirely from the Lord Jesus Christ. "Looking unto Jesus" by faith, is like removing the covering and opening the windows of a conservatory, to admit more freely the sun, beneath whose light and warmth the flowers and fruits expand and mature. Withdraw the veil that conceals the Sun of Righteousness, and let Him shine in upon your soul, and the mortification of all sin will follow, and the fruits of all holiness will abound.

NOVEMBER 4

"But of him are you in Christ Jesus, who of God is made unto us wisdom." 1 Corinthians 1:30

TO survey the effects of this manifold wisdom on individual character will exalt our views of Christ as the wisdom of God. To see a man "becoming a fool that he may be wise"—his reason bowing to revelation—his knowledge and attainments laid beneath the cross—his own righteousness surrendered—"counting all things but loss for the excellency of the knowledge of Christ Jesus the Lord"—and as a little child receiving the kingdom of God; oh, how glorious does appear in this the wisdom of God, the light of which shines in Jesus' face! Behold how determined is the Father, in every step of His grace, to humble the creature, and to exalt, magnify, and crown his co-equal Son, Lord of all!

We see Jesus the mediatorial Head of all wisdom and counsel to the Church. "It pleased the Father that in Him should all fullness dwell." "In whom," says the same apostle, "are hid all the treasures of wisdom and knowledge." He is the "Wonderful Counselor," of whom it was thus prophesied, "the spirit of the Lord shall rest upon Him, the spirit of wisdom and understanding, the spirit of counsel and might, the spirit of knowledge and of the fear of the Lord." O divine and precious truth! unutterably precious to a soul having no resources adequate to the great purposes of knowing self, Christ, and God; of salvation, sanctification, and guidance.

Reader, are you wanting the "wisdom that is profitable to direct" you at this moment? Acquaint now yourself with Jesus, in whom all the treasures of this wisdom are hid. What is His language to you? The same which Moses, the great legislator, spoke to the people of Israel: "The cause that is too hard for you, bring it unto me, and I will hear it." What a cheering invitation is this! A greater than Moses speaks it, and speaks it to you. You find your case baffling to human wisdom, too difficult for the acutest skill of man—take it, then, to Jesus. How sweetly He speaks—"bring it unto me." One simple exercise of faith upon His word will remove all that is difficult, make simple make simple all that is complex, and lucid all that is dark in your case. With Him nothing is impossible. To Him all is transparent. Knowing the end from the beginning, there can be nothing unforeseen in it to His mind; by His prescience all is known, and by His wisdom all is provided for. His precious promise is, "I will bring the blind by a way that they knew not: I will lead them in a path that they have not known. I will make darkness light before them, and crooked things straight. These things will I do unto them, and not forsake them." Thus is Jesus "made of God unto us wisdom," that all our perplexities may be guided, and all our doubts may be solved, and all our steps may be directed, by one on whom the anointing of the "spirit of wisdom and understanding" rests "without measure;" and who, from experience, is able to lead, having trod every step before us. "And when he puts forth His own sheep, he goes before them, and the sheep follow Him." "If any man lack wisdom, let him ask of God, that gives to all men liberally:" let him repair to Christ, whom God has set up from everlasting, "to the intent that now unto the principalities and powers in heavenly places might be known by the Church the manifold wisdom of God."

NOVEMBER 5

"For Christ is not entered into the holy places made with hands, which are the figures of the true; but into heaven itself, now to appear in the presence of God for us." Hebrews 9:24

IS it a privilege to be borne upon the affectionate and believing prayers of a Christian friend? Ah, yes! precious channels of heavenly blessing are the intercessions of the Lord's people on our behalf. But there is a Friend still closer to the Fountain of mercy, still nearer and dearer to the Father, than your dearest earthly friend; it is Jesus, "who ever lives to make intercession for them who come unto God by Him." Oh, how precious is that declaration upon which in any assault, or trial, or perplexity, you may calmly and confidently repose: "I have prayed for you"! Yes, when from confusion of thought, or pain of body, or burning fever, you can not pray for yourself, and no friend is near to be your mouth to God, then there is one, the Friend of friends, the ever-skillful Advocate and never-weary Intercessor—no invocating saint, nor interceding angel—but the Son of God himself, who appears in the presence of God moment by moment for you. Oh, keep, then, the eye of your faith immovably fixed upon Christ's intercession; He intercedes for weak faith, for tried faith, for tempted faith—yes, for him who thinks he has no faith. There is not a believer who is not borne upon His heart, and whose prayers and needs are not presented in His ceaseless intercession. When you deem yourself neglected and forgotten, a praying Savior in heaven is thinking of you. When you are tried and cast down, tempted and stumble, the interceding High Priest at that moment enters within the holiest, to ask on your behalf strength, consolation, and upholding grace. And when sin has wounded, when guilt distresses, and unbelief beclouds, who is it that stands in the breach, that makes intercession, that removes the darkness, and brings back the smile of a forgiving Father?—the Lord Jesus, the interceding Savior. Oh, look up, tried and assaulted believer! you have a Friend at court, an Advocate in the chancery of heaven, an Intercessor curtained within the holiest of holies, transacting all your concerns, and through whom you may have access to God with boldness.

NOVEMBER 6

"Verily I say unto you, Among those who are born of women there has not risen a greater than John the Baptist: notwithstanding he that is least in the kingdom of heaven is greater than he." Matthew 11:11

IF there are degrees of glory—and we see no reason to question the fact—we believe that those degrees will be graduated, not by the strength or capacity of the intellect, but according to the measure and standard of holiness which the believer attained in this life. If glory is the perfection of grace, then it follows, that proportioned to the degree of grace here will be the degree of glory hereafter. If the great and grand perfection of God be His holiness, then the more clearly I approximate to that holiness, the more deeply must I partake of the glory of God, and the higher must be my degree of glory. It is acquaintance with, and conformity to, God's moral, and not His intellectual being, that will constitute the highest source of our happiness in heaven. That our enlarged intellectual capacity will be a vast inlet to expanded views of God we do not dispute; but it will be the conformity of our moral nature to His that will constitute and augment our perceptions of glory. Were we asked to pass through the Church of God, and from its various communions select the individual whom we should regard as the richest heir of glory, whose degree of happiness would, perhaps, transcend that of the glorified philosopher, we should, it may be, find him the inmate of some obscure hut, dwelling amid lonely poverty, sickness, and neglect; yet holding communion with God, so filial, so endearing, and so close, as to present to our eye his soul's uplifted and soaring pinions, "as the wings of a dove covered with silver, and her feathers with yellow gold." We should go to him whose heart thus breathing after holiness, whose spirit thus imbibing more and more of the mind of Christ, who in this lowly and suffering school was learning more deeply of God, and what God is, and who thus was gathering around him the beams of that glory whose unclouded visions were so soon to burst upon his view; and we would unhesitatingly point to him as the man whose degree of glory will be transcendently great—grace enriching and encircling him with more glory than gift. Do you, my reader, desire to be a star of the first magnitude and luster in heaven? then aim after a high degree of grace on earth. The nearer your present walk with God, the nearer will be your future proximity to God. The closer your resemblance to Christ, the deeper your holiness, the more spiritual and heavenly-minded you become on earth, be assured of this, the higher and the more resplendent will be your glory in heaven. As the ungodly man is treasuring up wrath against the day of wrath, and is growing more and more meet for hell; so the godly man is laying up glory against the day of glory, and is growing more and more meet for heaven. We need not speculate and surmise about the future. Let the child of God be careful as to his degrees towards fitness for glory, and he may calmly and safely leave his degrees of glory to the period when that glory shall be revealed.

NOVEMBER 7

"God has not cast away his people which he foreknew." Romans 11:2

IN this place the word "foreknew" assumes a particular and explicit meaning. In its wider and more general application it must be regarded as referring not simply to the Divine prescience, but more especially to the Divine prearrangement. For God to foreknow is, in the strict meaning of the phrase, for God to foreordain. There are no guesses, or conjectures, or contingencies with God as to the future. Not only does He know all, but He has fixed, and appointed, and ordered "all things after the counsel of His own will." In this view there exists not a creature, and there transpires not an event, which was not as real and palpable to the Divine mind from eternity as it is at the present moment. Indeed, it would seem that there were no future with God. An Eternal Being, there can be nothing prospective in His on-looking. There must be an eternity of perception, and constitution, and presence; and the mightiest feature of His character—that which conveys to a finite mind the most vivid conception of His grandeur and greatness—is the simultaneousness of all succession and variety and events to His eye. "He is of one mind; and who can turn Him?" But the word "foreknew," as it occurs in the text, adds to this yet another, a more definite, and to the saints, a more precious signification. The foreknowledge here spoken of, it will be observed, is limited to a particular class of people, who are said to be "conformed to the image of God's Son." Now this cannot, with truth, be predicated of all creatures. The term, therefore, assumes a particular and impressive signification. It includes the everlasting love of God to, and His most free choice of, His people to be His especial and peculiar treasure. We find some examples of this: "God has not cast away His people which He foreknew." Here the word is expressive of the two ideas of love and choice. Again, "Who verily was foreordained (Greek, foreknown) before the foundation of the world." "Him being delivered by the determinate counsel and foreknowledge of God." Clearly, then, we are justified in interpreting the phrase as expressive of God's especial choice of, and His intelligent love to, His Church—His own peculiar people. It is a foreknowledge of choice—of love—of eternal grace and faithfulness.

NOVEMBER 8
"He also did predestinate." Romans 8:29

THIS word admits of but one natural signification. Predestination, in its lowest sense, is understood to mean the exclusive agency of God in producing every event. But it includes more than this: it takes in God's predeterminate appointment and fore-arrangement of a thing beforehand, according to His divine and supreme will. The Greek is so rendered: "For to do whatever Your hand and Your counsel determined beforehand to be done." Again, "Having predestinated us unto the adoption of children by Jesus Christ to Himself, according to the good pleasure of His will." It is here affirmed of God, that the same prearrangement and predetermination which men in general are agreed to ascribe to Him in the government of matter, extends equally, and with yet stronger force, to the concerns of His moral administration. It would seem impossible to form any correct idea of God, disassociated from the idea of predestination. And yet how marvelously difficult is it to win the mind to a full, unwavering acquiescence in a truth which, in a different application, is received with unquestioning readiness! And what is there in the application of this law of the Divine government to the world of matter, which is not equally reasonable and fit in its application to the world of mind? If it is necessary and proper in the material, why should it not be equally, or more so, in the spiritual empire? If God is allowed the full exercise of a sovereignty in the one, why should He be excluded from an unlimited sovereignty in the other? Surely it were even more worthy of Him that He should prearrange, predetermine, and supremely rule in the concerns of a world over which His more dignified and glorious empire extends, than that in the inferior world of matter He should fix a constellation in the heavens, guide the gyrations of a bird in the air, direct the falling of an autumnal leaf in the pathless desert, or convey the seed, borne upon the wind, to the spot in which it should grow. Surely if no fortuitous ordering is admitted in the one case, on infinitely stronger grounds it should be excluded from the other. Upon no other basis could Divine foreknowledge and providence take their stand than upon this. Disconnected from the will and purpose of God, there could be nothing certain as to the future; and consequently there could be nothing certainly foreknown. And were not Providence to regulate and control people, things, and events—every dispensation in fact—by the same preconstructed plan, it would follow that God would be exposed to a thousand contingencies unforeseen, or else that He acts ignorantly, or contrary to His will. What, then, is predestination but God's determining will?

Now all this will apply with augmented beauty and force to the idea of a predestinated Church. How clearly is this doctrine revealed! "According as He has chosen us in Him before the foundation of the world." "Whose names are written in the book of life, from the foundation of the world." "Elect according to the foreknowledge of God the Father." "Who has saved us, and called us with an holy calling, not according to our works, but according to His own purpose and grace, which was given us in Christ Jesus before the world began." What an accumulation of evidence in proof of a single doctrine of Scripture! Who but the most prejudiced can resist, or the most skeptical deny, its overwhelming force? Oh, to receive it as the word of God! To admit it, not because reason can understand, or man can explain it—for all truth flowing from an infinite source must necessarily transcend a finite mind—but because we find it in God's holy word. Predestination must be a Divine verity, since it stands essentially connected with our conformity to the Divine image.

NOVEMBER 9

"To be conformed to the image of his Son." Romans 8:29

NO standard short of this will meet the case. How conspicuous appears the wisdom and how glorious the goodness of God in this—that in making us holy, the model or standard of that holiness should be Deity itself! God would make us holy, and in doing so He would make us like Himself. But with what pencil—dipped though it were in heaven's brightest hues—can we portray the image of Jesus? The perfection of our Lord was the perfection of holiness. His Deity, essential holiness; His humanity without sin, the impersonation of holiness; all that He was, and said, and did, was as coruscations of holiness emanating from the Fountain of essential purity, and kindling their dazzling and undying radiance around each step He trod. How lovely, too, His character! How holy the thoughts He breathed, how pure the words He spoke, how humble the spirit He exemplified, how tender and sympathizing the outgoings of His compassion and love to man! "The chief among ten thousand, the altogether lovely." Such is the believer's model. To this he is predestinated to be conformed. And is not this predestination in its highest form? Would it seem possible for God to have preordained us to a greater blessing, to have chosen us to a higher distinction? In choosing us in Christ before the foundation of the world, that we should be holy, He has advanced us to the loftiest degree of honor and happiness to which a creature can be promoted—assimilation to His own moral image. And this forms the highest ambition of the believer. To transcribe those beauteous lineaments which, in such perfect harmony and lovely expression, blended and shone in the life of Jesus, is the great study of all His true disciples. But in what does this conformity consist? The first feature is a conformity of nature. And this is reciprocal. The Son of God, by an act of divine power, became human; the saints of God, by an act of sovereign grace, become divine. "Partakers of the Divine nature." This harmony of nature forms the basis of all conformity. Thus grafted into Christ, we grow up into Him in all holy resemblance. The meekness, the holiness, the patience, the self-denial, the zeal, the love, traceable—faint and imperfect indeed—in us are transfers of Christ's faultless lineaments to our renewed soul. Thus the mind that was in Him is in some measure in us. And in our moral conflict, battling as we do with sin and Satan and the world, we come to know a little of fellowship with His sufferings, and conformity to His death. We are here supplied with a test of Christian character. It is an anxious question with many professors of Christ, "How may I arrive at a correct conclusion that I am among the predestinated of God?—that I am included in His purpose of grace and love?—that I have an interest in the Lord's salvation?" The passage under consideration supplies the answer— conformity to the image of God's Son. Nothing short of this can justify the belief that we are saved. No evidence less strong can authenticate the fact of our predestination. The determination of God to save men is not so fixed as to save them be their character what it may. Christ's work is a salvation from sin, not in sin. "According as He has chosen us in Him, before the foundation of the word, that we should be holy." In other words, that we should be conformed to the Divine image. That we should be like Christ—like Christ in His Divine nature—like Christ in the purity of His human nature—like Christ in the humility He exemplified, in the self-denial He practiced, in the heavenly life He lived; in a word, in all that this expressive sentence comprehends—"conformed to the image of His Son." And as we grow day by day more holy, more spiritually-minded, more closely resembling Jesus, we are placing the truth of our predestination to eternal life in a clearer, stronger light, and consequently the fact of our salvation beyond a misgiving and a doubt. In view of this precious truth, what spiritual heart will not breathe the prayer, "O Lord! I cannot be satisfied merely to profess and call myself Your. I want more of the power of vital religion in my soul. I pant for Your image. My deepest grief springs from the discovery of the little real resemblance which I bear to a model so peerless, so divine—that I exemplify so little of Your patience in suffering; Your meekness in opposition; Your forgiving spirit in injury; Your gentleness in reproving; Your firmness in temptation; Your singleness of eye in all that I do. Oh, transfer Yourself wholly to me."

NOVEMBER 10

"That he might be the firstborn among many brethren." Romans 8:29

THE Son of God sustains to us the relation of the Elder Brother. He is emphatically the "Firstborn." In another place we read, "Forasmuch then as the children are partakers of flesh and blood, He also Himself likewise took part of the same." He is the "Brother born for adversity." Our relation to Him as our Brother is evidenced by our conformity to Him as our model. We have no valid claim to relationship which springs not from a resemblance to His image. The features may be indistinctly visible, yet one line of holiness, one true lineament, drawn upon the heart by the Holy Spirit, proves our fraternal relationship to Him the "Firstborn." And how large the brotherhood!—"many brethren."

What the relative proportion of the Church is to the world—how many will be saved—is a question speculative and profitless. But this we know—the number will be vast, countless. The one family of God is composed of "many brethren." They are not all of the same judgment in all matters, but they are all of the same spirit. The unity of the family of God is not ecclesiastical nor geographical, it is spiritual and essential. It is the "unity of the Spirit." Begotten of one Father, in the nature of the Elder Brother, and through the regenerating grace of the one Spirit, all the saints of God constitute one church, one family, one brotherhood—essentially and indivisibly one. Nor is this relationship difficult to recognize. Take an illustration. Two brethren in the Lord of widely different sections of the Church, and of much dissonance of sentiment on some points of truth, meet and converse together. Each wonders that, with the Word of God in his hand, the other should not read it as he reads it, and interpret it as he interprets it. But they drop the points of difference, and take up the points of agreement. They speak of Christ—the Christ who loves them both, and whom they both love. They talk of the one Master whom they serve; of their common labors and infirmities, trials and temptations, discouragements, failures, and success; they talk of the heaven where they are journeying; of their Father's house, in which they will dwell together for ever; they kneel in prayer; they cast themselves before the cross; the oil of gladness anoints them; their hearts are broken, their spirits are humbled, their souls are blended; they rise, and feel more deeply and more strongly than ever, that they both belong to the same family, are both of the "many brethren," of whom the Son of God is the "Firstborn," the Elder Brother. Oh, blessed unity! What perfect harmony of creed, what strict conformity of ritual, what sameness of denominational relation, is for a moment to be compared with this? Have you, my reader, this evidence that you belong to the "many brethren"?

NOVEMBER 11

"But God forbid that I should glory, save in the cross of our Lord Jesus Christ, by whom the world is crucified unto me, and I unto the world." Gal. 6:14

CONFORMITY to the death of Christ can only be obtained by close, individual, realizing views of the cross. It is in the cross sin is seen in its exceeding sinfulness. It is in the cross the holiness of God shines with such ineffable luster. This is the sun that throws its light upon these two great objects—the holiness of God, the sinfulness of the sinner. Veil this sun, remove the cross, blot out the Atonement, and all our knowledge of holiness and sin vanishes into distant and shadowy views. Faith, dealing much and closely with the cross of Christ, will invariable produce in the soul conformity to His death. This was the great desire of the apostle: "That I may know Him, and the power of His resurrection, and the fellowship of His sufferings, being made conformable unto His death." This was the noble prayer of this holy man. He desired crucifixion with Christ; a crucifixion to sin, to indwelling sin, to sin in its every shape—to sin in principle, sin in temper, sin in worldly conformity, sin in conversation, sin in thought, yes, sin in the very glance of the eye. He desired not only a crucifixion of sin, of one particular sin, but of all sin; not only the sin that most easily beset him, the sin that he daily saw and felt, and mourned over, but the sin that no eye saw but God's—the sin of the indwelling principle; the root of all sin—the sin of his nature. This is to have fellowship with Christ in His sufferings. Jesus suffered as much for the subduing of the indwelling principle of sin, as for the pardon of the outbreakings of that sin in the daily practice. Have we fellowship with Him in these sufferings? There must be a crucifixion of the indwelling power of sin. To illustrate the idea: if the root be allowed to strengthen and expand, and take a deeper and firmer grasp, what more can we expect than that the tree will shoot upward and branch out on either hand? To cut off the outward branches is not the proper method to stay the growth of the tree: the root must be uncovered, and the axe laid to it. Outward sins may be cut off, and even honestly confessed and mourned over, while the concealed principle, the root of the sin, is overlooked, neglected, and suffered to gather strength and expansion.

That the inherent evil of a believer will ever, in his present existence, be entirely eradicated, we do not assert. To expect this would be to expect what God's Word has not declared; but that it may be greatly subdued and conquered, its power weakened and mortified, this the Word of God leads us to hope for and aim after. How is this to be attained? Faith dealing frequently and closely with Christ—the atoning blood upon the conscience—the "fountain opened" daily resorted to—the believer sitting constantly at the foot of the cross, gazing upon it with an eye of steady, unwavering faith—"looking unto Jesus." In this posture sin, all sin—the sin of the heart, the sin of the practice—is mourned over, wept over, confessed, mortified, crucified. Let the reader again be reminded that all true crucifixion of sin springs from the cross of Christ.

NOVEMBER 12

"Blessed are the poor in spirit: for theirs is the kingdom of heaven." Matt. 5:3

CULTIVATE above all spiritual conditions, most assiduously, prayerfully, earnestly, and fervently, poverty of spirit. Rest not short of it. This is the legitimate fruit and the only safe evidence of our union to Christ and the indwelling of the Spirit in our hearts. Nothing can suffice for it. Splendid talent, versatile gifts, profound erudition, gorgeous eloquence, and even extensive usefulness, are wretched substitutes for poverty of spirit. They may dazzle the eye, and please the ear, delight the taste, and awake the applause of man, but, dissociated from humiliation of mind, God sees no glory in them. What says He? "To this man"—to him only, to him exclusively—"will I look, even to him that is poor and of a contrite spirit, and trembles at my word." We may think highly of gifts, but let us learn their comparative value and true place from the words of our Lord, spoken in reference to John: "Verily I say unto you, Among them which are born of women, there has not risen a greater than John the Baptist: "notwithstanding he that is least in the kingdom of heaven is greater than he." Behold the true position which Christ assigns to distinction of office, of place, and of gifts—subordinate to lowliness of spirit. This is their proper rank; and he who elevates them above profound self-abasement, deep lowliness of spirit, sins against God, impeaches His wisdom, and denies the truth of His word. But how shall we adequately describe this blessed state? How draw the portrait of the man that is "poor, and of a contrite spirit"? Look at him as he appears in his own apprehension and judgment—"the chief of sinners"—"less than the least of all saints"—"though I be nothing." Prostrate, where others exalt him; condemning, where others approve him; censuring, where others applaud him; humbling himself, where others have put upon him the greatest honor. Confessing in secret, and in the dust before God, the flaws, the imperfections, and the sins of those things which have dazzled the eyes, and awoke to trembling ecstasy the souls of the multitude. Look at him in the place he assumes among others—taking the low position; in honor preferring others; washing the disciples' feet; willing to serve, rather than be served; rejoicing in the distinction, the promotion, the gifts, the usefulness, and the honor put upon his fellow-saints; and ready himself to go up higher at his Master's bidding. Look at him under the hand of God—meek, patient, resigned, humbled, drinking the cup, blessing the hand that has smitten, justifying the wisdom, the love, and the gentleness which mark the discipline, and eager to learn the holy lessons it is sent to teach. Look at him before the cross—reposing all his gifts, attainments, and honors at its foot, and glorying only in the exhibition it presents of a holy God pardoning sin by the death of His Son, and as the hallowed instrument by which he becomes crucified to the world, and the world to him.

NOVEMBER 13

"Take my yoke upon you, and learn of me; for I am meek and lowly in heart: and you shall find rest unto your souls. For my yoke is easy, and my burden is light." Matthew 11:29, 30

HOW shall we array, in their strongest light, before you, the motives which urge the cultivation of this poverty of spirit? Is it not enough that this is the spiritual state on which Jehovah looks with an eye of exclusive, holy, and ineffable delight? "To this man I will look." Splendid gifts, brilliant attainments, costly sacrifices, are nothing to me. "To this man will I look, that is poor and of a contrite spirit, and that trembles at my word." To this would we add, if you value your safe, happy, and holy walk—if you prize the manifestations of God's presence—the "kisses of His mouth, whose love is better than wine"— the teaching, guiding, and comforting influence of the Holy Spirit, seek it. If you would be a "savor of Christ in every place"—if you would pray with more fervor, unction, and power—if you would labor with more zeal, devotedness, and success, seek it. By all that is dear, and precious, and holy, by your own happiness, by the honor of Christ, by the glory of God, by the hope of heaven, seek to be found among those who are "poor and of a contrite spirit," who, with filial, holy love, tremble at God's word, whom Jesus has pronounced blessed here, and meet for glory hereafter. And though in approaching the Great High

Priest, you have no splendid and costly intellectual offerings to present, yet with the royal penitent you can say, "You desire not sacrifice, else would I give it: you delight not in burned offering. The sacrifices of God are a broken spirit: a broken and a contrite heart, O God, you will not despise." "This, Lord, is all that I have to bring You." Avoid a spurious humility. True humility consists not in denying the work of the Holy Spirit in our hearts, in under-rating the grace of God in our souls, in standing afar off from our heavenly Father, and in walking at a distance from Christ, always doubting the efficacy of His blood, the freeness of His salvation, the willingness of His heart, and the greatness of His power to save. Oh no! this is not the humility that God delights to look at, but is a false, a counterfeit humility, obnoxious in His sight. But to "draw near with a true heart, in full assurance of faith," in lowly dependence upon His blood and righteousness; to accept of salvation as the gift of His grace; to believe the promise because He has spoken it; gratefully and humbly to acknowledge our calling, our adoption, and our acceptance, and to live in the holy, transforming influence of this exalted state, giving to a Triune God all the praise and glory; this is the humility which is most pleasing to God, and is the true product of the Holy Spirit.

NOVEMBER 14

"My son, give me your heart." Proverbs 23:26

THE human heart is naturally idolatrous. Its affections once supremely centered in God: but now, disjoined from Him, they go in quest of other objects of attachment, and we love and worship the creature rather than the Creator. The circle which our affections traverse may not indeed by a large one; there are, perchance, but few to whom we fully surrender our heart; no, so circumscribed may the circle be, that one object alone shall attract, absorb, and concentrate in itself our entire and undivided love—that one object to us as a universe of beings, and all others comparatively indifferent and insipid. Who cannot see that, in a case like this, the danger is imminent of transforming the heart—Christ's own sanctuary—into an idol's temple, where the creature is loved, and reverenced, and served more than He who gave it. But from all idolatry our God will cleanse us, and from all our idols Christ will wean us. The Lord is jealous, with a holy jealousy, of our love. Poor as our affection is, He asks its complete surrender. That He requires our love at the expense of all creature attachment, the Bible nowhere intimates. He created our affections, and He it is who provides for their proper and pleasant indulgence. There is not a single precept or command in the Scriptures that forbids their exercise, or that discourages their intensity. Husbands are exhorted to "love their wives, even as Christ loved His church." Parents are to cherish a like affection toward their children, and children are bound to render back a filial love not less intense to their parents. And we are to "love our neighbors as ourselves." Nor does the word of God furnish examples of Christian friendship less interesting and devoted. One of the choicest and tenderest blessings with which God can enrich us, next to Himself, is such a friend as Paul had in Epaphroditus, a "brother and companion in labor, and fellow-soldier;" and such an affectionate friendship as John, the loving disciple, cherished for his well-beloved Gaius, whom he loved in the truth, and to whom, in the season of his sickness, he thus touchingly poured out his heart's affectionate sympathy: "Beloved, I wish above all things that you may prosper and be in health, even as your soul prospers." Count such a friend and such friendship among God's sweetest and holiest bestowments. The blessings of which it may be to you the sanctifying channel are immense. The tender sympathy—the jealous watchfulness—the confidential repose—the faithful admonition—above all, the intercessory prayer, connected with Christian friendship, may be placed in the inventory of our most inestimable and precious things.

It is not therefore the use, but the abuse, of our affections—not their legitimate exercise, but their idolatrous tendency—over which we have need to exercise the greatest vigilance. It is not our love to the creature against which God contends, but it is in not allowing our love to Himself to subordinate all other love. We may love the creature, but we may not love the creature more than the Creator. When the Giver is lost sight of and forgotten in the gift, then comes the painful process of weaning. When the heart burns its incense before some human shrine, and the cloud as it ascends veils from the eye the beauty and the excellence of Jesus, then comes the painful proves of weaning. When the absorbing claims and the engrossing attentions of some loved one are placed in competition and are allowed to clash with the claims of God, and the service due from us personally to His cause and truth, then comes the painful process of weaning. When creature devotion deadens our heart to the Lord, lessens our interest in His cause, congeals our zeal and love and liberality, detaches us from the public means of grace, withdraws from the closet, the Bible, and the communion of saints, thus propagating leanness of soul, and robbing God of His glory, then comes the painful process of weaning. Christ will be the first in our affections—God will be supreme in our service—and His kingdom and righteousness must take precedence of all other things.

NOVEMBER 15

"In whom we have redemption through his blood, the forgiveness of sins, according to the riches of his grace." Ephesians 1:7

LET not the reader be satisfied to rest upon the mere surface of the truth, that Christ has made an atonement for sin; this may be believed, and yet the full blessedness, peace, and sanctification of it not enjoyed. Any why? Because he enters not fully into the experience of the truth. Shall we not say, too, because his views of sin rest but on the surface of sin's exceeding sinfulness? Deep views of sin will ever result in deep views of the Sacrifice for sin; inadequate knowledge of sin, inadequate knowledge of Christ; low views of self, high views of Christ. Be satisfied, then, not to rest upon the surface of this wondrous truth. The completeness of Christ's atonement arises from the infinite dignity of His Person: His Godhead forms the basis of His perfect work. It guarantees, so to speak, the glorious result of His atonement. It was this that gave perfection to His obedience, and virtue to His atonement: it was this that made the blood He shed efficacious in the pardon of sin, and the righteousness He wrought out complete in the justification of the soul. His entire work would have been wanting but for His Godhead.

The pardon of a believer's sins is an entire pardon: it is the full pardon of all his sins. It were no pardon to him, if it were not an entire pardon. If it were but a partial blotting out of the thick cloud—if it were but a partial canceling of the bond—if it were but a forgiveness of some sins only, then the gospel were no glad tidings to his soul. The law of God has brought him in guilty of an entire violation. The justice of God demands a satisfaction equal to the enormity of the sins committed and of the guilt incurred. The Holy Spirit has convinced him of his utter helplessness, his entire bankruptcy.

What rapture would kindle in his bosom at the announcement of a partial atonement—of a half Savior—of a part payment of the debt? Not one throb of joyous sensation would it produce. On the contrary, this very mockery of his woe would but deepen the anguish of his spirit. But, go to the soul, weary and heavy laden with sin, mourning over its vileness, its helplessness, and proclaim the gospel. Tell him that the atonement which Jesus offered on Calvary was a full satisfaction for his sins. That all his sins were borne and blotted out in that awful moment. That the bond which divine justice held against the sinner was fully cancelled by the obedience and sufferings of Christ, and that, appeased and satisfied, God was "ready to pardon." How beautiful will be the feet that convey to him tidings so transporting as these! And are not these statements perfectly accordant with the declarations of God's own word? Let us ascertain: what was the ark symbolical of, alluded to by the apostle in the ninth chapter of his Epistle to the Hebrews, which contained the manna, Aaron's rod, and the tables of the covenant, over which stood the Cherubim of glory, shadowing the mercy-seat? What, but the entire covering of sin? For, as the covering of the ark did hide the law and testimony, so did the Lord Jesus Christ hide the sins of His chosen, covenant people— not from the eye of God's omniscience, but from the eye of the law. They stand legally acquitted. So entire was the work of Jesus, so infinite and satisfactory His obedience, the law of God pronounces them acquitted, and can never bring them into condemnation. "There is therefore now no condemnation to those who are in Christ Jesus." "Who is he that condemns? It is Christ that died." How could the apostle, with any truth, have made a declaration so astounding, and uttered a challenge so dauntless as this, if the point we are now endeavoring to establish were not strictly as we affirm it to be?

NOVEMBER 16

"Even the righteousness of God which is by faith of Jesus Christ unto all and upon all those who believe." Romans 3:22

THE righteousness wrought out by the incarnation, obedience, sufferings, and death of Christ, is a most glorious righteousness. It took in the whole law of God. It did not soften down or ask for a compromise of its claims. It took the law in its utmost strictness, and honored it. It gave all the law demanded, all it could demand. And what stamped this righteousness with a glory so great? what enabled the Redeemer to offer an obedience so perfect?—what, but that He was God in our nature! The Law-giver became the Law-fulfiller. The God became the Substitute— the Judge became the Surety. Behold, then, the justification of a believing sinner! He stands accepted in the righteousness of Christ, with full and entire acceptance. What says the Holy Spirit? "In the Lord shall all the seed of Israel by justified, and shall glory." "And by Him (the Lord Jesus) all that believe are justified from all things, from which you could not be justified by the law of Moses." "And you are complete in Him, which is the head of all principality and power." "Christ loved the Church, and gave Himself for it, that He might sanctify and cleanse it with the washing of water by the Word, that He might present it to Himself a glorious Church, not having spot, or wrinkle, or any such thing; but that it should be holy and without blemish." "He has made Him to be sin for us, who knew no sin; that we might be made the righteousness of God in Him." Mark the expression, "made the righteousness of God"! So called because the righteousness which Christ wrought out was a divine righteousness—not the righteousness of a created being, of an angel, or of a superior prophet, else it were blasphemy to call it "the righteousness of GOD." Oh no! the righteousness in which you stand, if you are "accepted in the Beloved," is a more costly and glorious righteousness than Adam's, or the highest angel's in glory: it is "the righteousness of God." The righteousness of the God-man—possessing all the infinite merit, and glory, and perfection of Deity. And what seems still more incredible, the believer is made the righteousness of God in Christ. So that beholding him in Christ, the Father can "rest in His love, and rejoice over Him with singing." Is it not then, we ask, a perfect, a complete justification? what can be more so? Do not the passages we have quoted prove it? Can any other meaning be given to them, without divesting them of their beauty and obvious sense? Would it not be to turn from God's word, to dishonor and grieve the Spirit, and to rob the believer of a most influential motive to holiness, were we to take a less expanded view of this subject than that which we have taken? Most assuredly it would. Then let the Christian reader welcome this truth. If it is God's truth—and we humbly believe we have proved it to be so—it is not less his privilege than his duty to receive it.

NOVEMBER 17

*"To the praise of the glory of his grace, wherein he has
made us accepted in the beloved." Ephesians 1:6*

THE holy influence which a believer is called to exert around him will
be greatly augmented, and powerfully felt, by an abiding realization of his
full and entire acceptance in Christ. The child of God is "the salt of the
earth," "the light of the world," surrounded by moral putrefaction and
darkness. By his holy consistent example, he is to exert a counteracting
influence. He is to be purity where there is corruption, he is to be light
where there is darkness. And if his walk is consistent, if his life is holy, his
example tells, and tells powerfully, upon an ungodly world. Saints of God
catch, as it were, the contagion of his sanctity. The worldling acknowledges
the reality of the gospel he professes, and the bold skeptic falls back
abashed, and feels "how awful goodness is!" What, then, will so elevate
his own piety, and increase the power of his influence, as a realization of
his justification by Christ? Oh how this commends the religion of Jesus! We
will suppose a Christian parent surrounded by a large circle of unconverted
children. They look to him as to a living gospel: they look to him for an
exemplification of the truth he believes: they expect to see its influence
upon his principles, his temper, his affections, his whole conduct. What,
then, must be their impression of the gospel, if they behold their parent
always indulging in doubts as to his acceptance, yielding to unbelieving
fears as to his calling? Instead of walking in the full assurance of faith,
saying with the apostle, "I know whom I have believed"—instead of living
in the holy liberty, peace, and comfort of acceptance, there is nothing
but distrust, dread, and tormenting fear. How many a child has borne
this testimony, "the doubts and fears of my parent have been my great
stumbling-block"! Oh, then, for the sake of those around you—for the sake
of your children, your connections, your friends, your domestics—realize
your full, free, and entire acceptance in Christ.

Is it any marvel, then, that in speaking of His beloved and justified
people, God employs in His word language like this: "You are all fair, my
love: there is no spot in you." "He has not beheld iniquity in Jacob, neither
has He seen perverseness in Israel"? Carry out this thought. Had there
been no iniquity in Jacob? had there been no perverseness in Israel? Read

their histories, and what do they develop but iniquity and perverseness of the most aggravated kind? And yet, that God should say He saw no iniquity in Jacob, and no perverseness in Israel, what does it set forth but the glorious work of the adorable Immanuel—the glory, the fitness, the perfection of that righteousness in which they stand "without spot, or wrinkle, or any such thing"? In themselves vile and worthless, sinful and perverse, deeply conscious before God of possessing not a claim upon His regard, but worthy only of His just displeasure, yet counted righteous in the righteousness of another, fully and freely justified by Christ. Is this doctrine startling to some? Is it considered too great a truth to be received by others? Any other gospel than this, we solemnly affirm, will never save the soul! The obedience, sufferings, and death of the God-man, made over to the repenting, believing sinner, by an act of free and sovereign grace, is the only plank on which the soul can safely rest—let it attempt the passage across the cold river of death on any other, and it is gone! On this it may boldly venture, and on this it shall be safely and triumphantly carried into the quiet and peaceful haven of future and eternal blessedness. We acknowledge the magnitude of this doctrine; yet it is not to be rejected because of its greatness. It may be profound, almost too deeply so for an angel's mind—the cherubim may veil their faces, overpowered with its glory, while yet with eager longings they desire to look into it—still may the weakest saint of God receive it, live upon it, walk in it. It is "a deep river, through which an elephant might swim, and which a lamb may ford."

NOVEMBER 18

"And I will bring the third part through the fire, and will refine them as silver is refined, and will try them as gold is tried: they shall call on my name, and I will hear them: I will say, It is my people: and they shall say, The Lord is my God." Zechariah 13:9

THE believer often commences his spiritual journey with shallow and defective views of the perfect fitness and glory of the Redeemer's justifying righteousness. There is, we admit, a degree of self-renunciation—there is a reception of Christ—and there is some sweet and blessed enjoyment of His acceptance. Yet his views of himself, and of the entire, absolute, supreme necessity, importance, and glory of Christ's finished work, are as nothing compared with his after experience of both. God will have the righteousness of His Son to be acknowledged and felt to be everything. It is a great work, a glorious work, a finished work, and He will cause His saints to know it. It is His only method of saving sinners; and the sinner that is saved shall acknowledge this, not in his judgment merely, but from a deep heartfelt experience of the truth, "to the praise of the glory of His grace."

It is, then, we say, in the successive stages of his experience, that the believer sees more distinctly, adores more profoundly, and grasps more firmly, the finished righteousness of Christ. And what is the school in which he learns his nothingness, his poverty, his utter destitution? the school of deep and sanctified affliction. In no other school is it learned, and under no other teacher but God. Here his high thoughts are brought low, and the Lord alone is exalted. Here he forms a just estimate of his attainments, his gifts, his knowledge, and that which he thought to be so valuable he now finds to be nothing worth. Here his proud spirit is abased, his rebellious spirit tamed, his restless, feverish spirit soothed into passive quietude; and here, the deep humbling acknowledgment is made, "I am vile!" Thus is he led back to first principles. Thus the first step is retaken, and the first lesson is relearned. The believer, emptied entirely of self, of self-complacency, self-trust, self-glorying, stands ready for the full Savior. The blessed and eternal Spirit opens to him, in this posture, the fitness, the fullness, the glory, the infinite grandeur of Christ's finished righteousness; leads him to it afresh, puts it upon him anew, causes him to enter into it more fully, to rest upon it more entirely; breaks it up to the soul, and discloses its perfect fitness to his case. And what a glory he sees in it! He saw it before, but not as he beholds it now. And what a resting-place he finds beneath the cross! He rested there before, but not as he rests now. Such views has he now of Christ—such preciousness, such beauty, such tenderness he sees in Immanuel—that a new world of beauty and of glory seems to have opened before his view. A new Savior, a new righteousness, appear to have been brought to his soul. All this has been produced by the discipline of the covenant—the afflictions sent and sanctified by a good and covenant God and Father. Oh, you tried believers! murmur not at God's dispensations; repine not at His dealings. Has He seen fit to dash against you billow upon billow? Has He thought proper to place you in the furnace? Has He blasted the fair prospect— dried up the stream—called for the surrender of your Isaac? Oh, bless Him for the way He takes to empty you of self, and fill you with His own love. This is His method of teaching you, schooling you, and fitting you for the inheritance of the saints in light. Will you not allow Him to select His own plan—to adopt His own mode of cure? You are in His hands; and could you be in better? Are you now learning your own poverty, destitution, and helplessness? and is the blood and righteousness of Jesus more precious and glorious to the eye of your faith? Then praise Him for your afflictions, for all these cross dispensations are now, yes, at this moment, working together for your spiritual good.

NOVEMBER 19

"Charity suffers long, and is kind; charity envies not; charity boasts not itself, is not puffed up, does not behave itself unseemly, seeks not her own, is not easily provoked, thinks no evil; rejoices not in iniquity, but rejoices in the truth; bears all things, believes all things, hopes all things, endures all things." 1 Corinthians 13:4—7

TRUE Christian love will excite in the mind a holy jealousy for the Christian reputation of other believers. How sadly is this overlooked by many professors! What sporting with reputation, what trifling with character, what unveiling to the eyes of others the weaknesses, the infirmities, and the stumblings of which they have become cognizant, marks many in our day. Oh! if the Lord had dealt with us as we have thoughtlessly and uncharitably dealt with our fellow-servants, what shame and confusion would cover us! We should blush to lift up our faces before men. But the exercise of this divine love in the heart will constrain us to abstain from all envious, suspicious feelings, from all evil surmisings, from all wrong construing of motives, from all tale-bearing—that fruitful cause of so much evil in the Christian Church—from slander, from unkind insinuations, and from going from house to house retailing evil, and making the imperfections, the errors, or the doings of others the theme of idle, sinful gossip—"busy-bodies in other men's matters." All this is utterly inconsistent with our high and holy calling. It is degrading, dishonoring, lowering to our character as the children of God. It dims the luster of our piety. It impairs our moral influence in the world. Ought not the character of a Christian professor to be as dear to me as my own? And ought I not as vigilantly to watch over it, and as zealously to promote it, and as indignantly to vindicate it, when unjustly aspersed or maliciously assailed, as if I, and not he, were the sufferer? How can the reputation of a believer in Jesus be affected, and we not be affected? It is our common Lord who is wounded—it is our common salvation that is injured—it is our own family that is maligned. And our love to Jesus, to His truth, and to His people, should caution us to be as jealous of the honor, as tender of the feelings, and as watchful of the character and reputation, of each member of the Lord's family, be his denomination what it may, as of our own. "Who is weak," says the apostle, "and I am not weak? who is offended, and I burn not?" Oh how graciously, how kindly does our God deal with His people! Laying His hand upon their many spots, He seems to say, "No eye but mine shall see them." Oh! let us in this particular be "imitators of God, as dear children." Thus shall we more clearly evidence to others, and be assured ourselves, that have "passed from death unto life."

NOVEMBER 20

"God, who quickens the dead." Romans 4:17

THE commencement of spiritual life is sudden. We are far from confining the Spirit to a certain prescribed order in this or any other part of His work. He is a Sovereign, and therefore works according to His own will. But there are some methods He more frequently adopts than others. We would not say that all conversion is a sudden work. There is a knowledge of sin, conviction of its guilt, repentance before God on account of it; these are frequently slow and gradual in their advance. But the first communication of divine light and life to the soul is always sudden—sudden and instantaneous as was the creation of natural light—"God said, Let there be light, and there was light." It was but a word, and in an instant chaos rolled away, and every object and scene in nature was bathed in light and glory—sudden as was the communication of life to Lazarus—"Jesus cried with a loud voice, Lazarus, come forth!" it was but a word, and in an instant "he that was dead came forth, bound hand and foot with grave-clothes." So is it in the first communication of divine light and life to the soul. The eternal Spirit says, "Let there be light," and in a moment there is light. He speaks again, "Come forth," and in a moment, in the twinkling of an eye, the dead are raised.

Striking illustrations of the suddenness of the Spirit's operation are afforded in the cases of Saul of Tarsus and of the thief upon the cross. How sudden was the communication of light and life to their souls! It was no long and previous process of spiritual illumination—it was the result of no lengthened chain of reasoning—no labored argumentation. In a moment, and under circumstances most unfavorable to the change, as we should think—certainly, at a period when the rebellion of the heart rose the most fiercely against God, "a light from heaven, above the brightness of the sun," poured its transforming radiance into the mind of the enraged persecutor; and a voice, conveying life into the soul, reached the conscience of the dying thief. Both were translated from darkness into light, "in a moment, in the twinkling of an eye." How many who read this page may say, "Thus it was with me!" God the Eternal Spirit arrested me when my heart's deep rebellion was most up in arms against Him. It was a sudden and a short work, but it was mighty and effectual. It was unexpected and rapid, but deep and thorough. In a moment the hidden evil was brought to view—the deep and dark fountain broken up; all my iniquities passed before me, and all my secret sins seemed placed in the light of God's countenance. My soul sank down in deep mire—yes, hell opened its mouth to receive me."

Overlook not this wise and gracious method of the blessed Spirit's operation in regeneration. It is instantaneous. The means may have been simple; perhaps it was the loss of a friend—an alarming illness—a word of reproof or admonition dropped from a parent or a companion—the singing of a hymn—the hearing of a sermon—or some text of Scripture winged with his power to the conscience; in the twinkling of an eye, the soul, "dead in trespasses and sins," was "quickened" and translated into "newness of life." Oh blessed work of the blessed and Eternal Spirit! Oh mighty operation! Oh inscrutable wisdom! What a change has now passed over the whole man! Overshadowed by the Holy Spirit, that which is begotten in the soul is the divine life—a holy, influential, never-dying principle. Truly he is a new creature, "old things are passed away; behold, all things are become new." For this change let it not be supposed that there is, in the subject, any previous preparation. There can be no preparation for light or life. What preparation was there is chaos? What preparation was there in the cold clay limbs of Lazarus? What in Paul? What in the dying thief? The work of regeneration is supremely the work of the Spirit. The means may be employed, and are to be employed, in accordance with the Divine purpose, yet are they not to be deified. They are but means, "profiting nothing" without the power of God the Holy Spirit. Regeneration is His work, and not man's.

NOVEMBER 21

"Verily, verily, I say unto you, He that hears my word, and believes on him that sent me, has everlasting life, and shall not come into condemnation; but is passed from death unto life." John 5:24

IF, then, the first implantation of the divine life in the soul is sudden; the advance of that work is in most cases gradual. Let this be an encouragement to any who are writing hard and bitter things against themselves in consequence of their little progress. The growth of divine knowledge in the soul is often slow—the work of much time and of protracted discipline. Look at the eleven disciples—what slow, tardy scholars were they, even though taught immediately from the lips of Jesus; and "who teaches like Him?" They drank their knowledge from the very Fountain. They received their light directly from the Sun itself. And yet, with all these superior advantages—the personal ministry, instructions, miracles, and example of our dear Lord—how slow of understanding were they to comprehend, and how "slow of heart to believe," all that He so laboriously, clearly, and patiently taught them! Yes, the advance of the soul in the divine life, its knowledge of sin, of the hidden evil, the heart's deep treachery and intricate windings, Satan's subtlety, the glory of the gospel, the preciousness of Christ, and its own interest in the great salvation, is not the work of a day, nor of a year, but of many days, yes, many years of deep ploughing, long and often painful discipline, of "windy storm and tempest."

But this life in the soul is not less real, nor less divine, because its growth is slow and gradual: it may be small and feeble in its degree, yet, in its nature, it is the life that never dies. How many of the Lord's beloved ones, the children of godly parents, brought up in the ways of God, are at a loss, in reviewing the map of their pilgrimage, to remember the starting-point of their spiritual life. They well know that they left the city of destruction—that by a strong and a mighty arm they were brought out of Egypt; but so gently, so imperceptibly, so softly, and so gradually were they led—"first a thought, then a desire, then a prayer"—that they could no more discover when the first dawning of divine life took place in their soul, than they could tell the instant when natural light first broke upon chaos. Still it is real. It is no fancy that he has inherited an evil principle in the heart; it is no fancy that that principle grace has subdued. It is no fancy that he was once a child of darkness; it is no fancy that he is now a child of light. He may mourn in secret over his little advance, his tardy progress, his weak faith, his small grace, his strong corruption, his many infirmities, his startings aside like "a broken bow," yet he can say, "Though I am the 'chief of sinners,' and the 'least of all saints'—though I see within so much to abase me, and without so much to mourn over, yet this 'one thing I know, that whereas I was blind, now I see.' I see that which I never saw before—a hatefulness in sin, and a beauty in holiness; I see a vileness and emptiness in myself, and a preciousness and fullness in Jesus." Do not forget, then, dear reader, that feeble grace is yet real grace. If it but "hungers and thirsts," if it "touches but the hem," it shall be saved.

NOVEMBER 22

"Leaning upon her Beloved." Solomon's Song, 8:5

WHAT more appropriate, what more soothing truth could we bring before you, suffering Christian, than this? You are sick—lean upon Jesus. His sick ones are peculiarly dear to His heart. You are dear to Him. In all your pains and languishings, faintings and lassitude, Jesus is with you; for He created that frame, He remembers that it is but dust, and He bids you lean upon Him, and leave your sickness and its issue entirely in His hands. You are oppressed—lean upon Jesus. He will undertake your cause, and committing it thus into His hands, He will bring forth your righteousness as the light, and your judgment as the noonday. You are lonely—lean upon Jesus. Sweet will be the communion and close the fellowship which you may thus hold with Him, your heart burning within you while He talks with you by the way. Is the ascent steep and difficult? lean upon your Beloved. Is the path strait and narrow? lean upon your Beloved. Do intricacies and perplexities and trials weave their network around your feet? lean upon your Beloved. Has death smitten down the strong arm and chilled the tender heart upon which you were used to recline? lean upon your Beloved. Oh! lean upon Jesus in every strait, in every want, in every sorrow, in every temptation. Nothing is too insignificant, nothing too mean, to take to Christ. It is enough that you want Christ, to warrant you in coming to Christ. No excuse need you make for repairing to Him; no apology will He require for the frequency of your approach; He loves to have you quite near to Him, to hear your voice, and to feel the confidence of your faith and the pressure of your love. Ever remember that there is a place in the heart of Christ sacred to you, and which no one can fill but yourself, and from which none may dare exclude you. And when you are dying, oh! lay your languishing head upon the bosom of your Beloved, and fear not the foe, and dread not the passage; for His rod and His staff, they will comfort you. On that bosom the beloved disciple leaned at supper; on that bosom the martyr Stephen laid his bleeding brow in death; and on that bosom you, too, beloved, may repose, living or dying, soothed, supported, and sheltered by your Savior and your Lord.

NOVEMBER 23

"God is not a man, that he should lie; neither the son of man, that he should repent: has he said, and shall he not do it? Or has he spoken, and shall he not make it good?" Numbers 23:19

GOD has done the utmost which His infinite wisdom dictated, to lay the most solid ground for confidence. He has made all the promises of the covenant of grace absolute and unconditional. Were faith simply to credit this, what "strong consolation" would flow into the soul! Take, for example, that exceeding great and precious promise, "Call upon me in the day of trouble: I will deliver you, and you shall glorify me." What a sparkling jewel, what a brilliant gem is this! How many a weeping eye has caught the luster, and has forgotten its misery, as waters that pass away! While others, perhaps, gazing intently upon it, have said, "This promise exactly suits my case, but is it for me? is it for one so vile as I? Who by my own indiscretion and folly and sin have brought this trouble upon myself? May such an one call upon God, and be answered?" What is this unbelieving reasoning, but to render this divine and most exhilarating promise, as to any practical influence upon your mind, of none effect? But the promise stands in God's word absolute and unconditional. There is not one syllable in it upon which the most unworthy child of sorrow can reasonably found an objection. Is it now with you a "day of trouble"?—God makes no exception as to how, or by whom, or from where your trouble came. It is enough that it is a time of trouble with you—that you are in sorrow, in difficulty, in trial—God says to you, "Call upon me in the day of trouble, I will deliver you." Resign, then, your unbelief, embrace the promise, and behold Jesus showing Himself through its open lattice. Take yet another glorious promise, "Him that comes unto me I will in no wise cast out." "This is just the promise that my poor, guilty, anxious heart needs," exclaims a trembling, sin-distressed soul; "but dare I with all my sin, and wretchedness, and poverty, take up my rest in Christ? What! may I, who have been so long an enemy against God, such a despiser of Christ, such a neglecter of my soul, and scoffer at its great salvation, approach with a trembling yet assured hope that Christ will receive me, save me, and not cast me out?" Yes! You may. The promise is absolute and unconditional, and, magnificent and precious as it is, it is yours. "Him that comes unto me I will in no wise cast out. Satan shall not persuade me, sin shall not prevail with me, my own heart shall not constrain me, yes, nothing shall induce me, to cast out that poor sinner who comes to me, believes my word, falls upon my grace, and hides himself in my pierced bosom: I will in no wise cast him out."

NOVEMBER 24

"Nevertheless I tell you the truth; It is expedient for you that I go away: for if I go not away, the Comforter will not come unto you; but if I depart, I will send him unto you." John 16:7

THERE is no sorrow of the believing heart of which the Holy Spirit is ignorant, to which He is indifferent, or which His sympathy does not embrace, and His power cannot alleviate. The Church in which He dwells, and whose journeyings he guides, is a tried Church. Chosen in the furnace of affliction, allied to a suffering Head, its course on earth is traced by tears, and often by blood. Deeply it needs a Comforter. And who can compute the individual sorrows which may crowd the path of a single traveler to his sorrowless home? What a world of trial, and how varied, may be comprised within the history of a single saint! But if sorrows abound, consolation much more abounds, since the Comforter of the Church is the Holy Spirit. What a mighty provision, how infinite the largess, the God of all consolation has made in the covenant of grace for the sorrows of His people, in the appointment of the Third Person of the blessed Trinity to this office! What an importance it attaches to, and with what dignity it invests, and with what sanctity it hallows, our every sorrow! If our heavenly Father sees proper in His unerring wisdom and goodness to send affliction, who would not welcome the message as a sacred and precious thing, thus to be soothed and sanctified? Yes, the Spirit leads the sorrowful to all comfort. He comforts by applying the promises—by leading to Christ—by bending the will in deep submission to God—and by unveiling to faith's far-seeing eye the glories of a sorrowless, tearless, sinless world. And oh, who can portray His perfection as a Comforter? With what promptness and tenderness He applies Himself to the soothing of each grief—how patiently He instructs the ignorant—how gently He leads the burdened—how skillfully He heals the wounded—how timely He meets the necessitous—how effectually He speaks to the mourner! When our heart is overwhelmed within us, through the depth and foam of the angry waters, He leads us to the Rock that is higher than we.

He leads to glory. There He matures the kingdom, and perfects the building, and completes the temple He commenced and occupied on earth. No power shall oppose, no difficulty shall obstruct, no contingency shall thwart the consummation of this His glorious purpose and design. Every soul graced by His presence, every heart touched by His love, every body sanctified as His temple, He will lead to heaven. Of that heaven He is the pledge and the earnest. While Jesus is in heaven, preparing a place for His people, the Spirit is on earth, preparing His people for that place. The one is maturing glory for the Church, the other is maturing the Church for glory.

NOVEMBER 25

"What? know you not that your body is the temple of the Holy Spirit which is in you, which you have of God, and you are not your own? For you are bought with a price: therefore glorify God in your body, and in your spirit, which are God's." 1 Corinthians 6:19, 20

AS a temple of the Holy Spirit, yield yourself to His divine and gracious power. Bend your ear to His softest whisper—your will to His gentlest sway—your heart to His holy and benign influence. In not hearkening to His voice, and in not yielding to His promptings, we have been great losers. Often has He incited to communion with God, and because the time was not seasonable, or the place not convenient, you stifled His persuasive voice, resisted His proffered aid, and, thus slighted and grieved, He has retired. And lo! when you have risen to pray, God has covered Himself as with a cloud that your prayer could not pass through. Oh, seek to have an ear attuned to His softest accents, and a heart constrained to an instant compliance with His mildest dictates. The greatest blessing we possess is the possession of the Spirit.

And oh, to be Christ's—to be His gift, His purchase, His called saint, His lowly disciple—what an inestimable privilege! But how may we be quite sure that this privilege is ours? If we have the Spirit of Christ, we are in very deed Christians. It is the superscription of the King, the mark of the Shepherd, the Lord's impress of Himself upon the heart. And how sanctifying this privilege! "Those who are Christ's have crucified the flesh, with its affections and lusts." "Let every one that names the name of Christ depart from iniquity." And if we are Christ's now, we shall be Christ's to all eternity. It is a union that cannot be dissolved. Every believer in Jesus is "sealed with that Holy Spirit of promise which is the earnest of our inheritance." And as we have the earnest of the inheritance, we shall as assuredly possess the inheritance itself. The Spirit of Christ is an active, benevolent Spirit. It bore the Savior, when He was in the flesh, from country to country, from city to city, from house to house, preaching His own gospel to lost man. "He went about doing good." If we have the Spirit of Christ, we shall be prompted to a like Christian love and activity on behalf of those who possess not the gospel, or who, possessing it, slight and reject the mercy. The Spirit of Christ is essentially a missionary Spirit. It commenced its labor of love at Jerusalem, and from that its center, worked its way with augmenting sympathy and widening sphere until it embraced the world as the field of its labor. Ah! that we manifest so little of this Spirit, ought to lead us to deep searchings of heart, and stir us up to earnest prayer: "Lord, make me more earnest for the salvation of souls, for the advancement of Your kingdom. Grant me this evidence of being Your—the possession of Your Spirit, constraining me to a more simple and unreserved consecration of my talents, my substance, my rank, my influence, my time, myself, to the establishment of Your truth, the advancement of Your cause, and thus to the wider diffusion of Your glory in the earth."

NOVEMBER 26

"Blessed be the God and Father of our Lord Jesus Christ, which according to His abundant mercy has begotten us again unto a lively hope by the resurrection of Jesus Christ from the dead." 1 Peter 1:3

TO be sensible of this amazing power in the soul is to be born again—to be raised from the grave of corruption—to live on earth a heavenly, a resurrection-life—to have the heart daily ascending in the sweet incense of love and prayer and praise, where its risen Treasure is. It possesses, too, a most comforting power. What but this sustained the disciples in the early struggles of Christianity, amid the storms of persecution, which else had swept them from the earth? They felt that their Master was alive. They needed no external proof of the fact. They possessed in their souls God's witness. The truth authenticated itself. The three days of His entombment were to them days of sadness, desertion, and gloom. Their sun had set in darkness and in blood, and with it every ray of hope had vanished. All they loved, or cared to live for, had descended to the grave. They had now no arm to strengthen them in their weakness, no bosom to sympathize with them in sorrow, no eye to which they could unveil each hidden thought and struggling emotion. But the resurrection of their Lord was the resurrection of all their buried joys. They now traveled to him as to a living Savior, conscious of a power new—born within them, the power of their Lord's resurrection. "Then were the disciples glad when they saw the Lord." But is this truth less vivifying and precious to us? Has it lost anything of its vitality to quicken, or its power to soothe? Oh, no! truth is eternal and immutable. Years impair not its strength, circumstances change not its character. The same truths which distilled as dew from the lips of Moses, which awoke the seraphic lyre of David, which winged the heaven—soaring spirit of Isaiah, which inspired the manly eloquence of Paul, which floated in visions of sublimity before the eye of John, and which in all ages have fed, animated, and sanctified the people of God, guiding their counsels, soothing their sorrows, and animating their hopes, still are vital and potent in the chequered experiences of the saints, hastening to swell the cloud of witnesses to their divinity and their might. Of such is the doctrine of Christ's resurrection. Oh, what consolation flows to the Church of God from the truth of a living Savior—a Savior alive to know and to heal our sorrows—to inspire and sanctify our joys—to sympathize with and supply our need! Alive to every cloud that shades the mind, to every cross that chafes the spirit, to every grief that saddens the heart, to every evil that threatens our safety or imperils our happiness! What power, too, do the promises of the gospel derive from this truth! When Jesus speaks by these promises, we feel that there is life and spirit in His word, for it is the spoken word of the living Savior. And when He invites us to Himself for rest, and bids us look to His cross for peace, and asks us to deposit our burdens at His feet, and drink the words that flow from His lips, we feel a living influence stealing over the soul, inspiriting and soothing as that of which the trembling evangelist was conscious, when the glorified Savior gently laid His right hand upon him, and said, "Fear not: I am the first and last: I am he that lives, and was dead; and behold, I am alive for evermore, Amen; and have the keys of hell and of death." Is Jesus alive? Then let what else die, our life, with all its supports, consolations, and hopes, is secure in Him. "Because I live, you shall live also." A living spring is He. Seasons vary, circumstances change, feelings fluctuate, friendships cool, friends die, but Christ is ever the same. Oh, the blessedness of dealing with a risen, a living Redeemer! We take our needs to Him—they are instantly supplied. We take our sins to Him—they are immediately pardoned. We take our griefs to Him—they are in a moment assuaged.

NOVEMBER 27

"Because the creature itself also shall be delivered from the bondage of corruption into the glorious liberty of the children of God." Romans 8:21

THEY are already in possession of a liberty most costly and precious. Is it no true liberty to stand before God accepted in the Beloved? Is it no liberty to draw near to Him with all the confidence of a child reposing in the boundless affection of a loving father? Is it no liberty to travel day by day to Jesus, always finding Him an open door of sympathy the most exquisite, of love the most tender, and of grace the most overflowing? Is it, in a word, no real liberty to be able to lay faith's hand upon the everlasting covenant, and exclaim, "There is now no condemnation"? Oh, yes! This is the liberty with which Christ has made us free. But the glorious liberty of the children of God is yet to come. Glorious it will be, because more manifest and complete. Including all the elements of our present freedom, it will embrace others not yet enjoyed. We shall be emancipated from the body of sin and of death. Every fetter of corruption will be broken, and every tie of sense will be dissolved. All sadness will be chased from our spirit, all sorrow from our heart, and all cloud from our mind. Delivered from all sin, and freed from all suffering, we shall wander through the many mansions of our Father's house, and tread the star-paved streets of the celestial city, repose beneath the sylvan bowers of the upper Paradise, and drink of the waters, clear as crystal, that flow from beneath the throne—our pure, and blissful, and eternal home—exulting the in the "glorious liberty of the children of God." How striking and solemn is the contrast between the present and the future state of the believer and the unbeliever! Yours, too, unregenerate reader, is a state of vanity. But, alas! it is a most willing subjection, and the bondage of corruption which holds you is uncheered by one ray of hope of final deliverance. What a terrible and humiliating bondage—a willing slave to sin and Satan! All is vanity which you so eagerly pursue. "The Lord knows the thoughts of man, that they are vanity." Were it possible for you to realize all the schemes of wealth and distinction, of pleasure and happiness, which now float in gorgeous visions before your fevered fancy, still would your heart utter its mournful and bitter complaint, "All is vanity and vexation of spirit." Oh, turn you from these vain shadows to Jesus, the substance of all true wealth, and happiness, and honor. That fluttering heart will never find repose until it rests in Him. That craving soul will never be satisfied until it be satisfied with Christ. At His feet then cast you down, and with the tears of penitence, the reliance of faith, and the expectation of hope, ask to be numbered among the adopted, who shall before long be delivered from the bondage of corruption into the glorious liberty of the children of God.

NOVEMBER 28

"As many as were ordained to eternal life believed." Acts 13:48

THERE can be nothing in the Bible adverse to the salvation of a sinner. The doctrine of predestination is a revealed doctrine of the Bible; therefore predestination cannot be opposed to the salvation of the sinner. So far from this being true, we hesitate not most strongly and emphatically to affirm, that we know of no doctrine of God's word more replete with encouragement to the awakened, sin-burdened, Christ-seeking soul than this. What stronger evidence can we have of our election of God than the Spirit's work in the heart? Are you really in earnest for the salvation of your soul? Do you feel the plague of sin? Are you sensible of the condemnation of the law? Do you come under the denomination of the "weary and heavy laden"? If so, then the fact that you are a subject of the Divine drawings—that you have a felt conviction of your sinfulness—and that you are looking wistfully for a place of refuge, affords the strongest ground for believing that you are one of those whom God has predestinated to eternal life. The very work thus begun is the Spirit's first outline of the Divine image upon your soul—that very image to which the saints are predestinated to be conformed.

But while we thus vindicate this doctrine from being inimical to the salvation of the anxious soul, we must with all distinctness and earnestness declare, that in this stage of your Christian course you have primarily and mainly to do with another and a different doctrine. We refer to the doctrine of the Atonement. Could you look into the book of the Divine decrees, and read your name inscribed upon its pages, it would not impart the joy and peace which one believing view of Christ crucified will convey. It is not essential to your salvation that you believe in election; but it is essential to your salvation that you believe in the Lord Jesus Christ. In your case, as an individual debating the momentous question how a sinner may be justified before God, your first business is with Christ, and Christ exclusively. You are to feel that you are a lost sinner, not that you are an elect saint. The doctrine which meets the present phase of your spiritual condition is, not the doctrine of predestination, but the doctrine of an atoning Savior. The truth to which you are to give the first consideration and the most simple and unquestioning credence is, that "Christ died for the ungodly"—that He came into the world to save sinners— that He came to call, not the righteous, but sinners to repentance—that in all respects, in the great business of our salvation, He stands to us in the relation of a Savior, while we stand before Him in the character of a sinner. Oh, let one object fix your eye, and one theme fill your mind— Christ and His salvation. Absorbed in the contemplation and study of these two points, you may safely defer all further inquiry to another and a more advanced stage of your Christian course. Remember that the fact of your predestination, the certainty of your election, can only be inferred from your conversion. We must hold you firmly to this truth. It is the subtle and fatal reasoning of Satan, a species of atheistical fatalism, to argue, "If I am elected I shall be saved, whether I am regenerated or not." The path to eternal woe is paved with arguments like this. Men have cajoled their souls with such vain excuses until they have found themselves beyond the region of hope! But we must rise to the fountain, by pursuing the stream. Conversion, and not predestination, is the end of the chain we are to grasp. We must ascend from ourselves to God, and not descend from God to ourselves, in settling this great question. We must judge of God's objective purpose of love concerning us, by His subjective work of grace within us. In conclusion, we earnestly entreat you to lay aside all fruitless speculations, and to give yourself to prayer. Let reason bow to faith, and faith shut you up to Christ, and Christ be all in all to you. Beware that you come not short of true conversion—a changed heart, and a renewed mind, so that you become a "new creature in Christ Jesus." And if as a poor lost sinner you repair to the Savior, all vile and guilty, unworthy and weak as you are, He will receive you and shelter you within the bosom that bled on the cross to provide an atonement and an asylum for the very chief of sinners.

NOVEMBER 29

"But I certify you, brethren, that the gospel which was preached of me is not after man. For I neither received it of men, neither was I taught it, but by the revelation of Jesus Christ." Galatians 1:11, 12

THE great and distinctive truth thus so broadly, emphatically, and impressively stated is the divinity of the gospel—a truth, in the firm and practical belief of which the Church of God needs to be established. The gospel is the master-work of Jehovah, presenting the greatest display of His manifold wisdom, and the most costly exhibition of the riches of His grace. In constructing it He would seem to have summoned to His aid all the resources of His own infinity; His fathomless mind, His boundless love, His illimitable grace, His infinite power, His spotless holiness—all contributed their glory, and conspired to present it to the universe as the most consummate piece of

Divine workmanship. It carries with it its own evidence. The revelations it makes, the facts it records, the doctrines it propounds, the effects is produces, speak it to be no "cunningly devised fable," of human invention and fraud, but what it truly is, the "revelation of Jesus Christ," the "glorious gospel of the blessed God." What but a heart of infinite love could have conceived the desire of saving sinners? And by what but an infinite mind could the expedient have been devised of saving them in such a way—the incarnation, obedience, and death of His own beloved Son? Salvation from first to last is of the Lord. Here we occupy high vantage ground. Our feet stand upon an everlasting rock. We feel that we press to our heart that which is truth—that we have staked our souls upon that which is divine—that Deity is the basis on which we build: and that the hope which the belief of the truth has inspired will never make ashamed. Oh, how comforting, how sanctifying is the conviction that the Bible is God's word, that the gospel is Christ's revelation, and that all that it declares is as true as Jehovah Himself is true! What a stable foundation for our souls is this! We live encircled by shadows. Our friends are shadows, our comforts are shadows, our defenses are shadows, our pursuits are shadows, and we ourselves are shadows passing away. But in the precious gospel we have substance, we have reality, we have that which remains with us when all other things disappear, leaving the soul desolate, the heart bleeding, and the spirit bowed in sorrow to the dust. It peoples our lonely way, because it points us to a "cloud of witnesses." It guides our perplexities, because it is a "lamp to our feet." It mitigates our grief, sanctifies our sorrow, heals our wounds, dries our tears, because it leads us to the love, the tenderness, the sympathy, the grace of Jesus. The gospel reveals Jesus, speaks mainly of Jesus, leads simply to Jesus, and this makes it what it is, "glad tidings of great joy," to a poor, lost, ruined, tried, and tempted sinner.

NOVEMBER 30

"For I am not ashamed of the gospel of Christ: for it is the power of God unto salvation to every one that believes." Romans 1:16

TO what but the divinity of its nature are we to attribute the miraculous success which has hitherto attended the propagation of the gospel? Systems of religious opinion have risen, flourished for a while, then languished and disappeared. But the gospel, the most ancient, as it is the most sublime of all, has outlived all other systems. It has beheld the rise and the fall of many, and yet it remains. What religion has ever encountered the fierce and persevering opposition which Christianity has endured? Professed friends have endeavored to corrupt and betray it. Avowed enemies have sworn utterly to annihilate it. Kings and legislatures have sought to arrest its progress, and to banish it from the earth. The fires of persecution have consumed its sanctuaries and its preachers; and behold! it yet lives! The "divinity within" has kept it. He who dwelt in the bush has preserved it. Where are the French Encyclopedists—the men of deep learning and brilliant genius, of moving eloquence, caustic wit, and untiring energy, who banded themselves together with a vow to exterminate Christ and Christianity? Where is the eloquent Rosseau, the witty Voltaire, the ingenious Helvetius, the sophistical Hume, the scoffing D'Alembert, and the ribaldist Paine? Their names have rotted from the earth, and their works follow them. And where is the Savior, whom they sought to annihilate? Enthroned in glory, robed in majesty, and exalted a Prince and a Savior, encircled, worshiped, and adored by countless myriads of holy beings, the crown of Deity on His head, and the scepter of universal government in His hand, from whose tribunal they have passed, tried, sentenced, and condemned, while He yet lives, "to guard His Church and crush His foes." And where is the gospel, which they confederated and thought to overthrow? Pursuing its widening way of mercy through the world; borne on the wings of every wind, and on the crest of every billow, to the remotest ends of the earth, destroying the temples and casting down the idols of heathenism, supplanting superstition and idolatry with Christian sanctuaries and Christian churches; softening down the harshness of human barbarism, turning the instruments of cruelty into implements of husbandry; above all, and the grandest of all its results, proclaiming to the poorest, neediest, vilest of our race, salvation—full, free salvation by Christ—the pardon of the greatest sins by His atoning blood, the covering of the greatest deformity and unworthiness by His justifying righteousness, and the opening of the kingdom of heaven to all that believe. Thus is the glorious gospel now blessing the world. It goes and effaces the stains of human guilt, it gives ease to the burdened conscience, rest to the laboring spirit, the sweetest comfort under the deepest sorrow, dries the mourner's tear, exchanges the "garment of praise for the spirit of heaviness," and all because it speaks of Jesus. Oh, this gospel were no glad tidings, it were no good news, did it not testify of Jesus the Savior. He that sees not Christ the sum, the substance, the wisdom, the power of the gospel, is blind to the real glory of the word. He that has never tasted the love of Jesus is yet a stranger to the sweetness of the truth.

Yes! the gospel is divine! it is of God's own creation. He gave the word, and great is the company of those who preach it. Infidelity may oppose, and infidels may scorn it; false professors may betray, and sworn enemies may assail it; yet it will survive, as it has done, the fiercest assaults of men and of devils; like the burning bush it will outlive the flame, and like the rock of the ocean it will tower above the storm—God, who originated and who guards it, exclaiming to all their rage, "Hitherto shall you come, but no farther; and here shall your proud waves be stayed."

DECEMBER

DECEMBER 1

"He shall sit as a refiner and purifier of silver: and he shall purify the sons of Levi, and purge them as gold and silver, that they may offer unto the Lord an offering in righteousness." Malachi 3:3

"Take away the dross from the silver, and there shall come forth a vessel for the refiner." Proverbs 25:4

MARK the great and glorious end of this fiery process—a righteous offering to the Lord; and a vessel formed, prepared, and beautified for the Refiner; a "vessel unto honor, meet for the Master's use." Blessed result! Oh the wonders wrought by the fire of God's furnace! Not only is "God glorified in the fire," but the believer is sanctified. Have you ever observed the process of the artificer in the preparation of his beautiful ornament? After removing it from its mold, skillfully and properly formed, he then traces upon it the design he intended it should bear, dipping his pencil in varied hues of the brightest coloring. But the work is not yet finished. The shape of that ornament is yet to be fixed, the figures are to be set, the colors perpetuated, and the whole work consolidated. By what process?—by passing through the fire. The fire alone completes the work. Thus is it with the chastened soul—that beautifully constructed vessel, which is to adorn the palace of our King through eternity—the gaze, the wonder, the delight of every holy intelligence. God has cast it into the Divine mold, has drawn upon it the "image of His Son," with a pencil dipped in heaven's own colors—but it must pass through the furnace of affliction, thus to stamp completeness and eternity upon the whole. Calmly, then, repose in the hands of your Divine Artificer, asking not the extinguishment of a spark until the holy work is completed. God may temper and soften—for He never withdraws His eye from the work for one moment—but great will be your loss, if you lose the affliction unsanctified! Oh! could we with a clearer vision of faith but see the reason and the design of God in sending the chastisement, all marvel would cease, all murmur would be hushed, and not a painful dispensation of our Father would afford us needless trouble.

David's pen never wrote more sweetly than when dipped in the ink of affliction. And never did his harp send forth deeper, richer melody than when the breath of sadness swept its strings. This has been the uniform testimony of the saints of God in every age. "It is good for me that I have been afflicted; for before I was afflicted I went astray, but now have I kept your law." Learn to see a Father's hand, yes, a Father's heart, in every affliction. It is not a vindictive enemy who has chastened you, but a loving Friend: not an unfeeling stranger, but a tender Father, who, though He may cast you down in the dust, will never cast you off from His love. The Captain of your salvation— Himself made perfect through suffering—only designs your higher spiritual promotion in His army, by each sanctified affliction sent. You are on your way to the mansion prepared for you by the Savior, to the kingdom bestowed upon you by God. The journey is short, and time is fleeting; what though the cross is heavy and the path is rough—you have not far nor long to carry it. Let the deep-drawn sigh be checked by the throb of gladness which this prospect should create. "He will not always chide, neither will he retain his anger forever." The wind will not always moan, nor the waters be always tempestuous; the dull vapor will not forever float along the sky, nor the sunbeams be forever wreathed in darkness. Your Father's love will not always speak in muffled tones, nor your Savior hide Himself forever behind the wall or within the lattice. That wind will yet breathe music, those waters will yet be still; that vapor will yet evaporate; that sun will yet break forth; your Father's love will speak again in unmuffled strains, and your Savior will manifest Himself without a veil. Pensive child of sorrow! Weary pilgrim of grief! timid, yet prayerful; doubting, yet hoping; guilty, yet penitent; laying your hand on the head of the great appointed Sacrifice, you look up with tears, confessing your sin, and pleading in faith the blood of sprinkling. Oh, rejoice that this painful travail of soul is but the Spirit's preparation for the seat awaiting you in the upper temple, where the days of your mourning will be ended. You may carry the cross to the last step of the journey—weeping even up to heaven's gate—but there you shall lay that cross down, and the last bitter tear shall there be wiped away forever! Truly we may exclaim, "Blessed is the man whom You chastens, O Lord, and teach him out of Your law."

DECEMBER 2

"The Lord will strengthen him upon the bed of languishing:
you will make all his bed in his sickness." Psalm 41:3

WHAT a view this touching expression gives of the consideration of our heavenly Father— stooping down to the couch of his sick child—softening the sickness by a thousand nameless kindnesses—alleviating suffering, and mitigating pain. Would you learn the Lord's touching tenderness towards His people? Go to the sick chamber of one whom He loves! Ten thousand books will not teach you what that visit will. Listen to the testimony of the emaciated sufferer—"His left hand is under my head, His right hand does embrace me." What more can we desire? what stronger witness do we ask? What! is Jesus there? Is His loving bosom the pillow, and is His encircling arm the support, of the drooping patient? Is Christ both the physician and the nurse? Is His finger upon that fluttering pulse, does His hand administer that draught, does He adjust that pillow, and make all that bed in sickness? Even so. Oh, what glory beams around the sick one whom Jesus loves! Trace it, too, in the grace which He measures out to the languid sufferer. The season of sickness is a season, in the Christian's life, of especial and great grace. Many a child of God knew his adoption but faintly, and his interest in Christ but imperfectly, until then. His Christianity was always uncertain, his evidences vague, and his soul unhealthy. Living, perhaps, in the turmoil of the world secular, or amid the excitement of the world religious, he knew but little of communion with his own heart, or of converse with the heart of God. No time was extracted from other and all-absorbing engagements, and consecrated to the high and hallowed purposes of self-examination, meditation, reading, and prayer—elements entering essentially and deeply into the advancement of the life of God in the soul of man. But sickness has come, and with it some of the costliest and holiest blessings of his life. A degree of grace, answerable to all the holy and blessed ends for which it was sent, is imparted. And now, how resplendent with the glory of Divine grace has that chamber of sickness become! We trace it in the spirit and conduct of that pale, languid sufferer. See the patience with which he possesses his soul; the fervor with which he kisses the rod; the meekness with which he bows to the stroke; the subduing, softening, humbling of his spirit, once, perhaps, so lofty, fretful, and sensitive to suffering. These days of weariness and pain, these nights of sleeplessness and exhaustion, how slowly, how tediously they dray along! and yet not an impatient sigh, nor a murmuring breath, nor an unsubmissive expression breaks from the quivering lip. This is not natural—this is above nature. What but Divine and especial grace could effect it? Oh, how is the Son of God, in His fullness of grace and truth, glorified thereby!

DECEMBER 3

"Was then that which is good made death unto me? God forbid. But sin, that it might appear sin, working death in me by that which is good; that sin by the commandment might become exceeding sinful." Romans 7:13

NO child of God, if he is advancing in the divine life, but must mourn over his defective views of sin. The holier he grows, the more sensible he is of this: yes, may we not add, the deeper the view of his own vileness, the stronger the evidence of his growth in sanctification. A growing hatred of sin, of little sins, of great sins, of all sin—sin detected in the indwelling principle, as well as sin observable in the outward practice—oh, it is one of the surest symptoms of the onward progress of the soul in its spiritual course. The believer himself may not be sensible of it, but others see it; to him it may be like a retrograde, to an observer it is an evidence of advance. The child of God is not the best judge of his own spiritual growth. He may be rapidly advancing when not sensible of it; the tree may be growing downwards, it roots may be expanding and grasping more firmly the soil in which they are concealed, and yet the appearance of growth do not be very apparent. There is an inward, concealed, yet effectual growth of grace in the soul; the believer may not be sensible of it, and even others may overlook it, but God sees it: it is His own work, and He does not think meanly of it. God, in His gracious dealings with the believer, often works by contraries. He opens the eye of His child to the deep depravity of the heart, discloses to him the chamber of imagery, reveals to him the sin unthought of, unsuspected, unrepented, unconfessed, that lies deeply embedded there—and why? only to make His child more holy; to compel him to repair to the mercy-seat, there to cry, there to plead, there to wrestle for its subjection, its mortification, it crucifixion. And through this, as it were, circuitous process, the believer presses on to high and higher degrees of holiness. In this way, too, the believer earnestly seeks for humility, by a deep discovery which the Lord gives him of the pride of his heart—for meekness, by a discovery of petulance, for resignation to God's will, by a sense of restlessness and impatience—and so on, through all the graces of the blessed Spirit. Thus there is a great growth in grace, when a believer's views of sin's exceeding sinfulness and the inward plague are deepening.

But how are these views of sin to be deepened? By constant, close views of the blood of Christ—realizing apprehensions of the atonement. This is the only glass through which sin is seen in its greater magnitude. Let the Christian reader, then, deal much and often with the blood of Christ. Oh! that we should need to be urged to this!—that once having bathed in the "fountain opened," we should ever look to any other mode of healing, and of sanctification! For let it never be forgotten, that a child of God is as much called to live on Christ for sanctification as for pardon. "Sanctify them through your truth." And who is the truth? Jesus Himself answers, "I am the truth." Then we are to live on Jesus for sanctification: and happy and holy is he who thus lives on Jesus. The fullness of grace that is treasured up in Christ, why is it there? for the sanctification of His people—for the subduing of all their sins. Oh, do not forget, then, that He is the Refiner as well as the Savior—the Sanctifier as well as the Redeemer. Take your indwelling corruptions to Him; take the easy besetting sin, the weakness, the infirmity, of whatever nature it is, at once to Jesus: His grace can make you all that He would have you to be. Remember, too, that this is one of the great privileges of the life of faith; living on Christ for the daily subduing of all sin. This is the faith that purifies the heart, and it purifies by leading the believer to live out of himself upon Christ. To this blessed and holy life our Lord Jesus referred, when speaking of its necessity in order to the spiritual fruitfulness of the believer: "Abide in me, and I in you. As the branch cannot bear fruit of itself, except it abide in the vine; no more can you, except you abide in me. I am the vine, you are the branches: he that abides in me, and I in him, the same brings forth much fruit; for without me you can do nothing."

DECEMBER 4

"The Holy Spirit was not yet given; because that
Jesus was not yet glorified." John 7:39

OUR Lord's triumphant entrance into glory was the signal of the Holy Spirit's descent. Scarcely had He crossed the threshold of the heavenly temple, the august ceremonies of His enthronement, amid the songs of adoring millions, had but just ceased, when the promise of the Father was fulfilled, and the orphan Church of Jerusalem was baptized with the Spirit from on high. Oh! how soon was that promise fulfilled! How soon did Jesus make good the pledges of His love! The outpouring of the Holy Spirit on the Day of Pentecost transpired fifty days after Christ's resurrection. Forty days He was seen of the disciples, "to whom He showed Himself alive after His passion, by many infallible proofs;" consequently but ten days elapsed from the period of His return to His kingdom before the Spirit came down in all the plenitude of His glorifying, witnessing, awakening, and sanctifying power! And why were even ten days allowed to intervene between the glorification of Jesus and the descent of the Spirit? Doubtless to place the Church in a state of preparedness to receive so vast, so holy, and so rich a blessing. The Lord would have them found in a posture suited to the mercy. It was that of prayer, of all postures this side of glory the most blessed and holy. Thus did the Spirit find them on the Day of Pentecost. Returning from the mount of Olivet, where they had caught the last glimpse of the receding form of their ascending Lord, they came to Jerusalem, and "went up into an upper room," where abode the rest of the disciples. "These all continued with one accord in prayer and supplication." And while "they were all with one accord in one place," breathing forth their souls in fervent petition, "suddenly there came a sound from heaven as of a rushing mighty wind, and it filled all the house where they were sitting. And there appeared unto them cloven tongues, like as of fire, and it sat upon each of them. And they were all filled with the Holy Spirit."

And now how manifestly and how illustriously was Jesus glorified—with what overpowering effulgence did His Godhead shine forth—how gloriously did He appear in the eyes of the awe—stricken multitude, wearing the crown, not of painful thorns, and invested with the robe, not of mock-majesty, but of His real Divinity! With what majestic mien and stately step would He now walk amid the assembled throng, the God confessed! And all this divine glory would be seen arrayed on the side of Redemption—its conquests would be those of Grace—its manifestations those of Love—its signals those of Mercy. Was it not so? See how they crowd the temple! Some, their hands scarcely cleansed from the blood they had been shedding on Calvary; others with the dark scowl of malignity yet lingering on their brows. Mark how intently they gaze! how breathlessly they listen! how fearfully they tremble! and with what anguish they smite upon their breasts, and cry, "Men and brethren, what shall we do?" Nor did the Spirit rest its triumph here; it paused not until it led three thousand heart-broken sinners to the Fountain which some of them had been instrumental in opening for "sin and uncleanness," from thence to emerge washed, sanctified, and saved—the heirs of God, the joint-heirs with Christ Jesus. Now was Jesus glorified—now was a crown of pure gold placed upon His head— and now was fulfilled His own prophetic words, "At that day you shall know that I am in my Father, and He in me, and I in you."

DECEMBER 5

"As you therefore received Christ Jesus the Lord, so walk you in him: rooted and built up in him, and established in the faith, as you have been taught, abounding therein with thanksgiving." Colossians 2:6, 7

BY simple, close, and crucifying views of the cross of Christ does the Spirit most effectually sanctify the believer. This is the true and great method of gospel sanctification. Here lies the secret of all real holiness, and, may I not add, of all real happiness. For, if we separate happiness from holiness, we separate that which, in the covenant of grace, God has wisely and indissolubly united. The experience of the true believer must testify to this. We are only happy as we are holy—as the body of sin is daily crucified, the power of the indwelling principle weakened, and the outward deportment more beautifully and closely corresponding to the example of Jesus. Let us not, then, look for a happy walk, apart from a holy one. Trials we may have; yes, if we are the Lord's covenant ones, we shall have them, for He Himself has said, "in the world you shall have tribulation;" disappointments we may meet with—broken cisterns, thorny roads, wintry skies; but if we are walking in fellowship with God, dwelling in the light, growing up into Christ in all things, the Spirit of adoption witnessing within us, and leading to a filial and unreserved surrender—oh, there is happiness unspeakable, even though in the very depth of outward trial. A holy walk is a happy walk: this is God's order, it is His appointment, and therefore must be wise and good.

Seek high attainments in holiness. Do not be satisfied with a low measure of grace, with a dwarfish religion, with just enough Christianity to admit you into heaven. Oh, how many are thus content—satisfied to leave the great question of their acceptance to be decided in another world, and not in this—resting upon some slight evidence, in itself faint and equivocal, perhaps a former experience, some impressions, or sensations, or transient joys, long since passed away; and thus they are content to live, and thus content to die. Dear reader, be you not satisfied with anything short of a present Christ, received, enjoyed, and lived upon. Forget the things that are behind—reach forth unto higher attainments in sanctification—seek to have the daily witness, daily communion with God; and for your own sake, for the sake of others, and for Christ's sake, "give all diligence to make your calling and election sure."

DECEMBER 6

"God is faithful, by whom you were called unto the fellowship of his Son Jesus Christ our Lord." 1 Corinthians 1:9

FAITH has something still more substantial and firm to rest upon than even the Divine asseverations of the truth, something superior to the averment of the promise—even the faithfulness of the Divine Promiser Himself. Here it is that faith has its stronghold—not the word of God merely, but the God of the word. God must be faithful because He is essentially true and immutable. "He cannot deny Himself." "God that cannot lie." "It is impossible for God to lie." What asseverations of any truth can be stronger? And now, O believer, have faith in God, as true to His word, and faithful to His promise. Has the Spirit, the Comforter, caused your soul to rely upon His promises, to hope in His word? Have you nothing but the naked declaration to bear you up? Stand fast to this word, for God, who cannot lie, stands by to make it good. Have faith in His faithfulness. In doubting Him you cannot dishonor him more. If to discredit the word of man were an impeachment of his veracity, and that impeachment were the darkest blot that you could let fall upon his character; what must be the dishonor done to God by a poor sinful mortal distrusting His faithfulness, and questioning His truth! But "God is faithful." Have faith in Him as such. He is engaged to perfect that which concerns you, to supply all your need, to guide your soul through the wilderness, to cover your head in the day of battle, and to conduct you to ultimate victory and rest. Oh, trust Him. It is all that He asks of you. Is it now with you a day of trouble? a season of pressure? Is your position perilous? Are your present circumstances embarrassed? Now is the time to trust in the Lord. "Call upon me in the day of trouble: I will deliver you, and you shall glorify me." Oh, if God were to speak audibly to you at this moment, methinks these would be the words that He would utter: "Have faith in my faithfulness. Have I ever been untrue to my engagements, false to my word, forgetful of my covenant, neglectful of my people? Have I been a wilderness to you? What evil have you found in me, what untruth, what wavering, what instability, what change, that you do not now trust me in this the time of your need? Oh, let your soul be humbled that you should ever have doubted the veracity, have distrusted the faithfulness of your God." But "if we believe not, yet He abides faithful: He cannot deny Himself." "A God of truth and without iniquity, just and right is He."

DECEMBER 7

"For I delight in the law of God after the inward man: but I see another law in my members, warring against the law of my mind, and bringing me into captivity to the law of sin which is in my members. O wretched man that I am! who shall deliver me from the body of this death?" Romans 7:22—24

REGENERATION does not transform flesh into spirit. It proposes not to eradicate and expel the deep-seated root of our degenerate nature; but it imparts another and a superadded nature— it implants a new and an antagonistic principle. This new nature is divine; this new principle is holy: and thus the believer becomes the subject of two natures, and his soul a battle-field, upon which a perpetual conflict is going on between the law of the members and the law of the mind; often resulting in his temporary captivity to the law of sin which is in his members. Thus every spiritual mind is painfully conscious of the earthly tendency of his evil nature, and that from the flesh he can derive no sympathy or help, but rather everything that discourages, encumbers, and retards his spirit in its breathings and strugglings after holiness. A mournful sense of the seductive power of earthly things enters deeply into this state of mind. As we bear about with us, in every step, an earthly nature, it is not surprising that its affinities and sympathies should be earthly; that earthly objects should possess a magnetic influence, perpetually attracting to themselves whatever is congenial with their own nature in the soul of the renewed man. Our homeward path lies through a world captivating and ensnaring. The world, chameleon-like, can assume any color, and, Proteus-like, any shape, suitable to its purpose and answerable to its end. There is not a mind, a conscience, or a taste, to which it cannot accommodate itself. For the gross, it has sensual pleasures; for the refined, it has polished enjoyments; for the thoughtful, it has intellectual delights; for the enterprising, it has bold, magnificent schemes. The child of God feels this engrossing power; he is conscious of this seductive influence. Worldly applause—who is entirely proof against its power? Human adulation—who can resist its incense? Creature power—who is free from its captivation? Love of worldly ease and respectability, influence, and position—a liking to glide smoothly along the sunny tide of the world's good opinion—who is clad in a coat of mail so impervious as to resist these attacks? Have not the mightiest fallen before them? Such are some only of the many ensnaring influences which weave themselves around the path of the celestial traveler, often extorting from him the humiliating acknowledgment—"My soul cleaves unto the dust." In this category we may include things which, though they are in themselves of a lawful nature, are yet of an earthly tendency, deteriorative of the life of God in the soul. What heavenly mind is not sadly sensible of this? Our ever-foremost, sleepless, subtle foe stands by and says, "This is lawful, and you may freely and unrestrictedly indulge in it." But another and a solemn voice is heard issuing from the sacred oracle of truth—"All things are lawful unto me, but all things are not expedient." And yet how often are we forced to learn the lesson, that things lawful may, in their wrong indulgence and influence, become unlawful, through the spiritual leanness which they engender in the soul! Oh, it is a narrow path which conducts us back to Paradise. But our Lord and Master made it so; He Himself has trodden it, "leaving us an example that we should follow His steps;" and He, too, is sufficient for its straitness. Yes; such is the gravitating tendency to earth of the carnal nature within us, we are ever prone and ever ready, at each bland smile of the world, and at each verdant, sunny spot of the wilderness, to retire into the circle of self—complaisance and self-indulgence, and take up our rest where, from the polluted and unsatisfying nature of all earthly things, real rest can never be found. Thus may even lawful affections and lawful enjoyments, lawful pursuits and pleasures, wring the confession from the lips of a heavenly-minded man—"My soul cleaves unto the dust."

DECEMBER 8

"And God shall wipe away all tears from their eyes; and there shall be no more death, neither sorrow, nor crying, neither shall there be any more pain: for the former things are passed away." Revelation 21:4

IN heaven we shall be freed from the in-being of evil, and be delivered from the tyranny of corruption. Sin, now our torment, and our burden, will then enslave, distress, and oppress us no more. The chain which now binds us to our dead, loathsome body of sin will be broken, and we shall be forever free! To you who cry, "O wretched man that I am!" who know the inward plague, and feel that there is not one moment of the day in which you do not come short of the Divine glory—whose heaviest burden, whose bitterest sorrow, whose deepest humiliation springs from the consciousness of sin—what a glorious prospect is this! "It does not yet appear what we shall be: but we know that, when He shall appear, we shall be like Him; for we shall see Him as He is." The absence of all evil, and the presence of all good, constitute elements of the heavenly state, which place its blessedness beyond the conception of the human mind. Assure me that in glory all the effects and consequences of the curse are done away—that the heart bleeds no more, that the spirit grieves no more, that temptation assails no more, that sickness and bereavement, separation and disappointment, are forms of suffering forever unknown—and let the Spirit bear His witness with my spirit, that I am a child of God, and a door is open to me in heaven, through which a tide of "joy unspeakable and full of glory" rushes in upon my soul. And this is heaven.

But heaven is not a place of negative blessedness merely. There is the positive presence of all good. "In Your presence is fullness of joy; at Your right hand there are pleasures for evermore." The soul is with Christ, in the presence of God, and in the complete enjoyment of all that He has from eternity prepared for those who love Him. All soul, all intellect, all purity, all love—"eye has not seen, nor ear heard" the inconceivable blessedness in the full ocean of which it now rejoices. Its society is genial, its employments are delightful, its joys are ever new. How deeply does it now drink of God's everlasting love, with what wondering delight it now surveys the glory of Immanuel, how clearly it reads the mysterious volume of all the Divine conduct below, and how loud its deep songs of praise, as each new page unfolds the "height, and depth, and length, and breadth of the love of Christ," which even then "passes knowledge"! Truly we may call upon the "saints to be joyful in glory." Sing aloud, for you are now with Christ, you see God, and are beyond the region of sin, of pain, of tears, of death—"forever with the Lord." But we cannot conceive, still less describe, the glorious prospects of believers; for "eye has not seen, nor ear heard, neither have entered into the heart of man, the things which God has prepared for those who love Him." We shall soon go home, and experience it all. Then the eye will have seen, and the ear will have heard, and the heart will have realized, the things which from eternity God has laid up in Jesus, and prepared in the everlasting covenant for the poorest, meanest, feeblest child, whose heart faintly, yet sincerely, thrilled in a response of holy love to His.

DECEMBER 9

"Therefore being justified by faith, we have peace with God through our Lord Jesus Christ: by whom also we have access by faith into this grace wherein we stand, and rejoice in hope of the glory of God." Romans 5:1, 2

WHAT a ground of rejoicing have the saints of God! You may see within and around you—in your soul, in your family, and your circumstances—much that saddens, and wounds, and discourages you; but behold the truth which more than counterbalances it all—your freedom from condemnation. What if you are poor—you are not condemned. What if you are afflicted— you are not condemned! What if you are tempted—you are not condemned! What if you are assailed and judged by others, you yet are not forsaken and condemned by God; and ought you not then to rejoice? Go to the condemned cell, and assure the criminal awaiting his execution that you bear from his sovereign a pardon; and what, though he emerge from his imprisonment and his manacles to battle with poverty, with sorrow, and contempt, will he murmur and repine, that in the redemption of his forfeited life there is no clause that exempts him from the ills to which that life is linked? No! life to him is so sweet and precious a thing, that though you return it trammeled with want, and beclouded with shame, you have yet conferred upon him a boon which creates sunshine all within and around him. And why should not we "rejoice with joy unspeakable and full of glory," for whom, "through the redemption that is in Christ Jesus," there is now no condemnation? Christ has "redeemed our life from destruction;" and although it is "through much tribulation we are to enter the kingdom," yet shall we not quicken our pace to that kingdom, rejoicing as we go, that "there is now no condemnation to those who are in Christ Jesus"? "These things have I spoken unto you, that my joy might remain in you, and that your joy might be full."

Be earnest and diligent in making sure to yourself your discharge from the sentence and penalty of the law. Sue out the great fact in the Lord's own court by fervent prayer and simple faith. Your Surety has cancelled your debt, and purchased your exemption from death. Avail yourself of the comfort and the stimulus of the blessing. You may be certain, yes, quite certain, of its truth. No process is more easy. It is but to look from off yourself to Christ, and to believe with all your heart that He came into the world to save sinners, and assurance is yours. The order is—"We believe, and are sure." Oh, do not leave this matter to a bare peradventure. Make sure of your union with Christ, and you may be sure of no condemnation from Christ.

DECEMBER 10

"Jesus says unto him, I am the way, the truth, and the life:
no man comes unto the Father but by me." John 14:6

NOT the least costly blessing, flowing from the vital power of the atoning blood, is the life and potency which it imparts to true prayer. The believer's path to communion with God is called the "new and living way" because it is the way of the life-blood of the risen and living Savior. There could be no spiritual life in prayer but for the vitality in the atoning blood, which secures its acceptance. Not even could the Holy Spirit inspire the soul with one breath of true prayer, were not the atonement of the Son of God provided. Oh, how faintly do we know the wonders that are in, and the blessings that spring from, the life-procuring blood of our incarnate God! Touching the article of prayer—I approach to God, oppressed with sins, my heart crushed with sorrow, my spirit trembling; shame and confusion covering my face, my mouth dumb before Him. At that moment the blood of Jesus is presented, faith beholds it, faith receives it, faith pleads it! There is life and power in that blood, and lo! in an instant my trembling soul is enabled to take hold of God's strength and be at peace with Him, and it is at peace. Of all the Christian privileges upon earth, none can surpass, none can compare with, the privilege of fellowship with God. And yet how restricted is this privilege in the experience of multitudes! And why? simply in consequence of their vague, imperfect, and contracted views of the connection of true prayer with the living blood of Jesus. And yet, oh, what nearness to, what communion with, the Father, may the meanest, the feeblest, the most unworthy child at all times and in all circumstances have, who simply and believingly makes use of the blood of Christ! You approach without an argument or a plea. You have many sins to confess, sorrows to unveil, many requests to urge, many blessings to crave; and yet the deep consciousness of your utter vileness, the remembrance of mercies abused, of base, ungrateful requitals made, seals your lips, and you are dumb before God. Your overwhelmed spirit exclaims, "Oh that I knew where I might find him! that I might come even to his seat! I would order my cause before him, and fill my mouth with arguments." And now the Holy Spirit brings atoning blood to your help. You see this to be the one argument, the only plea that can prevail with God. You use it—you urge it—you wrestle with it. God admits it, is moved by it, and you are blest! Let, then the life-power of the blood encourage you to cultivate more diligently habitual communion with God. With sinking spirits, with even discouragement and difficulty, you may approach His Divine Majesty, and converse with Him as with a Father, resting your believing eye where He rests His complacent eye—upon the blood of Jesus. Oh the blessedness, the power, the magic influence of prayer! Believer! you grasp the key that opens every chamber of God's heart, when your tremulous faith takes hold of the

blood of the covenant, and pleads it in prayer with God. It is impossible
that God can then refuse you. The voice of the living blood pleads louder
for you than all other voices can plead against you. Give yourself, then,
unto prayer—this sacred charm of sorrow, this divine talisman of hope.

DECEMBER 11

*"And beginning at Moses and all the prophets, he expounded unto
them in all the Scriptures the things concerning himself." Luke 24:27*

THE perfect harmony of the Old and the New Testament confirms our
faith in the Divine authenticity of the Scriptures of truth. Upon what other
ground can we account for this singular agreement of the Word with itself,
and for this exact and literal fulfillment of its predictions, but on that of
its Divinity? "Your word is truth" is the glorious and triumphant inference
fairly deducible from a fact so striking and self-evident at this. And in
what particular is this beautiful harmony especially seen? In exalting
the Lamb of God. The Old and the New Testament Scriptures of truth
do for Christ what Pilate and Herod did against Him—they confederate
together. They unite in a holy alliance, in a sublime unity of purpose, to
show forth the glory of the incarnate God. Divine book! Precious volume!
Behold an illustration of what the Church of the living God should be—a
transparent body, illumined with the glory of Immanuel, and scattering its
beams of light and beauty over the surface of a lost and benighted world.
How much does a perfect representation of the glory of the Redeemer
by the Church depend upon her visible union! A mirror broken into a
thousand fragments cannot reflect the glory of the sun with the same
brilliancy, power, and effect as if a perfect whole. Neither can the Church
of God, dismembered, divided, and broken, present to the world the same
harmonious, convincing, and effective testimony to the glory of Jesus,
as when, in her unimpaired oneness, she is seen "looking forth as the
morning, fair as the moon, clear as the sun, and terrible as an army with
banners." Oh then, by all that is precious in the name of Jesus, by all that
is sanctifying in His glory, and attractive in His cross, by all that is sweet
and persuasive in Christian love, by all that is solemn in the near approach
of death and eternity, and by all that is blissful in the hope of eternal life,
springing from the one atonement, reader, seek to promote the visible unity

of Christ's Church. Resolve beneath the cross, and by the grace of God, that you will not be a hindrance to the accomplishment of so blessed, so holy an end. Hold the faith with a firm hand, but hold it in righteousness. Speak the truth with all boldness, but speak it in love. Concede to others what you claim for yourself—the right of private judgment, and the free exercise of an enlightened conscience. And where you see the image of Jesus reflected, the love of Jesus influencing, and the glory of Jesus simply and solely sought, there extend your hand, proffer your heart, breathe your blessing and your prayer. Oh, this were to be like Christ; and to be like Christ is grace below and glory above!

DECEMBER 12

"But he was wounded for our transgressions, he was bruised for our iniquities: the chastisement of our peace was upon him; and with his stripes we are healed." Isaiah 53:5

A SPIRITUAL and continued contemplation of the Redeemer's humiliation supplies a powerful check to sin. What is every sin committed, but opening afresh the wounds, and reacting anew the humiliation, of Jesus? Oh, how hateful must that sin appear in our serious moments, which shut out the sun of God's countenance from the soul of Christ, and sank Him to such inconceivable depths of humiliation! We need every view of divine truth calculated to sanctify. At present, the deepest sanctification of the believer is imperfect; his loftiest soarings towards holiness never reaching the goal. And yet to be ever thirsting, panting, wrestling, and aiming after it, should be classed among our highest mercies. We too much forget this truth, that the thirsting for holiness is as much the Holy Spirit's creation, as it is His work to quench that thirst. "Blessed are those who hunger and thirst after righteousness;" or, blessed are they who have the desire for Divine conformity, who long to know Christ, and to resemble Christ more perfectly. They may never reach the mark, yet ever pressing towards it—they may never attain to their standard, yet ever aiming for it, they are truly blessed. Here, then, is one powerful means of attaining to holiness—the spiritual eye brought in close and frequent contact with the lowly life of God's dear Son. But for our sins, His mind had never been shaded with clouds, His heart had never been wrung with sorrow, His eye had never been bedewed with tears, He had never suffered and died, had never known the wrath of an offended God. How fraught with soothing and consolation is this subject to the bereaved and tried believer! It tells you, weeping mourner, that having drained His wrath, and poured it on the head of your Surety, nothing is reserved for you in the heart of God but the deep fountain of tender mercy and loving-kindness. Then where springs your present trial, but from the loving heart of your Father? In the life of Jesus all was humiliation; in the life of the believer all is glory; and all this glory springs from the headship of Christ. In every step that He trod, he is one with Him—the only difference being that Jesus changes positions with the believer, and thus what was bitter to Him becomes sweet to us; what was dark to Him appears light to us; and what was His ignominy and shame becomes our highest honor and glory.

Humbling as may be the way God is now leading you, forget not that the great end is to bring you into a fellowship with Christ's humiliation—into a more realizing oneness with your tried head. How contracted were the believer's view of, and how limited his sympathy with, the abasement of God's dear Son, but for the humiliation of His life, but for the way the Lord leads him about in order to humble him! To be brought into sympathy with you in all the gloomy stages of your journey, "He humbled Himself;" and that this feeling might be reciprocal, bringing you into a sympathy with the dark stages of His life, He humbles you. But deep as your present humiliation may be, you cannot sink so low but you will find He sunk yet lower, and is therefore able to sustain and bear you up. "I was brought low, and He helped me." Never can Christians sink beneath the everlasting arms; they will always be underneath you. You may be sorely tried—painfully bereaved—fearfully tempted—deeply wounded. Saints and sinners, the Church and the world, may each contribute some bitter ingredient to your cup; nevertheless, the heart of Jesus is a pavilion within whose sacred enclosure you may repose until these calamities be overpast. Your greatest extremity can never exceed His power or sympathy, because He has gone before His people, and has endured what they never shall endure. Behold what glory thus springs from the humiliation and sufferings of our adorable Redeemer!

DECEMBER 13

"Who has saved us, and called us with an holy calling, not according to our works, but according to his own purpose and grace, which was given us in Christ Jesus before the world began." 2 Timothy 1:9

THERE is an external and an internal call of the Spirit. The external call is thus alluded to: "I have called, and you refused;" "Many are called, but few are chosen." This outward call of the Spirit is made in various ways. In the word, in the glorious proclamation of the gospel, through the providences of God—those of mercy and those of judgment—the warnings of ministers, the admonitions of friends, and, not less powerful, the awakening of the natural conscience. By these means does the Holy Spirit "call sinners to repentance." In this sense, every man who hears the gospel, who is encircled with the means of grace, and who bears about with him a secret but ever-faithful monitor, is called by the Spirit. The existence of this call places the sinner in an attitude of fearful responsibility; and the rejection of this call exposes him to a still more fearful doom. God has never poured out His wrath upon man, without first extending the olive-branch of peace. Mercy has invariably preceded judgment. "I have called, and you have refused." "All day long I have stretched forth my hands." "Behold, I stand at the door and knock." He reasons, He argues, He expostulates with the sinner. "Come, let us reason together," is His invitation. He instructs, and warns, and invites; He places before the mind the most solemn considerations, urged by duty and interest; He presses His own claims, and appeals to the individual interests of the soul; but all seems ineffectual. Oh, what a view does this give us of the patience of God toward the rebellious! That He should stretch out his hand to a sinner— that instead of wrath, there should be mercy—instead of cursing, there should be blessing— that, instead of instant punishment, there should be the patience and forbearance that invites, and allures, and reasons!"—Oh, who is a God like unto our God? "I have called, and you refused; I have stretched out my hand, and no man regarded."

But there is the special, direct, and effectual call of the Spirit, in the elect of God, without which all other calling is in vain. God says, "I will put my Spirit within them." Christ says, "The hour is coming and now is, when the dead shall hear the voice of the Son of God; and those who hear shall live." And in the following passages reference is made to the effectual operation of God the Spirit. "Whereof I was made a minister, according to the gift of the grace of God given unto me by the effectual working of His power." "The word of God which effectually works in you that believe." Thus, through the instrumentality of the truth, the Spirit is represented as effectually working in the soul. When He called before, there was no inward, supernatural, secret power accompanying the call to the conscience. Now there is an energy put forth with the call, which awakens the conscience, breaks the heart, convinces the judgment, opens the eye of the soul, and pours a new and an alarming sound upon the hitherto deaf ear. Mark the blessed effects. The scales fell from the eyes, the veil is torn from the mind, the deep fountains of evil in the heart are broken up, the sinner sees himself lost and undone—without pardon, without a righteousness, without acceptance, without a God, without a Savior, without a hope! Awful condition! "What shall I do to be saved?" is his cry: "I am a wretch undone! I look within me, all is dark and vile; I look around me, everything seems but the image of my woe; I look above me, I see only an angry God: whichever way I look, is hell!—and were God now to send me there, just and right would He be." But, blessed be God, no poor soul that ever uttered such language, prompted by such feelings, ever died in despair. That faithful Spirit who begins the good work, effectually carries it on, and completes it. Presently He leads him to the cross of Jesus—unveils to his eye of glimmering faith a suffering, wounded, bleeding, dying Savior— and yet a Savior with outstretched arms! That Savior speaks—oh, did ever music sound so melodious?—"All this I do for you—this cross for you—these sufferings for you—this blood for you—these stretched-out arms for you. Come unto me, all you that labor and are heavy laden, and I will give you rest—Him that comes to me, I will in no wise cast out—Look unto me, and be you saved—only believe. Are you lost? I can save you. Are you guilty? I can cleanse you. Are you poor? I can enrich you. Are you low sunk? I can raise you. Are you naked? I can clothe you. Have you nothing to bring with you—no price, no money, no goodness, no merit? I can and will take you to me, just as you are, poor, naked, penniless, worthless; for such I came to seek, such I came to call, for such I came to die." "Lord, I believe," exclaims the poor convinced soul, "Help You mine unbelief." You are just the Savior that I want. I wanted one that could and would save me with all my vileness, with all my rags, with all my poverty—I wanted one that would save me fully, save me freely, save me as an act of mere unmerited, undeserved grace—I have found Him whom my soul loves—and will be His through time, and His through eternity." Thus effectually does the blessed Spirit call a sinner, by His especial, direct, and supernatural power, out of darkness into marvelous light. "I will work," says God, "and who shall let it?" (marg. turn it back.)

DECEMBER 14

"For all things are for your sakes, that the abundant grace might though the thanksgiving of many redound to the glory of God. For which cause we faint not; but though our outward man perish, yet the inward man is renewed from day to day." 2 Corinthians 4:15, 16

CHRISTIAN sufferer! you marvel why the Lord keeps you so long upon the couch of solitariness and upon the bed of languishing—why the "earthly house of this tabernacle" should be taken down by continued and pining sickness, the corrodings of disease, and the gradual decay of strength. Hush every reasoning, anxious, doubtful thought. Your heavenly Father has so ordained it. He who built the house, and whose the house is, has a right to remove it by what process He sees fit. The mystery of His present conduct will, before long, be all explained. Yes, faith and love can even explain it now—"Even so, Father, for so it seems good in Your sight!" Yours is an honorable and a responsible post. God has still a work for you to do. You have been waiting year by year, in the quietness of holy submission, the summons to depart. But God has lengthened out your period of weariness and of suffering, for the work is not done in you and by you, to effect which this sickness was sent. Oh, what a witness for God may you now be! What a testimony for Christ may you now bear! What sermons—converting the careless, confirming the wavering, restoring the wandering, comforting the timid—may your conversation and your example now preach from that sick bed! And oh, for what higher degrees of glory may God, through this protracted illness, be preparing you! That there are degrees of glory in heaven, as there are degrees of suffering in hell, and degrees of grace on earth, admits of not a doubt. "As one star differs from another star in glory," so does one glorified saint differ from another. Will there be the absence in heaven of that wondrous variety of proportion which throws such a charm and beauty around the beings and the scenery of earth? Doubtless not. Superior grace below is preparing for superior glory above. And the higher our attainments in holiness here, the loftier our summit of blessedness hereafter. For these high degrees of heavenly happiness your present lengthened sickness may, by God's grace, be preparing you. Sanctified by the Spirit of holiness, the slow fire is but the more perfectly refining; and the more complete the refinement on earth, the more perfectly will the sanctified soul mirror forth the Divine Sun in heaven. Be, then, your beautiful patience of spirit, meek and patient sufferer, increasingly that of the Psalmist, "I have behaved and quieted myself as a child that is weaned of his mother: my soul is even as a weaned child."

DECEMBER 15

"But when the Comforter is come, whom I will send unto you from the Father, even the Spirit of truth, which proceeds from the Father, he shall testify of me." John 15:26

WITH regard to the spiritual sorrows of a child of God—those peculiar only to a believer in Jesus—we believe that a revelation of Jesus is the great source of comfort to which the Spirit leads the soul. Here is the true source of comfort. What higher comfort need we? What more can we have? This is enough to heal every wound, to dry up every tear, to assuage every grief, to lighten every cross, to fringe with brightness every dark cloud, and to make the roughest place smooth—that a believing soul has Jesus. Having Jesus, what has a believer? He has the entire blotting out of all his sins. Is not this a comfort? Tell us, what can give comfort to a child of God apart from this? If this fail, where can he look? Will you tell him of the world—of its many schemes of enjoyment—of its plans for the accumulation of wealth—of its domestic happiness? Wretched sources of comfort to an awakened soul! Poor empty channels to a man made acquainted with the inward plague! That which he needs to know is the sure payment of the ten thousand talents—the entire cancelling of the bond held against him by stern justice— the complete blotting out, as a thick cloud, of all his iniquity. And, until this great fact is made sure and certain to his conscience, all other comfort is but as a dream of boyhood, a shadow that vanishes, a vapor that melts away. But the Holy Spirit comforts the believer by leading him to this blessed truth—the full pardon of sin. This is the great controversy which Satan has with the believer. To bring him to doubt the pardon of sin, to unhinge the mind from this great fact, is the constant effort of this arch-enemy. And, when unbelief is powerful, and inbred sin is strong, and outward trials are many and sore, and, in the midst of it all, the single eye is removed from Christ, then is the hour of Satan to charge home upon the conscience of the believer all the iniquity he ever committed. And how does the blessed Spirit comfort at that moment? By unfolding the greatness, perfection, and efficacy of the one offering by which Jesus has forever blotted out the sins of His people, and perfected those who are sanctified. Oh, what comfort does this truth speak to a fearful, troubled, anxious believer, when, the Spirit working faith in his heart, he can look up, and see all his sins laid upon Jesus in the solemn hour of atonement, and no condemnation remaining! Dear child of God! poor, worthless as you feel yourself to be, this truth is even for you. Oh, rise to it, welcome it, embrace it, think it not too costly for one so unworthy. It comes from the heart of Jesus, and cannot be more free. "Blessed is he whose transgression is forgiven, whose sin is covered." Having Jesus, what has the believer more?

He possesses a righteousness in which God views him complete and accepted, from the beginning of the year to the end of the year. Is not this a comfort? To stand "complete in Him"—in the midst of many and conscious imperfections, infirmities, flaws, and proneness to wander, yet for the sorrowing and trembling heart to turn and take up its rest in this truth, "that he that believes is justified from all things," and stands accepted in the Beloved, to the praise of the glory of Divine grace, what a comfort! That God beholds him in Jesus without a spot, because He beholds His Son, in whom He is well pleased, and viewing the believing soul in Him can say, "You are all fair, my love; there is no spot in you"! The blessed Comforter conveys this truth to the troubled soul, brings it to take up its rest in it; and, as the believer realizes his full acceptance in the righteousness of Christ, and rejoices in the truth, he weeps as he never wept, and mourns as he never mourned, over the perpetual bias of his heart to wander from a God that has so loved him. The very comfort poured into his soul from this truth lays him in the dust, and draws out the heart in ardent breathings for holiness.

DECEMBER 16

"Knowing that a man is not justified by the works of the law, but by the faith of Jesus Christ, even we have believed in Jesus Christ, that we might be justified by the faith of Christ, and not by the works of the law: for by the works of the law shall no flesh be justified." Galatians 2:16

THE term is forensic—employed in judicial affairs, transacted in a court of judicature. We find an illustration of this in God's word. "If there be a controversy between men, and they come into judgment, that the judge may judge them, then they shall justify the righteous, and condemn the wicked." It is clear from this passage that the word stands opposed to a state of condemnation, and in this sense it is employed in the text under consideration. To justify, in its proper and fullest sense, is to release from all condemnation. Now, it is important that we do not mix up this doctrine, and the Church of Rome has done, with other and kindred doctrines. We must clearly distinguish it from that of sanctification. Closely connected as they are, they yet entirely differ. The one is a change of state, the other a change of condition. By the one we pass from guilt to righteousness, by the other we pass from sin to holiness. In justification we are brought near to God; in sanctification we are made like God. The one places us before Him in a condition of non-condemnation; the other transforms us into His image. Yet the Church of Rome blends the two states together, and in her formularies teaches an imputed sanctification, just as the Bible teaches an imputed justification. It is to be distinguished, too, from pardon. Justification is a higher act. By the act of pardon we are saved from hell; but by the decree of justification we are brought to heaven. The one discharges the soul from punishment; the other places in its hand a title-deed to glory.

The Lord Jesus Christ is emphatically the justification of all the predestined and called people of God. "By Him all that believe are justified from all things." The antecedent step was to place Himself in the exact position of His Church. In order to do this, it was necessary that He should be made under the law; for, as the Son of God, He was above the law, and could not therefore be amenable to its precept. But when He became the Son of man, it was as though the sovereign of a vast empire had relinquished his regal character for the condition of the subject. He, who was superior to all law, by His mysterious incarnation placed Himself under the law. He, who was the King of Glory, became by His advent the meanest of subjects. What a stoop was this! What a descending of the Son of God from the height of His glory! The King of kings, the Lord of lords, consenting to be brought under His own law, a subject to Himself, the Law-giver becoming the law-fulfiller. Having thus humbled Himself, He was prepared, as the sacrificial Lamb, to take up and bear away the sins of His people. The prophecy that predicted that He should "bear their iniquities," and that He should "justify many," received in Him its literal and fullest accomplishment. Thus upon Jesus were laid all the iniquities, and with the iniquities the entire curse, and added to the curse, the full penalty, belonging to the Church of God. This personal and close contact with sin affected not His moral nature; for that was essentially sinless, and could receive no possible taint from His bearing our iniquity. He was accounted "accursed," even as was Israel's goat, when upon its head Aaron laid the sins of the people; but as that imputation of sin could not render the animal to whom it was transferred morally guilty, though by the law treated as such, so the bearing of sin by Christ could not for a single instant compromise His personal sanctity. With what distinctness has the Spirit revealed, and with what strictness has He guarded, the perfect sinlessness of the atoning Savior! "He has made Him to be sin for us, who knew no sin, that we might be made the righteousness of God in Him." Oh blessed declaration to those who not only see the sin that dwells in them, but who trace the defilement of sin in their holiest things, and who lean alone for pardon upon the sacrifice of the spotless Lamb of God! To them, how encouraging and consolatory the assurance that there is a sinless One who, coming between a holy God and their souls, is accepted in their stead, and in whom they are looked upon as righteous! And this is God's method of justification.

DECEMBER 17

"Being justified freely by his grace through the redemption that
is in Christ Jesus; whom God has set forth to be a propitiation
through faith in his blood." Romans 3:24, 25

By a change of place with the Church, Christ becomes the "Lord our
Righteousness," and we are "made the righteousness of God in Him." There
is the transfer of sin to the innocent, and, in return, there is the transfer
of righteousness to the guilty. In this method of justification, no violence
whatever is done to the moral government of God. So far from a shade
obscuring its glory, that glory beams forth with an effulgence which must
have remained forever veiled, but for the redemption of man by Christ.
God never appears so like Himself as when He sits in judgment upon
the person of a sinner, and determines his standing before Him upon
the ground of that satisfaction to His law rendered by the Son of God in
the room and stead of the guilty. Then does He appear infinitely holy, yet
infinitely gracious; infinitely just, yet infinitely merciful. Love, as if it had
long been panting for an outlet, now leaps forth and embraces the sinner;
while justice, holiness, and truth gaze upon the wondrous spectacle with
infinite complacence and delight. And shall we not pause and bestow a
thought of admiration and gratitude upon Him, who was constrained to
stand in our place of degradation and woe, that we might stand in His
place of righteousness and glory? What wondrous love! what stupendous
grace! that He should have been willing to have taken upon Him our sin,
and curse, and woe! The exchange to Him how humiliating! He could only
raise us by Himself stooping. He could only emancipate us by wearing
our chain. He could only deliver us from death by Himself dying. He
could only invest us with the spotless robe of His pure righteousness by
wrapping around Himself the leprous mantle of our sin and curse. Oh,
how precious ought He to be to every believing heart! What affection, what
service, what sacrifice, what devotion, He deserves at our hands! Lord,
incline my heart to yield itself supremely to You! But in what way does
this great blessing of justification become ours? In other words, what is
the instrument by which the sinner is justified? The answer is at hand, in
the text, "through faith in His blood." Faith, and faith alone, makes this

righteousness of God ours. "By Him all that believe are justified." And why is it solely and exclusively by faith? The answer is at hand, "Therefore it is of faith, that it might be by grace." Were justification through any other medium than by believing, then the perfect freeness of the blessing would not be secured. The expressions are, "Justified freely by His grace;" that is, gratuitously—absolutely for nothing. Not only was God in no sense whatever bound to justify the sinner, but the sovereignty of His law, as well as the sovereignty of His love, alike demanded that, in extending to the sinner the greatest boon of His government, He should do so upon no other principle than as a perfect act of grace on the part of the Giver, and as a perfect gratuity on the part of the recipient—having "nothing to pay." Therefore, whatever is associated with faith in the matter of the sinner's justification—whether it be baptism, or any other rite, or any work or condition performed by the creature—renders the act entirely void and of none effect. The justification of the believing sinner is as free as the God of love and grace can make it.

DECEMBER 18

"Jesus answered, Verily, verily, I say unto you, Except a man be born of water and of the Spirit, he cannot enter into the kingdom of God." John 3:5

THE utter impossibility of the sinner's admission into heaven with the carnal mind unchanged is most clear. Suppose an opposite case. Imagine an unrenewed soul suddenly transported to heaven. In a moment it finds itself in the light and holiness and presence of God. What a scene of wonder, purity, and glory has burst upon its gaze! But, awful fact! horror of horrors! it is confronted face to face with its great enemy—the God it hated, loathed, and denied! Is it composed? Is it at home? Is it happy? Impossible! It enters the immediate presence of the Divine Being, its heart rankling with the virus of deadly hate, and its hand clutching the uplifted weapon. It carries its sworn malignity and its drawn sword to the very foot of the throne of the Eternal. "Take me hence," it exclaims, "this is not my heaven!" And then it departs to its "own place." But we are supposing an impossible case. For it is written of the heavenly city, "There shall in no wise enter into it anything that defiles, neither whatever works abomination, or makes a lie; but they who are written in the Lamb's book of life." Listen to the declaration of the Great Teacher sent from God—"except a man be born again, he cannot see the kingdom of God." Ask you what this new birth means? We reply, you must become a new creature in Christ Jesus. You must ground your arms before the Eternal God of heaven and earth. You must give up the quarrel. You must relinquish the controversy. You must cease to fight against God. You must submit to the law and government of Jehovah. Your will must bow to God's will. Your heart must beat in unison with God's heart. Your mind must harmonize with God's mind. Implacable hatred must give place to adoring love—deep ungodliness to a nature breathing after holiness—stern opposition to willing obedience—the creature to the Creator—yourself to God. Oh blissful moment! when the controversy ceases, and God and your soul are at agreement through Christ Jesus. When, dropping the long-raised weapon, you grasp His outstretched hand, and rush into His expanded arms, fall a lowly, believing penitent upon His loving bosom, take hold of His strength, and are at peace with Him. Oh, happy moment! No more hatred, no more enmity, no more opposition now! It is as though all heaven had come down and entered your soul—such joy, such peace, such love, such assurance, such hope do you experience! What music now floats from these words, "No condemnation in Christ Jesus"! How blessed now to lean upon the breast which once you hated, and find it a pillow of love; to meet the glance which once you shunned, and find it the expression of forgiveness; to feel at home in the presence of Him to whom once you said, "Depart from me, for I desire not the knowledge of Your ways"!

What an evidence of the reign of grace in the soul, when the mind fully acquiesces in the moral government of God! "The Lord God omnipotent reigns" is the adoring anthem of every heart brought into subjection to the law of God. To the Christian how composing is the thought, that the government is upon Christ's shoulders, and that He sits upon the throne judging right. From hostility to the law of God, his heart is now brought to a joyful acquiescence in its precepts, and to a deep delight in its nature. "I delight in the law of God after the inward man." "O Lord," he exclaims, "my holiness is in submission to Your authority. My happiness flows from doing and suffering Your will. I rejoice that the scepter is in Your hands, and I desire that the thoughts of my mind and the affections of my heart may be brought into perfect obedience to Yourself. Be my soul Your kingdom, by my heart Your throne, and let grace reign through righteousness unto eternal life."

DECEMBER 19

"But if we walk in the light, as he is in the light, we have fellowship one with another, and the blood of Jesus Christ his Son cleanses us from all sin." 1 John 1:7

NOT only is Jesus the actual, but He is also the relative life of the believer—the life of his pardon and acceptance. See it in reference to the blood of Immanuel. It is the blood of Him who was essential life. And, although springing from His pure humanity, essential life gave it all its virtue and its power. The resurrection of Jesus confirmed forever the infinite value and sovereign efficacy of His atoning blood. Oh what virtue has it now, flowing from the life of Jesus! It has removed transgression to the distance of infinity, and for ever from the Church. Washed whiter than snow, forgiven all iniquity, blotted out all sin, the believer stands before God a pardoned soul. And, oh! what life does he find in the constant application to his conscience of the atoning blood! One drop, what peace does it give! what confidence does it inspire! what vigor does it impart to faith, and power to prayer, and cheerfulness to obedience! Oh, it is living blood. He who spilt it lives to plead it, lives to apply it, lives to sustain its virtue, until there shall be no more sins to cancel, and no more sinners to save. "The blood of Jesus Christ cleanses from all sin," and "speaks better things than the blood of Abel," because it possesses undying life. Behold then, beloved, how manifestly is Jesus the life of your pardon. Oh! as fresh, as efficacious, as precious is that blood at this moment as when it spring warm and gushing from the pierced side of the glorious Redeemer. It is life-giving and life-sustaining blood. Here we see the antitype of the "living bird dipped in the blood of the bird slain," and then suffered to go free, suspended mid-heaven upon the wing of unrestricted and joyous life. As the living bird bore upon its plumage the crimson symbol of atonement—death and life thus strangely blended—what was the glorious gospel truth it shadowed forth, but the close and indissoluble union of the pardoning blood with the resurrection life of our incarnate God? And, O believer, lose not sight of the deep significance of the "running water" over which the bird was slain. That flowing stream was the image of the perpetual life of the blood of Jesus. And it bids you, in language too expressive to misunderstand, and too persuasive to resist, to draw near and wash. Glorious truth that it teaches! Precious privilege that it enforces!—the repeated, the perpetual going to Immanuel's atoning, life-giving, life-sustaining blood, thus keeping the conscience clean and at peace with God.

My beloved reader, no experimental and practical truth does this work enforce of greater effect, of more precious nature, and more closely interwoven with your happy, holy walk than this. Your peace of mind—your confidence in God—your thirsting for holiness—your filial access—your support in the deepest trial—spring from your soul's constant repose beneath the cross. What is your present case? what is the sin that wounds your spirit? what guilt burdens your conscience? what the grief that bows your heart? what the fearfulness and trembling that agitate and rock your mind? what gives you anxious days and sleepless nights? See yonder stream! It is crimson, it is flowing, it is vivifying with the life-blood of Jesus. Repair to it by faith. Go now—go at this moment. Have you gone before? go yet again. Have you bathed in it once? bathe in it yet again. See! it is a "running stream." Cast your sin, your guilt, your burden, your sorrow upon its bosom; it shall bear it away, never, never more to be found. Oh, deal closely with the atoning, life-giving blood! When you do rise in the morning, and when you do lie down at night, wash in the blood. When you go to duties, and when you come from duties, wash in the blood. When your deepest sigh has been heaved, when your holiest tear has been shed, when your most humbling confession has been made, when your sincerest resolution has been formed, when your solemn covenant has been renewed, when body, soul, and spirit have again been fully, freely, unreservedly dedicated—wash in the blood. When you draw near to the Holy Lord God, and spread out your case before Him, plead the blood. When Satan accuses, and conscience condemns, when death terrifies, and judgment alarms, flee to the blood. Oh! nothing, save the atoning blood of the spotless Lamb, gives you acceptance at any moment with God. And this, at any moment, will conduct you into the secret chamber of His presence, and bow His ear and heart to your faintest whisper and to your deepest want.

DECEMBER 20

"For Christ is the end of the law for righteousness
to every one that believes." Romans 10:4

BEHOLD, what an open door does this subject set before the humble, convinced sinner. It encircles the whole future of his being with the covenant bow of hope. Beneath its gorgeous and expanding arch he is safe. The law, now honored as it never was before, invested with a luster in view of which its former glory pales, and at the brightness of which angels veil their faces, the utmost glory brought to the Divine government, do you think, penitent reader, that the Lord will reject the application of a single sinner who humbly asks to be saved? What! after the Son of God had stooped so low to save the lowest, had suffered so much to save the vilest, will the Father refuse to enfold to His reconciled heart the penitent who flees to its blessed asylum? Never! Approach, then, bowed and broken, weary and burdened spirit. There is hope for you in Jesus, there is forgiveness for you in Jesus, there is acceptance for you in Jesus, there is rest for you in Jesus, there is a heaven of bliss and glory awaiting you—all in Jesus, the law's great fulfiller. Oh, how welcome will the heart of Christ make you! How full and free will be the pardon of God extended to you! How deep and rich the peace, and joy, and hope, which, like a river, will roll its gladdening waves into your soul the moment that you receive Christ into your heart! "Believe in the Lord Jesus Christ, and you shall be saved." "He that believes shall not come into condemnation, but is passed from death unto life."

Saints of God, keep the eye of your faith intently and immovably fixed upon Christ, your sole pattern. Our Lord did not keep that law that His people might be lawless. He did not honor that law that they might dishonor its precepts. His obedience provided no license for our disobedience. His fulfillment releases us not from the obligation—the sweet and pleasant, yet solemn obligation—to holiness of life. Our faith does not make void the law, but rather establishes the law. The "righteousness of the law is fulfilled in us" when we "walk after the Spirit," in lowly conformity to Christ's example. Was He meek and lowly in heart? Did He bless when cursed? Did He, when reviled, revile not again? Did He walk in secret with God? Did He always seek to do those things which pleased His Father? Did He live a life of faith, and prayer, and toil? So let us imitate Him, that of us it may be said, "These are they who follow the Lamb withersoever He goes." What richer comfort can flow into the hearts of the godly than that which springs from this truth? "The righteousness of the law fulfilled in us." What wondrous, blessed words! You are often in fear that the righteousness of the law will rise against you; and when you consider your many failures and short-comings, you justly tremble. But fear not; for in Christ the law is perfectly fulfilled, and fulfilled in your stead, as much as if you had obeyed in your own person. Is not this a sure ground of comfort? You see the imperfection of your own obedience, and you are alarmed; but have you not an eye also for the perfection of Christ's obedience, which He has made yours by imputation? "There is therefore now no condemnation to them who are in Christ Jesus," because He has fulfilled the law's righteousness in their behalf. You are cast down because of the law of sin, but the Spirit of life has freed you from the law. You are troubled because of the law of God, but that law, by Christ's perfect obedience, is fulfilled in you. You desire a righteousness that will present you without spot before God; you have it in Him who is the "Lord our righteousness." Christian! Christ's whole obedience is yours. What can sin, or Satan, or conscience, or the law itself allege against you now? Be humble, and mourn over the many flaws and failures in your obedience; yet withal rejoice, and glory, and make your boast in the fullness, perfection, and unchangeableness of that righteousness on the Incarnate God which will place you without fault before the throne.

Sinner! if the righteousness of the law is not fulfilled in you now, that righteousness will be exhibited in your just condemnation to all eternity! Flee to Jesus, "the end of the law for righteousness to every one that believes."

DECEMBER 21

"For even hereunto were you called: because Christ also suffered for us, leaving us an example, that you should follow his steps." 1 Peter 2:21

BUT imperfectly, perhaps, beloved reader, are you aware of the high privilege to which you are admitted, and of the great glory conferred upon you, in being identified with Jesus in His life of humiliation. This is one of the numerous evidences by which your adoption into the family of God is authenticated, and by which your union with Christ is confirmed. It may be you are the subject of deep poverty—your circumstances are straitened, your resources are limited, your necessities are many and pressing. Perhaps you are the "man that has known affliction;" sorrow has been your constant and intimate companion; you have become "acquainted with grief." The Lord has been leading you along a path of painful humiliation. You have been "emptied from vessel to vessel." He has brought you down, and laid you low; step by step, and yet, oh, how wisely and how gently, He has been leading you deeper and yet deeper into the valley! But why all this leading about? why this emptying? why this descending? Even to bring you into a union and communion with Jesus in His life of humiliation! Is there a step in your abasement that Jesus has not trodden with you—ah! and trodden before you? Is there a sin that He has not carried, a cross that He has not borne, a sorrow that has not affected Him, and infirmity that has not touched Him? Even so will He cause you to reciprocate this sympathy, and have fellowship with Him in His sufferings. As the Head did sympathize with the body, so must the body sympathize with the Head. Yes, the very same humiliation which you are now enduring the Son of God has before endured. And that you might learn something what that love and grace and power were which enabled Him to pass through it all, He pours a little drop in your cup, places a small part of the cross upon your shoulder, and throws a slight shadow on your soul! Yes, the very sufferings you are now enduring are, in a faint and limited degree, the sufferings of Christ. "Who now rejoice in my sufferings for you," says the apostle, "and fill up that which is behind of the afflictions of Christ in my flesh, for His body's sake, which is the Church." There is a two-fold sense in which Jesus may be viewed as a sufferer. He suffered in His own person as the Mediator of His Church; those sufferings were vicarious and complete, and in that sense He can suffer no more! "for by one offering He has perfected forever them that are sanctified." The other now presents Him as suffering in His members: in this sense Christ is still a sufferer; and although not suffering to the same degree, or for the same end, as He once did, nevertheless He who said, "Saul, Saul, why persecute you me?" is identified with the Church in all its sufferings; in all her afflictions, He being afflicted. The apostle therefore terms the believer's present sufferings the "afflictions of Christ."

DECEMBER 22

"It is a faithful saying: For if we be dead with him, we shall also live with him: if we suffer, we shall also reign with him." 2 Timothy 2:11, 12

BEHOLD, then, your exalted privilege, you suffering sons of God! See how the glory beams around you, you humble and afflicted ones! You are one with the Prince of sufferers, and the Prince of sufferers is one with you! Oh! to be one with Christ—what tongue can speak, what pen can describe the sweetness of the blessing, and the greatness of the grace? To sink with Him in His humiliation here is to rise with Him in His exaltation hereafter. To share with Him in His abasement on earth is to blend with Him in His glory in heaven. To suffer shame and ridicule, persecution and distress, poverty and loss for Him now, is to wear the crown, and wave the palm, to swell the triumph, and shout the song, when He shall descend the second time in glory and majesty, to raise His Bride from the scene of her humiliation, robe her for the marriage, and make her manifestly and eternally His own.

Oh! laud His great name for all the present conduct of His providence and grace. Praise Him for all the wise though affecting discoveries He gives you of yourself, of the creature, of the world. Blessed, ah! truly blessed and holy is the discipline that prostrates your spirit in the dust. There it is that He reveals the secret of His own love, and draws apart the veil of His own loveliness. There it is that He brings the soul deeper into the experience of His sanctifying truth; and, with new forms of beauty and expressions of endearment, allures the heart, and takes a fresh possession of it for Himself. And there, too, it is that the love, tenderness, and grace of the Holy Spirit are better known. As a Comforter, as a Revealer of Jesus, we are, perhaps, more fully led into an acquaintance with the work of the Spirit in seasons of soul-abasement than at any other time. The mode and time of His divine manifestation are thus beautifully predicted: "He shall come down like rain on the mown grass; as showers that water the earth." Observe the gentleness, the silence, and the sovereignty of His operation—"He shall come down like rain." How characteristic of the blessed Spirit's grace! Then mark the occasion on which He descends—it is at the time of the soul's deep prostration. The waving grass is mowed—the lovely flower is laid low—the fruitful stem is broken—that which was beautiful, fragrant, and precious is cut down—the fairest first to fade, the loveliest first to die, the fondest first to depart; then, when the mercy is gone, and the spirit is bowed, when the heart is broken, the mind is dejected, and the world seems clad in wintry desolation and gloom, the Holy Spirit, in all the softening, reviving, comforting, and refreshing influence of His grace, descends, speaks of the beauty of Jesus, leads to the grace of Jesus, lifts the bowed soul, and reposes it on the bosom of Jesus.

Precious and priceless, then, beloved, are the seasons of a believer's humiliation. They tell of the soul's emptiness, of Christ's fullness; of the creature's insufficiency, of Christ's all—sufficiency; of the world's poverty, of Christ's affluence; they create a necessity which Jesus supplies, a void which Jesus fills, a sorrow which Jesus soothes, a desire which Jesus satisfies. They endear the cross of the incarnate God, they reveal the hidden glory of Christ's humiliation, they sweeten prayer, and lift the soul to God; and then, "truly our fellowship is with the Father, and with His Son, Jesus Christ." Are you as a bruised flower? are you as a broken stem? Does some heavy trial now bow you in the dust? Oh never, perhaps, were you so truly beautiful— never did your grace send forth such fragrance, or your prayers ascend with so sweet an odor— never did faith, and hope, and love develop their hidden glories so richly, so fully as now! In the eye of a wounded, a bruised, and a humbled Christ, you were never more lovely, and to His heart never more precious than now—pierced by His hand, smitten by His rod, humbled by His chastisement, laid low at His feet, condemning yourself, justifying Him, taking to yourself all the shame, and ascribing to Him all the glory.

DECEMBER 23

"Now he which establishes us with you in Christ, and has anointed us, is God; who has also sealed us, and given the earnest of the Spirit in our hearts." 2 Corinthians 1:21, 22

IT is, and has long been, the solemn conviction of the writer, that much of the spiritual darkness, the little comfort and consolation, the dwarfish piety, the harassing doubts and fears, the imperfect apprehensions of Jesus, the feeble faith, the sickly, drooping state of the soul, the uncertainty of their full acceptance in Christ, which mark so many of the professing people of God in this our day, may be traced to the absence of a deep sealing of the Spirit. Resting satisfied with the faint impression in conversion, with the dim views they then had of Christ, and the feeble apprehension of their acceptance and adoption, is it any marvel that all their lifetime they should be in bondage through slavish doubts and fears?—that they should never attain to the "stature of perfect men in Christ Jesus"—that they should never rise to the humble boldness, the unwavering confidence, the blest assurance, and the holy dignity of the sons of God? Oh no! They rest short of this blessing. They hang upon the door of the ark—they remain upon the border of the goodly land, and not entering fully in, the effects are as we have described. But, beloved reader, the richest ore lies buried the deepest—the sweetest fruit is on the higher branches—the strongest light is near the sun. In other words, if we desire more knowledge of Christ—of our full pardon, and complete acceptance—if we desire the earnest of our inheritance, and even now would taste the "grapes of Eshcol," we must be "reaching forth unto those things that are before," we must "press toward the mark," and rest not until that is found in a clear, unclouded, immoveable, and holy assurance of our being in Christ; and this is only experienced in the sealing of the Spirit. Again we say, with all the earnestness which a growing sense of the vastness of the blessing inspires, seek to be sealed of the Spirit—seek the "earnest of the Spirit"— seek to be "filled with the Spirit"—seek the "anointing of the Spirit"— seek the "Spirit of adoption." Say not, it is too immense a blessing, to high an attainment for one so small, so feeble, so obscure, so unworthy as you. Oh, impeach not thus the grace of God. All His blessings are the bestowments of grace; and grace means free favor to the most unworthy. There is not one lowly, weeping eye that falls on this page, but may, under the blessed sealing of the Spirit, look up through Jesus to God as a Father. Low views of self, deep consciousness of vileness, poverty of state or of spirit, are no objections with God, but rather strong arguments that prevail with Him why you should have the blessing. Only ask—only believe—only persevere, and you shall attain unto it. It is in the heart of the Spirit to seal "unto the day of redemption" all that believe in Jesus. May it be in the heart of the reader to desire the blessing, seeing it is so freely and richly offered!

Reader, whose superscription do you bear? It may be your reply is—"I want Christ; I secretly long for Him; I desire Him above all beside." Is it so? Then take courage, and go to Jesus. Go to Him simply, go to Him unhesitatingly, go to Him immediately. That desire is from Him; let it lead you to Him. That secret longing is the work of the Spirit; and having begotten it there, do you think that He will not honor it, and welcome you when you come? Try Him. Bring Him to the touch-stone of His own truth. "Prove me now herewith," is His gracious invitation. Take His promise, "Him that comes to me I will in no wise cast out," and plead it in wrestlings at the mercy-seat, and see if He will not "open the windows of heaven, and pour you out a blessing, that there shall not be room enough to receive it." Go to Him just as you are; if you cannot take to Him a pure heart, take an impure one; if you cannot take to Him a broken heart, take a whole one; if you cannot take to Him a soft heart, take a hard one—only go to Him. The very act of going will be blessed to you. And oh, such is the strength of His love, such His yearning compassion and melting tenderness of heart for poor sinners, such His ability and willingness to save, that He will no more cast you out than deny His own existence. Precious Jesus! Set us as a seal upon Your heart, and by Your Spirit seal Yourself upon our hearts; and give us, unworthy though we are, a place among "those who are sealed."

DECEMBER 24

"This Jesus has God raised up, whereof we all are witnesses. Therefore being by the right hand of God exalted, and having received of the Father the promise of the Holy Spirit, he has shed forth this, which you new see and hear." Acts 2:32, 33

THE day of Pentecost, with its hallowed scenes, cannot be too frequently brought before the mind. Were there a more simple looking to Christ upon the throne, and a stronger faith in the promise of the outpouring of the Spirit, and in the faithfulness of the Promiser to make it good, that blessed day would find its prototype in many a similar season enjoyed by the Church of God to the end of time. The effects of the descent of the Spirit on that day upon the apostles themselves are worthy of our especial notice. What a change passed over those holy men of God, thus baptized with the promised Spirit! A new flood of divine light broke in upon their minds. All that Jesus had taught them while yet upon earth recurred to their memory, with all the freshness and glory of a new revelation. The doctrines which He had propounded concerning Himself, His work, and His kingdom, floated before their mental eye like a newly—discovered world, full of light and beauty. A newness and a freshness invested the most familiar truths. They saw with new eyes; they heard with new ears; they understood as with recreated minds: and the men who, while He was with them, teaching them in the most simple and illustrative manner, failed fully to comprehend even the elementary doctrines and the most obvious truths of the gospel, now saw as with the strength of a prophet's vision, and now glowed as with the ardor of a seraph's love. Upon the assembled multitudes who thronged the temple how marvelous, too, the effects! Three thousand as in one moment were convinced of sin, and led to plunge in the "Fountain opened to the house of David and the inhabitants of Jerusalem, for sin and uncleanness." And how does the apostle explain the glorious wonder?—"This Jesus," says he, "has God raised up, whereof we all are witnesses. Therefore being by the right hand of God exalted, and having received of the Father the promise of the Holy Spirit, he has shed forth this which you now see and hear."

This, and this only, is the blessing which the Church of God now so greatly needs—even the baptism of the Holy Spirit. She needs to be confirmed in the fact, that Jesus is alive and upon the throne, invested with all power, and filled with all blessing. The simple belief of this would engage her heart to desire the bestowment of the Spirit; and the Spirit largely poured down would more clearly demonstrate to her the transcendent truth in which all her prospects of glory and of happiness are involved, that the Head of the Church is triumphant. Oh, let her but place her hand of faith simply, solely, firmly, on the glorious announcement—Jesus is at the right hand of the Father, with all grace and love in His heart, with all authority in His hand, with all power at His disposal, with all blessing in His gift, waiting to open the windows of heaven, and pour down upon her such a blessing as there shall not be room enough to receive it—prepared so deeply to baptize her with the Holy Spirit as shall cause her converts greatly to increase, and her enterprises of Christian benevolence mightily to prosper; as shall heal her divisions, build up her broken walls, and conduct her to certain and triumphant victory over all her enemies— let her but plant her faith upon the covenant and essential union of these two grand truths—An exalted Redeemer and a descending Spirit—and a day on which, not three thousand only, but a nation shall turn to the Lord, and all flesh shall see His glory!

DECEMBER 25

"Who shall separate us from the love of Christ?" Romans 8:35

OF whose love does the apostle speak? The believer's love to Christ? On the contrary, it is Christ's love to the believer. And this view of the subject makes all the difference in its influence upon our minds. What true satisfaction and real consolation, at least how small its measure, can the believer derive from a contemplation of his love to Christ? It is true, when sensible of its glow, and conscious of its power, he cannot but rejoice in any evidence, the smallest, of the work of the Holy Spirit in his soul. Yet this is not the legitimate ground of his confidence, not the proper source of his comfort. It is Christ's love to him! And this is just the truth the Christian mind needs for its repose. To whom did Paul originally address this letter? To the saints of the early and suffering age of the Christian Church. And this truth—Christ's love to His people—would be just the truth calculated to comfort, and strengthen, and animate them. To have declared that nothing should prevail to induce them to forsake Christ would have been but poor consolation to individuals who had witnessed many a fearful apostasy from Christ in others, and who had often detected the working of the same principle in themselves. Calling to mind the strong asseveration of Peter, "Although all shall be offended, yet will not I," and remembering how their Master was denied by one, betrayed by another, and forsaken by all His disciples, their hearts would fail them. But let the apostle allure their minds from a contemplation of their love to Christ, to a contemplation of Christ's love to them, assuring them, upon the strongest grounds, that whatever sufferings they should endure, or by whatever temptations they should be assailed, nothing should prevail to sever them from their interest in the reality, sympathy, and constancy of that love, and he has at once brought them to the most perfect repose. The affection, then, of which the apostle speaks, is the love of God which is in Christ Jesus.

The love of Christ! such is our precious theme. Of it can we ever weary? Its greatness can we fully know? Its plenitude can we fully contain? Never. Its depths cannot be fathomed, its dimensions cannot be measured. It "passes knowledge." All that Jesus did for His Church was but the unfolding and expression of His love. Traveling to Bethlehem—I see love incarnate. Tracking His steps as He went about doing good—I see love laboring. Visiting the house of Bethany—I see love sympathizing. Standing by the grave of Lazarus—I see love weeping. Entering the gloomy precincts of Gethsemane—I see love sorrowing. Passing on to Calvary—I see love suffering, bleeding, and expiring. The whole scene of His life is but an unfolding of the deep, awful, and precious mystery of redeeming love.

DECEMBER 26

"For I am persuaded, that neither death, nor life, nor angels, nor principalities, nor powers, nor things present, nor things to come, nor height, nor depth, nor any other creature, shall be able to separate us from the love of God, which is in Christ Jesus our Lord." Romans 8:38, 39

THE love of the Father is seen in giving us Christ, in choosing us in Christ, and in blessing us in Him with all spiritual blessings. Indeed, the love of the Father is the fountain of all covenant and redemption mercy to the Church. It is that river the streams whereof make glad the city of God. How anxious was Jesus to vindicate the love of the Father from all the suspicions and fears of His disciples! "I say not unto you that I will pray the Father for you; for the Father Himself loves you." "God so loved the world that He gave his only begotten Son." To this love we must trace all the blessings which flow to us through the channel of the cross. It is the love of God, exhibited, manifested, and seen in Christ Jesus; Christ being, not the originator, but the gift of His love; not the cause, but the exponent of it. Oh, to see a perfect equality in the Father's love with the Son's love! Then shall we be led to trace all His present mercies, and all His providential dealings, however trying, painful, and mysterious, to the heart of God; thus resolving all into that from where all alike flow—everlasting and unchangeable love.

Now it is from this love there is no separation. "Who shall separate us from the love of Christ?" The apostle had challenged accusation from every foe, and condemnation from every quarter; but no accuser rose, and no condemnation was pronounced. Standing on the broad basis of Christ's finished work and of God's full justification, his head was now lifted up in triumph above all his enemies round about. But it is possible that, though in the believer's heart there is no fear of impeachment, there yet may exist the latent one of separation. The aggregate dealings of God with His Church, and His individual dealings with His saints, may at times present the appearance of an alienated affection of a lessened sympathy. The age in which this epistle was penned was fruitful of suffering to the Church of God. And if any period or any circumstances of her history boded a severance of the bond which bound her to Christ, that was the period, and those were the circumstances. But with a confidence based upon the glorious truth on which he had been descanting—the security of the Church of God in Christ—and with a persuasion inspired by the closer realization of the glory about to burst upon her view—with the most dauntless courage he exclaims, "I am persuaded that neither death, nor life, nor angels, nor principalities, nor powers, nor things present, nor things to come, nor height, nor depth, nor any other creature, shall be able to separate us from the love of God, which is in Christ Jesus our Lord."

DECEMBER 27

"Our Savior Jesus Christ, who has abolished death, and has brought life and immortality to light through the gospel." 2 Timothy 2:10

THAT there is a separating power in death is a truth too evident and too affecting to deny. It separates the soul from the body, and man from all the pursuits and attractions of earth. "His breath goes forth, in that very day his thoughts perish." All his thoughts of ambition—his thoughts of advancement—his thoughts of a vain and Pharisaical religion—all perish on that day. What a mournful sublimity is there in this vivid description of the separating power of death over the creature! What a separating power, too, has it, as felt in the chasms it creates in human relationships! Who has not lost a friend, a second self, by the ruthless hand of death? What bright home has not been darkened, what loving heart has not been saddened, by its visitations? It separates us from the husband of our youth—from the child of our affections— from the friend and companion of our earlier and riper years. It comes and breaks the link that bound us so fondly and so closely to the being whose affection, sympathy, and communion seemed essential elements of our being, whose life we were used to regard as a part of our very existence. But there is one thing from which death cannot separate us—the love of God which is in Christ Jesus, and all the blessings which that love bestows. Death separate us! No; death unites us the more closely to those blessings, by bringing us into their more full and permanent possession. Death imparts a realization and a permanence to all the splendid and holy antic-ipations of the Christian. The happiest moment of his life is its last. All the glory and blessing of his existence cluster and brighten around that solemn crisis of his being. Then it is he feels how precious the privilege and how great the distinction of being a believer in Jesus. And the day that darkens his eye to all earthly scenes opens it upon the untold and unimaginable and ever-increasing glories of eternity. It is the birth-day of his immortality. Then, Christian, fear not death! It cannot separate you from the Father's love, nor can it, while it tears you from an earthly bosom, wrench you from Christ's. You shall have in death, it may be, a brighter, sweeter manifestation of His love than you ever experienced in life. Jesus, the Conqueror of death, will approach and place beneath you His almighty arms, and your head upon His loving bosom. Thus encircled and pillowed, you "shall not see death," but, passing through its gloomy portal, shall only realize that you had actu-ally died, from the consciousness of the joy and glory into which death had ushered you.

DECEMBER 28

"But thanks be to God, which gives us the victory,
through our Lord Jesus Christ." 1 Corinthians 15:57

DOES the ear of some dear departing saint of God lend itself to the recital of these closing words? Beloved of the Lord, beloved in the Lord, what a blessed opportunity have you now of leaning the entire weight of your soul, with all its sins and sorrows, upon the finished work of Jesus, your Almighty Savior, your God, your Redeemer! The great debt is cancelled. Justice exacts not a second payment, the first from your Surety, the second from you. No! justice itself is on your side; every perfection of God is a wall of fire round about you. You stand complete in the righteousness of the incarnate God. The blood of Jesus Christ, the Father's own Son, cleanses you from all sin. Many and aggravated you now see to have been your flaws, your derelictions, your departures, your backslidings, your stumblings; sin appears now as it never did before; the sense of your utter unworthiness presses you to the earth. Well, who is on the eager watch for the first kindlings of godly sorrow in the heart of the prodigal? Who welcomes his return with joy, with music, with honors? Whose heart has not ceased to love, whose eye has not ceased to follow, amid all the waywardness and wandering of that child? Oh, it is the Father! "When he was yet a great way off, his father saw him, and had compassion, and ran, and fell on his neck, and kissed him." Behold your God, your covenant God and Father in Christ Jesus! This reconciled Father is yours. Throw yourself in His arms, and He will fall on your neck, and will seal upon your heart afresh the sense of His free forgiveness and His pardoning love. Heaven is before you. Soon will you be freed, entirely and forever freed, from all the remains of sin. Soon the last sigh will heave your breast, the last tear will fall from your eye, and the last pang will convulse your body. Soon, oh, how soon, will you "see the King in His beauty," the Jesus who loved you, died for you, ransomed you, and loves you still! Soon you will fall at His feet, and be raised in His arms, and be hushed to rest in His bosom. Soon you will mingle, a pure and happy spirit, with patriarchs and prophets, apostles and martyrs, and with all who sleep in Jesus, who have gone but a little before you. See how they line the shores on the other side, and wait to welcome you over! See how they beckon you away! Above all, sweetest and most glorious of all, behold Jesus standing at the right hand of God, prepared to receive you to Himself! Jesus has gone before, to make ready for the glorification of His Church. "I go to prepare a place for you." Oh sweet words! A place prepared—a mansion set apart for each individual believer! "In my Father's house are many mansions." A mansion in His heart, a mansion in His kingdom, a mansion in His house, for the weakest babe in Christ. The Forerunner is for us entered, even Jesus! How sure is heaven! How certain the eternal happiness of every pardoned and justified soul!

DECEMBER 29

"For you are my lamp, O Lord; and the Lord
will lighten my darkness." 2 Samuel 22:29

BLESSED Lord! You are my light. Accepted in Your righteousness, I am "clothed with the sun." Dark in myself, I am light in You. Often have You turned my gloomy night into sunny day. Yes, Lord, and with a love not less tender, You have sometimes turned my "morning of joy" into a "night of weeping." Yet have You made my very griefs to sing. Many a dark cloud of my pilgrimage has You fringed with Your golden beams. "In Your light have I seen light" upon many a gloomy and mysterious dispensation of my covenant God. "By Your light I have walked through darkness," many a long and lonely stage of my journey. Oh, how have You gone before me each step You do bid me to travel. You, too, did pass through Your night of solitude, suffering, and woe. But You were deprived of the alleviations which You do so graciously and tenderly vouchsafe to me. Not a beam illumined, not a note cheered, the midnight of Your soul. The light of the manifested Fatherhood was hidden from Your view, and in bitter agony did You exclaim, "My God, my God, why have You forsaken me?" And all this did You willingly endure, that I might have a song in the night of my grief. Thus Your darkness becomes my light; Your suffering my joy; Your humiliation my glory; Your death my life; Your curse my crown.

O Lord! that is a blessed night of weeping in which I can sing of Your sustaining grace, of Your enlivening presence, of Your unfaltering faithfulness, of Your tender love. In Your school how well have You instructed me! How patiently and skillfully have You taught me! I could not have done without Your teaching and Your discipline. With not one night of suffering, with not one chastising stroke, with not one ingredient in my cup of sorrow, could I safely have dispensed. All was needful. And now I can see, as faith, with a reflex action, surveys all the past, with what infinite wisdom and skill, integrity and gentleness, You were appointing all, and overruling all the incidents and windings of my history. With not less shame and self—abhorrence do I cover my face, and lay my mouth in the dust before You, because You has brought light out of my darkness, and educed good from my evil, and overruled all my mistakes and departures for my greater advance and Your richer glory, and are now "pacified towards me for all that I have done." I have stumbled, and You have upheld me. I have fallen, and You have raised me up. I have wandered, and You have restored. I have wounded myself, and You have healed me. Oh, what a God have You been to me! What a Father! What a Friend! Shall I ever distrust You, ever disbelieve You, ever wound You, ever leave You more? Ah! Lord, a thousand times over, yes, this very moment, but for Your restraining grace. "Hold You me up, and I shall be safe."

DECEMBER 30

"You shall guide me with your counsel, and afterward receive me to glory." Psalm 73:24

LORD, give me more clearly to see Your love in all Your dealings. Anoint my eye of faith afresh, that, piercing the dark cloud, it may observe beneath it Your heart, all beating with an infinite and a deathless affection towards me. The cup which my Father has prepared and given me, shall I not drink in deep submission to His holy will? O Lord, I dare not ask that it may pass my lips untasted: I may find a token of Your love concealed beneath the bitter draught. Your will be done. Nearer would I be to You. And since You, my blessed Lord, were a sufferer—Your sufferings now are all passed—I would have fellowship with You in Your sufferings, and thus be made conformable to Your death. Grant me grace, that patience may have her perfect work, wanting nothing. Calm this perturbed mind. Tranquillize this ruffled spirit. Bind up this bruised and broken heart. Say to these troubled waters in which I wade, "Peace, be still." Jesus, I throw myself upon Your gentle bosom. To whom can I, to whom would I, tell my grief, to whom unveil my sorrow, but to You? Lord! it is too tender for any eye, too deep for any hand, but Your. I bless You that I am shut up to You, my God. "Whom have I in heaven but You? and there is none upon earth that I desire beside You." You did hear my prayer, and have answered me, "though as by fire." I asked for health of soul, and You gave sickness of body. I asked You to possess my entire heart, and You broke my idol. I asked that I might more deeply drink of the fountain of Your love, and You did break my cistern. I asked to sit beneath Your shadow with greater delight, and You smote my gourd. I asked for deeper heart-holiness, and

You did open to me more widely the chambers of imagery. But it is well; it is all well. Though You do slay me, yet will I trust in You. Divine and holy Comforter, lead me to Jesus, my comfort. Witness to my spirit that I am a child of God, though an erring and a chastened one. Lord! I come to You! My soul would sincerely expand her wings, and fly to its home. Let me go, for the day breaks. Come to me, or let me come to You. Ever with You, Lord, oh! that will be heaven indeed. Why do Your chariot wheels so long tarry? Hasten, blessed Savior, and dissolve my chain, and let me spring into glory, and see Your unclouded face, and drink of the river of Your love, and drink—forever.

DECEMBER 31

"Let not your heart be troubled: you believe in God, believe also in me. In my Father's house are many mansions: if it were not so, I would have told you. I go to prepare a place for you." John 14:1, 2

GOING home! what a soothing reflection! what an ecstatic prospect! The heart throbs quicker—the eye beams brighter—the spirit grows elastic—the whole soul uplifts its soaring pinion, eager for its flight, at the very thought of heaven. "I go to prepare a place for you," was one of the last and sweetest assurances that breathed from the lips of the departing Savior; and though uttered eighteen hundred years ago, those words come stealing upon the memory like the echoes of by-gone music, thrilling the heart with holy and indescribable transport. Yes! He has passed within the veil as our Forerunner; He has prepared heaven for us, and by His gentle, wise, and loving discipline He is preparing us for heaven. Amid the perpetually changing scenes of earth, it is refreshing to think of heaven as our certain home. "In hope of eternal life, which God, that cannot lie, promised before the world began." This is no quicksand basis for faith— no mirage of hope. Heaven is a promised "rest"—exquisitely expressive image! And that promise is the word of Him who cannot lie. Nothing can surpass, nothing can compare with this! Human confidences—the strong and beautiful—have bent and broken beneath us. Hopes, bright and winning, we too fondly fed, have, like evening clouds of summer, faded away, draping the landscape they had painted with a thousand variegated hues in the somber pall of night. But heaven is true! God has promised it—Christ has secured it—the Holy Spirit is its earnest—and the joys we now feel are its pledges and "first-fruits." The home to which we aspire, and for which we pant, is not only a promised, it is also a perfect and permanent home. The mixed character of those seasons we now call repose, and the shifting places and changing dwellings we here call home, should perpetually remind us that we are not, as yet, come to the perfect rest and the permanent home of heaven. Most true indeed, God is the believer's present home, and Jesus his present rest. Beneath the shadow of the cross, by the side of the mercy-seat, within the pavilion of a Father's love, there is true mental repose, a real heart's ease, a peace that passes all understanding, found even here, where all things else are fleeting as a cloud, and unsubstantial as a dream. "Come unto me, all you that labor and are heavy laden, and I will give you rest." But it is to heaven we look for the soul's perfect and changeless happiness. With what imagery shall I portray it? How shall I describe it? Think of all the ills of your present condition—not one exists in heaven! Bereaved one! death enters not, slays not, sunders not there. Sick one! disease pales not, enfeebles not, wastes not there. Afflicted one! sorrow chafes not, saddens not, shades not there. Oppressed one! cruelty injures not, wounds not, crushes not there. Forsaken one! inconstancy disappoints not, chills not, mocks not there. Weeping one! tears spring not, scald not, dim not there. "The former things are passed away." There rests not upon that smooth brow, there lingers not upon those serene features, a furrow or line or shade of former sadness, languor, or suffering—not a trace of wishes unfulfilled, of fond hopes blighted. The desert is passed, the ocean is crossed, the home is reached, and the soul finds itself in heaven, where all is the perfection of purity and the plenitude of bliss. Ages move on in endless succession, and still all is bright, new and eternal. Oh, who would not live to win and enjoy a heaven so fair, so holy, and so changeless as this? He who has Christ in his heart enshrines there the inextinguishable, deathless hope of glory.

Enough that God is my Father, my Sun, and Shield; that He will give grace and glory, and will withhold no good and needed thing. Enough that Christ is my Portion, my Advocate, my Friend, and that, whatever else may pass away, His sympathy will not cease, His sufficiency will not fail, nor His love die. Enough that the everlasting covenant is mine, and that that covenant, made with me, is ordered in all things, and sure. Enough that heaven is my rest, that towards it I am journeying, and that I am one year nearer its blessed and endless enjoyment.

If you enjoyed *Morning Thoughts*
you'll love Winslow's Evening devotional

Available at:
www.greatchristianbooks.com

THE MISSION OF GREAT CHRISTIAN BOOKS

The ministry of Great Christian Books was established to glorify The Lord Jesus Christ and to be used by Him to expand and edify the kingdom of God while we occupy and anticipate Christ's glorious return. Great Christian Books will seek to accomplish this mission by publishing Gospel literature which is biblically faithful, relevant, and practically applicable to many of the serious spiritual needs of mankind upon the beginning of this new millennium. To do so we will always seek to boldly incorporate the truths of Scripture, especially those which were largely articulated as a body of theology during the Protestant Reformation of the sixteenth century and ensuing years. We gladly join our voice in the proclamations of— Scripture Alone, Faith Alone, Grace Alone, Christ Alone, and God's Glory Alone!

Our ministry seeks the blessing of our God as we seek His face to both confirm and support our labors for Him. Our prayers for this work can be summarized by two verses from the Book of Psalms:

"...let the beauty of the LORD our God be upon us, And establish the work of our hands for us; Yes, establish the work of our hands." —Psalm 90:17

"Not unto us, O LORD, not unto us, but to your name give glory." —Psalm 115:1

Great Christian Books appreciates the financial support of anyone who shares our burden and vision for publishing literature which combines sound Bible doctrine and practical exhortation in an age when too few so-called "Christian" publications do the same. We thank you in advance for any assistance you can give us in our labors to fulfill this important mission. May God bless you.

For a catalog of other great
Christian books including
additional titles by
Octavius Winslow—

contact us in
any of the following ways:

write us at:
Great Christian Books
160 37th Street
Lindenhurst, NY 11757

call us at:
(631) 956-0998

find us online:
www.greatchristianbooks.com

email us at:
mail@greatchristianbooks.com

Printed in Great Britain
by Amazon